MANIFEST MADNESS

Manifest Madness

Mental Incapacity in Criminal Law

ARLIE LOUGHNAN

OXFORD
UNIVERSITY PRESS

Great Clarendon Street, Oxford, OX2 6DP,
United Kingdom

Oxford University Press is a department of the University of Oxford.
It furthers the University's objective of excellence in research, scholarship,
and education by publishing worldwide. Oxford is a registered trade mark of
Oxford University Press in the UK and in certain other countries

© A. Loughnan 2012

The moral rights of the author have been asserted

First Edition published in 2012

Impression: 2

All rights reserved. No part of this publication may be reproduced, stored in
a retrieval system, or transmitted, in any form or by any means, without the
prior permission in writing of Oxford University Press, or as expressly permitted
by law, by licence or under terms agreed with the appropriate reprographics
rights organization. Enquiries concerning reproduction outside the scope of the
above should be sent to the Rights Department, Oxford University Press, at the
address above

You must not circulate this work in any other form
and you must impose this same condition on any acquirer

Crown copyright material is reproduced under Class Licence
Number C01P0000148 with the pemission of OPSI
and the Queen's Printer for Scotland

British Library Cataloguing in Publication Data
Data available

Library of Congress Cataloging in Publication Data
Library of Congress Control Number 2012932677

ISBN 978–0–19–969859–2

Printed in Great Britain
on acid-free paper by
CPI Group (UK) Ltd, Croydon, CR0 4YY

Links to third party websites are provided by Oxford in good faith and
for information only. Oxford disclaims any responsibility for the materials
contained in any third party website referenced in this work.

For my family, with love.

General Editor's Preface

In this monograph Arlie Loughnan examines the criminal law's response to what she terms 'mental incapacity'. This takes her beyond a study of the 'defence of insanity' to consider a wider range of doctrines including infancy and intoxication, infanticide and diminished responsibility. Drawing on historical research and on legal theory, the author challenges various orthodoxies in criminal law scholarship, and reconceptualizes the relationship between the criminal law and forms of mental incapacity. The book casts new light on established topics, and does so at a time when law reform agencies in this country and elsewhere are turning their attentions to this part of the criminal law. This monograph should therefore be an important resource both for legal scholarship and for law reformers.

Andrew Ashworth

Acknowledgements

This book has been several years in the formation. It is based on a doctoral thesis, completed at the London School of Economics. I am deeply indebted to my supervisors, Nicola Lacey and Jill Peay, for their invaluable guidance, support and encouragement. I would also like to thank the examiners of the thesis, Lindsay Farmer and Alan Norrie, whose helpful comments and suggestions greatly assisted me in the process of writing this book.

Parts of this book were written while I held a Visiting Fellowship in the Law Department, LSE, on sabbatical from the Faculty of Law, University of Sydney. During this visit, I was able to present some of the thoughts that are contained in this book to various audiences, and I benefited from the discussions that ensued. I would like to thank Martin Loughlin and Neil Duxbury for making that visit possible and Emmanuel Melissaris, Mike Redmayne, and Charlie Webb for fruitful conversations on the topic of mental incapacity and crime.

I am grateful to Thomas Crofts, Jesse Elvin, Nicola Lacey, and Kevin Walton, who generously gave their time to read parts of this book, and who provided valuable feedback on draft chapters. I would like to thank Graeme Coss, Mark Findlay, Tanya Mitchell, Michelle Momdjian, and Julie Stubbs for the support they gave me while I was working on this project. I would also like to thank Adriana Edmeades and Katherine Connolly for their assistance in preparing the manuscript for publication. A special thank you is reserved for Sabine Selchow, with whom I have had many stimulating discussions, and whose encouragement and intellectual companionship played a vital role in this project.

The editorial team at Oxford University Press, including Alex Flach, Natasha Flemming, and Sally Pelling-Deeves, has been a pleasure to work with, and I appreciate the team's efforts on this book. Helpful comments and suggestions came from the three referees consulted by OUP. I would like to express my gratitude to them and to Andrew Ashworth for the General Editor's Preface.

Parts of this book draw from the following articles: '"Manifest Madness": Towards a New Understanding of the Insanity Defence' (2007) 70(3) *Modern Law Review* 379; '"In a Kind of Mad Way": A Historical Perspective on Evidence and Proof of Mental Incapacity' (2011) 35(3) *Melbourne University Law Review* 1047; and 'Putting Mental Incapacity Together Again' (2012) 15(1) *New Criminal Law Review* 1. I thank the editors and publishers of these journals for allowing me to reuse the materials.

Arlie Loughnan
University of Sydney,
January 2012

Contents

Table of Cases	xv
Table of Old Bailey Proceedings	xix
Table of Legislation	xxi
List of Abbreviations	xxiii

PART I

1. The Terrain of Mental Incapacity in Criminal Law   3

Why Examine Mental Incapacity?	3
Carving Out a Useful Approach to Mental Incapacity in Criminal Law	7
Overview of the Book	12

2. Putting Mental Incapacity Together Again   16

Reconstructing Mental Incapacity in Criminal Law	17
The Category of Mental Incapacity Doctrines in Criminal Law	26
Difference within Criminal Law	34

3. 'Manifest Madness': The Intersection of 'Madness' and Crime   39

The Terrain of Mental Incapacity in Criminal Law	40
The Ontology of 'Madness' at the Point of Intersection with Crime	49
The Epistemology of 'Madness' at the Point of Intersection with Crime	57

PART II

4. Dynamics of Inclusion and Exclusion: Unfitness to Plead and Infancy   67

Informal Legal Practices and the Emergence of the Doctrines	68
Formalization of Unfitness to Plead and Infancy I: Dangerousness and Disposal	75
Formalization of Unfitness to Plead and Infancy II: Fairness and Special Treatment	81
Formalization of Unfitness to Plead and Infancy III: the Rise of a Dynamic of Exclusion	92

5. Incapacity and Disability: the Exculpatory Doctrines of Insanity and Automatism   103

Of Unsound Minds and Wild Beasts: Insanity before *M'Naghten*	104
The Cleaving Apart of Insanity and Automatism	109

A 'fierce and fearful delusion': Daniel M'Naghten and the
  Creation of the *M'Naghten Rules* 113
Insanity As We Know It: the M'Naghten Rules 116
The Appearance of a Discrete Automatism Doctrine and the
  Rise of Disability as a Basis for Insanity 122
The Persistence of Incapacity: the Requirements of the
  Doctrine of Automatism 125
On the Eve of Reform? 133

6. **Knowing and Proving Exculpatory Mental Incapacity** 136
The Naturalization of 'Madness' and the Role of Common
  Knowledge of 'Madness' 137
'As a medical man, I have no hesitation in saying so': Expert
  Knowledges of 'Madness' 143
'I have seen a great many insane persons, and I should put
  him down as such': the Significance of Prudential Knowledge
  and the Ongoing Role of Lay Knowledge 150
Knowing More Than They Can Say: Experts (and Non-Experts)
  in the Current Era 155
Proving Exculpatory 'Madness': Reconstruction and Due Process .. 159

PART III

7. **'Since the days of Noah': the Law of Intoxicated Offending** 173
The Emergence of an Informal Intoxication Plea 174
'The nature of her mania was madness from drink': the
  Development of Expertise on Intoxication 178
The Formalization of the Law of Intoxicated Offending 181
The Apogee of Formalization?: *DPP v Majewski* 186
Beyond the Bounds of *Majewski*: Amoral Intoxication 191
Lay Knowledge of Intoxication in Criminal Law 195
The Janus-face of the Law of Intoxicated Offending 198

8. **Gender, 'Madness', and Crime: the Doctrine of Infanticide** 202
Proscribing Infanticide: 'Lewd Women' and 'Bastard' Children ... 203
'Out of her usual senses': Infanticide and Incapacity 209
Liability, Responsibility, and the 'Infanticidal' type 214
Of Imbalance and Disturbance: the Current Law of Infanticide ... 216
'[T]his sad case': What Legal Actors Know about Infanticide ... 221

9. **Differences of Degree and Differences of Kind: Diminished
Responsibility** 226
'Without being insane in the legal sense': the Development
  of Diminished Responsibility in Scotland 227

'In the light of modern knowledge': the Introduction of
  Diminished Responsibility in England and Wales   232
The Current Doctrine of Diminished Responsibility   235
Professional Actors and Expert Knowledge: Deciding
  Diminished Responsibility   245
The Difference Diminished Responsibility Makes   253

Bibliography   259
Index   275

Table of Cases

All cases are from England and Wales unless otherwise specified.

A v DPP [1997] 1 Cr App R 27 90–1
Attorney-General for Jersey v Holley [2005] 2 AC 580 .... 23, 28, 194, 246, 253, 257–8
Attorney-General for Northern Ireland v Gallagher [1963] AC 349 .... 118, 185
Attorney-General's Reference (No 2 of 1992) [1994] QB 91 126
Attorney-General's Reference (No 3 of 1998) [2000] QB 401 95–6

Beverley's Case (1603) 4 Co Rep 123; (1550) 1 Plowd 1 174
Bratty v Attorney-General for Northern Ireland [1963] AC 386 .. 5, 26–7, 118–19, 127–31, 156–8, 160–3, 185, 196, 217, 247
Broome v Perkins (1987) 85 Cr App R 321 .... 126, 132, 161

C (A Minor) Appellant v DPP [1996] AC 1 .... 30, 68, 78, 88–90, 92–3
C v DPP [1994] 3 WLR 888 92–3
Carraher v HM Advocate 1946 JC 108 (Scotland) 231
CC (A Minor) v DPP [1996] 1 Cr App R 375 78
Crown Court at Maidstone ex parte London Borough of Harrow [2000] 1 Cr App R 117 158

DPP v Beard [1920] 1 AC 479 .... 43, 118, 122, 174–5, 182–3, 185–6, 190, 194
DPP v Camplin [1978] AC 705 .... 30, 256
DPP v H [1997] 1 WLR 1406 .... 121, 134
DPP v Majewski [1977] AC 443 .... 31, 131, 183, 185–91, 193–4, 196, 199–200
DPP v Morgan [1976] AC 182 187
DPP v Newbury [1977] AC 500 190
DPP v P [2008] 1 WLR 1005 .... 90, 93

Galbraith v HM Advocate (No 2) 2002 JC 1 (Scotland) 231
Governor of Stafford Prison, ex parte Emery [1909] 2 KB 81 81

Habib Ghulam [2010] 1 WLR 891 87
Hill v Baxter [1958] 1 QB 277 .... 27, 119, 128, 131, 157, 163–4
HM v McLean (1876) 3 Couper 334 229–30
HM Advocate v Dingwall (1867) 5 Irv 466 229–30
HM Advocate v Savage 1923 SLT 659 (Scotland) 231–2

JM (A Minor) v Runeckles (1984) 79 Cr App R 255 90–1

Kennedy v HM Advocate (1944) JC 171 (Scotland) 196

L (A Minor) v DPP [1996] 2 Cr App R 501 91

M'Naghten's case (1843) 10 Cl & Fin 200 ...... 8, 22, 42–3, 54, 74, 113–17, 120–4, 129, 145, 147, 161, 164–5, 169, 185, 188, 226, 238, 241
Moyle v R [2008] EWCA Crim 3059 102

Queen v Berry (1876) 1 QBD 447 .... 83, 99

Table of Cases

Queen v O'Connor [1980] 146 CLR 64 (Australia) 196
Queen v Shickle [2005] EWCA Crim 1881.. 245

R v Ahluwalia (1993) 96 [2003] 1 AC 1209 236
R v Allen [1988] Crim LR 698 192
R v Antoine [2001] 1 AC 340 .... 95–6, 99
R v Arnold's case (1724) 16 St Tr 695 .... 106, 113, 141
R v B, W, S, H and W [2009] 1 Cr App R 261 97
R v Bailey [1983] 1 WLR 760 .... 132, 190, 193–4
R v Benyon [1957] 2 QB 111 83
R v Bingham [1991] Crim LR 433 128–9
R v Bree [2008] QB 131.. 192
R v Budd [1962] Crim LR 49.. 128, 161
R v Burgess [1991] 2 QB 92.. 118–19, 130, 161
R v Burles [1970] 2 WLR 597... 99
R v Burns (1973) 58 Cr App R 364... 163, 190
R v Byrne [1960] 2 QB 396 .... 28, 117, 123, 146, 236–8, 240–1, 248
R v Caldwell [1982] AC 341.. 188, 190
R v Campbell (1987) 84 Cr App R 255.. 245–6
R v Campbell [1997] Crim LR 495 234
R v Carr-Briant [1943] KB 607 163
R v Chard (1971) 56 Cr App R 268 157
R v Charlson [1955] 1 WLR 317.. 127, 163, 167
R v Clarke (1972) 56 Cr App R 225 117
R v Codère (1916) 12 Cr App R 21 120–1
R v Coulburn (1988) 87 Cr App R 309 .... 78, 90
R v Cox [1968] 1 WLR 308 .... 158, 247–8
R v Davies (1853) 3 C & K 328 82
R v Davies [1913] 1 KB 573.. 122
R v Davis (1881) 14 Cox CC 563 .... 185, 194
R v Diamond [2008] EWCA Crim 923.. 245
R v Dietschmann [2003] 1 AC 1209 .... 236, 239, 243
R v Dix (1982) 74 Cr App R 306 249
R v Dunbar [1958] 1 QB 1 246
R v Durante [1972] 3 All ER 962 190
R v Eatch [1980] Crim LR 650 .... 190, 192
R v Egan [1992] 4 All ER 470 .... 95–6, 243
R v Erskine; Williams [2010] 1 WLR 183 244–5
R v Felstead [1914] AC 534... 111
R v Ferrers (1760) 19 St Tr 885 .... 74, 141
R v Friend [1997] 1 WLR 1433 99
R v Gore (Lisa Therese) (Deceased) [2007] EWCA Crim 2789 .... 28, 218
R v Gorrie (1918) 83 JP 136 90
R v Graddock [1981] Current L Ybk 476 236
R v Graham [1982] 1 All ER 801 22
R v Grant [1960] Crim LR 424 .... 162, 246
R v Grant [2002] QB 1030 .... 85, 96–7, 99
R v Grindley (1819) 1 C & M 8.. 182–3
R v H [2003] UKHL 1 .... 61, 83, 86, 97
R v Hadfield (1800) 27 St Tr 1281 .... 75, 109, 113
R v Hale, The Times, 22 July 1936 217
R v Hardie (1985) 80 Cr App R 157 .... 131, 188, 193–4, 199
R v Harrison-Owen [1951] 2 All ER 726 .... 103, 126, 158, 163

R v Hasan [2005] 2 Cr App R 22 22
R v Heard [2007] 3 WLR 475 ......183, 188, 190
R v Hennessy [1989] 1 WLR 287 ......5, 118, 126, 129–30
R v Hobson [1998] 1 Cr App R 31 236
R v Holman (Unreported) CA, 27 April 1994 99
R v Holmes [1953] 2 All ER 324 157
R v Horseferry Road Magistrates, ex parte K [1997] QB 23 133–4
R v Inseal (CA, 10 May 1991) 195
R v Ireland (1910) 9 Cr App R 139 111
R v Isitt (1978) 67 Cr App R 44 ......126, 132
R v James; R v Karimi [2006] 1 Cr App R 440 ......23, 258
R v Jennion [1962] 1 WLR 317 248
R v JTB [2009] 2 Cr App R 500 ......74, 93
R v Kai-Whitewind (Chaha'oh Niyol) [2005] 2 Cr App R 457 ......211, 221–2
R v Kemp [1957] 1 QB 399 ......117–18, 128, 162
R v Kershaw (1902) 18 TLR 357 ......78, 90
R v Khan (Dawood) [2010] 1 Cr App R 74 248
R v Kingston [1995] 2 AC 355 192–3
R v Kooken (1982) 74 Cr App R 30 246
R v Kopsch (1925) 19 Cr App Rep 50 123
R v Lambert [2002] QB 1112 164
R v Latus [2006] EWCA Crim 3187 245
R v Lawrence [1981] 2 WLR 524 ......173, 197
R v Lewis (1989) 11 Cr App R (S) 577 224–5
R v Lincoln (Kesteven) Justices, ex parte O'Connor [1983] 1 WLR 335 87
R v Lipman [1970] 1 QB 152 ......131, 193
R v Lloyd [1967] 1 QB 175 241
R v M [2003] EWCA Crim 3452 ......99, 101
R v M (Edward) & Ors [2002] 1 Cr App R 25 97
R v Martin [2003] 2 Cr App R 322 ......96, 99
R v Matheson [1958] 1 WLR 474 248
R v Meade [1909] 1 KB 895 185
R v Monkhouse (1849) 4 Cox CC 55 182
R v Neaven [2007] 2 All ER 891 245
R v O'Connell [1996] EWCA Crim 1552 238
R v O'Connor (1994) 15 Cr App R 473 196
R v O'Donoghue (1927) 20 Cr App R 132 217
R v O'Driscoll (1977) 65 Cr App R 50 190
R v Pearson's case (1835) 2 Lew 144 192
R v Pinfold and Mackenney [2004] 2 Cr App R 5 157
R v Podola [1960] 1 QB 325 ......61, 81–3, 99, 162
R v Price [1963] 2 QB 1 162
R v Quick [1973] 57 Cr App R 722 ......120, 128–30, 133
R v Ramchurn [2010] 2 Cr App R 3 243
R v Reniger v Feogossa (1551) 75 ER 1 174
R v Reynolds (Gary) [2004] EWCA Crim 1834 236
R v Richardson and Irwin (1999) 1 Cr App Rep 392 189
R v Rivett (1950) 34 Cr App R 87 82
R v Roach [2001] EWCA Crim 2698 129
R v Roberts [1954] 2 QB 329 ......83, 99
R v Robertson [1968] 1 WLR 1767 ......99, 101
R v Sainsbury (1989) 11 Cr App R (S) 533 224
R v Sanderson (1994) 98 Cr App R 325 238–9

R v Secretary of State for the Home Department, ex parte Doody (1994) 1 AC 57 89
R v Seers (1984) 79 Cr App R 261 236–7
R v Sharp [1960] 1 QB 357 ...... 82, 99
R v Sheehan; R v Moore [1975] 1 WLR 739 ...... 45, 187, 192
R v Smith [1979] 1 WLR 1445 157
R v Smith (Morgan) [2001] 1 Cr App R 31 ...... 23, 28, 252, 257–8
R v Soderman (1935) AC 462 163
R v Spriggs [1958] 1 QB 270 236
R v Stapleton (1952) 86 CLR 358 121
R v Stewart [2009] 2 Cr App R 500 ...... 195, 240
R v Stripp (1979) 69 Cr App R 318 ...... 127, 157, 161
R v Sullivan [1984] 1 AC 156 ...... 26, 111, 118–19, 127, 130
R v Sutcliffe, The Times, 30 April 1981 247
R v T [1990] Crim LR 256 ...... 128, 133
R v Tandy [1989] 1 WLR 350 ...... 194–5, 239, 248
R v Tolson (1889) 23 QBD 168 130
R v Turner [1975] QB 834 157
R v Walden [1959] 1 WLR 1008 242
R v Weekes [1999] 2 Cr App R 520 236
R v Windle [1952] 2 QB 826 121
R v Wood [2010] 1 Cr App R (S) 6 241
R v Wood (Clive) [2009] 1 WLR 496 ...... 195, 240
R v Woods (1982) 74 Cr App Rep 312 189
Rabey v R (1980) 15 CR (3d) 225 (Canada) 128
Reg v Cruse (1838) 8 C & P 541 182
Reg v Smith (Sidney) (1845) 1 Cox CC 260 78
Reg v Turton (1854) 6 Cox 395 82
Reniger v Feogossa (1551) 75 ER 1 174
Rex v Carroll (1835) 7 C & P 145 182
Rex v Dashwood [1943] KB 1 ...... 61, 86
Rex v Dyson (1831) 7 C & P 305 ...... 77, 81, 99
Rex v Meakin (1836) 173 ER 132 182
Rex v North (1937) 1 Criminal Law Journal 84 156
Rex v Pritchard (1836) 7 C & P 303 ...... 75, 77, 81, 99–100
Rex v Smith (1910) 6 Cr App R 19 162
Rose v R [1961] AC 496 237
Ruse v Read [1949] 1 KB 377 190

SC v United Kingdom (2004) 40 EHRR 10 (ECHR) 93

T v United Kingdom (2000) 30 EHRR 121; V v United Kingdom (2000) EHRR 121
  (Application No 24724/94) (ECHR) 89, 93

Watmore v Jenkins [1962] 2 QB 572 ...... 126, 161
Wheeler and Batsford v Alderson (1831) 3 Hog Ecc 574 184
Winterwerp v The Netherlands (1979) 2 EHRR 387 (ECHR) 85
Woolmington v DPP [1935] All ER 1 ...... 78, 122–3, 161, 163–5, 189

Table of Old Bailey Proceedings

Allen, Benjamin, 24 February 1768 (t17680224–73) 107
Allnutt, William Newton, 13 December 1847 (t18471213–290) 78, 143
Baggot, Thomas, 28 June 1780 (t17800628–113) 177
Barlow, Thomas, Morris, Oliver, 13 January 1688 (t16880113–41) 71
Barnelly, William, 9 July 1729 (t17290709–64) 107
Barry, Julia, 8 December 1825 (t18251208–16) 209
Bennet, John, 23 February 1683 (t16830223–5) 69
Bromfield, Edward, 9 September 1696 (t16960909–27) 108
Brown, Emma, 6 May 1878 (t18780506–499) 178, 184
Buckham, Isabella, 4 December 1755 (t17551204–27) 207
Burrams, William, 13 January 1796 (t17970113–97) 72
Campion, Mary, 11 December 1689 (t16891211–26) 205
Carroll, Patrick, 11 May 1835 (t18350511–1119) 57
Clifford, Henry, 13 January 1688 (t16880113–30) 108
Crouch, William, 6 May 1844 (t18440506–1363) 148
Cuthbert, John, 25 October 1875 (t18751025–588) 147
Draper, Thomas, 17 May 1727 (t17270517–12) 107
Edwards, William, 20 October 1784 (t17841020–10) 176
Farrell, Harriet, 19 February 1829 (t18290219–62) 211
Francis, John, 26 November 1849 (t18491126–41) 146
Gardner, Ann, 15 January 1708 (t17080115–1) 206
Greenwood, Richard, 29 April 1767 (t17670429–50) 107
Hall, Alice, 17 January 1709 (t17090117–19) 141
Harrington, Jane, 18 September 1854 (t18540918–1068) 209
Haycock, Thomas, 28 June 1780 (t17800628–34) 177
Hoddinott, James, 3 April 1854 (t18540403–563) 184
Horton, William, 7 July 1784 (t17840707–77) 70
Huggins, James, 7 July 1851 (t18510707–1502) 148, 153
Hunt, Mary Ann, 16 August 1847 (t18470816–1797) 146-7
Hunter, Sarah, 28 June 1769 (t17690628–27) 207
Jenkins, Maria, 18 September 1765 (t17650918–40) 204
Jones, Mary, 18 May 1768 (t17680518–39) 177
Layton, Thomas, 6 April 1687 (t16870406–36) 69
Mabe, Ann, 27 February 1718 (t17180227–25) 204
Mac-Yennis, Coustantine, 26 February 1724 (t17240226–78) 108
Mayaffree, John Peter, 26 February 1746 (t17460226–36) 78
McKenzie, Susannah, 2 July 1855 (t18550702–723) 184
Milesent, Susannah, 11 November 1794 (t17941111–1) 57, 63, 73
Mills, James Alexander, 18 September 1871 (t18710918–695) 181
Montgomery, Richard, 30 August 1727 (t17270830–29) 109
Murray, William, 12 July 1869 (t18690712–652) 181
Nash, Thomas, 12 April 1727 (t17270412–21) 141-2
Oxford, Edward, 6 July 1840 (t18400706–1877) 153
Parker, Diana, 17 September 1794 (t17940917–46) 207
Parker, Philip, 8 December 1708 (t17081208–34) 141
Parker, William, 12 January 1874 (t18740112–123) 147
Pate, Robert, 8 July 1850 (t18500708–1300) 150

Poulton, Maria, 17 May 1832 (t18320517–65) 210
Reed, Thomas, 4 December 1723 (t17231204–20) 141
Smith, John, 5 April 1676 (t16760405–3) 72
Smith, William, 24 November 1851 (t18511124–61) 184
Stirn, Francis David, 10 September 1760 (t17600910–19) 108
Stone, George, 12 September 1787 (t17870912–15) 176
Sweetland, James, 28 June 1880 (t18800628–423) 147
Taplin, Thomas, 28 June 1780 (t17800628–18) 178
Tirey, John, Tirey, William, Tirey, James, 23 May 1787 (t17870523–30) 74
Tuchet, William, 21 October 1844 (t18441021–2396) 147
Vyse, Ann Cornish, 7 July 1862 (t18620707–745) 152
Walker, William, 21 April 1784 (t17840421–13) 108
Watson, John Selby, 8 January 1872 (t18720108–117) 152
Westron, Charles Broadfoot, 4 February 1856 (t18560204–263) 147
Wright, Charles, 30 November 1863 (t18631130–77) 184
'young Lad, Apprentice in London', 10 October 1677 (t16771010–4) 69

Table of Legislation

An Act for the Further Prevention of Malicious Shooting and Attempting to Discharge Loaded Fire-arms 1803.....................209–10, 215
An Act for the Safe Custody of Insane Persons Charged with Offences *see* Criminal Lunatics Act 1800
An Act to Prevent the Destroying and Murthering of Bastard Children *see* Concealment of Birth of Bastards Act 1624
Articles of Union 1707.................................227
Black Act (1723) (9 Geo. 1 c.22)................106
Children and Young Persons Act 1933 (23 & 24 Geo.5 c.12) 70, 88
s 53(1)..88–9
Children and Young Persons Act 1963, s 16................30, 88
Children and Young Persons Act 1969..........88
Children's Act 1908 88
ss 103–104..88
Concealment of Birth of Bastards Act 1624 (21 Jac.I. c.27) 204–6, 208–9
Coroners and Justice Act 2009..........28, 32, 48, 54, 123, 202, 217–18, 224, 235–6, 239, 241–2, 246, 256
s 52 .... 27, 30, 54, 94, 226, 235
s 52(1B) 242
s 54 ....23, 256
s 54(1)(c)..256
ss 55–56...23, 256
Crime and Disorder Act 1998, s 34 93
Criminal Appeal Act 1968
s 23 244
s 23(2)..223
Criminal Evidence Act 1898 .... 79, 142, 149
Criminal Justice Act 1961 88
Criminal Justice Act 1963 70
Criminal Justice Act 1967, s 8 187
Criminal Justice Act 1982 89
Criminal Justice Act 1991 88
Criminal Justice Act 2003, Sch 21 89
Criminal Justice and Licensing Act 2010.....231
Criminal Justice and Licensing (Scotland) Act 2010 88
Criminal Lunatics Act 1800 (39 & 40 Geo.3, c.94) 29, 75–7, 82–3, 95, 98, 110–12, 133–4, 166, 227

s 1 ....76, 110
s 2 ....75–6, 81
Criminal Lunatics Act 1884 (47 & 48 Vict. c.64) 154
Criminal Procedure (Insanity) Act 1964 .... 32, 82–4, 87, 99, 111, 168
ss 1–2...111
s 4...61, 83
s 4(2)..83
s 5..167
s 5(1)..83
s 5(4)..83
s 6 ....31, 162, 246
Criminal Procedure (Insanity and Unfitness to Plead) Act 1991............83–5, 87, 95, 99, 125, 156, 159, 166–9
s 1(1)..156
s 4..97
s 4(6)..83
s 4A...83, 95–7
s 4A(2)...84, 96
s 5..84, 97
s 5(2)..84
s 5(2)(b)(iii)..168
s 5(3)..168
Sch 1, para 4(2)..84
Criminal Procedure (Scotland) Act 1995, s 41A..88
Crown Cases Act 1848 (11 & 12 Vict. c.43) 79, 149
Domestic Violence, Crime and Victims Act 2004 ....84–5, 98, 168
s 22...98
s 24 ....84–5, 168
European Convention on Human Rights 1950.......................96, 134, 156
Art 3 89
Art 5 ....85, 89
Art 6 ....93, 97
Habitual Drunkards Act 1879......................180
Homicide Act 1957.............. 23, 48, 233, 235, 239, 246, 248, 252
s 2 .... 27, 54, 123, 233, 235, 238, 242, 246
s 2(1).............................. 48, 226, 235, 241, 246, 249–50
s 3 ....23, 256

Human Rights Act 1998 ....96, 134
    Art 5(1)(e) 85
Inebriates Act 1898 180
Infanticide Act 1922 ....28, 122, 216–18
Infanticide Act 1938 ....28, 122,
                           217–18, 220, 222
    s 1(1) 32, 202, 217
    s 1(2) 202, 217
Insane Prisoners Act 1840 (3 & 4
    Vict. c. 54) 110, 133, 153
Insane Prisoners (Amendment)
    Act 1864 (27 & 28 Vict. c.29) 154
Juvenile Offenders Act 1847 79
Juvenile Offenders Act 1850 79
Mental Capacity Act 2005 ....29, 100
    s 1(3) 29, 100
    s 3(1) 29, 100
Mental Deficiency Act 1927 238–9
    s 1(2) 238
Mental Health Act 1959 125
Mental Health Act 1983 ....85, 87
    s 37(1) 87
    s 37(3) 87, 134
Mental Health Act 2007, s 1 87

Misuse of Drugs Act 1971 199
Offences Against the Person
    Act 1861 132
    s 18 190
    s 20 190
    s 60 209
'Poor Law' Act 1576 (18 Eliz. I c.3) 203
Prisoners' Counsel Act 1836 (6 & 7
    Will IV c.114) 79, 113,
                                     142, 149
Prosecution of Offences Act 1879
    (42 & 43 Vict. c.22) 79, 149
Reformatory Schools (Youthful
    Offenders Act) 1854 79
Sexual Offences Act 2003 190
    s 3 190
    s 13 91
Transportation Act 1718 (4 Geo. I c.11) 105
Treason Trials Act 1696 142
Trial of Lunatics Act 1883 (46 & 47
    Vict. c.38) 32, 95, 111
    s 2(1) 95
Vagrancy Act 1744 (17 Geo. II c.5) 112

List of Abbreviations

AC	Appeal Cases Law Reports
All ER	All England Law Reports
C & K	Carrington & Kirwin's Nisi Prius Reports
C & P	Carrington & Payne's Nisi Prius Reports
CLRC	Criminal Law Revision Committee
Cox CC	Cox's Criminal Cases
Cr App R	Criminal Appeal Reports
EHRR	European Human Rights Reports
OBPs	Old Bailey Proceedings
QB	Queen's Bench Law Reports
St Tr	State Trials
WLR	Weekly Law Reports

PART I

1
The Terrain of Mental Incapacity in Criminal Law

This book offers a study of the terrain of mental incapacity in criminal law. I am particularly interested in the relationship between legal doctrines, practices, and knowledge about mental incapacity. I suggest that the terrain of mental incapacity in criminal law is traversed by a set of mental incapacity doctrines, and marked out by particular legal practices concerning evidence and proof, which themselves rest on different types of knowledges of mental incapacity. I argue that this terrain has a distinctive character, which I analyse under the label 'manifest madness'. And by introducing the concept of 'manifest madness', I invite scholars to engage in a rethinking of this area of criminal law.

My study of mental incapacity is based on the criminal law of England and Wales. It advances our understanding of mental incapacity in three main ways. First, I develop a theorized account of the scope of the mental incapacity terrain, based on a rethinking of what it is that particular criminal law doctrines share, and on what basis they are connected. Second, the book provides a careful socio-historical study of each of the legal doctrines classed as mental incapacity doctrines on my account. In doing this, I focus on a particular mental incapacity doctrine, its attendant practices of evidence and proof, and the different types of knowledge enlisted in those practices. Last, based on my close and systematic study of each doctrine, and with a view to the mental incapacity terrain as a whole, I offer an analysis of the deep structures of the terrain, presented as 'manifest madness'.

Why Examine Mental Incapacity?

Mental incapacity has come to occupy a prominent place in the contemporary criminal law. From the question of the age below which a child cannot be held liable for any offending behaviour, to the attribution of criminal responsibility to defendants with mental illnesses, mental incapacity raises concerns for legal actors, policy makers and legislators. Individuals' claims based on mental incapacity raise fundamental issues—concerning criminal responsibility and subjectivity—which go to the core of criminal law. When mental incapacity is raised at trial—whether for the purposes of exculpation, or for some other reason, such as to prevent a normal trial proceeding—it is often assumed to raise distinctive (and difficult) issues of evidence and proof. The point of intersection between crime and mental incapacity attracts a high degree of social and political interest. In short, mental incapacity has a symbolic significance in the criminal law that stretches beyond its role in particular cases.

In broad brush strokes, and at the risk of caricature, the usual story told about this area proceeds along the following lines: mental incapacity in criminal law is a rag-bag area of criminal law, featuring intricate legal constructs (such as 'disease of the mind') and unusual rules of evidence and procedure (such as the reverse burden of proof). The development of mental incapacity doctrines—typically labelled mental incapacity defences—was and continues to be characterized by conflict, either explicit or implicit, between expert medical and legal knowledges. It is this conflict that has resulted in the creation of what is generally understood as an uneasy middle ground between legal and medical norms when it comes to mental incapacity in the criminal law. Medical and legal types of expert knowledge are usually regarded as mutually exclusive and thought to together cover the field of knowledge practices related to mental incapacity in criminal law. In terms of their operation, however, individual mental incapacity doctrines are typically considered practically functional even if theoretically confused.

While there is no question about the value of much of the literature on mental incapacity, there are reasons to think that a close analysis may tell a different story. In this story, mental incapacity has a greater significance than hitherto realized. For instance, as it articulates with criminal non-responsibility, the development of principles and practices concerning mental incapacity is connected to the historical existence of the exculpatory criminal trial—whereby defendants were in effect presumed guilty and required to prove their innocence. This connection meant that claims to exculpation based on incapacity were crucial in the formalization of criminal law defences, and in the cleaving apart of defences and factors in mitigation, as well as in the development of the particular rules of evidence and procedure that accompanied this movement. Later, the rise to prominence of a professional body of 'alienists' and a discipline of psychiatry made criminal trials about insanity prominent *fora* for discussion about the meaning, significance, and means of identifying abnormal mental states. The deployment of the criminal law as an instrument of moralization in the late Victorian era provoked what has turned out to be sustained social and political anxiety about individuals who seek to 'get off' on claims of incapacity. The different types of knowledge now covering the field of mental incapacity in criminal law interrelate with each other and are mediated through legal institutions such as the jury and the trial. Expert knowledges must be seen to share the field with lay or non-expert knowledge of mental incapacity, an unsystematized body of knowledge that encompasses attitudes and beliefs held by non-experts. Even these brief points suggest that a careful study of the development of the law on mental incapacity seems likely to reveal the interest of this topic for criminal law more generally.

The starting point of this book is the distinctiveness of a part of criminal law that I call the mental incapacity terrain. It is this terrain that forms the focus of this book. As I discuss in Chapter 2, this terrain includes, but is not limited to, what are usually called mental incapacity defences. In Chapter 3, I argue that this terrain has a particular character, which I analyse under the label 'manifest madness'. With the label 'manifest madness', I refer to the specific character of 'madness' at the point of intersection with crime. I argue that it has two formal features, one ontological and one epistemological (according to which, 'madness' is constructed as both dispositional and 'readable'). Together, these features constitute the topography of the mental incapacity terrain. Turning to examine individual parts of this terrain—particular mental incapacity doctrines—in the remaining chapters of this book, I subject each to a close socio-historical assessment. These assessments reveal the dynamic nature of the topic of mental incapacity, with reconfiguration of the merciful space marked out by mental incapacity over time. As I discuss at different junctures in the book, the terrain of mental incapacity is marked out by *both* expert and non-expert knowledges, and their interaction constitutes a distinctive dimension of this area of criminal law.

Part of what makes mental incapacity an intriguing topic is that, although it is often treated as if it were straightforward, it is complex. One reason why mental incapacity is complex is that it is a disciplinary hybrid. As the Royal Commission on Capital Punishment stated about insanity, it is 'usually regarded by lawyers as a medical term and by doctors as a legal, or at any rate a medico-legal term'.[1] Although it is a legal term, in that it is a term vested with meaning in legal discourse, it has a close connection to what in the current era might be thought to be a medical referent, an individual's non-normal mental condition.[2] When considered alongside the way in which legal doctrines are organized across the mental incapacity terrain—almost wholly around disability—it is clear that these criminal law doctrines invoke a non-legal body of knowledge. This body of knowledge is a type of medical knowledge, epitomized by psychiatric and psychological knowledge (knowledges which have been labelled 'psy-knowledge'[3]). The part played by psy-knowledge in the criminal law domain marks this area out from other areas, and the notions associated with psy-knowledge—such as objectivity, victimhood, amorality, and non-responsibility—have particular significance in legal practices of evaluation and adjudication.

Another reason why mental incapacity is intriguing is that it refers to something abstract, albeit in a way that we might feel confident to say we know to what it refers. Although it might be thought to describe a condition or set of conditions, strictly speaking, mental incapacity refers to the *consequences* of certain conditions. It is for this reason that mental incapacity has been analysed

---

[1] See United Kingdom Royal Commission on Capital Punishment 1949–1953 Report (Cmd 8932, 1953) para 212.
[2] In terms of medical language referents, the term mental incapacity encompasses mental disorder, mental illness, intellectual disability, and physical disorders that have an effect on mental functioning. For discussion of the meaning of some of these terms, see United Kingdom *Report of the Committee on Mentally Abnormal Offenders* (Cmnd 6244, 1975) ('Butler Report') para 1.12. Examples of physical illnesses that have an effect on mental functioning include hyperglycaemia (*R v Hennessy* [1989] 1 WLR 287) and psychomotor epilepsy (referred to in *Bratty v Attorney-General for Northern Ireland* [1963] AC 386, 403).
[3] I use the term 'psy knowledge' following Nikolas Rose. For further discussion, see N Rose *Inventing Our Selves: Psychology, Power and Personhood* (Cambridge: CUP, 1996).

by criminal law scholars in terms of its effects, that is, as an absence of, or impairment in, the moral, cognitive, and volitional capacities both assumed and required by the law.[4] As the reference to such capacities suggests, mental incapacity is intimately related to the foundational concepts of subjectivity and individual responsibility in criminal law, and to processes, such as the criminal trial, dependent on such subjectivity and tasked with evaluating responsibility. This connection to the foundational concepts of criminal law and core criminal processes suggests the place of mental incapacity at the heart of criminal law.

Mental incapacity is also intriguing because it is something of an umbrella term—it enjoys a wide reach. It is possible to gain a sense of this by slicing mental incapacity in different ways. If it is sliced according to medical referents, it includes difficulties of communication as well as comprehension (under unfitness to plead) and also affective conditions such as depression (under diminished responsibility). Although several parts of the terrain of mental incapacity in criminal law continue to reflect a bias toward cognitive capacities, taken as a whole, the reach of mental incapacity extends far beyond this. If we slice mental incapacity according to less technical descriptors of the type of incapacitation covered, it includes moderate or severe, temporary or permanent, externally-induced or endogenous incapacitation. For instance, as I discuss in Chapter 2, the law on intoxicated offending may be included within the scope of mental incapacity in criminal law. The reach of mental incapacity indicates the diversity of conditions criminal law doctrines cover, and also suggests that much more is captured by mental incapacity than it might be taken to suggest on its face.

These different dimensions of mental incapacity hint at the particular meanings that mental incapacity generates in criminal law. I make the case for taking seriously the specific kind of difference encoded in criminal law doctrines—which I call abnormality—as this is a feature of each of the doctrines that make up the mental incapacity terrain (in Chapter 2). The particular ways in which the mentally incapacitated subject is imagined as abnormal is the flipside of the legal construction of the 'normal' individual, a capacitous subject, and one to whom ordinary principles of responsibility, liability, and punishment apply. Having made a case about the significance of the kind of difference encoded in mental incapacity doctrines, I expand the viewpoint, beyond legal doctrines, to encompass legal practices concerning evidence and proof of mental incapacity. Adopting a multi-dimensional approach to the terrain of mental incapacity (taking into account evidence and proof as well as legal doctrines) prompts me to adopt the term 'madness' in my analysis because there is something more complex and multi-layered that I seek to capture under my 'manifest madness' label (in Chapter 3). The meanings produced in and through criminal law doctrines and practices concerning mental incapacity are what make this area an exciting subject of study.

---

[4] Antony Duff argues that mental disorder is best understood in terms of 'an impairment of the capacities for rational thought, emotion and action that constitute responsible agency': see R A Duff *Answering for Crime: Responsibility and Liability in the Criminal Law* (Oxford: Hart, 2007) 286. See also V Tadros *Criminal Responsibility* (Oxford: OUP, 2005).

Carving Out a Useful Approach to Mental Incapacity in Criminal Law

As a result of its connection to criminal responsibility, scholars have analysed mental incapacity principally as a basis for exculpation. Broadly, scholarship on mental incapacity in criminal law falls into one of two camps—philosophical studies (which typically adopt broad frames of reference and examine the connections between legal and extra-legal norms and practices) and doctrinal studies (which typically adopt narrow frames of reference and examine legal doctrines and practices).[5] However, both these types of studies share a focus on mental incapacity as a basis for exculpation, where exculpation is understood in a non-technical way to mean not holding a person liable for an offence. This shared focus dovetails with the significance of individual responsibility in the late modern era and reflects its profile in the academic realm. Individual responsibility for crime has come to act as a lynchpin in criminal law in the late modern era.[6] Where mental incapacity forms the basis for exculpation or partial exculpation, it grounds findings of non- or partial responsibility, and is implicated in constructing 'a barrier beyond which responsibility could not go in the case of those who were not rational', as Alan Norrie puts it in relation to the law of insanity.[7]

Perhaps in part because of the rather incoherent nature of the criminal law corpus in the common law world, and because of the connection between moral norms and legal norms (wrongs, harms, justifications etc), philosophical analyses of criminal law precepts and concepts have been popular and philosophical approaches make up a significant slice of the criminal law academic domain. In relation to mental incapacity, the bulk of the relevant philosophical works offer a conceptual analysis of responsibility (and thus, by default, non-responsibility, which I would suggest is only part of mental incapacity).[8] Thus, the focus is on what Lindsay Farmer refers to as the 'abstract structure of responsibility', and the conditions necessary for an individual to be held accountable for his or her actions under the criminal law.[9] Here, the preoccupation with the role of mental incapacity

---

[5] By way of philosophical studies, see eg, Tadros *Criminal Responsibility* and J Horder *Excusing Crime* (Oxford: OUP, 2004). By way of doctrinal studies, see, eg, R D Mackay *Mental Condition Defences in the Criminal Law* (Oxford: Clarendon Press, 1995).

[6] See, eg, L Farmer *Criminal Law, Tradition and Legal Order: Crime and the Genius of Scots Law 1747 to the Present* (Cambridge: CUP, 1997); N Lacey 'Responsibility and Modernity in Criminal Law' (2001) 9(3) *Journal of Political Philosophy* 249; and A Norrie *Crime, Reason and History: A Critical Introduction to Criminal Law* (London: Butterworths, 2001). Re late modernity, see, for instance, D Garland *Culture of Control: Crime and Social Order in Contemporary Society* (Oxford: OUP, 2002) and A Giddens *Modernity and Self-Identity: Self and Society in the Late Modern Age* (Stanford: Stanford University Press, 1991).

[7] See Norrie *Crime, Reason and History* 176.

[8] A prominent example of this type of scholarship is H L A Hart *Punishment and Responsibility: Essays in the Philosophy of Law (With an Introduction by John Gardner)* (Oxford: OUP, 2008).

[9] Farmer *Criminal Law, Tradition and Legal Order* 181. As Nicola Lacey puts it, the conditions of criminal responsibility are thought to 'reside in fundamental aspects of *human agency*'. See Lacey 'Responsibility and Modernity in Criminal Law' 255.

as a basis for exculpation is reflected in the normative tenor of this type of scholarship, and expressed in its main concern with the status of the mentally incapacitated as non- or less than full subjects of the criminal law, or improper targets of criminal sanctions. So, for instance, in relation to insanity, the focus has been on the concept of insanity, or non-responsibility, rather than on *M'Naghten* insanity per se. Insanity and other legal provisions are positioned across various classificatory schemes popular in philosophical scholarship. As I discuss in Chapter 2, in an analysis of criminal law defences by normative type, for instance, insanity and diminished responsibility may find themselves either in categories of excuse or exemption (also known as denials of responsibility), or, on a functional account of defences, they may sit together within a broader category of 'disability excuses'. Non-exculpatory mental incapacity provisions are generally marginalized in these philosophical studies.[10]

In doctrinal scholarship, the dominance of the idea that mental incapacity is a basis for exculpation is reflected in reliance on the category of mental incapacity or mental condition defences. The idea that the particular claims advanced by individuals with mental incapacities represent a distinct subcategory of criminal defences appears to enjoy some acceptance among legal commentators.[11] The 'usual suspects' found in this category are insanity, automatism, diminished responsibility, infanticide and, sometimes, intoxication (and unfitness to plead).[12] However, the otherwise rich vein of commentary on the operation and construction of these particular defences has not generated a robust account of the category itself—the category of mental incapacity defences has remained curiously undefined. This might be taken to suggest that this is perhaps less a category, comprising defences united in a particular, thoroughly-understood way, and more a term which is in relatively common use. Even on a straightforwardly descriptive level, it is not clear that the category of mental incapacity defences has any particular scope. For instance, is the rule about voluntary intoxication—related to the admissibility of evidence, rather than a defence per se—properly included within the category? What about procedural provisions, such as unfitness to plead, which are typically grouped alongside this category of defences and regarded as allied to the defences in some way (although their conceptual interrelations are usually assumed rather than explained)? The elasticity of the scope of this category suggests that what it is that unites mental incapacity defences *qua* mental incapacity defences is either elusive or contested.

With the emphasis on either criminal responsibility (in philosophical studies) or on criminal defences based on mental incapacity (in doctrinal studies), the scholarly

---

[10] A notable exception is R A Duff *Trials and Punishments* (Cambridge: CUP, 1986), which contains a close and persuasive discussion of unfitness to plead. See also A Duff et al *The Trial on Trial (Vol. 3): Towards a Normative Theory of the Criminal Trial* (Oxford: Hart, 2007) 179–81.

[11] This classification of defences features in academic monographs on the criminal law: see Mackay *Mental Condition Defences*, and N Walker *Crime and Insanity in England (Vol. 1: The Historical Perspective)* (Edinburgh: Edinburgh University Press, 1968).

[12] In the seminal work in this area, R D Mackay does not seek to account for the inclusion of these topics: see Mackay *Mental Condition Defences*.

focus to date has been consistently trained on the role of mental incapacity as a basis for exculpation. The effect of the dominance of the idea that mental incapacity is a basis for exculpation is that this role has come to be the principal one for mental incapacity in criminal law. This has marginalized other roles played by mental incapacity, with any other role being understood in relation to exculpation or indeed as derivative of exculpation. As a result, we do not have a thorough understanding of mental incapacity in criminal law. I take up this point in Chapter 2. As I suggest there, a reconstruction of the mental incapacity terrain permits a reconceptualization of the role of mental incapacity in criminal law.

Taken as a whole, the existence of both philosophical and doctrinal studies means there is a rich literature on mental incapacity in criminal law. There seem to be aspects of this area that escape these scholarly camps, however, including the dynamic relationship between legal doctrines and procedures of evidence and proof, and their broader interaction with extra-legal knowledges. Further, what seems to be an unusually sharp bifurcation between philosophical and doctrinal approaches to mental incapacity has occluded insights that might be generated by their mingling. There is room for an approach to mental incapacity in criminal law that seeks to carve out a space between these approaches, to consider the analytical insights to be gained from a close historical study of the legal provisions and the attendant practices of evidence and proof.

Socio-historical studies provide a means of buttressing the academic space that exists between doctrinal and theoretical approaches to criminal law. The relative dominance of one or other of the philosophical or doctrinal approaches should not be taken to indicate that the middle ground between the two is unoccupied terrain. Rather, it is a rich arena in which I am pitching my scholarly tent. Reflecting the long-lasting influence of legal realism, and the rise to prominence of socio-legal studies scholarship, this ground is well-traversed. Indeed, because mental incapacity in criminal law lies at the intersection of two vectors of state power—welfare and punishment—it has been of particular interest to scholars working within these traditions. Thus, there is a vibrant and growing body of socio-historical studies concerning mental incapacity, broadly conceived. On the one hand, there are texts focused on the historical operation and development of legal doctrines and practices.[13] On the other hand, there are social histories of the law of insanity,[14] which are not specifically concerned with either doctrinal analysis or in tracing the relevance of historical developments into the current era. This book draws on both of these categories of scholarship in terms of either subject matter or methodological approach, but it is distinct in that its focus is the relationship

---

[13] Examples in this category include M J Wiener *Reconstructing the Criminal: Culture, Law and Policy in England, 1830–1914* (Cambridge: CUP, 1990); K J M Smith *Lawyers, Legislators and Theorists: Developments in English Criminal Jurisprudence 1800–1957* (Oxford: Clarendon Press, 1998) and D Rabin *Identity, Crime and Legal Responsibility in Eighteenth Century England* (New York: Palgrave Macmillan, 2004).
[14] Examples include J P Eigen *Witnessing Insanity: Madness and Mad Doctors in the English Court* (New Haven: Yale University Press, 1995) and *Unconscious Crime: Mental Absence and Criminal Responsibility in Victorian London* (Baltimore: Johns Hopkins University Press, 2003).

between legal doctrines, practices, institutions, and knowledge concerning mental incapacity.

The systematic analysis of mental incapacity in criminal law that I offer in this book is based on a socio-historical approach. Such an approach situates the relevant doctrinal, evidentiary, and procedural developments within their particular social, historical, and institutional contexts.[15] This approach evidences a commitment to examining law as a social phenomenon, which means that the development of conceptual frameworks is itself the object of study.[16] As Markus Dirk Dubber suggests in advocating a historical analysis of law, this approach seeks to 'understand principles and practices in their relation to other principles and practices'.[17] And as Nicola Lacey argues with respect to criminal responsibility and criminalization, the scholarly research agenda benefits from appreciation of historical and social scientific as well as legal and philosophical scholarship.[18]

There are reasons to think that this methodological approach is a particularly appropriate one for the study of mental incapacity in criminal law. This approach provides a means of capturing the dynamic nature of the terrain of mental incapacity in criminal law. Even on what has been called the level of weak historical argument,[19] such an approach exposes the major changes in criminal law and process that have taken place over time, and it is notable that the terrain of mental incapacity is marked by significant continuities, as well as change. The durability of some component parts of this area of law—such as the *M'Naghten Rules* and the criteria for a finding of unfitness—is particularly striking. On another level, a socio-historical analysis of the criminal trial opens the way for a *historicized* account that incorporates the principles and practices of criminal law, evidence, and procedure that pertain at particular junctures. As Farmer suggests, rather than looking at the object of legal definitions, scholars should look more broadly to encompass the relations between that object and the defining process.[20]

A study employing a socio-historical approach to mental incapacity is more than an intellectual history of legal principles or paradigms. In relation to my particular

---

[15] According to this approach, in a particular temporal and spatial context, the colonial context of criminal justice may be relevant. For an example of a study of the operation of the criminal law in a colonial context, see M J Wiener 'Criminal Law at the Fault Line of Imperial Authority: Interracial Homicide Trials in British India' in M D Dubber and L Farmer (eds) *Modern Histories of Crime and Punishment* (2007) 252.

[16] See N Lacey 'Philosophy, History and Criminal Law Theory' (1998) 1 *Buffalo Criminal Law Review* 295, 311, and N Lacey 'Philosophical Foundations of the Common Law: Social not Metaphysical' in J Horder (ed) *Oxford Essays in Jurisprudence* (Oxford: OUP, 2001) 17, 19.

[17] M D Dubber 'Historical Analysis of Law' (1998) 16(1) *Law and History Review* 159, 160–2. See also Dubber and Farmer 'Introduction: Regarding Criminal Law Historically' 1.

[18] See N Lacey 'Space, Time and Function: Intersecting Principles of Responsibility Across the Terrain of Criminal Justice' (2007) 1(2) *Criminal Law and Philosophy* 233 and 'Historicising Criminalisation: Conceptual and Empirical Issues' (2009) 72(6) *Modern Law Review* 936. See also M D Dubber and L Farmer 'Introduction: Regarding Criminal Law Historically' in M D Dubber and L Farmer (eds) *Modern Histories of Crime and Punishment* (Berkeley: Stanford University Press, 2007) 1.

[19] See N Lacey 'In Search of the Responsible Subject: History, Philosophy and Social Sciences in Criminal Law Theory' (2001) 64(3) *Modern Law Review* 350, 357.

[20] See L Farmer 'The Obsession with Definition: The Nature of Crime and Critical Legal Theory' (1996) 5 *Social and Legal Studies* 57.

interests in this book—the interaction of doctrines, practices, and knowledge about mental incapacity—the specific value of a socio-historical approach also lies in filling in the open-textured nature of abnormality, and understanding the significance of the different types of knowledge—lay and expert—that are brought to bear on mental incapacity in criminal law. As I discuss in Chapter 2, while the meanings generated by the legal doctrines covered in this book coalesce around a specific idea of difference—abnormality—it is a dynamic notion, taking on a different hue in different corners of the mental incapacity terrain and at different times. In relation to knowledge, persistent controversy about the place of expert medical evidence in the courtroom hints at the contingent nature of the relationship between different knowledges about incapacity. The expert knowledges governing the field of mental incapacity in criminal law interrelate with each other in a dynamic way, mediated through legal institutions such as the lay jury and the adversarial criminal trial. I take up this issue in Chapter 6, on knowing 'madness', and at different points throughout the book as relevant to particular mental incapacity doctrines.

My socio-historical approach, and my aim to provide a close analysis of mental incapacity, leads me to draw on particular sources in this book. The most significant of these is the *Old Bailey Proceedings* (*OBPs*).[21] The *OBPs* record many although not all of the trials that took place at the Old Bailey Criminal Court (which was the main felony trial court in London) from 1674 to 1913. The *OBPs* database contains almost 200,000 trial records. I use these records selectively in order to back up my analysis of the development of mental incapacity doctrines over time. Unlike the State Trial reports, *State Trials*, which recorded a small number of celebrated treason trials (which had distinctive procedural features[22]), the records from the Old Bailey provide information about a large number of trials concerning different offences, giving a sense of the everyday processing of criminal matters. Similarly, unlike private reports, the Old Bailey records provide a series that is substantially complete from the beginning and entirely complete from 1729. As with any source material, it is necessary to be cautious in relying on the *OBPs* for evidence about criminal trials in the relevant period and, as several scholars note, these sources call for a careful and reflective approach.[23] Overall, even mindful of

---

[21] The *OBPs* are available at <http://www.oldbaileyonline.org> (last accessed on 30 November 2011). The *OBPs* are a selection of a larger collection of trials, generally known as the *Old Bailey Sessions Papers*, which have not been digitized.
[22] See J H Langbein *The Origins of the Adversary Criminal Trial* (Oxford: OUP, 2003) 14–15, 97–102.
[23] See generally Eigen *Witnessing Insanity* 7s–8; Langbein *The Origins of the Adversary Criminal Trial* 180–90 in relation to the *Old Bailey Sessions Papers*. The Old Bailey records initially targeted a popular rather than legal audience, and this meant that legal proceedings were not always recorded in detail. As a result, the records focused on the circumstances of the crime and its detection, rather than on judicial pronouncements, criminal procedure, or evidence. In addition, because the Old Bailey tried matters arising from offences that took place in and around London, the *OBPs* skew the picture they present of the criminal trial process towards the capital, affecting the type of offences prosecuted as well as their number in the records. Last, the Old Bailey records compressed some of the trials they recorded and it is not possible to know what was deleted or why. John Langbein concludes that these features of the records mean that, although negative inferences from them are hazardous, positive inferences are

their limitations, the Old Bailey records are a vital resource for my purposes because they facilitate a close examination of the ordinary operation of the practices relating to mental incapacity in a way that is not permitted by reliance on other sources. The *OBPs* records provide a useful companion to the historical writings of criminal law theorists and reformers, such as Matthew Hale and James Fitzjames Stephens, which have been examined by a number of legal scholars.[24]

Having analysed this area of the law via this approach, I am able to offer a synthesized assessment of the mental incapacity terrain, drawing connections both across the doctrines that traverse this terrain and across developments over time. This approach enables me to demonstrate the ways in which mental incapacity doctrines have been and continue to be interrelated, both conceptually (evidenced by the applicability of the right/wrong test to insanity and infancy, for instance) and in practice (evidenced by the interaction of diminished responsibility and insanity, for instance), and to draw out what I understand to be the most important analytical features of this area of law.

Overview of the Book

This book is organized into three parts. In Part I, comprising Chapters 1, 2 and 3, I look across the terrain of mental incapacity as a whole in order to provide a synthesized assessment of mental incapacity in criminal law. In Chapter 2, I mark out the boundary of mental incapacity in criminal law—determining what's in and what's out. The precise boundary I advance is not itself novel (with the exception of the inclusion of infancy or non-age within it), but making a theoretical case for it is new. In this chapter, I suggest an approach to mental incapacity in criminal law whereby the relevant substantive and procedural provisions are understood as doctrines (not defences), some of which are exculpatory. The significance of this reconstruction of the terrain of mental incapacity is that it permits a reconceptualization of the roles of mental incapacity in criminal law—to include imputation, inculpation, and a procedural role, as well as exculpation. This reconstruction introduces the conceptual tools—such as exculpatory and non-exculpatory mental incapacity doctrines—which I employ throughout this book. In addition, this chapter reveals that the scope of this book is itself an argument—for the placement of particular legal doctrines, which share certain formal features, on the terrain of mental incapacity.

Having made an argument about the scope of the terrain of mental incapacity, in Chapter 3, I turn to analyse the terrain itself. This chapter presents the argument that gives the book its title, an argument which is the outcome of my close study of the doctrines and practices that make up the terrain of mental incapacity. In this chapter, I expand the scholarly frame beyond the legal doctrines, to encompass

---

safe because fabrication or invention of content was unlikely: Langbein *The Origins of the Adversary Criminal Trial* 185.

[24] See, eg, Lacey 'In Search of the Responsible Subject'; Smith *Lawyers, Legislators and Theorists*.

attendant legal practices concerning evidence and proof, enabling me to examine the deep features of the mental incapacity terrain. Here with the label 'manifest madness', I refer to the specific character of 'madness' at the point of intersection with crime. I argue that 'madness' has two formal features, one ontological (whereby it is constructed as dispositional) and one epistemological (whereby it is constructed as 'readable'). Together, these features constitute the topography of the mental incapacity terrain. As I discuss in detail in this chapter, as 'dispositional', 'madness' is regarded as subsisting and evident in conduct extending beyond the external component of the criminal offence, and, as 'readable', 'madness' can be 'read off' conduct by different participants in the criminal justice process. It is to capture this dual aspect of 'madness' for criminal law purposes that I use the adjective 'manifest'.

Armed with the necessary conceptual tools, and having assessed the mental incapacity terrain as a whole, I turn to engage in a close socio-historical study of each of the mental incapacity doctrines. This part of the book is divided into two. In Part II, I examine the law on unfitness to plead and infancy, and the law concerning exculpatory 'madness' (now marked out by the doctrines of insanity and automatism). These doctrines are brought together in this part of the book on the basis that they concern either the fundamental issue of the subject of criminal law and process, on the one hand, or the paradigmatic mental incapacity doctrine, insanity, on the other.

In Chapter 4, I juxtapose two mental incapacity doctrines—unfitness to plead and infancy—that are facially quite dissimilar, but which define, by a process of exclusion, those who can be subjected to criminal law process and sanctions. Although infancy is not typically incorporated into studies of mental incapacity in criminal law, in my view, its historical, conceptual, and procedural features make it a proper inclusion. I show that infancy and unfitness to plead have both developed along a trajectory of formalization. In this chapter, I suggest that formalization was shaped by a deep dynamic of inclusion—whereby the scope of these mental incapacity doctrines was drawn broadly—but, more recently, has also come to be structured by a dynamic of exclusion, whereby the scope of the doctrines is more circumscribed. As I discuss in this chapter, the change in the dynamics structuring the process of formalization itself reflects changing concerns with matters such as dangerousness. As a result of these changing concerns, in the current era, formalization of these mental incapacity doctrines is now structured by these two dynamics of inclusion and exclusion.

In both Chapters 5 and 6, I examine insanity and automatism, now two discrete exculpatory doctrines. I examine insanity and automatism side by side in order to give play to their interdependent development in criminal law. In Chapter 5, I focus on the substantive law of insanity and automatism. Here, I suggest that, when a loose, broad, and partially moralized notion of incapacity—defined largely by extra-legal norms—pertained as a basis for exculpation, claims now falling across the bounds of insanity and automatism were accommodated within an informal insanity doctrine and under a flexible criminal process. However, gradually, as mental incapacity came to be the subject of expert medical knowledge—a change that took place as much beyond as within criminal law—this broad notion of incapacity ossified into a narrower notion of disability, ushering in a more circumscribed approach to insanity. It was in this context that a discrete automatism doctrine appeared in the second half of the twentieth century.

In Chapter 6, I turn from the substantive law of insanity and automatism to the rules and practices of evidence and proof. This chapter provides an epistemological analogue to the discussion in the preceding chapter. Here, I analyse the way in which claims to exculpatory mental incapacity are governed. The rules of evidence and procedure relating to automatism are able to be distinguished from those relating to insanity, in a way that usefully throws each into relief. There are two main points made in this chapter. The first of these is that more than one type of knowledge informs the evidentiary practices attending exculpatory incapacity. Both expert or specialized knowledge of 'madness' and non-expert or lay knowledge are relevant for understanding how exculpatory incapacity claims are adjudicated in criminal law. The second main point is that the rules of evidence and proof applying to insanity and automatism reflect the different eras in which they formalized from informal practices. As I discuss in detail, while the rules related to insanity crystallized in the era of the 'reconstructive' criminal trial, the appearance of a discrete automatism doctrine in the second half of the twentieth century coincides with a version of the adversarial criminal trial concerned with due process and the effective processing of criminal cases.

Chapters 7, 8, and 9 make up the third and final part of this book. Here, in Part III, I examine specific components of the mental incapacity terrain. In the first chapter in this part, Chapter 7, I examine the law on intoxicated offending, according to which incapacity resulting from intoxication by alcohol or drugs can form the basis for imputed criminal liability.[25] The first of two main arguments made in this chapter is that while technical and complex rules appear to dominate, criminal law practices relating to intoxicated offending continue to depend on lay or non-expert knowledge of intoxication. This type of knowledge plays a significant part in criminal law practices concerning intoxicated offending into the current era—broadly, to block certain arguments about what is known and not known about intoxication. The second of the two main arguments advanced in this chapter relates to the meanings given to intoxicated offending in criminal law. I suggest that, in the law on intoxicated offending, intoxication is simultaneously constructed as exculpatory abnormality and morally culpable conduct, two sets of meanings that are held in a fine balance in law and process.

Chapter 8 takes up the issue of the relationship between gender, 'madness', and crime via an examination of the specific case of the infanticide doctrine. Broadly, I suggest that a dense network of meanings about the interrelationship between

---

[25] For this reason, voluntary intoxication has been referred to as a 'doctrine of imputation'. Paul Robinson argues that doctrines of imputation impute missing offence elements, providing an 'alternative means of holding the defendant liable as if the required elements were satisfied': see P Robinson *Structure and Function in Criminal Law* (Oxford: Clarendon Press, 1997) 67. See further my Chapter 2.

gender, 'madness', and crime has sustained what is widely regarded as a peculiar or strange legal doctrine into the current era, permitting women who rely on infanticide to slide between the categories of offence and defence, or, more precisely, between charge and plea (and meaning that the doctrine itself is most accurately understood as either/both partially exculpatory and partially inculpatory). According to my analysis, a particular social type—the infanticidal woman—has come to determine the legal issue of the defendant's criminal responsibility, and the act of infanticide has come to be read as an instantiation of abnormality for criminal law purposes. In the current era, the doctrine of infanticide is sustained by a lay or non-expert knowledge about the interrelation of gender, childbirth, and 'madness', which over-determines the legal evaluation of infanticidal women and their acts in criminal law.

In the final chapter of the book, Chapter 9, I examine the doctrine of diminished responsibility. As I foreshadow in Chapter 2, useful insights are to be gained by viewing diminished responsibility as Janus-faced, both partially exculpatory and partially inculpatory. In Chapter 9, I take up this point again, with the aim of examining what kind of difference is encoded in the diminished responsibility doctrine, or, put another way, examining what kind of difference diminished responsibility makes to the individual who raises it. Supported by my assessment of the development of a doctrine of diminished responsibility from its origins in nineteenth-century Scotland, I make the case in this chapter that the sort of difference encoded in diminished responsibility is usefully conceptualized as one of kind, as opposed to one of degree.

2
Putting Mental Incapacity Together Again

In this chapter, I reassemble the terrain of mental incapacity in criminal law. As I discuss in the previous chapter, while philosophical and doctrinal scholarly approaches have dominated legal studies of this area of criminal law, such studies have not produced a thorough understanding of mental incapacity. As a result of its connection to criminal responsibility, legal scholars have analysed mental incapacity principally as a basis for exculpation, reflecting the significance of individual responsibility in the late modern era and its corresponding profile in the academic realm.[1] The dominance of the idea that mental incapacity is a basis for exculpation in the legal literature means that this role has come to be the principal one for mental incapacity in criminal law. This has marginalized other roles played by mental incapacity, with any other role understood in relation to exculpation or as derivative of exculpation. In this chapter, I suggest that significant insights are to be gained through an alternative approach to the mental incapacity terrain. As it sets out the boundaries of the terrain of mental incapacity, this chapter also explains the scope of this book. As will become clear, the scope of this book is itself an argument—for a theorized boundary of the terrain of mental incapacity.

The discussion in this chapter unfolds in three steps. First, in order to develop the conceptual tools to understand mental incapacity in criminal law afresh, this chapter provides a reconstruction of the legal terrain concerned with mental incapacity. In my reconstruction, the terrain is traversed by a set of mental incapacity doctrines, a subset of which is exculpatory. On my account, mental incapacity doctrines share two formal features: each doctrine invokes a particular kind of difference, which I call abnormality, and, where the doctrines are exculpatory, the evaluative inquiry is not indexed to the reasonable person. This reconstruction of mental incapacity in criminal law—as mental incapacity doctrines—cuts across existing categorizations of the doctrines on this terrain and, as such, offers a rethinking of this area of the criminal law. This reconstruction prompts a reconceptualization of the role of mental incapacity in criminal law, which represents the second step in my discussion. Here, it becomes clear that mental incapacity doctrines play a multiplicity of roles—inculpation, imputation, and a

---

[1] See, for discussion, L Farmer *Criminal Law, Tradition and Legal Order: Crime and the Genius of Scots Law 1747 to the Present* (Cambridge: CUP, 1997); N Lacey 'Responsibility and Modernity in Criminal Law' (2001) 9(3) *Journal of Political Philosophy* 249; and A Norrie *Crime, Reason and History: A Critical Introduction to Criminal Law* (London: Butterworths, 2001).

procedural role—beyond exculpation. In the third step in my discussion, I analyse the kind of difference—abnormality—invoked by mental incapacity doctrines.

Reconstructing Mental Incapacity in Criminal Law

As the first step in my discussion, I offer a reconstruction of mental incapacity in criminal law. Without assuming the necessary priority of exculpation on the basis of mental incapacity, and taking seriously the moral import, function, and formal structure of different legal provisions, I reconsider what parts of the criminal law belong together and on what basis they are connected. Viewed from the perspective of the existing literature, my reconstruction involves three moves: from defences to doctrines, from moral evaluation to function, and from function to form. The resulting reconstructed terrain depicts mental incapacity as a set of doctrines, sub-classified into exculpatory and non-exculpatory doctrines. This reconstruction provides a basis for a reconceptualization—beyond exculpation—of the role that mental incapacity plays in criminal law.

From Defences to Doctrines

Perhaps the most notable feature of my reconstruction of the terrain of mental incapacity in criminal law, traversed by a set of mental incapacity doctrines, is that I do not use the label defence to refer to the subset of doctrines that are exculpatory (or partially exculpatory). In plotting out my reconstruction of mental incapacity in criminal law, I start with this point. As is well known, the term defence is sometimes used in a 'casual' sense by criminal lawyers to denote any part of a defendant's case that, if advanced successfully, would warrant an acquittal.[2] However, by contrast with criminal lawyers, criminal law scholars tend to use the term defence in a stricter sense, to refer to a claim that is in a causal sense 'compatible with the defendant's conceding that the offence charged was committed'.[3] That is, a defence is a claim that, for some reason related to the defendant or his or her circumstances, he or she should be acquitted, despite the commission of the offence. On this basis, defence is at least a facially plausible label for claims to exculpation based on mental incapacity—indeed, its acceptability is borne out by the bulk of doctrinal scholarship on mental incapacity, which revolves around defences.

There are, however, reasons to reject the label defence in favour of the more cumbersome label, exculpatory mental incapacity doctrine. Here, I refer to exculpation in a broad, non-technical way to denote not holding an individual liable for

---

[2] P Robinson 'Criminal Law Defences: A Systematic Analysis' (1982) 82(2) *Columbia Law Review* 199. In this sense, criminal defences include denial of the *mens rea* or *actus reus* elements of the offence and claims that the relevant statute of limitations has expired, as well as claims like self-defence and duress.
[3] J Gardner *Offences and Defences: Selected Essays in the Philosophy of Criminal Law* (Oxford: OUP, 2007) 141.

an offence. There are three reasons to prefer the label exculpatory mental incapacity doctrine to the label defence.[4] The first reason is the strength of arguments, made by advocates of the categorization of defences by normative type, about the difference between exemptions (also known as 'denials of responsibility') and excuses. The organization of defences by normative type, which is arguably the most popular way of categorizing criminal defences, entails classifying defences either as justifications or excuses, or justifications, exemptions, or excuses.[5] As these terms suggest, this categorization of defences tracks social practices of responsibility attribution.[6] Over recent years, a significant weight of authority has come to locate exculpation on the basis of mental incapacity within the confines of exemptions. On this approach, claims based on incapacity are denials of responsibility rather than excuses because individuals who cannot 'believe and feel as reason demands, and because reasons demand it...do not need to bother making excuses'.[7] An alternative formulation is put forward by Antony Duff. In the context of his argument about criminal responsibility as answerability, Duff argues that excuses admit responsibility but deny liability, while exemptions (such as insanity based on 'serious disorder') mean that the exempted person is not, or should not be, expected to answer for her actions.[8] On this approach, the categorization of a particular doctrine as an exemption indicates that those who are seeking to rely on it are not individuals to whom the criminal law—as a normative system—speaks. Accepting the premises of this normative classificatory scheme, and, for the moment, the implied neutrality of not being 'called to answer', the effect of this is that, where a claim to exculpation based on mental incapacity is an exemption, it is a misnomer to refer to it as a defence.

Now, it might be argued that, even if some claims to exculpation on the basis of mental incapacity are most accurately thought of as exemptions, some such claims may be best regarded as excuses, and thus have a stronger claim to the defence label. Reflecting back to the idea that mental incapacity refers to an absence of or *impairment* in the moral, cognitive, and volitional capacities both assumed and

---

[4] See also A Loughnan 'Mental Incapacity Doctrines in Criminal Law' (2012) 15(1) *New Criminal Law Review* 1.

[5] This approach to criminal defences was advanced in Anglo-American criminal law in large part by the work of George Fletcher: see G P Fletcher *Rethinking Criminal Law* (New York: OUP, 2000) and G P Fletcher 'The Nature of Justification' in J Horder and J Gardner (eds) *Action and Value in Criminal Law* (Oxford: Clarendon Press, 1993).

[6] For discussion of these social practices, see M Baron 'Excuses, Excuses' (2007) 1 *Law and Philosophy* 21 and V Tadros 'The Scope and Grounds of Responsibility' (2008) 11 *New Criminal Law Review* 91.

[7] Gardner *Offences and Defences* 131–2. See also J Horder *Excusing Crime* (Oxford: OUP, 2004) 105; S Kadish 'Excusing Crime' (1987) 75(1) *California Law Review* 257, 262–3. According to Gardner, while other defences may be at base about the defendant's fitness for his or her role, defences such as insanity and infancy are straightforwardly about capacity (112). See also J Gardner 'The Gist of Excuses' (1998) 1(2) *Buffalo Criminal Law Review* 575, 589.

[8] See R A Duff *Answering for Crime: Responsibility and Liability in the Criminal Law* (Oxford: Hart, 2007) 284–91. Thus, according to Duff, exemptions are not actually defences because the latter are 'exculpatory answers for the commission of the offence for which responsibility has been proved' (263). On this approach, the question of the defendant's responsibility is prior to any question of a defence.

required by the law (discussed in Chapter 1), it might be argued that some claims to exculpation or partial exculpation are genuine excuses.[9] On this basis, they might then be thought of as genuine defences in that they are indeed 'answers' given by individuals.[10] Without deciding one way or the other about the most accurate label for such claims, I suggest that it is still advisable to reject the term defence in relation to claims to exculpation based on mental incapacity. This has the advantage of avoiding what is a deceptively sharp contrast between 'defences' and 'denials of responsibility' where exculpatory mental incapacity is concerned, and, further, such an approach deflects a potential over-emphasis on the distinction between exculpatory and non-exculpatory mental incapacity doctrines, obscuring what these doctrines share.

The second reason for jettisoning the label defence for claims to exculpation based on mental incapacity flows from the analysis developed by Duff in the context of his broader argument on criminalization and responsibility as answerability. Duff argues that denials of responsibility (or 'agent exemptions') are granted rather than pleaded: it falls to a third party—someone other than the defendant—to make the case for an exemption.[11] In relation to claims based on mental incapacity, this is most likely to be a psychiatrist or psychologist. This feature of claims based on mental incapacity accords with Duff's view that they are not properly thought of as defences—they do not involve the defendant him or herself answering for his or her conduct. The reason for jettisoning the term defence in my own analysis looks at this feature of exemptions from a different angle. From this angle, the type of knowledge enlisted in mental incapacity claims is a relevant consideration. Because exemptions are granted rather than pleaded, they rely on an alternative (ie as opposed to legal) expert body of knowledge, which we might call (broadly) psychiatric, psychological, or 'psy-knowledge'.[12] When medical professionals give evidence in relation to an individual's claim to exculpation (or for a reason other than exculpation), they bring with them a distinctive expert knowledge about mental incapacity. This distinctive knowledge is evident in, for instance, the particular language, certain notions of cause and effect, and specific professional authority structures those whom we may call psy-experts bring with them into the courtroom. This concern with the types of knowledge brought to bear on mental

---

[9] For instance, Fletcher makes a convincing case that, over centuries, insanity has drifted from being a general condition (compatible with the idea of exemption) to an excuse: see Fletcher *Rethinking Criminal Law* 837–9. For an opposing argument to the effect that insanity is an exemption, see, for example, Gardner 'The Gist of Excuses' 588 and S Kadish 'Excusing Crime' 257.
[10] This sort of thinking seems to have motivated Jeremy Horder, who advocates classification not in terms of exemptions and excuses, but in terms of excusatory claims, diminished capacity claims, and denials of responsibility. For Horder, these three categories appeal to different types of reasons for conduct: those with respect to which defendants are morally active, mixed reasons for conduct where defendants are both morally active and morally passive, and reasons for conduct with respect to which the defendant is morally passive, respectively: see Horder *Excusing Crime* 103–8. On this basis, Horder concludes diminished responsibility is most accurately thought of as a partial excuse rather than a partial exemption.
[11] See Duff *Answering for Crime* 286–7.
[12] I use the term 'psy-knowledge' following N Rose *Inventing our Selves: Psychology, Power and Personhood* (Cambridge: CUP, 1996).

incapacity in turn connects to the notion of abnormality, and I return to this issue below.

The third reason for rejecting the label defence for claims to exculpation based on incapacity is derived from the rules of procedure and evidence that apply to such claims. As I argue elsewhere, the rules of evidence and procedure that apply to the law of insanity, for example, are distinctive.[13] For instance, the most notable feature of the law on insanity is the special verdict, which, since 1800, has meant that, where a defendant's claim is successful, he or she is liable to an alternative set of disposal measures.[14] Beyond insanity, it is notable that, as well as defence counsel, the prosecution and the judge may raise a number of claims based on mental incapacity. For example, the prosecution may raise diminished responsibility (where the defence has raised insanity), or infanticide (which is an offence as well as a defence in England and Wales), each of which I discuss below. Either the judge or the prosecution or defence counsel may raise unfitness to plead, which I also discuss below. That legal actors other than the defence may raise claims to exculpation based on mental incapacity marks these claims out from criminal law defences such as self-defence, and suggests that the straightforward idea of a defence, in use in the broader criminal law, is obfuscating in this specific context.

From Moral Evaluation to Function

The argument thus far is based on a new sense of what knowledge (expert medical knowledge), and whose knowledge (expert medical professionals), counts, on the relevance of how arguments are initiated in the courtroom (not only by defence counsel), and on the effect of at least some successful claims to mental incapacity (exemption). Having explained why my reconstruction of mental incapacity in criminal law employs the label exculpatory doctrines, rather than defences, I turn now to the second feature of my reconstruction. Here, relative to the bulk of the existing scholarship, the move is from moral evaluation to function and I am relying on the literature concerned not with the relations between extra-legal and legal norms and practices of responsibility (as per the normative scholarship, canvassed above) but with relations between parts of the criminal law corpus. As this implies, a functional approach commences from a different starting point to that of normative approaches but this difference is attractive—a functional approach focuses on what work different criminal law doctrines *do* within the criminal law corpus.

A functional approach to the criminal law has been developed most fully by Paul Robinson as part of a project relating to criminal codes in the US context.[15] The categorization of parts of the criminal law (defences, offences, or other doctrines) by

---

[13] See A Loughnan 'Manifest Madness: Towards A New Understanding of the Insanity Defence' (2007) 70(3) *Modern Law Review* 397. See also my Chapter 6. See also A Loughnan '"In a Kind of Mad Way": A Historical Perspective on Evidence and Proof of Mental Incapacity' (2011) 35(3) *Melbourne University Law Review* 1047.

[14] For discussion, see E Colvin 'Exculpatory Defences in Criminal Law' (1990) 10 *Oxford Journal of Legal Studies* 381, 392.

[15] See P Robinson *Structure and Function in Criminal Law* (New York: Clarendon Press, 1997).

function depends not on a moral-evaluative assessment of particular conduct but on the role of the defence or offence or doctrine in the 'functional structure' of the criminal law. In relation to defences in particular, Robinson suggests that the popularity of the categorization of defences by normative type has obscured important distinctions between defences and between defence groups.[16] Rather than classifying the criminal law in terms of *actus reus* and *mens rea* requirements and defences, Robinson proposes an analysis based on the varying functions—rule articulation, liability assignment, and grading—that different criminal law doctrines perform. According to Robinson, doctrines with a rule articulation function define the prohibited conduct, while, by contrast, doctrines with a liability assignment function set out 'the minimum requirements of liability for a violation' of the law, and, by contrast again, doctrines with a grading function serve to aggravate an actor's liability.[17]

This approach promises a different and potentially more fine-tuned analysis of mental incapacity in criminal law. Initially, however, this promise is unfulfilled: Robinson's functional approach leads him to propose a five-part categorization of criminal law doctrines, but he places exculpation on the basis of mental incapacity wholly within the category of excuses—a category he borrows from the categorization of defences by normative type.[18] More helpfully, for my purposes, however, under Robinson's analysis, the function performed by various excuse defences is more precisely identified. According to Robinson, excuse defences may be subdivided into 'mistake excuses' and 'disability excuses', with the latter relying on a 'disabling abnormality'. In distinguishing between 'disability excuses' (such as insanity) and 'mistake excuses' (such as reliance on an official misstatement of law), Robinson argues that, in the former, 'the disabling abnormality sets the actor apart from the general population'.[19] Unlike 'mistake excuses', which involve a claim that 'the actor should not be punished because in fact he or she has acted in a way that anyone else would have acted in the same situation', 'disability excuses' exculpate (or partially exculpate) according to the defendant's difference from others. In Robinson's words, the 'disability requirement' 'serves to distinguish the actor . . . and allows the law to acquit the actor *because* he is different'.[20] Thus, in Robinson's scheme, as well as defining instances in which an individual is not liable for a criminal offence (liability assignment, a function shared by other excuses), 'disability excuses' serve to separate out those individuals who seek to rely on these excuses from individuals making other kinds of claims to exculpation (thus forming a subset of excuse defences).

---

[16] *Structure and Function in Criminal Law* 68.
[17] *Structure and Function in Criminal Law* 128, and, more generally, 127–42.
[18] Robinson's five-part categorization encompasses absent element defences (eg alibi), offence modification defences (eg renunciation in attempts or conspiracy), justifications, excuses, and non-exculpatory defences (eg diplomatic immunity): see *Structure and Function in Criminal Law* 14–15, 68–71. The last three are general defences that apply to all offences—they exist to bar liability unrelated to the criminalization decisions embodied in the offence definition.
[19] *Structure and Function in Criminal Law* 83.
[20] *Structure and Function in Criminal Law* 84 (emphasis added).

As Robinson acknowledges, the categories of 'disability excuses' and 'mistake excuses' *look* different from each other. But, for Robinson, despite the apparent differences between 'disability excuses' and 'mistake excuses', they are in fact analogous because, in both types of excuses, an individual is excused if, due to 'special conditions', he or she could not have been expected to avoid a violation of the law.[21] That is, the function of both types of excuses is the same. Although in the next section of the chapter I take issue with Robinson's position on the irrelevance of the particular 'special conditions' which give rise to an excuse, at base, a functional approach to mental incapacity in criminal law is useful to me because it reveals that, like 'disability excuses', what I call exculpatory mental incapacity doctrines share a role in the criminal law: they distinguish individuals on the basis of their difference from others. In relation to exculpatory mental incapacity doctrines, exculpation is a product of, and contingent on, the individual's difference from others. This is a specific idea of difference, and it extends to non-exculpatory mental incapacity doctrines, and has a particular character and significance, which I discuss below. Before turning to this, I explain how this idea of a shared function provides the basis for my own analysis about what doctrines in this area of the law have in common, which forms the basis of my own categorization—something that becomes apparent in the third and final move comprising my reconstruction.

From Function to Form

Accepting my preference for doctrines over defences, and function over moral evaluation, it is then necessary to explain the third feature of my reconstruction of this area of the criminal law. Here, I am making a final move—from function to form. I make this move because of what I take to be the significance of the formal structures of those doctrines Robinson collects together in the category 'disability excuses'. By formal structures, I am referring to what might be called the mode or technique of exculpation. Here, in this third and final move comprising my reconstruction of the terrain of mental incapacity, I part company with Robinson: his category of 'disability excuses' and my category of exculpatory mental incapacity doctrines are not coextensive. For Robinson, what sets the actor apart from the 'general population'—his or her 'disabling abnormality'—may be either abnormal circumstances or characteristics.[22] Robinson does not see the distinction between circumstances and characteristics as relevant, arguing that, 'essentially', any claim of

---

[21] *Structure and Function in Criminal Law* 83. Indeed, for Robinson, '[j]ustifications, excuses, and non-exculpatory defences each represent a different kind of special condition' (14).

[22] *Structure and Function in Criminal Law* 83. Thus, Robinson's category of 'disability excuses' includes duress, where exculpation depends on the extraordinary coercive circumstances in which the defendant finds him or herself. Yet, duress is structured differently to other defences that Robinson identifies as 'disability excuses': it provides exculpation where a person of 'reasonable firmness' would have been unable to resist the coercion to which the defendant was subject (see *R v Graham* [1982] 1 All ER 801; *R v Hasan* [2005] 2 Cr App R 22). *Contra M'Naghten* insanity, for instance, the construction of duress requires that the defendant seeking to rely on the defence be *similar* to—rather than *different* from—the 'general population'.

excuse involves a claim that 'the reasonable person suffering a similar disability similarly would have been unable to avoid a violation' of the criminal law.[23] According to Robinson, the practical effect is likely to be the same whether a doctrine is formally structured along the lines of an 'individualized reasonable person test' (as in duress) or whether it is structured to require a sufficiently 'substantial' incapacitation to excuse an individual (evaluation absent the reasonable person comparator, as in the case of involuntariness or automatism, for example).[24] As will be clear, in keeping with Robinson's reliance on the normative idea of excuse in this part of his schema, this practical effect tracks normative lines of culpability in that the individual is not blameworthy whether for reasons internal or external to him or herself.

But there is something to be gained from breaking the category of 'disability excuses' down further. Even if the practical effect of constructing an exculpatory doctrine around the reasonable person standard and constructing it around a direct evaluation of capacity (as 'substantial') might be the same, and there is no appreciable difference detectable in the rather broad concept of excuse, these two doctrinal structures are different in a meaningful way—they rely on different constructions of the individuals raising them. For instance, an individual seeking to rely on either duress (or provocation or 'loss of control'[25]) is constructed as if he or she was making a claim as an ordinary person in extra-ordinary conditions. By contrast, an individual seeking to rely on insanity or infanticide, for example, is constructed as if he or she was making a claim as an other than ordinary person. That is, in these latter types of claims, exculpation is dependent on the individuals' difference—and the technique of exculpation is distinctive. It does not make sense to reference these latter claims to exculpation to the reasonable person standard. After all, such a standard is precluded by the logic of constructing defendants who make these claims as abnormal. As Eric Colvin argues, 'in situations of mental impairment, there is no good reason to insist upon any particular behavioural standards [such as reasonableness] being observed'.[26]

It is clear then that a specific notion of difference—which I call abnormality—is buried within the more generalized idea about difference from others that structures Robinson's category of 'disability excuses'. As noted above, according to Robinson, the 'disability requirement' 'serves to distinguish the actor... and allows the law to acquit the actor because he is different', and the relevant difference flows

---

[23] *Structure and Function in Criminal Law* 84. According to Robinson, the practical effect is likely to be the same whether a doctrine is structured along the lines of an 'individualized reasonable person test' (as in duress) (which Robinson includes in his category of 'disability excuses') or whether it is structured to require a sufficiently 'substantial' incapacitation to excuse an individual (evaluation absent the reasonable person comparator, as in the case of involuntariness or automatism, for example) (*Structure and Function in Criminal Law* 90–1).
[24] *Structure and Function in Criminal Law* 90–1.
[25] On provocation and loss of control, see *R v James* [2006] 1 Cr App R 440 and *Attorney-General for Jersey v Holley* [2005] 2 AC 580, which effectively overruled the decision of the House of Lords in *R v Smith (Morgan)* [2001] 1 Cr App R 31, each concerning Homicide Act 1957, s 3; see now Coroners and Justice Act 2009, ss 54–6, amending the Homicide Act 1957.
[26] Colvin 'Exculpatory Defences in Criminal Law' 403.

from either something about the defendant or his or her circumstances. But the apparent equivalence between self and circumstances obscures what is really at issue in this area of the law. The specific kind of difference, which I seek to capture by the term abnormality, and which flows from something about the individual rather than their circumstances, is distinctive. It maps onto the idea of mental incapacity—a substantive impairment of the standard cognitive, moral, and volitional capacities both assumed and required by the criminal law. This difference pertains to the individual who raises or relies on a mental incapacity doctrine. And, as I discuss below, this specific notion of difference, abnormality, constructs this individual as qualitatively, as opposed to merely quantitatively, different from others.[27]

Where this kind of difference—abnormality—is at issue, exculpation cannot be indexed to the reasonable person comparator because it does not make sense to evaluate the claim to exculpation on that basis. The absence of the reasonable person comparator in the formal structure of the exculpatory doctrines is a formal representation of the particular way mentally incapacitated subjects are imagined in criminal law. Traditionally this absence has been regarded as insignificant. The reasonable person has been thought to have a functional substitute in the requirement that incapacitation (for the insanity doctrine etc) be sufficiently substantial for exculpation (how disordered?; how intoxicated? etc).[28] However, some sort of comparison does exist within these exculpatory mental incapacity doctrines. As I suggest in the final section of this chapter, we can think of the comparison implied in exculpatory mental incapacity doctrines as drawn not so much with a 'normal' defendant but with a mythical, fictitious, constructed 'abnormal' person.

One particular point Robinson makes as part of his analysis of 'disability excuses' remains relevant to my own unit of study, mental incapacity doctrines. This point applies not at the level of categorization but at the level of the doctrines themselves. As Robinson argues in relation to his functional approach to criminal law, in defences such as insanity and intoxication, like most excuse defences, it is the cause of the excusing condition (such as mental disorder or drunkenness) rather than its results that determines which excuse defence is applicable.[29] Robinson suggests that the 'disability-organized system of excuses' may have evolved because disability is an 'independently observable phenomenon'.[30] As discussed above, for

---

[27] This difference, or abnormality, is a distinct state, although it may be a temporary one. Robinson argues that the durability of a defendant's incapacity is of little conceptual significance in the criminal law—what matters is its effect on his or her ability to understand and to control his or her conduct: Robinson *Structure and Function in Criminal Law* 71. Although Robinson concludes that, in addition to its conceptual irrelevance, the durability of the defendant's disabling condition has 'little' practical significance (71), it may be argued that the durability of the defendant's incapacity has a significant practical import as, for instance, it lies behind the special verdict, with attendant disposal orders, and the scope of the requirement of 'disease of the mind' in the *M'Naghten Rules*.

[28] See, for instance, *Structure and Function in Criminal Law* 90–1 and the discussion above.

[29] As Robinson points out, even where the result of a particular disability is the same as the result of insanity (such as a distortion in perception), if the disability is not mental disease, insanity is not the appropriate excuse: *Structure and Function in Criminal Law* 92.

[30] *Structure and Function in Criminal Law* 92.

Robinson, the significance of this lies in the way in which such defences distinguish individuals who seek to rely on them from others. For me, the implications of a 'disability-organized system of excuses' are different. Keeping in mind the ways in which meanings are accorded to behaviour and individuals under mental incapacity doctrines, the significance of a 'disability-organized system of excuses' is two-fold. First, this feature of mental incapacity doctrines invokes the idea that there is an objective aspect to these doctrines, and, by extension, to the process of evaluation of claims based on mental incapacity. Second, the 'disability' aspect of mental incapacity doctrines provides another sign of the role of expert medical knowledges in proof of mental incapacity. I take up these points in the final section of this chapter.

At this point, in advance of a full discussion, below, it is appropriate to offer some preliminary comments on the specific kind of difference—abnormality—that is invoked by mental incapacity doctrines. Abnormality is the label I give to the idea of difference specifically attendant to mental incapacity. This idea of difference is open-textured, and the particular meanings attached to abnormality vary from doctrine to doctrine and over time. This difference is a construct of the law; it is produced through doctrines and practices (with the aid of expert psychiatric and psychological knowledge adduced in relation to claims of mental incapacity). Although Robinson does not argue in this way, I suggest that, as is the case with his category of 'disability excuses', this specific kind of difference is both produced by the doctrine and a precondition of the individual's success in relying on it. That is, the difference of the legal subject is both assumed by and constructed through these legal doctrines. Viewed in this way, mental incapacity doctrines are based on a particular construction of incapacity. Recognizing that mental incapacity doctrines involve the construction of individuals relying on them as abnormal—a difference of kind, not a difference of degree—prepares the way for thinking about the doctrines in a nuanced way, exposing what might otherwise be thought to be neutral or natural aspects of criminal law principles and practices.

Taking seriously both the formal structure of exculpatory criminal law doctrines, and the attendant constructions of individuals seeking to rely on them, means that, in my reconstruction, exculpatory mental incapacity doctrines are a smaller set than Robinson's 'disability excuses'. The category of exculpatory mental incapacity doctrines on which this book is based encompasses only those doctrines which share two distinct but allied features: doctrines in which the evaluative inquiry is not indexed to the reasonable person standard and through which the individual is constructed as abnormal. Thus, in England and Wales, these doctrines are insanity and automatism, and diminished responsibility and infanticide (the latter two are also inculpatory, as I discuss below). Non-exculpatory mental incapacity doctrines are those that have only the second of these two features—that is, the individual relying on them is constructed as abnormal. In this subgroup, there are two procedural doctrines: unfitness to plead and infancy, and one doctrine of imputation: intoxication. These seven doctrines, and the terrain which they traverse, form the subject matter of this book.

The Category of Mental Incapacity Doctrines in Criminal Law

As foreshadowed above, my reconstruction of the terrain of mental incapacity permits a reconceptualization of the role of mental incapacity in criminal law—beyond exculpation. In what follows, I briefly discuss each of the doctrines that, on my approach, are classed as mental incapacity doctrines, with an eye to their functional aspect. Like any such effort, my categorization does not capture everything that might be said about this area of the law, and, as will be seen, it is intended to be a more flexible approach to the organization of legal doctrines than the normative and functional approaches discussed above.

Exculpatory Mental Incapacity Doctrines

Insanity is arguably the archetypal mental incapacity doctrine in criminal law and it is not surprising that it shares the two features that, on my account, denote exculpatory mental incapacity doctrines. As the *M'Naghten Rules* make clear, the success of an insanity plea is dependent on whether the defendant's incapacity is of the requisite type; exculpation is not indexed to the reasonable person standard.[31] In addition, an individual raising insanity is constructed as abnormal in and through the insanity doctrine. A sense of this particular construction is provided by Lord Morris who, in *Bratty*, cited with approval the trial judge's statement to the jury that it was open to them to conclude that Bratty 'behaved in these, perhaps minor, ways of "abnormality"'.[32] In relation to insanity in particular, the meaning given to the difference of those individuals raising the doctrine has had a specific import—for a long time, the insane defendant has been regarded as dangerous. In *Sullivan*, Lord Diplock stated that 'the purpose of the legislation relating to the defence of insanity, ever since its origin in 1800, has been to protect society against recurrence of the dangerous conduct'.[33] Arguably, it was this construction of insane defendants that legitimated the automatic indefinite detention that followed a successful insanity claim until 1990 (via the special verdict).[34] The connection between abnormality, an idea of difference, as it is invoked in the insanity doctrine, and dangerousness, is a contingent association and may be contrasted with the way

---

[31] See *Bratty v Attorney-General for Northern Ireland* [1963] AC 386. As is well known, the *M'Naghten Rules* require that an individual suffer from a 'defect of reason' caused by a 'disease of the mind', and, as a result, he or she must not know the 'nature and quality' of the act or that it was wrong. These requirements are discussed in Chapter 5.

[32] *Bratty v Attorney-General for Northern Ireland* [1963] AC 386 per Lord Morris.

[33] *R v Sullivan* [1984] 1 AC 156, 172. For a historical discussion of insanity and dangerousness, see R Moran 'The Punitive Uses of the Insanity Defence: The Trial for Treason of Edward Oxford (1840)' (1986) 9 *International Journal of Law and Psychiatry* 171.

[34] Since 1800, the special verdict resulting from a successful insanity defence has been inextricably connected with a particular set of disposal options. Until 1990, there was only one disposal option following a successful insanity defence: indefinite detention. For further discussion, see R D Mackay, B J Mitchell and L Howe 'Yet More Facts about the Insanity Defence' [2006] *Criminal Law Review* 399, 408 and my Chapter 6.

in which meaning is given to this idea of difference via other mental incapacity doctrines.

Automatism (or non-insane automatism) may seem at first glance to be an odd inclusion in a category of exculpatory mental incapacity doctrines. By contrast with insanity, automatism does not prescribe a particular disability as a baseline condition for exculpation.[35] The 'external cause' requirement of the doctrine, which has been used to mark the boundary between automatism and insanity, might be taken to mean that this exculpatory doctrine has little, if anything, to do with mental incapacity.[36] Yet, the automatistic individual is also constructed as abnormal; the 'external' factor must affect the individual raising automatism in a particular way, and exculpation is not referenced to the reasonable person comparator, making it an exculpatory mental incapacity doctrine on my account. Exculpation on the basis of automatism is available only to those individuals who are *un*conscious or acting *in*voluntarily—their loss of voluntary control must be total (albeit temporary)—and, in their total incapacitation, such individuals are constructed as qualitatively different from other defendants. Here, abnormality is given a contrasting set of meanings to that attendant to abnormality in insanity: automatism, arising from an external factor, is thought to mark out an individual who is less dangerous (or not dangerous at all) when compared with an insane individual. As Justice Devlin stated in *Hill v Baxter*, 'if there is some temporary loss of consciousness arising accidentally, it is reasonable to hope that it will not be repeated and that it is safe to let an acquitted man go entirely free'.[37]

Unlike insanity and automatism, diminished responsibility alters rather than abrogates criminal responsibility for killing. As a result, it is usually regarded as partially exculpatory. But, as I discuss below, viewed from another angle, diminished responsibility may also be thought to be partially inculpatory, or, to slide between my subcategories of exculpatory and non-exculpatory mental incapacity doctrines. As a result of changes made by the recent Coroners and Justice Act 2009, diminished responsibility is available where a killing is caused or explained by an 'abnormality of mental functioning', arising from a 'recognised medical condition', which has 'substantially impaired' the defendant's ability to understand the nature of his conduct, exercise self-control, or act rationally.[38] Again, exculpation via the doctrine is not indexed to the reasonable person, and the individual seeking partial

---

[35] As is well known, a defendant will be able to rely on automatism for exculpation if he or she meets three conditions: the cause of the automatic or automatistic behaviour is 'external', the defendant is not 'at fault' for getting into a state of automatism, and he or she lost 'total control' over his or her actions (again, there is no comparison with the reasonable person): see *Bratty v Attorney-General for Northern Ireland* [1963] AC 386. See Chapter 5 for a discussion of the law of automatism.

[36] This argument is probably strongest in relation to what has been referred to as conscious automatism, describing the kind of behaviour resulting from spasms or reflex actions, where it might be thought that an individual's mind is unaffected. However, as Andrew Ashworth argues, automatism is most accurately understood as a denial of authorship, thus encompassing situations in which the ordinary link between mind and body was absent: see A Ashworth *Principles of Criminal Law* (Oxford: OUP, 2009) 88–90. My notion of abnormality extends to cover such situations.

[37] *Hill v Baxter* [1958] 1 QB 277, 285. See also *Bratty v Attorney-General for Northern Ireland* [1963] AC 386.

[38] Coroners and Justice Act 2009, s 52, amending Homicide Act 1957, s 2.

exculpation via diminished responsibility is constructed as abnormal.[39] This construction of diminished defendants is invoked in the requirement of the newly formulated provision that an individual must suffer from an 'abnormality of mental functioning', or, in the rather infamous phrase it replaced, an 'abnormality of mind' (which was held to refer to 'a state of mind so different from that of ordinary human beings that the reasonable man would term it abnormal'[40]). Abnormality is also open-textured in relation to diminished responsibility, and, within the confines of the doctrine itself, it has accommodated a variety of meanings around reduced culpability (including supposedly altruistic lethal violence or lethal violence occurring in the context of sustained victimization[41]). As with other exculpatory mental incapacity doctrines, this specific kind of difference, which I am calling abnormality, is both a condition of exculpation and a construction of those individuals seeking to rely on these doctrines.

Like diminished responsibility, where it operates as an exculpatory doctrine, infanticide is partially exculpatory and it is available only to certain offences. In addition, as is both well known and controversial, infanticide is restricted by the type of defendant who can rely on it. In England and Wales, the provision operates to substitute liability for infanticide in place of murder or manslaughter where the 'balance' of the defendant woman's mind was disturbed at the time of the act or omission leading to the death of her child under the age of 12 months.[42] Again, the infanticidal woman is constructed as abnormal (evident in the language of disturbance and imbalance, for instance) and exculpation is not referenced to the reasonable person comparator, making infanticide an exculpatory mental

---

[39] By contrast, provocation, which was replaced by a partial defence of 'loss of control' in the Coroners and Justice Act 2009, is indexed to the reasonable person. Some commentators have suggested that the historical trajectory of provocation has been from a partial justification to a partial excuse; see, eg J Dressler 'Provocation: Partial Justification or Partial Excuse?' (1988) 51(4) *Modern Law Review* 467. Even if this means provocation should be best thought of as an excuse, nonetheless, on my reconstruction, it is not an exculpatory mental incapacity doctrine because exculpation via the doctrine is referenced to the reasonable person standard.

[40] See *Byrne* [1960] 2 QB 396, 403 per Lord Parker. Something of what is at stake in criminal law investment in a notion of abnormality is reflected in the hard-fought academic and practice debate about the difference between provocation and diminished responsibility, where the latter has been regarded as the appropriate preserve of an individual who is abnormal in some way. For a flavour of this debate, see B J Mitchell et al 'Pleading for Provoked Killers: In Defence of Morgan Smith' (2008) 124 *Law Quarterly Review* 675 and T Macklem and J Gardner 'Provocation and Pluralism' (2001) 64(6) *Modern Law Review* 815 and, in relation to legal practice, see *Attorney-General for Jersey v Holley* [2005] 2 AC 580 and *R v Smith (Morgan)* [2001] 1 Cr App R 31.

[41] See discussion in *R v Smith (Morgan)* [2001] 1 Cr App R 31. See also N Lacey 'Partial Defences to Homicide: Questions of Power and Principle in Imperfect and Less Imperfect Worlds' in A Ashworth and B J Mitchell (eds) *Rethinking English Homicide Law* (Oxford: OUP, 2000) 107.

[42] Infanticide Act 1938, as amended by Coroners and Justice Act 2009. With its particular wording, the Infanticide Act 1922 and the subsequent 1938 Act 'simplified' the legal relationship between mental disturbance and the *actus reus* of the offence—a mere temporal connection between the disturbance and the killing suffices for partial exculpation. See N Walker *Crime and Insanity in England (Vol 1: The Historical Perspective)* (Edinburgh: Edinburgh University Press, 1968) 131. The recent Coroners and Justice Act 2009 amended the infanticide provision such that it is now clear that it is an alternative offence and a partial defence to both murder and manslaughter: see *Gore (Lisa Therese) (Deceased)* [2007] EWCA Crim 2789. The 2009 Act also altered the wording of the provisions in a minor way. Infanticide is discussed in my Chapter 8.

incapacity doctrine on my account. The creation and retention of this unique doctrine in the criminal law has been the subject of a thoroughgoing critique by feminist theorists.[43] For my purposes in thinking about the kind of difference of mental incapacitated subjects, one particular aspect of this exculpatory doctrine is of note: in providing that women's mental disturbance has a physical base in common reproductive practices (giving birth and breastfeeding), infanticide achieves a naturalization of the construction of abnormality for criminal law purposes. This in turn supports two facially contradictory effects: inculpation via the offence of infanticide, which I discuss below, as well as partial exculpation.

Non-Exculpatory Mental Incapacity Doctrines

Mental incapacity is a basis for doctrines which perform other roles in criminal law, beyond exculpation. The most prominent of these other roles is a procedural role, which the doctrine of unfitness to plead performs. Unfitness to plead is a procedural provision exempting a defendant from an ordinary trial (at least temporarily) on the basis that he or she cannot understand or participate in it.[44] Unfitness to plead is often swept up alongside exculpatory mental incapacity in academic studies, on the basis that exemption from trial via unfitness is a procedural cognate of exculpation. However, in thinking about unfitness to plead, it would be inaccurate to reduce its role to the ways in which it is similar to exculpation. Historically, unfitness to plead (as insanity on arraignment) had connections to the substantive criminal law, and, as is the case with insane defendants, the particular abnormality of unfit defendants has been closely connected with dangerousness.[45] But, as reflected in the way in which it is now decided (by a judge rather than a jury), the doctrine has come to be intimately connected with the progress of the trial and, as such, with due process.[46] With its increasingly technical identity as a procedural provision, unfitness to plead is now more closely connected to the integrity of the criminal trial process than to the role of mental incapacity as a basis for exculpation.

---

[43] See, eg, H Allen *Justice Unbalanced: Gender, Psychiatry and Judicial Decisions* (Milton Keynes: Open University Press, 1987) and F E Raitt and M S Zeedyk *The Implicit Relation of Psychology and Law: Women and Syndrome Evidence* (London: Routledge, 2000).

[44] The Law Commission has recently proposed that the current, narrow cognitive criteria of unfitness be replaced with a broader test that assesses whether the accused has decision-making capacity for trial: see *Unfitness to Plead: A Consultation Paper* (Law Com No 197, 2010) para 3.41 for discussion. The Law Commission's proposal is based on the civil law on decision-making capacity. The Mental Capacity Act 2005 provides that a person is unable to make a decision for him or herself if he or she is unable to understand the information relevant to the decision, retain that information, use or weigh it as part of the process of making the decision or communicate the decision (s 3(1)). The Act also provides that a person is not to be treated as unable to make a decision 'unless all practicable steps to help him to do so have been taken without success' (s 1(3)). I discuss unfitness to plead in Chapter 4.

[45] On the historical connections to the substantive law of insanity, see Walker *Crime and Insanity in England (Vol 1)* for discussion. On dangerousness, the Criminal Lunatics Act 1800 provided that the unfit as well as the insane could be kept in 'strict custody until his Majesty's pleasure shall be known': see Moran 'The Punitive Uses of the Insanity Defence'. I take up both these issues in Chapter 5.

[46] See R D Mackay et al 'A Continued Upturn in Unfitness to Plead—More Disability in Relation to the Trial Under the 1991 Act' [2007] *Criminal Law Review* 530 for discussion.

This discussion of unfitness to plead as a procedural provision leads me to consider the status of infancy and suggest it is appropriately included in my category of non-exculpatory mental incapacity doctrines. In criminal law, infancy or non-age refers to the principle that, below a certain age, an individual is beyond the reach of the criminal law. The exemption is provided to children who are considered to be insufficiently mature to be subject to criminal sanction.[47] Interestingly, infancy is usually identified as a *sui generis* provision and rarely included in studies of mental incapacity in criminal law—perhaps because it is thought of as a non-exculpatory defence (like diplomatic immunity in Robinson's account). While infancy cannot be considered an exculpatory doctrine as it blocks an inquiry into criminal responsibility, it might be thought of as a procedural doctrine, implicated in the legitimacy of the criminal process.[48] Infancy also relies on a construction of defendants as abnormal, although I acknowledge that, as is the case with intoxication, discussed below, this is something of an unstable construction.[49] The claim that young defendants are constructed as abnormal seems counter-intuitive because, as Lord Diplock stated in relation to age and the law of provocation, 'nothing could be more ordinary or normal than to be aged 15'.[50] Yet, to the extent that it is regarded as an insufficiently developed or mature state, the criminal law doctrine of infancy invokes an idea of young people as abnormal (mentally and physically).[51]

In addition to these procedural doctrines, mental incapacity is also the basis of what Robinson has termed a 'doctrine of imputation': the law relating to voluntary intoxication.[52] In academic texts, the rules relating to intoxicated offending (which

---

[47] See *C (A Minor) v DPP* [1996] AC 1. The age of criminal responsibility has varied over time, and from jurisdiction to jurisdiction. In England and Wales, the age of criminal responsibility is currently 10 years: Children and Young Persons Act 1963, s 16. Significantly, infancy is a status; so, unlike unfitness to plead, there is no inquiry into the individual mental state of a child below the age of criminal responsibility and no possibility of a criminal trial and punishment. Infancy, and its close cousin, *doli incapax*, are discussed in Chapter 4.

[48] See G Maher 'Age and Criminal Responsibility' (2004–05) 2 *Ohio State Journal of Criminal Law* 493.

[49] The strongest evidence in support of this construction seems to be the historical connection between the development of the principles relating to infancy and those related to the substantive law of insanity: see A Platt and B L Diamond 'The Origins of the "Right and Wrong" Test of Criminal Responsibility and its Subsequent Development in the United Sates: An Historical Survey' (1966) 53 *California Law Review* 1227.

[50] *DPP v Camplin* [1978] AC 705, 718. A notion of 'normal immaturity' motivated the Government to reject the Law Commission's proposal to include 'developmental immaturity' in the new diminished responsibility provision contained in Coroners and Justice Act 2009, s 52, discussed above: see HL Deb 30 June 2009, vol 712, col 185–8.

[51] In criminal law scholarship, the conceptual connections between insanity and infancy are reflected in Michael Moore's theory that insanity, intoxication and infancy all belong in the category of 'status excuse': see M S Moore 'Causation and the Excuses' (1985) 73 *California Law Review* 1091, 1098. In a way that has long since fallen away for insane defendants, for instance, this abnormality is associated with vulnerability (warranting immunity from the rigours of the criminal law): see, eg, N Jareborg *Scraps of Penal Theory* (Uppsala: Iustus Forlag, 2002) 119–20. However, the House of Lords rather animated discussion of *doli incapax* in *C (A Minor) v DPP* [1996] AC 1, which led to legislative abolition of the doctrine, and recurrent debates about the appropriate age at which a child should be exposed to criminal liability, suggests that this notion of vulnerability is not all one way.

[52] According to Robinson, doctrines of imputation impute missing offence elements, providing an 'alternative means of holding the defendant liable as if the required elements were satisfied': see

include rules on involuntary intoxication) are sometimes included along with mental incapacity doctrines, although it has not been clear that this is not just because intoxication does not seem to belong elsewhere. As is well known, if controversial, the *Majewski* rules provide that voluntary intoxication is evidence that may be adduced in support of a defence argument that the prosecution has not proved that the defendant formed the requisite *mens rea* in offences of 'specific intent'.[53] As Robinson argues, although there is no suggestion that the actor in fact satisfied the required offence element, 'the special conditions required by the doctrine of imputation are said to justify treating the actor as if he satisfies the imputed element'.[54] As it does the work of imputation, voluntary intoxication is properly regarded as a mental incapacity doctrine because it is based on the abnormality of the intoxicated defendant, even if this abnormality is temporary and is something a significant percentage of the population have experienced at least once.[55] The specific meaning given to intoxicated abnormality—something along the lines of a lay concept of recklessness—is suggested by the House of Lords in *Majewski*, where Lord Elwyn-Jones referred to a defendant who 'consciously and deliberately takes alcohol and drugs...in order to escape from reality...and thereby *disables* himself from taking the care he might otherwise take'.[56]

Beyond exculpation, imputation, and a procedural role, the last of the roles of mental incapacity doctrines in criminal law is that of inculpation. Here, I refer to the doctrines of diminished responsibility and infanticide. As it is not buttressed by the status of a distinct offence, diminished responsibility is a more controversial inclusion in this latter category than infanticide. As mentioned above, although typically regarded as partially exculpatory, viewed from the other side, diminished responsibility seems to be partially, or, more accurately, *differently* inculpatory, and thus to slide between my two subcategories of exculpatory and non-exculpatory doctrines. This approach to diminished responsibility is not common but it could follow from the idea that a manslaughter conviction may be contrasted with a special verdict based on insanity as well as with a murder conviction.[57] Indeed, existing analyses of diminished responsibility as an excuse wrestle with its unusual

---

Robinson *Structure and Function in Criminal Law* 67. In a similar analysis, Andrew Simester has argued that voluntary intoxication is specifically a form of constructive liability: see A P Simester 'Intoxication is Never a Defence' [2009] *Criminal Law Review* 3.

[53] *DPP v Majewski* [1977] AC 443. The law of intoxication forms the subject of Chapter 7.

[54] Robinson *Structure and Function in Criminal Law* 58. By contrast with voluntary intoxication, Robinson includes involuntary intoxication within his category of 'disability excuses' (71).

[55] The ubiquity of intoxication poses a challenge for a construction of the intoxicated defendant as abnormal and, so, this construction is perhaps a more tenuous one than that of the insane defendant, for example. However, the notion of abnormality subsists in the law of England and Wales, even as intoxication pleas are less uncommon than those of insanity. See Chapter 7 for further discussion.

[56] *DPP v Majewski* [1977] AC 443, 471 (emphasis added).

[57] That both insanity and diminished responsibility may be relevant in a murder trial has been recognised in Criminal Procedure (Insanity) Act 1964, s 6, which provides that, if the defence raises either insanity or diminished responsibility, the prosecution may raise the other as an alternative.

status as a partial doctrine, attempting to account for the fact that certain conditions affecting a defendant's mental capacity are relevant to conviction (not just to sentence), but merely reduce rather than abrogate his or her criminal responsibility.[58] It is possible that the ambiguity over whether diminished responsibility relates to the actor or the act, which has stalked the doctrine since its origins as a plea in mitigation in the late nineteenth-century Scots law, allows the doctrine to be Janus-faced in this respect.[59] Assessing the value of this way of looking at diminished responsibility awaits a fuller discussion of the doctrine in Chapter 9. For now, it is possible to suggest that, when the link between mental incapacity and exculpation is de-naturalized, different perspectives on what might be regarded as well-traversed territory become possible.[60]

As mentioned above, although not the subject of a large amount of academic analysis (and rarely a conviction), infanticide is an offence as well as an exculpatory mental incapacity doctrine.[61] Just as it is a unique kind of exculpatory doctrine, so it is a unique kind of offence. In Hillary Allen's words, as an offence, infanticide is distinctive because 'mental abnormality is a positive precondition for conviction'.[62] This distinctive feature has been largely occluded by the most prominent feature of infanticide—only mothers who kill their own children when the children are younger than 12 months may be convicted of it, a feature of the doctrine which I mentioned above.[63] As a 'positive precondition for conviction', it is notable that, as could also be said to be the case with diminished responsibility, abnormality is here functioning to inculpate the individual woman charged with infanticide. The legal formulation short-circuiting an inquiry into a woman's criminal responsibility (which is the most interesting aspect of the law of infanticide) is double-edged: the connection between a defendant woman's abnormality and particular (criminal) conduct (killing)—as constructed through the infanticide provision—sustains both an offence and an exculpatory doctrine. This inculpatory role for mental incapacity is diametrically opposed to its supposedly principal role of exculpation.

---

[58] See, eg, E Griew 'The Future of Diminished Responsibility' [1988] *Criminal Law Review* 75, 81–2 and R Sparks '"Diminished Responsibility" in Theory and Practice' (1964) 27(1) *Modern Law Review* 9, 16–18.

[59] For discussion of the historical development of diminished responsibility in Scotland, see J Chalmers and F Leverick, *Criminal Defences and Pleas in Bar of Trial* (Edinburgh: W Green, 2006) 221–4.

[60] See further my Chapter 9. This dual assessment of diminished responsibility—as either or both an exculpatory and an inculpatory doctrine—may also shed light on the history of the insanity doctrine, which was, for a significant period of time, at least formally the basis of a conviction. In the Trial of Lunatics Act 1883, the special verdict was repackaged as 'guilty but insane' thus technically altering its form to a conviction from an acquittal. For discussion, see R Moran 'The Origin of Insanity as a Special Verdict: The Trial for Treason of James Hadfield' (1985) 19(3) *Law and Society Review* 487, 519. The Criminal Procedure (Insanity) Act 1964 restored the form of the special verdict to 'not guilty by reason of insanity' (s 1).

[61] See Infanticide Act 1938, s 1(1) (as amended by the Coroners and Justice Act 2009) which makes infanticide an independent homicide offence.

[62] See Allen *Justice Unbalanced* 27.

[63] Explanations for the existence of a separate homicide offence—like the explanations for the exculpatory provision—are historical: see my Chapter 8; see also T Ward 'The Sad Subject of Infanticide: Law, Medicine and Child Murder 1860–1938' (1999) 8(2) *Social and Legal Studies* 163.

Taken together, exculpatory and non-exculpatory doctrines make up my category of mental incapacity doctrines. As will be clear by now, the significance of my reconstruction lies not in its radical departure from what parts of criminal law have been captured to date by the category of mental incapacity defences (with allied procedural provisions included). With the exception of infancy, my approach to the category of mental incapacity doctrines mirrors the operational, if unarticulated, basis on which the authors of major monographs on the English and Welsh law proceed.[64] However, it should be noted that one of the consequences of my approach is that, because of its sensitivity to the particular formal structure of criminal doctrines, the scope of the category of mental incapacity doctrines will vary from jurisdiction to jurisdiction.[65] This greater sensitivity to doctrinal forms suggests that my reconstruction has a more rough-and-ready character, and this in turn indicates that it is not intended to be as definitive as the normative and functional approaches discussed in the first section of the chapter. Rather, my reconstruction is intended as a rethinking of mental incapacity in criminal law. The value of my reconstruction lies in what it allows us to see about this area of criminal law: that doctrines based on mental incapacity perform a variety of functions beyond exculpation, evident when the terrain of mental incapacity is re-assembled around those doctrines that imagine the subject who relies on them as abnormal, and, where the doctrines are exculpatory, that exculpation is not indexed to the reasonable person.

At this point, it is useful to comment on the relationship between the terrain of mental incapacity in criminal law, as marked out above, and criminal non-responsibility, which refers to the outcome of some criminal law adjudication processes. Criminal non-responsibility is sometimes regarded as coextensive with mental incapacity, and thus it might be thought that this term is synonymous with the references to mental incapacity in criminal law made here. On my approach to mental incapacity in criminal law, the terrain of interest to me is not coterminus with non-responsibility. Rather, non-responsibility—marked out by exculpatory mental incapacity doctrines—is a 'terrain within a terrain', encompassed by but not coextensive with mental incapacity. As my category of non-exculpatory mental incapacity doctrines suggests, the terrain of mental incapacity in criminal law extends beyond non-responsibility. But, while criminal non-responsibility and mental incapacity are not flip sides of the same coin, appreciation of the principles and practices of non-responsibility assists in illuminating what I want to suggest is distinctive in the terrain of mental incapacity.[66]

---

[64] See R D Mackay *Mental Condition Defences in the Criminal Law* (Oxford: Clarendon Press, 1995) and Walker *Crime and Insanity in England (Vol 1)*.

[65] For instance, it might be possible to draft a duress doctrine in a way in which it would construct the defendant as abnormal and would not incorporate a comparison between the defendant and the reasonable person and, if this was the case, it would move into my category of mental incapacity doctrines.

[66] See Chapter 3 on 'manifest madness'.

Difference within Criminal Law

Thinking anew about mental incapacity in criminal law, without the assumed priority of mental incapacity as a basis for exculpation, entails questioning what certain criminal law doctrines share with others, and on what basis they are grouped together. As the first step in my discussion, this chapter has offered a reconstruction of the terrain of mental incapacity in criminal law as mental incapacity doctrines, a subset of which is exculpatory. This reconstruction was based on a new sense of what and whose knowledge counts (to include expert psychiatric and psychological knowledges of incapacity), on the relevance of how arguments are initiated in the courtroom (not only by defence counsel), and on the effect of at least some successful claims based on mental incapacity (exemption). This reconstruction also took the formal structure of criminal law doctrines seriously, and considered the kind of subject imagined by them to be a factor germane to the way in which this area of the criminal law is organized. This reconstruction prompts a reconceptualization of the role of mental incapacity in criminal law, which represents the second step in my discussion. Here, it becomes clear that mental incapacity performs a multiplicity of roles—inculpation, imputation, and a procedural role—beyond exculpation. My own effort at categorization cashed out that rethinking and exposed those aspects of mental incapacity doctrines that are illuminated by my reconstruction.

It is now possible to consider in more detail the specific kind of difference—abnormality—that I suggest has definitional or constitutive significance in relation to mental incapacity doctrines. The specific kind of difference that goes under the label abnormality is the outcome of legal evaluation—either processorial or adjudicative practices produce constructions of individuals relying on mental incapacity doctrines. As foreshadowed above, I suggest that according to this kind of difference, the individual is marked out as *qualitatively* different (different in kind) rather than quantitatively different (different in degree) from others. This qualitative difference is both a requirement of the doctrine and a construction of the individuals (diminished, abnormal, disabled) who seek to rely on them. The effect of this qualitative difference is that it has a precise and definite scope and is not subject to infinite gradations. The construction of individuals seeking to rely on mental incapacity doctrines as abnormal or qualitatively different from others also assists in the construction of the primary subject of the criminal law as 'always accountable', to borrow Dana Rabin's term.[67] The notion that an identifiable and delimited category of individuals lies beyond the reach of the criminal law preserves the norms of responsibility that the law encodes. By constructing the non-responsible subject as abnormal, the 'normal' individual becomes a responsible legal subject, one to whom ordinary principles of responsibility, liability, and punishment apply.

---

[67] D Rabin *Identity, Crime and Legal Responsibility in Eighteenth Century England* (New York: Palgrave Macmillan, 2004) 110.

Further, because the specific kind of difference I have called abnormality is open-textured, the particular meanings attached to this kind of difference vary from doctrine to doctrine and over time. As Nicola Lacey argues, the responsible subject of law is a particular and temporally contingent phenomenon.[68] I consider the particular contours of the notion of abnormality in relation to each of the mental incapacity doctrines discussed in this book. To give a flavour of this discussion, I mention just two points here. As I discuss in Chapter 5, these particular meanings include, for instance, dangerousness (in relation to insane defendants, for example) and not so dangerous (in relation to automatistic defendants). In relation to infanticide, which I discuss in Chapter 8, the infanticidal woman's abnormality is depicted as less dangerous or not dangerous at all. In addition, an infanticidal woman's difference is naturalized, and, as it is depicted as a product of her physiology, something which all women share, it suggests a 'natural maternal violence', which cannot be subject to the usual legal restraints.[69] The effect of these varying constructions is that what is actually a contingent set of meanings is portrayed as if they were given and unproblematic. Further, the particular meanings given to abnormality (such as dangerousness) are encoded in an individual's behaviour. This enhances the importance of behaviour or conduct in the context of legal evaluation and adjudication of mental incapacity claims, and I take up this point in my 'manifest madness' analysis in the next chapter.

Abnormality as a specific idea of difference, and the absence of the reasonable person standard in exculpatory doctrines (the second of the two constitutive features of the doctrines included in my reconstruction), are connected. The absence of the reasonable person standard in exculpatory mental incapacity doctrines may seem unimportant at first glance. Thus, noting that the 'reasonable person' plays an important role in the English and American criminal law, but not in the German criminal law, Hörnle argues that social expectations stand behind the 'reasonable person'; for Hörnle, these social expectations are relevant to judgments about wrongdoing but not judgments about personal responsibility, which she argues need to be shaped with a view to the individual offender.[70] Similarly, as discussed above, Robinson argues that the presence or absence of the reasonable person standard is merely a question of form rather than substance. Like scholars such as John Gardner, Robinson argues that, although excuses might be thought to be subjective, in that they are dependent on the actor rather than the act, they are structured according to some form of objective standard, such as the reasonable person.[71] According to Robinson, 'where a disabling abnormality exists, the claim

---

[68] See N Lacey 'In Search of the Responsible Subject: History, Philosophy and Social Sciences in Criminal Law Theory' (2001) 64(3) *Modern Law Review* 350 and N Lacey 'Space, Time and Function: Intersecting Principles of Responsibility Across the Terrain of Criminal Justice' (2007) 1 *Criminal Law and Philosophy* 233.
[69] Allen *Justice Unbalanced* 28.
[70] See T Hörnle 'Social Expectations in the Criminal Law: The "Reasonable Person" in a Comparative Perspective' (2008) 11 *New Criminal Law Review* 1.
[71] Robinson *Structure and Function in Criminal Law* 89–90; see also Gardner *Offences and Defences* 111.

of excuse is essentially a claim that the reasonable person suffering a similar disability would have been unable to avoid a violation'.[72] Other scholars have made arguments to similar effect.[73]

Is this all that might be said on this topic? What is the potential significance of exculpation and partial exculpation absent a reasonable person comparator? Something of a guide to this question is provided by the significance of the *presence* of this comparator elsewhere in the criminal law. As a number of scholars attest, the reasonable person occupies a central role in the criminal law. Indeed, the figure of the 'reasonable person' is arguably at the centre of the criminal law.[74] Lindsay Farmer's analysis of the 'reasonable person' in criminal law is most helpful here. Farmer regards the 'reasonable man' as the 'emblem of the modern criminal law', arguing that the 'concern with reasonableness is a feature of the modern law alone'.[75] As Farmer argues, the reasonable person is a device with a particular role in the modern criminal law. In Farmer's words, the 'reasonable man' is 'the means by which a governable community can be imagined by the modern law'. The criminal law 'does not express community values through this device, but seeks to create them'.[76] It is through this device that 'judges labour to connect the operation of the law to community feelings or community interests'.[77] The significance of the reasonable person in criminal law hints at something intriguing about its absence in the area of mental incapacity.

If the absence of the reasonable person comparator is significant, as I suggest it is, the challenging task of interpreting an absence (reading a silence) follows. If the figure of the 'reasonable person' may be thought to occupy a central place in the modern criminal law,[78] what is the significance of exculpation via formal structures

---

[72] *Offences and Defences* 84.
[73] Although he does not employ the same reasoning, Gardner reaches a similar conclusion. Referring to the tradition of placing a reasonableness requirement on excuses in criminal law, Gardner argues that the absence of this requirement in some excuses 'does not show a drift to a more purely "subjective" account of excuses' but rather indicates that some excuses 'may actually serve to negate an element of the offence rather than to excuse or justify its commission': see *Offences and Defences* 111. Following this logic would mean that exculpatory mental incapacity doctrines go exclusively to the absence of the elements of the offence, rather than the presence of additional exculpatory factors. Arguably, mental incapacity defences do not reduce to this but rather work both ways. For instance, a successful insanity defence may indicate that a defendant did not form the requisite *mens rea* for an offence, or that he or she did form it, but nonetheless met the requirements of the *M'Naghten Rules*. As several commentators have pointed out, knowledge of the wrongness of an act is not an application of the ordinary rules of *mens rea*: see for instance, T Ward 'Magistrates, Insanity and the Common Law' [1997] *Criminal Law Review* 796, 802. A defendant may have the *mens rea* for an offence, and yet, as a result of a defect of reason resulting from a disease of the mind, he or she may not know that the act was wrong. As a result, the insanity defence actually operates in two ways: it either negates an element of the offence (*mens rea*) or it excuses or exempts the defendant although he or she performed the *actus reus* with the requisite *mens rea*: see Colvin 'Exculpatory Defences in Criminal Law' 394.
[74] G P Fletcher 'The Right and the Reasonable' (1985) 98 *Harvard Law Journal* 949, 949.
[75] L Farmer 'The Obsession with Definition: The Nature of Crime and Critical Legal Theory' (1996) 5 *Social and Legal Studies* 57, 66.
[76] Farmer *Criminal Law, Tradition and Legal Order* 183.
[77] Farmer 'The Obsession with Definition' 57.
[78] Farmer 'The Obsession with Definition' 66.

other than a reasonable person comparator? One way of thinking about this is to suggest that, in the absence of the reasonable person comparator, exculpation on the basis of mental incapacity is coordinated and legitimated in distinctive ways.[79] This approach seems germane to the topic of mental incapacity. For instance, if exculpation on the basis of mental incapacity implicates expert and lay knowledge of incapacity, then both types of knowledge are required for the legitimation of verdicts relating to mental incapacity.[80] These arguments invite a close assessment of the relevance of different types of knowledge of mental incapacity brought to bear on mental incapacity claims in criminal law.[81]

My own study of mental incapacity in criminal law leads me to suggest that the adjudication of claims to exculpation based on mental incapacity involves a tacit comparison, but not one drawn to the 'reasonable person'. I suggest we might think of the comparison involved in adjudication of such claims as drawn not so much with a 'normal' defendant but with a mythical, fictitious, constructed 'abnormal' person, that is, an individual with the relevant condition but without the criminal act. As Robinson notes, and as discussed above, various incapacitating conditions are accommodated by the existence of various 'disability excuses', which are generally associated with a particular disability.[82] As I suggested above, the existence of exculpatory mental incapacity doctrines correlated with particular disabilities signals something objective about the process of evaluation of claims based on mental incapacity, as well as providing another sign of the role of expert medical knowledges in proof of mental incapacity. The combined effect of these two aspects of 'disability'-named doctrines is such as to conjure up a (mythical, fictional, constructed) mentally incapacitated individual and to invoke some sort of implicit comparison to him or her in the legal evaluation and adjudication process.

In this chapter, I offered a reorganization of mental incapacity in criminal law, which led to a reconceptualization of the roles played by mental incapacity. Thinking anew about what parts of the criminal law belong together and on what basis they are connected, I made a case for a particular theorized scope of the terrain of mental incapacity. I then examined closely the significance of what

---

[79] The notion that changes in the principles of criminal responsibility represent responses to problems of coordination and legitimation has been developed by Nicola Lacey. Lacey argues that these 'general problems' relate to the ways in which both the values expressed by the criminal law and the knowledge or belief in facts on which individual judgments depend are coordinated and legitimated: see Lacey 'In Search of the Responsible Subject' 368.

[80] Tony Ward suggests something along these lines in the 'dual authority of science and lay consensus', which he argues underpins the historical operation of mental incapacity doctrines such as insanity and diminished responsibility: see T Ward 'Observers, Advisors, or Authorities? Experts, Juries and Criminal Responsibility in Historical Perspective' (2001) 12 *Journal of Forensic Psychology* 105.

[81] I discuss this in Chapter 3, as part of my 'manifest madness' analysis, and in Chapter 6 regarding evidence and proof of insanity and automatism. For a discussion of the role of expert knowledge of mental incapacity, see, eg, M Lynch 'Circumscribing Expertise: Membership Categories in Courtroom Testimony' in S Jasanoff (ed) *States of Knowledge: The Co-production of Science and Social Order* (New York: Routledge, 2004) 161 and T Ward 'English Law's Epistemology of Expert Testimony' (2006) 33(4) *Journal of Law and Society* 572.

[82] Robinson *Structure and Function in Criminal Law* 92.

I regard as the definitional features of mental incapacity doctrines—the construction of the subject as abnormal, and the absence of the reasonable person comparator. This analysis exposed the distinctive features of mental incapacity doctrines when compared with other criminal law doctrines.

It now falls to analyse the mental incapacity terrain itself, on its own terms. This involves looking across each of the mental incapacity doctrines to capture something of the topography of this terrain taken as a whole. It also entails extending the inquiry from doctrines to doctrines and practices, that is, taking into account the evidentiary and procedural aspects of mental incapacity in assessing the mental incapacity terrain. In the next chapter, I examine the formal qualities of this terrain under my 'manifest madness' analysis.

3
'Manifest Madness': The Intersection of 'Madness' and Crime

This chapter sets out the analysis that gives the book its title. Having made an argument about the scope of the terrain of mental incapacity, and thus the focus of this book, in Chapter 2, I now analyse the terrain itself. This terrain represents the point of intersection between 'madness' and crime, or, between putative 'madness' and putative crime. In this chapter, I make the case that the terrain of mental incapacity has particular features, which I analyse under the label 'manifest madness'. Based on a close and systematic study of mental incapacity doctrines and practices, I suggest that, on this terrain, 'madness' is constructed as having two formal qualities: on the one hand, it is dispositional, and, on the other hand, it can be 'read off' conduct by different participants in the criminal justice process. These two formal qualities can be thought of as two topographical features of the mental incapacity terrain, one ontological and one epistemological. It is to capture this dual aspect of 'madness' for criminal law purposes that I use the adjective 'manifest'. As I discuss below, these features of the terrain of mental incapacity are significant as together they colour the legal evaluative and adjudicative practices associated with mental incapacity.

In turning to focus on the terrain of mental incapacity, as opposed to the content of the category of mental incapacity doctrines, a comment about the relationship between these two topics, and Chapters 2 and 3, is warranted. In Chapter 2, I make a case for a particular approach to the organization of criminal law doctrines based on mental incapacity. As discussed in the previous chapter, a specific kind of difference—one that I labelled abnormality—can be detected in doctrines based on mental incapacity. Here, I extend my line of sight, beyond legal doctrines, to encompass legal practices concerning evidence and proof of mental incapacity. This permits a closer and more nuanced view of what it is that distinguishes this area, enlarging the scholarly frame to produce a picture of the intricate internal pattern, logic, or coherence of the terrain of mental incapacity. Adopting a multidimensional approach to the terrain of mental incapacity (taking into account evidence and proof as well as legal doctrines) prompts me to adopt the term 'madness'—a thicker notion and a term that comes with its own baggage—because there is something more complex and multilayered that I seek to capture here. I am aware of the loaded nature of the term 'madness' but employ it consciously in order to convey the broader social and political relevance of this area of criminal law and by way of acknowledgment of the extra-legal scholarship on mental incapacity.[1]

The analysis presented in this chapter is the outcome of a careful socio-historical study of the doctrines and practices that make up the terrain of mental incapacity. I have come to the arguments put forward here through a systematic examination of each of the different parts of the mental incapacity terrain (its doctrines and attendant practices of evidence and proof) as well as a consideration of the terrain as a whole (following the argument advanced in Chapter 2). As such, the analysis in this chapter differs from that offered in the chapters that follow in Part II and Part III of this book. In those chapters, I provide a close tracing of the historical development of each of the doctrines that are classed as mental incapacity doctrines on my account. Here, however, I have a different aim in mind. I aim to introduce the reader to a distillation of what I regard as the most salient features of the mental incapacity terrain. It is this distilled assessment of the mental incapacity terrain that ensures this analysis adds to the existing scholarly literature on mental incapacity in criminal law.

The argument in this chapter unfolds in two main steps. First, by way of a link to the arguments made in Chapter 2, I make a case for thinking about the terrain of mental incapacity (not just its doctrines) in a way that sensitizes us to what marks it out. I do this from two different perspectives—from history and from knowledge. This discussion provides the ground for the 'manifest madness' analysis, which represents the second step in my argument. This analysis is outlined in two parts, each of which looks at one of the two formal qualities—ontological and epistemological—that together constitute the topography of the mental incapacity terrain. In order to support my 'manifest madness' analysis I make reference throughout to various aspects of different mental incapacity doctrines. The value of my 'manifest madness' analysis for the scholarly engagement with mental incapacity in criminal law derives from its capacity to capture deep dynamics structuring the mental incapacity terrain.

The Terrain of Mental Incapacity in Criminal Law

Change and Continuity in Mental Incapacity over Time

One of the ways of thinking about what marks out the terrain of mental incapacity in criminal law is to reflect on the historical development of criminal law principles and practices more broadly. My reflection leads me to detect something which I call the formalization account, so named to capture the trajectory in the criminal law towards the formalization of legal principles and practices. As I discuss below, this kind of account can be found in various sorts of historicized analyses of

---

[1] Most notably, M Foucault *History of Madness* (London: Routledge, 2006) (first published in English in 1965 as *Madness and Civilisation*), and *Discipline and Punish: The Birth of the Prison* (New York: Pantheon Books, 1977).

criminal law, but it is not usually expressly named or identified. This account of change over time is pitched at a rather general level. Identifying it is useful nonetheless because that provides a means of challenging the widespread, but typically tacit, belief that the development of criminal law principles and practices occurred in a more or less uniform way and in a unilinear direction.

According to the formalization account, the component parts of the law are most accurately understood as the product of broader processes by which, in a common law context, criminal law principles and practices solidified into the form they take in the current (late modern) era.[2] The central idea is that the discrete and technical rules that have come to comprise offences, defences, and rules of procedure and evidence are specific instances of a wider trend in the criminal law towards the formalization of legal principles and practices. The flexible and overtly moral-evaluative aspect of the early modern criminal law is seen as having gradually given way to rigid processes and technical and precise rules, dependent on, for instance, a clear conceptual separation of notions of motive and intent, a separation which is now well-established. This gradual process of formalization entailed the cleaving apart of notions of conduct and fault, fact and opinion, liability and responsibility, and conviction and sentencing. It has pushed individual mental states to a pre-eminent place in criminal law doctrines and practices of evaluation and adjudication, and produced the corresponding decline in significance of the conduct element of the offence, the *actus reus*, which, rather oddly, has come to be thought of as significant only as a preliminary point, a mere threshold issue for criminal liability.

This process of formalization has proceeded on multiple levels. On the level of law, the process has included the 'factualization' of a concept of fault,[3] and the subsequent elaboration of a subjective capacity concept of fault (*mens rea*)—which has meant that individual responsibility for criminal behaviour has come to form a lynchpin in the late modern criminal law[4]—along with the development of other doctrines of liability and attribution. On the level of evidence, the process of formalization has produced sophisticated rules of evidence and procedure (such as burdens of proof and rules about opinion evidence) governing the process of proof in criminal trials. On the institutional level, this process of formalization has

---

[2] Re late modernity, see for instance D Garland *Culture of Control: Crime and Social Order in Contemporary Society* (Oxford: OUP, 2002), and A Giddens *Modernity and Self-Identity: Self and Society in the Late Modern Age* (Stanford: Stanford University Press, 1991).

[3] N Lacey 'Responsibility and Modernity in Criminal Law' (2001) 9(3) *Journal of Political Philosophy* 249, 268; see also A Norrie *Crime, Reason and History: A Critical Introduction to Criminal Law* (London: Butterworths, 2001) and L Farmer *Criminal Law, Tradition and Legal Order: Crime and the Genius of Scots Law 1747 to the Present* (Cambridge: CUP, 1997).

[4] See, eg, *Criminal Law, Tradition and Legal Order*, Lacey 'Responsibility and Modernity in Criminal Law', and Norrie *Crime, Reason and History*. As Nicola Lacey argues, this development was accompanied by a profound change in the idea of criminal responsibility as a loose or thin formulation of criminal fault, whereby responsibility was assumed, which gave way to a thicker and more robust concept of fault or *mens rea*, which was itself the object of investigation at trial: see 'Responsibility and Modernity in Criminal Law' 261. More generally, regarding the accuracy of the story generally told about criminal responsibility, see N Lacey *Women, Crime and Character: From Moll Flanders to Tess of the D'Urbervilles* (Oxford: OUP, 2008).

included the 'lawyerization' of the criminal trial process and the subsequent professionalization of prosecution and defence, as well as the cut-and-thrust of the increasingly organized adversarial criminal process.[5] More broadly, the process of formalization has resulted in formalized enforcement practices, more organized reporting and a regularized appellate system, as well as the development of a complex administrative framework comprising the criminal justice system. Relating the formalization account to the issue of mental incapacity specifically, the mental incapacity doctrines of the current era are seen as the products of the broad movement over time from informal practices of exculpation, to informal standards for criminal responsibility and legal subjectivity, and then to discrete and technical legal rules constituting distinctive doctrines and specific procedures.

Looking at the scholarly literature, we see that what I have called the formalization account of the development of criminal law principles and practices has broad currency. As mentioned above, this formalization account forms the foundation of several sorts of historicized analyses of criminal law—albeit more often implicitly than explicitly. For instance, traces of the formalization account can be detected in normative argumentation about the development of criminal law. Such an argument runs along the lines that formalization has amounted to a 'positivization' of law in the common law world.[6] Similarly, formalization is a central part of more doctrinal studies of the development of the criminal law; Keith Smith's work is a prominent example here.[7] The formalization account also seems to be implicit in an analysis evidencing a more ideological bent, as we see in Alan Norrie's historicized analysis of criminal law.[8] Forming as it does the circumscribed and descriptive

---

[5] Re 'lawyerization', see J H Langbein *The Origins of the Adversary Criminal Trial* (Oxford: OUP, 2003) 145, and also A Duff et al *The Trial on Trial (Vol 3): Towards a Normative Theory of the Criminal Trial* (Oxford: Hart, 2007) 40–6. In relation to the professionalization of prosecution and defence and other procedural and institutional developments, see generally J M Beattie *Crime and the Courts in England 1660–1800* (Oxford: OUP, 1986).

[6] See M Constable *The Law of the Other: The Mixed Jury and Changing Conceptions of Citizenship, Law and Knowledge* (Chicago: University of Chicago Press, 1991). In the context of a discussion of the decline of the mixed jury in the USA by the early nineteenth century, Marianne Constable argues that broad notions of ethics, justice, and difference have given way to more positivistic notions of law, rationality, and indifference.

[7] K J M Smith *Lawyers, Legislators and Theorists: Developments in English Criminal Jurisprudence 1800–1957* (Oxford: OUP, 1998). See N Lacey 'In Search of the Responsible Subject: History, Philosophy and Social Sciences in Criminal Law Theory' (2001) 64(3) *Modern Law Review* 350 for a critical discussion.

[8] Norrie develops a nuanced argument about the 'juridification' of the modern criminal law, and suggests that the creation and maintenance of technical legal concepts (such as M'Naghten insanity) may be understood as an attempt to avoid 'open and contentious moral and political issues': see *Crime, Reason and History* 29; see also Lacey 'Responsibility and Modernity in Criminal Law' 267–8. In an analysis suggesting the strategic significance of expert medical knowledge in the current law, Norrie argues that 'the narrow rationalism' of the M'Naghten test for insanity works to 'withdraw the individual from the social conditions of his madness', while the use of psychiatric testimony stretches the practical operation of the test when a compassionate response is warranted (*Crime, Reason and History* 189–90). Further, in linking legal ideas about incapacity with the pre-eminent notion of individual criminal responsibility, Norrie connects the legal notion of insanity with the development of the idea of the subject of the criminal law as a 'reasoning being'. In Norrie's words, the reasoning individual has become a 'powerful mechanism of ideological legitimation' for the criminal law (*Crime, Reason and History* 176). For discussion of Norrie's analysis, see L Farmer 'The Obsession with

core of a number of powerful analyses of change over time across criminal law, it is clear that the formalization account has more than passing significance for understanding criminal law in historical relief.

The historical development of two specific mental incapacity doctrines—unfitness to plead and infancy—is particularly well explained by reference to the formalization account. This follows from the close connection these doctrines have with the criminal trial process. As procedural provisions, both unfitness to plead and infancy concern a defendant's understanding of, and engagement in, criminal proceedings, and the reach of the criminal law. In Chapter 4, I suggest that, as infancy and unfitness to plead have developed along a trajectory of formalization, doctrines that had been driven by a deep dynamic of inclusion—whereby their scope has been drawn broadly—have now come to be structured by a dynamic of exclusion as well, whereby the scope of the doctrines is more circumscribed. As I discuss in that chapter, the change in the dynamics structuring the process of formalization itself reflects changing concerns with matters such as dangerousness. Beyond unfitness to plead and infancy, formalization is also helpful elsewhere on the mental incapacity terrain. For instance, it is useful in understanding the broad trajectory of the law of insanity, which evolved from a capacious informal law, operating under a flexible criminal process, to a formal and more technical doctrine, which is grounded in a narrow, medicalized notion of disability.[9] Change in the scope of insanity was triggered in part by the formalization of other doctrines on the mental incapacity terrain.[10]

More generally, however, in relation to the mental incapacity terrain as a whole, the dynamic of formalization does not seem to have played out in the same way, or perhaps to the same extent. Although the formalization account assists in explaining the historical trajectory of mental incapacity doctrines in various respects, it does not seem to be able to capture it fully. This is because its emphasis on the degree and pace of change obscures certain significant dimensions of the terrain. For instance, the development of expert medical knowledge of insanity ushered in a more circumscribed approach to the law, and this resulted in a reconfiguration of the merciful space around exculpatory incapacity, which itself produced a discrete automatism doctrine. While this development represents a process of formalization, the outcome is not a thoroughly formalized new doctrine. By way of contrast with some other mental incapacity doctrines, but reflecting the persistence of a broad, moralized notion of incapacity on this part of the mental incapacity terrain, automatism is delimited via a tripartite construction, which tracks lines of

---

Definition: The Nature of Crime and Critical Legal Theory' (1996) 5 *Social and Legal Studies* 57; N Lacey 'Abstraction in Context' (1994) 14(2) *Oxford Journal of Legal Studies* 255.

[9] See Chapter 5 on insanity and automatism.

[10] As I discuss in Chapter 8, with the passage of the Infanticide Acts 1922 and 1938, all killings of newborn children by their mothers were taken outside the reach of the law of murder and the law of insanity. At around the same time, intoxicated offending was carved out from insanity when, in *Beard's Case*, the House of Lords dismissed the *M'Naghten* test as irrelevant to consideration of the effect of intoxication on an individual alleged to have committed a criminal offence: see *DPP v Beard* [1920] AC 479 and, more generally, Chapter 7.

non-culpability, catching a miscellaneous collection of cases in which individuals share little more than an absence of blameworthiness.[11]

Even just this one example of the persistence of overtly morally-evaluative concerns in relation to mental incapacity sensitizes us to the nuances of the historical development of this area of criminal law. In relation to what I call the formalization account, I am suggesting that change over time at the intersection of 'madness' and 'crime' is less wholesale and unidirectional than is typically assumed. That is, the story in relation to 'madness' for criminal law purposes may be as much one of continuity as of change.

Reflection on the historical development of criminal law principles and practices is one of the ways of thinking about what marks out the terrain of mental incapacity in criminal law. Another way of grasping what marks out the mental incapacity terrain arises from an examination of the types of knowledge enlisted in the legal practices that feature on this terrain, and it is to this I now turn.

Expert and Non-Expert Knowledges of 'Madness'

The discussion thus far suggests the value of looking at both change and continuity in the law on mental incapacity. A close analysis of the point of intersection between 'madness' and 'crime' also needs to give space to the broader practices, concerning proof and knowledge, for instance, in which the historical developments, canvassed above, are embedded. As suggested in Chapter 2, thinking afresh about what criminal law doctrines based on mental incapacity share reveals the significance of the type of knowledge that is brought to bear on such claims—both exculpatory and non-exculpatory.[12] Taking up the issue of the types of knowledge featured on the mental incapacity terrain again here provides another way of thinking about the distinctiveness of this terrain. Viewed from this knowledge perspective, I suggest that what marks out the terrain of mental incapacity in criminal law is not the presence of one particular type of knowledge, but the interaction of different types of knowledge.

At this point, a brief explanation of what I mean by knowledge is necessary. Within the literature on knowledge, spread across philosophy, sociology, and law, among other disciplines, knowledge and its study has been approached in different ways. For my purposes here, knowledge is approached as what Michael Bentley usefully calls 'paradigms of what was and what was not to count as worth knowing'.[13] What counts as knowledge, and who count as knowers, changes across time and space. This means that the linked concepts the study of knowledge often conjures up—such as truth, authority, and legitimacy—must be understood as

---

[11] See further Chapter 5.
[12] See Chapter 2 for a discussion of these terms, which represent subsections of the category of mental incapacity doctrines. See also A Loughnan 'Mental Incapacity Doctrines in Criminal Law' (2012) 15(1) *New Criminal Law Review* 1.
[13] See M Bentley 'The Evolution and Dissemination of Historical Knowledge' in M Daunton (ed) *The Organisation of Knowledge in Victorian Britain* (Oxford: OUP, 2005) 174–5.

both dynamic and contingent. In taking knowledge seriously in my examination of the mental incapacity terrain, I am following a rich scholarly tradition. What the recent scholarship on knowledge in socio-legal and law and society studies shares is a focus on the process or production of knowledges within legal contexts, rather than the particular content of that knowledge,[14] and this is also the focus that is of interest to me.

Other scholars have recognized the significance of knowledge for an understanding of criminal law principles and practices. For instance, Nicola Lacey analyses the influence of the development of psychiatric and psychological types of knowledge on the norms of criminal responsibility. As part of a larger argument about the way in which criminal responsibility principles and practices represent responses to 'problems of co-ordination and legitimation faced by systems of criminal law',[15] Lacey argues that the rise of psychological and psychiatric knowledges influenced the rise of a 'primarily capacity-based and heavily psychologised notion of *mens rea*' that marked 'the core of the late modern general part of the criminal law'.[16] Lacey suggests that the criminal law is marked by a shifting balance between capacity responsibility and outcome-based responsibility.[17] An illustration of the utility of her account is provided by the history of the recently altered but durable presumption that an individual intends the logical consequences of his or her actions.[18] Lacey argues that, 'particularly once the growth of psychological notions of individual responsibility began to pose intractable problems of proof for courts and juries', the presumption provided a solution to 'the problem of knowledge co-ordination',

---

[14] For discussion, see R Levi and M Valverde 'Knowledge on Tap: Police Science and Common Knowledge in the Legal Regulation of Drunkenness' (2001) 26(4) *Law and Social Inquiry* 819.

[15] Lacey 'In Search of the Responsible Subject' 350. These 'general problems' of coordination and legitimation relate to the ways in which both the values expressed by the criminal law and the knowledge or belief in facts on which individual judgments depend are coordinated and legitimated (368). For Lacey, the changing coordination and legitimation requirements of a modern criminal law prompted the 'search for a conception of criminal responsibility which could be explicated in legal, technical terms, and hence legitimated as a form of specialist knowledge underpinning an impersonal mode of judgment': 'Responsibility and Modernity in Criminal Law' 267–8. See also Farmer *Criminal Law, Tradition and Legal Order* 139–41.

[16] Lacey 'Responsibility and Modernity in Criminal Law' 266. These types of knowledge of criminal responsibility would eventually have a profound effect on conception of *mens rea* and ideas about fault. For instance, as Nigel Walker comments, by the time of the reception of a doctrine of diminished responsibility into English and Welsh criminal law, criminal responsibility was conceptualized as 'a quality of mind' and, as such, something that could be impaired: N Walker *Crime and Insanity in England (Vol 1: The Historical Perspective)* (Edinburgh: Edinburgh University Press, 1968) 151–2. I discuss diminished responsibility in Chapter 9.

[17] See N Lacey 'Character, Capacity, Outcome: Towards a Framework for Assessing the Shifting Pattern of Criminal Responsibility in Modern English Law' in M D Dubber and L Farmer (eds) *Modern Histories of Crime and Punishment* (Stanford: Stanford University Press, 2007) 14–41.

[18] This legal rule allowed a court to presume that a man [sic] may be taken to have intended the natural and probable consequences of his actions. This rule was changed by Criminal Justice Act 1967, s 8, which provided that the jury is not 'bound in law' to infer intention in this way, but is to determine what the defendant intended or foresaw 'by reference to all the evidence'. As a result of this statutory provision, the presumption about intention no longer exists as a matter of substantive law: *R v Sheehan; R v Moore* [1975] 1 WLR 739, 743; for analysis, see Lacey 'In Search of the Responsible Subject' 370.

permitting the courts to refer to a 'defendant's interior mental world' without requiring close investigation of that world.[19]

As prominent expert knowledges of 'madness', psychiatric and psychological knowledges are obviously relevant to a study of mental incapacity in criminal law. As I discuss in Chapter 2, in the current era, mental incapacity claims typically entail the introduction of expert psychiatric and psychological evidence, either in support or against the claims made by the defendant.[20] In the nineteenth century, the rise of an expert medical knowledge about 'madness' significantly altered the evidentiary and procedural practices governing mental incapacity claims in criminal law—it paved the way to the current era, in which expert psychiatric and psychological evidence may be just as likely to be adduced by prosecution or defence counsel. An expert medical knowledge about 'madness'—then as now—is based on a depiction of 'madness' as a genuine object of expertise, about which it is possible to offer intelligible explanations about cause and effect.[21] In the period since the appearance of an expert knowledge of 'madness', psychiatric and psychological knowledges have gradually risen to a position of dominance, such that they are the archetypal expertise about 'madness'.

Although it might be assumed that it is the presence or prominence of expert medical knowledge on the terrain of mental incapacity in criminal law that marks it out, in terms of knowledge I suggest that what marks out the terrain is the interaction of different types of knowledges. Here, I am referring to the interaction of both expert and non-expert knowledges. There are good reasons to consider both types of knowledge as each bears on legal evaluation and adjudication of mental incapacity claims. For instance, examining the history of the capacious informal insanity law, and the flexible criminal process that attended it, reveals the role played by ordinary people, and what was then common knowledge about 'madness', in animating legal evaluations of exculpatory insanity. As I discuss in Chapter 6, the rise to prominence of expert knowledge about exculpatory 'madness' was a slower and more uneven development than is typically assumed.[22] More generally, looking across the mental incapacity terrain, the point of intersection between 'madness' and crime appears to be the subject of

---

[19] 'In Search of the Responsible Subject' 370. The presumption permitted the court to focus on the objective meaning of the defendant's act, either ignoring or assuming what was going on in the defendant's mind.

[20] The relevance of expert evidence about an individual's mental incapacity led me to follow Anthony Duff in holding that mental incapacity claims are granted rather than pleaded. I then suggested that this is one of the reasons to jettison the term 'defence' in relation to mental incapacity. See further Chapter 2.

[21] See Chapter 6 for discussion.

[22] About the same time as an informal law of insanity formalized into the insanity doctrine recognizable in the current era, evidence from medical witnesses came to be significant in trials involving claims to exculpation on the basis of mental incapacity. I suggest that, in terms of proving 'madness' for legal purposes, the significance of expert medical knowledge—now predominantly psychiatric and psychological knowledge—lies as much in its prudential as in its ontological dimensions, a factor which has not been accorded due importance in accounts of how 'madness' is made known for criminal law purposes. See Chapter 6.

different types of knowledge, each of which is relevant to an understanding of both legal practices and legal constructions of mental incapacity.

How might this non-expert knowledge of mental incapacity be understood? As it is distinguished from expert knowledge, which emerged out of a body of common knowledge, I adopt the term 'lay' to refer to this non-expert knowledge. I do not use terms like 'common knowledge' or 'folk knowledge', each of which might be thought to be analogous. Such terms do not capture what is to me a significant dimension of this body of knowledge—it derives its meaning in opposition to expert knowledge. With the rise of an expert knowledge, the knowledge ordinary people had of 'madness' must be seen in a different light: the rise of expert or specialized knowledges about 'madness' produced a lay knowledge of 'madness'. Lay knowledge is distinct although related to lay evaluation (archetypally, the role of the jury in a serious criminal trial) because it refers to the kind of knowledge enlisted in legal practices as opposed to the roles of particular actors.[23]

This approach to non-expert knowledge means that, beyond the specific role of lay jurors in assessing certain types of claims, lay knowledge has a broader if more diffused role in relation to mental incapacity. The extent of the part played by lay knowledge becomes apparent if it is recognized that legal actors—judges, magistrates, prosecutors, and defence counsel—have lay knowledge when it comes to mental incapacity. This status as lay vis-à-vis knowledge of mental incapacity is not to deny legal actors their status as experts vis-à-vis legal practices and processes: rather, it is to acknowledge that, in Antony Giddens' words, as a result of specialization, 'all experts are themselves lay people most of the time'.[24] It is my suggestion that, in relation to matters involving mental incapacity, legal expertise is mixed with lay knowledge or non-expertise. Of course, unlike lay people (such as those comprising a jury in a criminal trial), legal actors are in positions of privilege in a way that changes the impact of their knowledge, if not its content. This in turn suggests that the attitudes and beliefs of judges, and prosecution and defence counsel, are an important site for analysis of knowledge practices in criminal law. Approached this way, the role of lay knowledge of mental incapacity extends beyond lay evaluation, because legal actors employ lay knowledge of mental incapacity in the execution of their roles. This is significant in that, even if lay people have come to have a reduced role in the procedures relating to mental incapacity, this does not entail a correspondingly minor role for the knowledge of 'madness' here labelled as lay knowledge.

As a non-expert form of knowledge, lay knowledge is both unsystematized and synthetic in that it is made up of different sources of understanding, such as suspicions and religious or other beliefs (and including knowledge that has entered the common domain from specialized arenas). Lay knowledge, which is a form of collective knowledge, is a broad and flexible construct, capturing the socially ratified attitudes and beliefs about 'madness' held by non-specialists. Beyond

---

[23] This distinction between knowledge and knowers is acknowledged by others. See N Lacey 'A Clear Concept of Intention? Elusive or Illusory?' (1993) 56(5) *Modern Law Review* 621, 635–6.
[24] See Giddens *Modernity and Self-Identity* 138, and, more generally, ch. 4.

acknowledging that lay attitudes and beliefs do not all flow in the same direction, the substance of these attitudes and beliefs is something of a black box. As Mariana Valverde has written of the common knowledge of alcohol held by inspectors, patrons, licensees, and hospitality staff, it has few intrinsic features.[25] It can be distinguished by its formal qualities—as with Valverde's 'common knowledge', it is qualitative, non-scientific, and non-numerical.[26] Lay knowledge encompasses experiential or firsthand knowledge (of alcohol, or mental illness, for instance), but extends beyond this empirical base to include social attitudes to 'madness'. The term lay knowledge is used here not with a view to investigating the content of lay knowledge of 'madness' but with the aim of conceptualizing it in order to be able to see what role it plays in criminal law.

Lay knowledge of mental incapacity (and also of other social objects) might be easily dismissed as a kind of generalized and nebulous knowledge background, against which more particular issues for determination (such as those discussed by experts) are foregrounded.[27] Yet what has been called the 'epistemological heterogeneity' of legal discourse extends further than just to other expert knowledges.[28] What I call lay knowledge of incapacity continues to be relevant across the mental incapacity terrain—as more than mere background knowledge. For instance, lay knowledge of mental incapacity was significant in the development of a jurisprudence of 'abnormality of mind' for the purposes of the recently amended doctrine of diminished responsibility.[29] This is suggested by the comments made when the doctrine was imported to England and Wales. As Major Lloyd-George stated in

---

[25] M Valverde *Law's Dream of Common Knowledge* (Princeton: Princeton University Press, 2003) 171. Valverde has written extensively about the types of knowledges implicated in alcohol licensing laws. See M Valverde '"Slavery from Within:" The Invention of Alcoholism and the Question of Free Will' (1997) 22(3) *Social History* 251; M Valverde *Diseases of the Will: Alcohol and the Dilemmas of Freedom* (Cambridge: CUP, 1998). In this body of work, Valverde examines the construction of a 'common knowledge' about alcohol possessed by untrained persons—knowledge that is simultaneously beyond the bounds of any one individual yet within the sphere of commonsense.

[26] M Valverde *Law's Dream of Common Knowledge* 170. As a result of these formal features of lay knowledge of intoxication, Valverde regards it as similar to police-power knowledges of disorder: see M D Dubber and M Valverde 'Introduction: Perspectives on the Power and Science of Police' in M D Dubber and M Valverde *The New Police Science: The Police Power in Domestic and International Governance* (Stanford: Stanford University Press, 2006).

[27] Indeed, scientific and allied knowledges (such as medical and forensic knowledges) have dominated scholarship on the parts played by extra-legal knowledges in legal practice, although it seems clear that extra-legal knowledges interact with legal knowledge in various ways. See M Valverde 'Authorizing the Production of Urban Moral Order: Appellate Courts and Their Knowledge Claims' (2005) 39(2) *Law and Society Review* 419, 420. Different expert knowledges seem to be treated differently in the legal context. For a discussion of historical and anthropological knowledge, see R van Krieken 'Law's Autonomy in Action: Anthropology and History in Court' (2006) 15 *Social and Legal Studies* 574. For a discussion of the contrasting treatment of scientific knowledge, see T Scheffer 'Knowing How to Sleepwalk: Placing Expert Evidence in the Midst of an English Jury Trial' (2010) 35(5) *Science, Technology & Human Values* 620. One way of addressing this scholarly imbalance, and an alternative to the argument presented here, is to approach lay knowledge as a form of expertise: see A Loughnan 'The Expertise of Non-Experts: Expert and Lay Knowledges of Intoxication in Criminal Law' in J Herring et al (eds) *Intoxication: Problematic Pleasures* (London: Routledge, 2012) (forthcoming).

[28] See M Valverde 'Authorizing the Production of Urban Moral Order' 423.

[29] See Homicide Act 1957, s 2(1), which was recently amended by the Coroners and Justice Act 2009. In Chapter 9, I suggest that the meaning of 'abnormality of mind' developed in a dialectical relation with both lay knowledge of mental incapacity and the technical legal meaning of insanity per the *M'Naghten Rules*.

introducing the Bill that became the Homicide Act 1957, diminished responsibility was to be open to those who were insane in the 'legal sense', the medical sense, and 'those who, not insane in either sense, are seriously abnormal'.[30] Looking across the mental incapacity terrain, it is the dynamic interaction of the multiple types of knowledge that govern mental incapacity in criminal law into the current era—expert medical, expert legal knowledge, and non-expert or lay knowledge—that marks out the mental incapacity terrain.

On the previous pages, I have sought to suggest the distinctiveness of the terrain of mental incapacity from two different perspectives—change and continuity over time, and the types of knowledge enlisted in legal assessment of mental incapacity claims. Together, these sections constituted the first of two steps in my overall argumentation and provided a connection to the conceptual argument developed in Chapter 2. My analysis is intended to generate a sense of the terrain of mental incapacity on its own terms, as *sui generis*. At the same time, it made clear that a close account of the contours of the point of intersection between 'madness' and 'crime' would need to give space to the broader practices, concerning evidence and proof, in which legal doctrines are embedded. These two approaches to the terrain of mental incapacity—from history and from knowledge—serve as the grounding for the following discussion of 'manifest madness', as they provide a bridge between Chapter 2 and 'manifest madness'. This 'manifest madness' analysis unfolds in two main parts, each of which looks at one of the two formal qualities—the ontological and epistemological—that together constitute the topography of the mental incapacity terrain. A key argument flowing from the following discussion is that the distinctiveness of the terrain of mental incapacity relates to both the principles and practices of mental incapacity, and evidence and proof of it. I show that at the point of intersection with crime, 'madness' is constructed as dispositional (the ontology of 'madness') and as able to be 'read off' the behaviour of an individual (the epistemology of 'madness').

The Ontology of 'Madness' at the Point of Intersection with Crime

'He was a man not accountable for his actions'[31]

Viewed ontologically, the main formal feature of the terrain of mental incapacity in criminal law—the point of intersection of 'madness' and 'crime'—is that, here, 'madness' is constructed as dispositional. By this, I mean that 'madness' is regarded as something like a condition or a status in that it exists over a length of time, and is displayed in behaviour taking place over that time. By referring to the constructed nature of this ontology of 'madness', I intend to suggest that this feature of 'madness' at the juncture with crime is a product of legal practices; in other words, it does not pre-exist legal practices or refer to a transcendent 'truth' about

---

[30] *Hansard*, HC vol 560, col 1154 (15 November 1956).
[31] *OBP*, Patrick Carroll, 11 May 1835 (t18350511-1119).

'madness'. Each of the roles of mental incapacity doctrines—exculpation, inculpation, imputation, and a procedural role—outlined in the previous chapter depend in distinct ways on a sense of 'madness' as dispositional, as subsisting. This idea of 'madness' as dispositional is fostered by the combined impact of different types of knowledges of 'madness', discussed below, which permit older patterns of meaning to persist into the current era.

My argument about the dispositional character of 'madness' at the point of intersection with crime specifically invokes the notions of time and space on which criminal law doctrines and practices depend. These notions of time and space have recently come to receive high-profile attention.[32] As Lindsay Farmer argues, criminal law doctrines and practices rest on particular temporal and spatial logics, which are central to the enforcement of proscribed conduct, the definitions of crimes, and conceptions of criminal responsibility.[33] In relation to criminal law defences in particular, Alan Norrie suggests that the defendant is recontextualized for the purposes of exculpation, having been decontextualized for the purposes of determining liability (whether he or she did the *actus reus* with the requisite *mens rea*).[34] These different analyses hint at the value of thinking closely about the role of time and space in criminal law.

In relation to the role of time and space in mental incapacity, some hints about the distinctive temporal inflection pertaining in this part of criminal law can be gleaned from the analysis of criminal responsibility developed by Victor Tadros. In the context of a broader normative analysis of the concept of criminal responsibility, in which he argues that ascription of criminal responsibility should be dependent on the accused's status as an agent, Tadros suggests that there is a problem in the way in which mental disorder defences have been understood. With reference to the case of a person who suffers a brain injury and undergoes a personality change, Tadros argues that the identity of that agent *qua* agent cannot be determined simply at the point in time at which she acts. As Tadros concludes, 'if the defendant's actions at a particular time are not reflective of her identity as constituted over time, she is not responsible for those actions'.[35] Taking up Tadros' exhortation, made in relation to mental disorder defences, that 'insufficient attention is given to the relationship between responsibility and time',[36] I turned my mind to the issue of mental incapacity and time. This entailed looking across

---

[32] See N Lacey 'Space, Time and Function: Intersecting Principles of Responsibility Across the Terrain of Criminal Justice' (2007) 1 *Criminal Law and Philosophy* 233 and L Farmer 'Time and Space in Criminal Law' (2010) 13 *New Criminal Law Review* 333.

[33] See Farmer 'Time and Space in Criminal Law'. The timeframe concept was first introduced into criminal law scholarship by Mark Kelman: see M Kelman 'Interpretive Construction in the Substantive Criminal Law' (1980–1981) 33 *Stanford Law Review* 591.

[34] Norrie *Crime, Reason and History*; see also Lacey 'A Clear Concept of Intention? Elusive or Illusory?' 621.

[35] V Tadros *Criminal Responsibility* (Oxford: OUP, 2005) 141. This argument could be harnessed for inculpatory purposes, on the basis that, say, failure to take medication prescribed for a diagnosed mental condition at one point in time, may then disqualify an individual from relying on the insanity doctrine when charged with an offence taking place at a later point in time: see E W Mitchell *Self-Made Madness: Rethinking Illness and Criminal Responsibility* (Aldershot: Ashgate, 2003).

[36] Tadros *Criminal Responsibility* 141.

mental incapacity doctrines—stretching beyond those relating to responsibility—to detect a deep structural dimension of the mental incapacity terrain. This leads me to my analysis of 'madness' as dispositional at the point of intersection with crime.

For my purposes in analysing mental incapacity closely, a particularly helpful analysis is the account of character-based criminal responsibility developed by Nicola Lacey. In relation to the historical development of criminal responsibility, Lacey argues that practices of responsibility-attribution founded in ideas of character remained significant for longer than is typically assumed (and indeed are making a resurgence in the current era).[37] For Lacey, the late Victorian era evidenced a conception of responsibility, and non-responsibility (the latter associated with claims to insanity for instance) that represented a mix of moral evaluative and factual assessment, 'of character and engaged psychological capacity'.[38] Lacey argues that character-based responsibility (or character-responsibility) produces a distinct formulation of the adjudication question: did the defendant's conduct 'express a settled disposition of hostility or indifference to the relevant norm of criminal law, or at least acceptance of such a disposition?', a question which opens up a different, longer relevant timeframe for the legal inquiry.[39] This analysis of criminal responsibility seems to have resonance for the way in which mental incapacity claims are evaluated (and as per the previous chapter, such claims extend beyond the bounds of non- or partial responsibility, to include the way mental incapacity relates to legal subjectivity). To me, the construction of 'madness' at the point of intersection with crime shares features with character-based conceptions of responsibility: that is, as it is constructed as dispositional, 'madness' for criminal law purposes is character-like.

A trigger for my thinking about the dispositional quality of 'madness' has been George Fletcher's landmark text, *Rethinking Criminal Law*.[40] In particular, I draw on Fletcher's analysis of what he calls 'manifest criminality', one of three conceptual structures or 'patterns of criminality' that he suggests account for the core content of criminal law.[41] According to Fletcher, taken together, his three patterns of

[37] See N Lacey 'Psychologising Jekyll, Demonising Hyde: The Strange Case of Criminal Responsibility' (2010) 4 *Criminal Law and Philosophy* 109; see also N Lacey 'In Search of the Responsible Subject'.
[38] Lacey 'Psychologising Jekyll, Demonising Hyde' 123.
[39] Lacey 'Space, Time and Function' 239. While retaining a focus on the specific allegation of criminal conduct that grounds conviction and punishment, it also situates the attribution of responsibility in a broader timeframe than implied by a capacity conceptualization of criminal responsibility (239).
[40] G P Fletcher *Rethinking Criminal Law* (Oxford: OUP, 2000). Fletcher's analysis enjoys a solid standing in criminal law academic discourse: it has been taken up by a number of criminal law scholars (see, for example, E Colvin 'Exculpatory Defences in Criminal Law' (1990) 10 *Oxford Journal of Legal Studies* 381) and seems to have been particularly useful in historicized discussions of the criminal law (see, for example, Farmer *Criminal Law, Tradition and Legal Order*; Lacey 'In Search of the Responsible Subject'; Lacey 'Space, Time and Function'; and Norrie *Crime, Reason and History*).
[41] The value of these abstract patterns is their explanatory power, in that they provide a means for understanding the content of criminal prohibitions at different points in time (Fletcher *Rethinking Criminal Law* 121). Fletcher begins from the premise that the criminal law is a 'polycentric body of principles' and, as a result, that no single formula will determine when conduct ought to be criminal

criminality or 'patterns of liability' 'generate an interpretive mode for understanding commonalities and contrasts among a wide variety of offenses'.[42] Fletcher argues that 'manifest criminality' was the dominant 'pattern of criminality' until the end of the eighteenth century and, since then, the 'subjective criminality' and the harmful consequences 'patterns of liability' have risen to the fore.[43] The 'manifest' 'pattern of criminality' resonates with my own reading of mental incapacity.[44] There are two aspects of Fletcher's 'manifest criminality' that prove useful to me, the first of which relates to the dispositional nature of 'madness' at the point of intersection with crime. The aspect of Fletcher's 'manifest criminality' analysis I wish to focus on for this purpose is the intimate connection between the conceptual and the evidentiary, which underpins the 'manifest' 'pattern of criminality'.

To explain the significance of this for my analysis, some more detail about Fletcher's 'manifest criminality' 'pattern of liability' is required. The central import of 'manifest criminality' can be explained by way of contrast with the other two of Fletcher's 'patterns of criminality'. Under the pattern of 'manifest criminality', the case for criminal liability starts with an 'objective standard', 'the manifestly criminal act'.[45] This means that the act manifests the actor's criminal purpose. By contrast, under the 'subjective criminality' pattern, 'the actor's intent is the central question in assessing liability'.[46] Thus, the act is of secondary importance: it is seen as a demonstration of the *firmness*, rather than the *content*, of the actor's resolve.[47] The focus of the court's inquiry into liability is on the intent behind the act. Under the harmful consequences 'pattern of liability', liability is independent of a human action or state of mind. Rather, it is dependent on an 'objective attribution' of a harmful event to a responsible person.[48] Overall, when compared with Fletcher's

---

(xxii). Nonetheless, the 'patterns of criminality' seem to have paradigmatic significance in Fletcher's account.

[42] *Rethinking Criminal Law* 60. Fletcher discusses his concept of 'manifest criminality' only in relation to criminal offences, and offers the concept as a way of understanding the core content of the criminal law. In extrapolating from his account to my own, I made two moves: from the doctrine or substance of the criminal law to the law of evidence and procedure, and from criminal offences to criminal defences: see A Loughnan '"Manifest Madness": Towards A New Understanding of the Insanity Defence' (2007) 70(3) *Modern Law Review* 379.

[43] Fletcher *Rethinking Criminal Law* 61.

[44] Elsewhere I have used Fletcher's argument as a jumping off point for a tripartite explication of 'manifest madness', see Loughnan 'Manifest Madness'. Although my 'manifest madness' analysis is explicated differently here, that tripartite explication of it may be read alongside the discussion in this chapter. I am aware of the critical reception Fletcher's work has received. As Lindsay Farmer points out, Fletcher's argument about the changing form of criminal liability is developed exclusively on an intellectual level. However, changes in criminal liability are not purely intellectual moments, but are closely linked to changes in the manner of state and social organization: see L Farmer *The Metamorphosis of Theft: Property and Criminalisation* (forthcoming).

[45] Fletcher *Rethinking Criminal Law* 89. So, for instance, when criminal liability is structured according to 'manifest criminality', 'thieves could be seen thieving; they could be caught in the act' (80).

[46] *Rethinking Criminal Law* 89.

[47] *Rethinking Criminal Law* 120.

[48] *Rethinking Criminal Law* 757.

other 'patterns of liability', 'manifest criminality' can be seen to have three essential features: criminal acts have meaning when viewed externally, that meaning is 'manifest' or evident to neutral observers or third parties, and crime is an organic category, arising from community experience of it.[49]

To reveal how this analysis connects to my point about the dispositional nature of 'madness' at the point of intersection with crime it is necessary to have a closer look at what Fletcher suggests about the intimate relation between the conceptual and evidentiary. The definitional feature of 'manifest criminality' is that, under that 'pattern of liability', the criminal act manifests the actor's criminal purpose and is treated as a substantive condition of liability.[50] For Fletcher, under the pattern of 'manifest criminality', there is an intimate connection between the *way* in which liability is proved and the content of *what* is to be proved.[51] As he writes in relation to the law of larceny, under the pattern of 'manifest criminality', the link between the manifest crime and a defendant's liability is conceptual as well as evidentiary: 'the issue of intent in larceny was not thought of separately from the manifestation of that intent in the external world'.[52] This does not mean, however, that the manifest nature of criminality is merely a rule of evidence, with the 'manifest' character of the act serving only as a presumption for establishing intent.[53] Rather, under 'manifest criminality', where the manifest act establishes the content of the defendant's intent, it is not possible to separate the evidentiary and substantive components of criminal liability.[54]

How does this analysis pertain at the point of intersection between 'madness' and crime? I suggest that a similar idea about the way meaning is given to 'madness' pertains at the point where 'madness' intersects with crime. My claim has two parts. The first is the relevant externality. In my thinking, the relevant externality is not the criminal act—the external element of an offence—but a broader notion of a 'mad' defendant's conduct, which seems to have a thick significance in criminal law doctrines and practices. By the term conduct, I refer to the criminal act as well as other aspects of a defendant's behaviour, such as his or her demeanour in court and aspects of his or her context. The second part of my claim relates to the connection between the conceptual and evidentiary. Compared with Fletcher's analysis, the intimate connection between the manner of proof and the content of *what* is to be proved does not link the criminal act and liability (as per 'manifest criminality') but conduct and criminal responsibility (for exculpatory mental incapacity doctrines) or conduct and capacity (for non-exculpatory doctrines). In each case, the conceptual

---

[49] *Rethinking Criminal Law* 115–16, 88, and 119 respectively.
[50] *Rethinking Criminal Law* 232.
[51] *Rethinking Criminal Law* 85.
[52] *Rethinking Criminal Law* 85.
[53] *Rethinking Criminal Law* 85. Rather, the requirement that criminal behaviour be manifest is an 'independent substantive requirement'—if the manifest act is not established, 'there is no point in inquiring further about the actor's intent' (85).
[54] By contrast, under 'subjective criminality', a variety of means other than a manifest act may be used to prove intent because the act demonstrates 'the *firmness* of the actor's resolve', rather than the content of his or her intent (*Rethinking Criminal Law* 120). Therefore, while the question of proof (and the law of evidence and procedure governing it) may now be thought of as distinct from the substantive criminal law, such a distinction was not applicable in the era of 'manifest criminality'.

and evidentiary are not wholly separated: meaning resides in conformity between the thing itself and the idea of the thing. That is, what counts as 'madness' for criminal law purposes is what is manifest as 'madness' within criminal doctrines and practices. Put another way, at the point of intersection with crime—and whether relating to exculpatory or non-exculpatory doctrines—'madness' is what 'madness' does.

Evidence in support of this dispositional dimension of 'madness' for criminal law purposes is to be found at a number of points across the mental incapacity terrain, in, for instance, the dependency different mental incapacity doctrines exhibit on generalized constructions of the capacities of individuals relying on these doctrines. Here, two examples suffice. In the newly formulated version of the doctrine of diminished responsibility, the statutory provision refers to an individual's 'ability' to understand the nature of his or her conduct, form a rational judgment or exercise self-control at the time of the killing.[55] Thus, while it is formally the actor's state at the moment of the killing that is at issue, the statutory reference to 'ability' references a more status-like condition, one that is not easily reduced to a mere moment in time. In relation to the law on intoxicated offending, it is notable that references to generalized ideas about capacity abound. The doctrine of 'specific intent' refers to a subjective mental state but actually rests on a generalized construction of the altered capacities of intoxicated individuals. In referring to capacity to form intent, the doctrine of 'specific intent' collapses a question of fact (did the defendant form the requisite intent?) into the question of ongoing capacity over time (was the defendant capable of forming the requisite intent?).[56]

Additional evidence in support of my analysis of the dispositional dimension of 'madness' for criminal law purposes is provided by the way in which, in relation to claims to exculpation, 'madness' interacts with the *actus reus* and *mens rea* of criminal offences. As mentioned above, a 'mad' defendant's conduct has a thick significance in criminal law, and this resists reduction to the dualistic paradigm of liability (*actus reus/mens rea*) otherwise largely taken for granted. We can see this in the multiple ways in which a mental condition can interact with criminal responsibility and thus criminal liability. For instance, it may be that the mental condition prevents the defendant from exercising control over his or her conduct (as per the doctrine of automatism), or the mental condition may affect an individual's understanding of the nature and quality, or the wrongness, of their act (as per *M'Naghten* insanity).[57] Just these two examples indicate that claims to exculpation based on mental incapacity can be understood to impact on an

---

[55] As a result of the recent Coroners and Justice Act 2009, diminished responsibility is available where a killing is caused or explained by an 'abnormality of mental functioning', arising from a 'recognised medical condition', which has 'substantially impaired' the defendant's 'ability' to understand the nature of his or her conduct, form a rational judgment or exercise self-control, and the 'abnormality provides an explanation for the defendant's act in doing or being a party to the killing': Coroners and Justice Act 2009, s 52, amending Homicide Act 1957, s 2. See further Chapter 9.

[56] See Chapter 7 in which I suggest that lay knowledge plays a role in underpinning the complex and technical rules making up the law of intoxication.

[57] See further Chapter 5.

individual in a way that traverses the *actus reus/mens rea* boundary, invoking an idea of a condition stretched out in time—beyond the narrow slice in time corresponding with the commission of the *actus reus*.

The construction of 'madness' as dispositional is achieved in part on the back of the distinct timeframes employed in expert systems of medical knowledge (which are also relevant to my discussion below). Psychiatry and psychology tend to operate with a different and broader notion of the relevant timeframe when compared with criminal law practices, which tend to adopt a snapshot view of the relevant time (generally, the moment of the commission of the *actus reus* of the alleged offence). Indeed, it is possible to refer to psychiatric time, which, depending on the circumstances, may well stretch back to, say, an adult defendant's childhood. The effect of the inclusion of expert medical discourses in courtroom evaluation processes is to expand the timeframe at issue in the legal inquiry into the criminal responsibility or the legal subjectivity of an individual making a claim to mental incapacity. Now, here, it might be pointed out that some criminal defences (such as provocation), and not just those in my category of mental incapacity doctrines, operate with an extended timeframe.[58] I suggest that, in relation to mental incapacity, the invocation of different knowledge systems in aid of this extended timeframe is significant, invoking as it does the distinct norms of proof referred to in relation to psychiatric and psychological knowledge, and the extended timeframes structurally embedded in these disciplines.

As the above analysis suggests, at the point of intersection between 'madness' and 'crime', the dispositional nature of 'madness' means it is possible for the alleged crime to be regarded as a symptom of mental disorder or disease, on the basis that the disorder predates the offence. This is the first of several effects of the construction of 'madness' as dispositional at the point of intersection with crime. Interpreting the alleged crime as a symptom of mental disorder or disease helps to account for the association of offending by mentally incapacitated individuals with motiveless crime, an association that can be traced back to the Victorian era.[59] This idea of crime as the symptom of 'madness' can be seen most clearly in relation to infanticide, where the defendant's act of killing her child is read as an instantiation of abnormality for criminal law purposes.[60] The idea that the crime is depicted as a symptom of disorder or disease is overlaid onto the different perspectives on time implied in criminal law practices versus those of psychiatry and psychology, in that this idea is premised on the subsisting nature of the mental condition. The idea that crime may be regarded as a symptom of disorder or disease is a deep-seated one, and may be found within both legal and psychiatric knowledge systems (and arguably in non-expert beliefs as well). This shared idea hints at the ways in

---

[58] Indeed this extended timeframe might be the temporal dimension of the recontextualization of the previously decontextualized defendant, for the purpose of exculpation. See Norrie *Crime, Reason and History*.

[59] See M J Wiener *Reconstructing the Criminal: Culture, Law and Policy in England, 1830–1914* (Cambridge: CUP, 1990).

[60] See further Chapter 8.

which criminal law and psychiatry and psychology each depend on a moralized discourse of deviance.[61]

The idea that the alleged crime may be regarded as a symptom of mental disorder or disease has a strange coda. It produces a complex relationship between the nature of the offence and the defendant's claim to non- or partial responsibility, or to non-subjectivity. In relation to allegations of offending at the more serious end of the spectrum (such as murder and other crimes of violence), this type of offence can be taken to suggest that the individual is 'becoming mad', as opposed to 'being mad'. That is, the offence itself can evidence the process of 'becoming mad', articulating with other factors such as the absence of motive, to encode a change in the defendant's condition. Of course, an empirical assessment of the content of social beliefs about 'madness', which lies beyond the aims of my book, would be required to bear out this claim. Here, I confine myself to pointing to a comment made by Edward Griew in speculating about the practical operation of diminished responsibility. Griew suggests that, in deciding whether to grant a plea of diminished responsibility, the jury may 'set the defendant's abnormality and its effects upon him against the character of the offence'.[62] It is possible that a similar kind of weighing up process occurs in relation to other mental incapacity doctrines, both exculpatory and non-exculpatory.

Another effect of constructing 'madness' as dispositional is that it feeds into a construction of the relevant individual as different in kind, exposing the ontological dimension of the argument about abnormality outlined in Chapter 2. For instance, an analysis of the historical development of diminished responsibility leads me to conclude that diminished responsibility relies on an idea of difference that is usefully conceptualized as one of kind rather than one of degree on the basis that this approach generates a closer understanding of the doctrine. Understanding diminished responsibility to connote a qualitative rather than a quantitative difference takes seriously the notion of abnormality, and helps to account for the prominence of expert medical evidence in decision-making around the doctrine.[63] Similarly, in relation to automatism, its tripartite construction (requiring a 'total loss of voluntary control', an external factor and no prior fault on the part of the defendant) ensures that those relying on automatism may be constructed as different in kind (*un*conscious or acting *in*voluntarily).[64]

The dispositional dimension of 'madness' at the juncture with crime also facilitates a conceptual slippage between 'crimes by the mad' and 'mad crimes'. For

---

[61] Indeed, in the development of a discipline of criminology, vocabulary, theories and strategies of intervention in the lives of individuals borrowed from the higher profile and longer standing specialism of psychiatry. See D Garland *Punishment and Welfare: A History of Penal Strategies* (Aldershot: Gower, 1985) and N Rafter 'The Unrepentant Horse-Slasher: Moral Insanity and the Origins of Criminological Thought' (2004) 42(2) *Criminology* 979.

[62] See E Griew 'The Future of Diminished Responsibility' [1988] *Criminal Law Review* 75, 83. See also J Horder *Excusing Crime* (Oxford: OUP, 2004) 155.

[63] It is this idea of difference—difference in kind rather than difference in degree—that can be seen to underpin the way in which diminished responsibility slides between a doctrine of exculpation and one of inculpation, which I discuss in Chapter 9.

[64] See further Chapter 5.

instance, as I discuss in Chapter 4, in the law on infancy, there is a slippage between childhood offending (a categorization by type of offending) and offending by children (a categorization by offender). The conceptual slippage between 'crimes committed by children' and 'childhood crimes' has rendered children who commit serious offences vulnerable to the exhaustion of mercy: at this point on the spectrum of offending, the special status granted to children seems to wear out.

In addition, the law of infanticide provides an illustration of the over-determining effect of the construction of 'madness' as dispositional. By eliding a distinction between the descriptive aspects of infanticide (a woman kills her infant at the same time as having a mind disturbed by childbirth or lactation) and its evaluative aspects (this action under these conditions warrants partial liability), a finding of partial responsibility for killing flows straightforwardly from the construction of the act of infanticide as an instantiation of abnormality. This specifically gendered idea of abnormality supports both partial inculpation and partial exculpation via the law of infanticide. According to my analysis, which I develop in Chapter 8, a particular social type, the infanticidal woman, has come to determine the legal issue of the defendant's criminal responsibility, and the act of infanticide has become an instantiation of abnormality for criminal law purposes.

To conclude this discussion, it is useful to return to the words, taken from the *Old Bailey Proceedings*, which I extracted at the beginning of this section—'he was a man not accountable for his actions'.[65] These words form part of the question the court addressed to Henry Parkin, a surgeon in the Royal Marines, who gave evidence that he had never seen the defendant, Patrick Carroll, in a 'state of lunacy'. What appears to us to be the archaic wording used by the judge helpfully captures the idea of the dispositional quality of 'madness' at the point of intersection with crime. While the court's specific interest was in the time of the stabbing that led to the death of Elizabeth Blake, the reference to the type of man the defendant was neatly conveys what I have sought to suggest about the ontological dimension of 'madness' for criminal law purposes.

The Epistemology of 'Madness' at the Point of Intersection with Crime

'Do you take her to be a mad woman? I do'[66]

Viewed epistemologically, the main feature of the mental incapacity terrain is that, here, 'madness' is constructed as 'readable'. Or put another way, the kind of *difference* invoked by mental incapacity doctrines is depicted as 'readable'. Again, it is worth repeating that, by the reference to the constructed nature of 'madness', I suggest that it is a product of legal practices; in other words, it does not pre-exist legal practices or refer to a transcendent 'truth' about 'madness'. In this section of

---

[65] *OBP*, Patrick Carroll, 11 May 1835 (t18350511-1119).
[66] *OBP*, Susannah Milesent, 11 November 1794 (t17941111-1).

the chapter, I discuss this idea of the 'readability' of 'madness' for criminal law purposes, on which the evidentiary and proof practices associated with each of the roles of mental incapacity in criminal law that I identified in Chapter 2—exculpation, inculpation, imputation, and a procedural role—depend. My argument about the epistemology of 'madness' is an analogue to the argument about the ontological features of 'madness', outlined above, in that the 'readability' of 'madness' at the point of intersection with crime is connected to its dispositional character.

At first, the suggestion that 'madness' is constructed as 'readable' at the point of intersection with crime might appear counter-intuitive because, over and above any connection to crime, 'madness' is now depicted as hidden to the ordinary observer. The hidden character of 'madness' is generally thought to be a product of the complex social, political, and economic changes associated with modernity. Modernity brought with it a set of expert systems, associated with distinctive competencies, claims to exclusive knowledge and specialization.[67] The effect of the rise of an expertise about 'madness' in particular has come to be understood in light of Michel Foucault's analysis of the historical development of institutions and professions devoted to the management of criminals and the insane in France.[68] A useful point made by scholars who have been inspired in different ways by Foucault's analysis is that, although, 'madness', had been both known and knowable in the early modern era, it is now hidden to the ordinary observer.[69]

The rise of expert psychiatric and psychological knowledge of 'madness' is regarded as effecting a change whereby medical professionals are equipped to provide insights into 'madness' that are hidden from the ordinary observer. Of course, this development has had significant impact well beyond the bounds of the criminal law and criminal process concerning mental incapacity. While I do not take issue with these analyses in general, I want to suggest that there are good reasons to think that, at the specific point marked out by the intersection of 'madness' with crime, this change has not been as wholesale or as unidirectional as is typically assumed. Within the space created by criminal law practices, it is possible to detect the persistence into the current era of older ideas about the way in which 'madness' becomes known. There remains a subsisting conviction, detectable in a close study of criminal law practices, that 'madness' is regarded as 'readable'—in conduct, and by ordinary people without specialist knowledge, as well as to those with specialist knowledge of 'madness'.

Here, again, my thinking about the formal quality of 'madness' as 'readable' has been triggered by Fletcher's 'manifest criminality' analysis, discussed above. There

---

[67] As Anthony Giddens argues, the deployment of expert knowledge—about personal life and collective life—as a constitutive element in social organization and social change, is part of the 'reflexivity of modernity' in the late modern era: see A Giddens *The Consequences of Modernity* (Cambridge: Polity Press, 1990). See also A Giddens 'Living in a Post-traditional Society' in U Beck et al (eds) *Reflexive Modernization: Politics, Tradition and Aesthetics in the Modern Social Order* (Stanford: Stanford University Press, 1994).

[68] See Foucault *History of Madness*, and *Discipline and Punish: The Birth of the Prison*.

[69] See generally Wiener *Reconstructing the Criminal*; J P Eigen *Witnessing Insanity: Madness and Mad Doctors in the English Court* (New Haven: Yale University Press, 1995); and N Rose *Governing the Soul: The Shaping of the Private Self* 2nd edn (London: Free Association Books, 1999).

are two aspects of Fletcher's 'manifest criminality' 'pattern of liability' that are useful, the first of which relates to my point about the dispositional nature of 'madness' for criminal law purposes, which I discussed above. The second point relates to the role of certain knowledges and certain knowers in legal practices concerning mental incapacity, and it is to this that I now turn. A little more detail about Fletcher's 'manifest criminality' analysis is needed here. Fletcher's 'manifest criminality' analysis depends on certain knowledge conditions. According to Fletcher, under 'manifest criminality', the 'assumption' is that the criminal nature of certain acts is intelligible as such to 'a neutral third-party observer' with 'no special knowledge about the offender's intention'.[70] Fletcher utilizes the notion of 'general knowledge', referring to the 'shared paradigms' through which criminal acts were perceived as such.[71] As Fletcher writes, the pattern of 'manifest criminality' rests on a 'stipulation' about the knowledge of observers: 'if someone hired a horse... his selling [it] would be suspect only if we should assume general knowledge of his status as a temporary possessor'.[72] Thus, as Fletcher argues, under 'manifest criminality', judgments of criminality depended on a community's 'general knowledge'.[73]

How does this analysis bear on the practices governing mental incapacity claims? Extrapolating to the mental incapacity terrain, 'neutral' observers viewing criminal behaviour without 'special knowledge' may be thought to be those who do not have an expert or specialist knowledge of mental incapacity. These observers play a role in criminal law practices: in lay evaluation by a jury, for instance. I suggest that expert knowledges of 'madness' have not covered the field of knowledge practices bearing on mental incapacity at the point of intersection with crime, and that 'madness' remains the subject of non-specialist knowledge. But, by contrast with Fletcher's terminology, I do not consider this 'general knowledge'. Rather, I refer to lay knowledge of incapacity, which as foreshadowed above, is explicitly contrasted with elite, expert, or specialist knowledge. As discussed above, the term lay knowledge is here employed to refer to socially ratified attitudes and beliefs about 'madness' held by non-experts. Lay knowledge of mental incapacity is non-expert knowledge of mental incapacity (that is, not medical knowledge where this is paradigmatically psychiatric and psychological knowledge). By contrast with expert knowledge, lay knowledge is unsystematized, incorporating a diverse array of attitudes and beliefs about 'madness'. Lay knowledge, as a form of collective knowledge, captures the social nature of knowledge about mental incapacity. Again, as discussed above, the term is used here not with a view to investigating the content of lay knowledge of 'madness' but in order to reveal that it plays a role in criminal law.[74]

---

[70] Fletcher *Rethinking Criminal Law* 116.
[71] *Rethinking Criminal Law* 82.
[72] *Rethinking Criminal Law* 82–3.
[73] *Rethinking Criminal Law* 82.
[74] See further Chapter 6 for a discussion in relation to the evidentiary and procedural aspects of insanity and automatism.

Evidence in support of this idea about the significance of lay knowledge of mental incapacity is provided by consideration of the law on intoxicated offending. In the current era, the law of intoxication comprises a complex set of rules in which the more moral-evaluative grounding of the law belies its technical neutrality and precision. The formalization of the law on intoxication, which produced a legal entity that is most accurately conceptualized as a 'doctrine of imputation', together with the development of a medical and psychiatric expertise about the effect of intoxication on individuals in the nineteenth century, went only some way toward covering the field of knowledge practices in criminal law. Space remained in criminal law practices for lay knowledge of intoxication. As I discuss in Chapter 7, stretching above its practical role in any particular decision, lay knowledge of intoxication has a further, more discursive part to play in criminal law. For instance, it bolsters the legal rules comprising the intoxication law in that it sustains the particularly complex and technical rules that make it up. In brief, viewed as a whole, the part played by lay knowledge in connecting the restrictions in the law of intoxicated offending with moral culpability and with genuinely different mental states may be interpreted as a bridge linking the law, which represents a half-way house of criminal liability (neither wholly subjective nor wholly objective), with the dominant subjective principles of *mens rea* or fault.[75]

Looking across the mental incapacity terrain, lay knowledge of 'madness' shares the field with expert knowledge, as both types of knowledge are enlisted in decision-making processes, and brought to bear on mental incapacity claims. As discussed above, when such claims are raised in court, the trial now typically entails the introduction of expert psychiatric and psychological evidence, either in support of or against the claims made by the individual. But, such expert knowledge does not form blanket coverage of mental incapacity, as lay knowledge is enlisted in these legal practices as well. It is the dynamic interaction between these types of knowledge that produces the distinctive epistemological contours of the mental incapacity terrain.

In what way does recognizing that lay knowledge of mental incapacity plays a role in criminal processes, alongside expert knowledge, connect to my argument about the 'readability' of 'madness'? The connection lies in recognizing that the role that lay knowledge of mental incapacity, and actors with that knowledge, play in criminal processes depends on the 'readability' of 'madness' at the point of intersection with crime. This insight is significant in two respects. First, it has been obscured in the extant scholarship on mental incapacity, which has not grasped the full implications of the social dimension of mental incapacity. Second, in unveiling the way in which legal processes rest on the 'readability' of 'madness', my analysis exposes the highly charged practice that structures the knowledge field on the topic of 'madness': on the one hand, 'madness' is framed as hidden to anyone without an expertise in it, and, on the other hand, legal practices depend on the 'manifest' nature of 'madness' to all involved in legal evaluation and adjudication—expert and

---

[75] See further Chapter 7.

non-expert actors. In this latter respect, 'madness' is like other 'facts' which are the subject of evidence and proof in the legal context. However, in contrast to these other 'facts', in relation to 'madness', 'readability' is significant because it simultaneously and somewhat contradictorily underpins the role played by both expert and lay knowledge, and experts and non-experts in legal processes. This older epistemological notion of 'readability' is embedded within modern knowledge practices, the lay actor playing a role alongside the expert.

My argument that 'madness' is constructed as 'readable' for criminal law purposes should not be taken to imply that the process of 'reading' is straightforward. Nor should my argument about the dispositional nature of 'madness' (provided above) be taken to suggest that the meanings given to 'madness' are devoid of internal conflict (homogenous) or separate from wider social and cultural dynamics (hermetically sealed).[76] Of course, any process of 'reading' meaning is complex, and I acknowledge what could be referred to as the instability of somatic or bodily signification. 'Reading' 'madness' in the criminal context is a nuanced process, influenced by broader social norms that affect deviance, culpability, and incapacity more generally.

Evidence in support of my argument about the 'readability' of 'madness' for criminal law purposes is provided by the law on unfitness to plead, and specifically by the way in which unfitness may be raised at trial, a practice which implicates both expert and lay knowledge of 'madness'. A legal assessment of an individual's unfitness depends on the 'readability' of his or her unfit status. Here, the (potentially unfit) accused's conduct at the time of the trial—including for instance his or her demeanour in court—is relevant to the legal inquiry. Historically, the situation seems to have been that anyone with knowledge about the individual's unfitness could raise the issue in court.[77] In a way that seems likely to have been reflective of established practice, in the mid-twentieth century, the court in *Dashwood* stated that, when a defendant may be unfit, 'the court acts in such a case on information conveyed to it from any quarter', including the defendant, his or her advisors, or the prosecution or an independent person.[78] This practice has since formalized into a particular rule about raising unfitness (according to which expert evidence is now mandatory).[79] But the rule about raising unfitness—by judges,

---

[76] Of course, the meanings given to 'madness' at the point of intersection with crime, and more generally, are inflected by gender, race, and class, among other factors. For historical discussion, see for instance, R Porter *Mind-Forg'd Manacles: A History of Madness in England from the Restoration to the Regency* (London: Athlone Press, 1987) 92–3 and D Rabin *Identity, Crime and Legal Responsibility in Eighteenth Century England* (Basingstoke: Palgrave Macmillan, 2004). For a discussion of gender and 'madness' in the context of infanticide, see Chapter 8.

[77] As John Beattie argues about this period, juries would gather evidence from 'those in court who had any dealings with the prisoner—magistrates, jailers and if there happened to be a doctor in the court he might be asked to examine the prisoner': see *Crime and the Courts in England* 337.

[78] *Rex v Dashwood* [1943] KB 1, 4; see also Walker *Crime and Insanity in England (Vol 1)* 231; Criminal Law Revision Committee *Third Report: Criminal Procedure (Insanity)* (Cmnd 2149, 1963) para 15; *R v H* [2003] UKHL 1, [4].

[79] Either the prosecution or defence may raise the issue of the accused's unfitness: Criminal Procedure (Insanity) Act 1964, s 4. The judge must raise the issue of unfitness if he or she believes it to be an issue and it has not been raised by either party: *Podola* [1960] 1 QB 325, 349–50 (Lord Parker CJ). As I discuss in Chapter 4, a judge may reject evidence of unfitness if his or her observations of the defendant in court are inconsistent with a finding of unfitness.

lawyers, and jurors, as well as medical experts—clearly rests on the 'readability' of unfitness. This interpretation of unfitness to plead also conjures up the other topographical feature of the mental incapacity terrain—the construction of 'madness' as dispositional—in that the rule about raising unfitness depends on the subsisting nature of the defendant's condition (at least over some of the time of the trial).

Regarding the expert knowledge side of the combination of types of knowledges about 'madness', I suggest that expert knowledges of 'madness' have a distinct significance in relation to the 'readability' of 'madness'. This is the case in at least two respects. Both of these are apparent when that type of knowledge is viewed as a subset of scientific knowledge, an umbrella term for the types of knowledge arising from the Scientific Revolution, and subsequently implicated in a vast array of political, social, and cultural changes.[80] The rhetorical force of these expert knowledges—presented as neutral, objective, and descriptive[81]—is such that the boundary between explanation and excuse, description and evaluation is blurred. Thus, in relation to infanticide, and as discussed above, the legal provision is constructed such that a distinction between the descriptive aspects of infanticide (a woman kills her infant at the same time as having a mind disturbed by childbirth or lactation) and its evaluative aspects (this action under these conditions warrants partial liability), is elided. As I discuss in Chapter 8, a finding of partial responsibility for killing then flows straightforwardly from the construction of the act of infanticide as an instantiation of abnormality.[82] There is a second dimension of the significance of the rhetorical associations of expert knowledge of 'madness'. The rhetorical associations of this body of scientific knowledge—to notions such as 'patient', 'suffering', 'illness', 'vulnerability', 'treatment', and to ideas such as victimhood and lack of agency—cut across the idea of the defendant as what might be called the villain of the piece and assist in associating mental incapacity with a lack of culpability, addressing precisely what is at issue in relation to exculpatory mental incapacity doctrines.

These points about the rhetorical associations of expert evidence about 'madness' provoke an insight about the structure of exculpatory mental incapacity doctrines, to which I also referred in Chapter 2. Exculpatory mental incapacity doctrines are those doctrines which, if successfully invoked, result in findings of non- or partial criminal responsibility. In Chapter 2, I suggest that one of the definitional features of exculpatory mental incapacity doctrines is that they do not reference the reasonable person. Rather, mental incapacity doctrines entail a tacit reference to the *non-criminal* mentally incapacitated individual. That is, the evaluation of the defendant who seeks to rely on a mental incapacity doctrine involves a comparison of sorts—but not one that is overtly countenanced in the legal

---

[80] See for discussion S Shapin *A Social History of Truth: Civility and Science in Seventeenth-century England* (Chicago: University of Chicago Press, 1994).

[81] For a critical discussion of the deployment of scientific knowledge in legal contexts, see C A Jones *Expert Witnesses: Science, Medicine and the Practice of Law* (Oxford: Clarendon Press, 1994).

[82] See further Chapter 8.

context.[83] Some evidence in support of this reading may be found in the recently repealed law relating to the rebuttable presumption of *doli incapax,* which involved a preliminary or circumscribed inquiry into the capacity of a defendant aged 10–14 years. As I discuss in Chapter 4, although the focus of the legal inquiry was on whether the child defendant him or herself could appreciate the difference between something 'seriously wrong' and something merely mischievous, that inquiry was dependent on generalized notions of child and adolescent development, and it was against these generalized notions (referent to non-criminal children) that the particular child defendant was compared.

This discussion of the epistemological dimension of the mental incapacity terrain, revolving around the 'readability' of 'madness', is intended to show that older ways of knowing inform the practices entailed in evaluative and adjudicative processes around mental incapacity. To conclude this discussion, it is again useful to return to the quote taken from the *Old Bailey Proceedings* with which this section began: 'do you take her to be a mad woman? I do'.[84] The quote is an extract from the evidence given in the trial of Susannah Milesent on the charge of theft of a petticoat in 1794. The words represent the court's question, and the answer of the witness, a servant, as recorded in the trial record. To me, both this question and the emphatic answer it elicited in response capture something of the 'readability' of 'madness' at the point of intersection with crime. The words convey a palpable sense of the way in which 'madness' is known—in conduct, and to ordinary people without specialist knowledge—for criminal law purposes.

This chapter has advanced a novel account of the terrain of mental incapacity in criminal law under the name 'manifest madness'. With the label 'manifest madness', I referred to the specific character of 'madness' at the point of intersection with crime. I argued that here, 'madness' has two formal features, one ontological (whereby it is constructed as dispositional) and one epistemological (whereby it is constructed as 'readable'). Together, these features constitute the topography of the mental incapacity terrain. My 'manifest madness' analysis revolves around the subsisting significance, in legal doctrines and practices, of older ideas about both the means by which certain types of human behaviour are evaluated, and the confidence with which evaluative judgments are made. I argued that, in relation to mental incapacity, these older ideas continue to be felt, and that this gives the terrain of mental incapacity distinctive features, which I conceptualized as broad ontological and epistemological contours. Particular ways of being and knowing inform both the principles and practices entailed in evaluative and adjudicative practices around mental incapacity. Each of the roles of mental incapacity doctrines—exculpation, inculpation, imputation, and a procedural role—outlined in the previous chapter depend on a sense of 'madness' as dispositional, and the

---

[83] My analysis of this aspect of the significance of expert knowledge of 'madness' helps to account for the relevance, both historical and into the current era, of expert evidence of a general nature about the mental disease or illness with which the defendant has been diagnosed. See Chapter 6 for a historical discussion in the context of insanity.
[84] *OBP*, Susannah Milesent, 11 November 1794 (t17941111–1). See also Chapter 4.

attendant practices of evidence and proof depend on a sense of 'madness' as 'readable'.

My analysis of the mental incapacity terrain is intended to be a contribution to scholarly understanding of this area of criminal law, and may serve as a corrective to existing studies of this area of criminal law. This argument about the topography of mental incapacity in criminal law is an explanatory rather than a normative one—'manifest madness' is offered to assist in understanding the structure of the terrain of mental incapacity in criminal law. The utility of 'manifest madness' lies in its ability to facilitate a fresh account of mental incapacity in criminal law, exposing and capturing the deep structures that inform this terrain.

PART II

4
Dynamics of Inclusion and Exclusion: Unfitness to Plead and Infancy

In this chapter, I examine unfitness to plead and infancy, both of which are non-exculpatory mental incapacity doctrines on my account of the mental incapacity terrain.[1] Unfitness to plead is a procedural provision exempting an individual from an ordinary trial, at least temporarily, on the basis that, at the time of the trial, he or she cannot understand or participate in it. Infancy refers to the minimum age at which criminal responsibility can be imposed (and is also known as non-age).[2] In discussing infancy, I also discuss the rules comprising *doli incapax* for children aged 10–14 years, which until recently, carved out a buffer zone for those, who, although above the age of criminal responsibility, did not have the full capacities of an adult. Taken together, unfitness to plead and infancy concern a defendant's understanding of, and engagement in, criminal proceedings, and the reach of the criminal law.

Unfitness to plead and infancy are not commonly examined alongside each other in legal scholarship. Indeed, because the sort of incapacity invoked by the law of infancy has come to be regarded as *sui generis*, it might at first seem to be a strange inclusion in a book on mental incapacity. While unfitness to plead is often swept up alongside exculpatory mental incapacity doctrines in academic studies (where it is usually, if implicitly, analysed as a procedural cognate of substantive criminal law doctrines such as insanity[3]), infancy is rarely so included, and, indeed, is often examined in isolation from other procedural provisions.[4] Feeding into its treatment

---

[1] See Chapter 2 for my reconstruction of the mental incapacity terrain and explanation of the category non-exculpatory mental incapacity doctrines.
[2] See G Maher 'Age and Criminal Responsibility' [2004–05] 2 *Ohio State Journal of Criminal Law* 493. In the Scots law, non-age has been labelled a plea in bar of trial, grouped together with entrapment, time limitations, and unfitness to plead: see J Chalmers and F Leverick *Criminal Defences and Pleas in Bar of Trial* (London: Routledge, 2006) 193.
[3] As a procedural provision, unfitness has been analysed beneath broad rationales for criminal procedural rules such as threat to the integrity of the justice system or unfairness to the accused. See, for instance, I Campbell *Mental Disorder and Criminal Law in Australia and New Zealand* (Sydney: Butterworths, 1988); D Chiswick 'Psychiatric Testimony in Britain: Remembering your Lines and Keeping to the Script' (1992) 15(2) *International Journal of Law and Psychiatry* 171; and I Freckelton 'Rationality and Flexibility in Assessment of Fitness to Stand Trial' (1996) 19(1) *International Journal of Law and Psychiatry* 39.
[4] The two most well-known studies of mental incapacity in criminal law (R D Mackay *Mental Condition Defences in the Criminal Law* (Oxford: Clarendon Press, 1995) and N Walker *Crime and Insanity in England (Vol 1: The Historical Perspective)* (Edinburgh: Edinburgh University Press, 1968)) include unfitness to plead but not infancy. Where it has not been examined in isolation, infancy has

in isolation, infancy is sometimes thought to have greater political and social than legal overtones.[5] But unfitness to plead and infancy interrelate with each other in intricate ways, and comparing them here usefully demonstrates the multifarious connections between the two, which stretch beyond their shared identity as procedural doctrines, safeguarding criminal process. The connections between unfitness to plead and infancy—historical, conceptual, and procedural—that I trace in this chapter not only provide some justification for their consideration side by side, but also reveal insights about the terrain of mental incapacity in criminal law.

The purpose of this chapter is two-fold. First, I show that infancy and unfitness to plead have both developed along a trajectory of formalization. By the term formalization, I refer to the process by which flexible and overtly moral-evaluative aspects of the law have gradually given way to rigid processes and technical and precise rules that mark out criminal law in the current era.[6] Both unfitness to plead and infancy are now discrete, procedural issues, but each trace their origins to the same broad set of morally evaluative principles and practices, which rested on largely undifferentiated ideas of incapacity. Second, I discuss the deep dynamics that have structured this process of formalization. While the process of formalization continues in the current era, the dynamics shaping it have altered over time. I suggest that formalization was shaped by a deep dynamic of inclusion—whereby the scope of these mental incapacity doctrines was drawn broadly—but, recently, has also come to be structured by a dynamic of exclusion, whereby the scope of the doctrines is more circumscribed. As I discuss in this chapter, the change in the dynamics structuring the process of formalization itself reflects changing concerns with matters such as dangerousness and fairness to the accused. As a result of these changes, in the current era, formalization of these mental incapacity doctrines is now structured by both dynamics of inclusion and exclusion.

Informal Legal Practices and the Emergence of the Doctrines

Although the absence of sources renders the early history of unfitness to plead and infancy opaque, it seems likely that what came to be called insanity on arraignment (and later unfitness to plead) and what would now be called infancy developed out of an informal practice of excusing certain individuals from trial. It is generally accepted that an informal practice of excusing young children via the means of a royal pardon, predated any formal prescription on a minimum age for criminal

---

been connected to criminal law and criminological examinations of youth justice, or family law relating to children, care, and custody. See, for example, A Bottoms and J Dignan 'Youth Justice in Great Britain' (2004) 31 *Crime and Justice* 21.

[5] As the House of Lords said of the treatment and punishment of young offenders in the context of their discussion of *doli incapax*, it is 'not so much a legal as a social problem, with a dash of politics thrown in': see *C (A Minor) Appellant v DPP* [1996] AC 1, 40.

[6] See further Chapter 3 for a discussion of the significance of formalization for my 'manifest madness' analysis.

responsibility.[7] Adults who were excused from trial included those who could not communicate, those who had intellectual disabilities, and those who were regarded as 'mad'.[8] These latter categories were loose, reflecting the limited way in which mental incapacity was disaggregated in the early modern era.[9] The scope of this informal practice—encompassing adults with both communication and comprehension impairments as well as children—prepared the ground for the subsequent development of the laws of unfitness and infancy.

The Role of Mercy in Criminal Process and the Significance of a Plea

In relation to the development of the law on infancy, the practice of according special treatment to young people charged with offences can be detected from the early modern period. Young children represented a statistically larger number of defendants than those who were unfit.[10] When young children came to the attention of the courts, the way they were dealt with was highly variable, affected by matters such as the circumstances of the victim, the type of offence, and the young person's social position. In the context of porous boundaries between what would now be factors affecting liability and factors in mitigation, age could be taken into account either in acquitting the defendant ('he being but a Youth, and no other Testimony than his own Confession, he was acquitted' of theft of a horse[11]), reducing the charge he or she faced (charged with theft but, 'taking pity of [sic] his youth', he was found guilty of the lesser charge of petty larceny[12]), or as a basis for a recommendation of mercy (convicted of high treason, but, 'in compassion to his Youth and Simplicity, he may have Mercie extended to him'[13]). In general, in the absence of specific laws or a regularized procedure for young people, the idea that a child could be excused from punishment on grounds of mercy seems to have had wide currency.

The special status of young defendants was recognized in legal commentary in the early modern era, in treatises which harked back to older legal traditions. This special status took the form of an irrebuttable presumption of *doli incapax* for very

---

[7] See for discussion Walker *Crime and Insanity in England (Vol 1)* 24–5.
[8] *Crime and Insanity in England (Vol 1)* 24–5. Walker argues that those individuals who had communication difficulties (who were referred to as 'deaf and dumb') featured prominently in this informal practice. Walker speculated that 'the practice of exempting the deaf-mute from trial may well have preceded... the practice of excusing the insane from either trial or punishment' (219). Individuals who, through informal practice, were excused from trial may have been remanded to prison until they were fit to be tried (220).
[9] Walker suggests that the term 'insane' included 'idiots as well as madmen': see *Crime and Insanity in England (Vol 1)* 225. The term *non compos mentis* was used as a generic term to cover all persons of unsound mind, including 'idiots' and 'lunatics': see F Woodbridge 'Some Unusual Aspects of Mental Irresponsibility in the Criminal Law' (1939) 29(6) *Journal of Criminal Law and Criminology* 822, 823.
[10] High mortality and short life expectancy meant that young people were a larger percentage of the population up to and including the Victorian era: see T E Jordan *Victorian Childhood: Themes and Variations* (New York, State University of New York Press, 1987) 271.
[11] OBP, Thomas Layton, 6 April 1687 (t16870406-36).
[12] OBP, John Bennet, 23 February 1683 (t16830223-5).
[13] OBP, 'young Lad, Apprentice in London', 10 October 1677 (t16771010-4).

young children and a rebuttable presumption of *doli incapax* for older children.[14] The idea that very young children should not be subject to criminal sanction seems to have been shared by a number of commentators, but there was variation in thinking about the age from which criminal sanction might be imposed.[15] Specification of a minimum age of criminal responsibility-cum-liability (then the two as yet unseparated) in legal treatises took on greater significance in the seventeenth century, when the system of registering births made it possible to be precise about an individual's age.[16] In the writings of Matthew Hale, whose *History of the Pleas of the Crown* was first published posthumously in 1736, the author refers to the *presumptio juris* that after 14 years children are *doli capaces*.[17] For a child aged between 12 and 14, 'if it appear to the court that he was *doli capax*, and could discern between good and evil at the time of the offence', he may be convicted.[18] As these words suggest, for children aged between 12 and 14, the assessment was flexible, taking into account the demeanour and appearance of the child. It was on the back of such dissertations on the law—as much aspirational as actual—that a systematic approach to young defendants would eventually emerge.

In relation to the development of unfitness to plead, the court processes of the medieval era that required an individual to enter a plea in response to a charge gave impetus to the development of the law on unfitness (and set up what would be an enduring link in the law of unfitness between inability to plead and inability to participate in a trial). At this juncture, court formalities meant that a defendant's inability or refusal to plead prevented his or her trial from proceeding. As John Langbein argues, this resulted from the perception that trial by jury was a 'consensual proceeding that the defendant had a right to decline'.[19] The significance of the

---

[14] See A W G Kean 'The History of the Criminal Liability of Children' (1937) 53 *Law Quarterly Review* 364, 366. For discussion, see T Crofts *The Criminal Responsibility of Children and Young Persons: A Comparison of English and German Law* (Aldershot: Ashgate, 2002) 6–11. It seems likely that, while references to mental processes and 'discretion' appear in the legal commentary, this two-tier approach to criminal responsibility originated with the physical process of puberty: see V D Sharma 'The Criminal Responsibility of Children in England' (1974) 3 *Anglo-American Law Review* 157, 161.

[15] The age of 14 seems to have come from Lord Coke's writings, which were taken up by Hale, who also stated that absolute immunity lay for a child under the age of seven. See Kean 'The History of the Criminal Liability of Children' 364–70 and Woodbridge 'Physical and Mental Infancy in the Criminal Law' 434. The age of criminal responsibility was raised to eight by the Children and Young Persons Act 1933 and to 10 by the Criminal Justice Act 1963.

[16] See Sharma 'The Criminal Responsibility of Children in England' 161–2.

[17] Matthew Hale, *Historia placitorum coronae* (The history of the pleas of the crown) (1st American edn by W A Stokes and E Ingersoll, Vol 1, Philadelphia, 1847) [25], in The Making of Modern Law database <http://galenet.galegroup.com/servlet/MOML> (last accessed 26 September 2011).

[18] Matthew Hale, *Historia placitorum coronae* [26]. Hale stated that a child under seven cannot be guilty of a felony. However, it is widely accepted that Hale's prescriptions were aspirational as much as actual, and it is not a surprise to find contradictory data in the *Old Bailey Proceedings*. For instance, in the trial of a young person for theft in 1784, the judge expressly rejected the idea of a minimum age of criminal responsibility, stating that the question in all cases is 'whether the Jury are satisfied that the child, of whatever age, has sufficient knowledge and discretion to understand that he is doing a criminal act? for if he has, he is answerable to the law for the consequences': see *OBP*, William Horton, 7 July 1784 (t17840707-77).

[19] J H Langbein *Torture and the Law of Proof: Europe and England in the Ancien Regime* (Chicago: University of Chicago Press, 1977) 75. According to Langbein, this perception dated from the earlier

requirement that individuals enter a plea in response to a charge meant that those who *would* not plead were grouped together with those who *could* not plead due to either communication or comprehension impairments.[20] In order to distinguish those defendants who were truly unfit from those who were merely obstructing the progress of the trial, medieval court process worked to separate those who were wilfully obstructionist. A jury was empanelled to decide if the defendant's muteness was the product of a genuine inability to communicate (in which case, he or she would be found 'mute by the visitation of God') or wilful choice (in which case, he or she would be found 'mute by malice').[21] This particular practice continued after the jury trial lost its consensual character.[22]

The practical significance of a defendant's plea to a charge increased over the period to the end of the seventeenth century, as a result of the type of criminal process then prevailing. The criminal trial in this era—typically referred to as 'trial by altercation'—centred on the idea that direct confrontation of the accused with his or her charge was the best means of discovering the truth of the allegation.[23] As Antony Duff and colleagues write, the accused was confronted by the accuser and the evidence, a practice which was the basis for the orality of the proceedings.[24] In his account of this trial process, which he calls the 'lawyer-free' or 'accused speaks' criminal trial, Langbein chronicles the factors, such as the absence of defence counsel and the rapidity of jury trials, which compelled the defendant to speak, 'either to hang himself or to clear himself'.[25] The trial was an exculpatory process—defendants were in effect presumed guilty and required to prove their innocence. Under these conditions, defendants who could not (or would not) plead presented a problem for criminal courts, obstructing the path to a verdict of either guilty or not guilty. This functional dependency on the accused seems to be behind the court

---

era in which trials by ordeal were the usual method of prosecution. In this era, individuals could avoid trial by ordeal by electing trial by jury.

[20] D Grubin 'What Constitutes Fitness to Plead?' [1993] *Criminal Law Review* 748, 750. Walker argues that defendants who would not plead presented a more common problem for medieval and Tudor judges than defendants who could not plead (*Crime and Insanity in England (Vol 1)* 220). According to Walker, remaining silent in response to a charge was a 'common gambit of men of property'—a silent defendant's property would not be forfeited to the Crown if he was executed (184); see also J M Beattie *Crime and the Courts in England 1660–1800* (Oxford: OUP, 1986) 337.

[21] If the defendant was found to be 'mute by malice', he or she would be subject to the practice of *peine forte et dure*, which involved weights pressed on the defendant's chest, in order to force him or her to enter a plea (see, for example, *OBP* Thomas Barlow, Oliver Morris, 13 January 1688 (t16880113-41). The category of those who were considered genuinely mute covered two groups of defendants: those who were 'deaf and dumb' and those who were 'insane': see Grubin 'What Constitutes Fitness to Plead?' 751.

[22] The associated practice of *peine forte et dure*—which reflected the at first prevailing and then subsisting ideas about proof in the form of divine judgment—continued into the eighteenth century. See Beattie *Crime and the Courts in England* 337.

[23] See A Duff et al *The Trial on Trial (Vol 3): Towards a Normative Theory of the Criminal Trial* (Oxford: Hart, 2007) 31, and 29–40 on the altercation criminal trial more generally. See also my Chapter 5 for a discussion of informal criminal processes then prevailing, and Chapter 6 for a discussion of the epistemological dimensions of this type of trial process.

[24] See *The Trial on Trial (Vol 3)* 34.

[25] J H Langbein *The Origins of the Adversary Criminal Trial* (Oxford: OUP, 2003) 36. I discuss the epistemological aspects of this criminal process in Chapter 6.

practice of inquiring into the defendant's mental ability to determine whether he or she could indeed be tried.[26] Because the defendant was an informational resource for the court in the 'accused speaks' trial process, guilty pleas were discouraged: even if conviction was certain, such a plea meant that the court could not consider mitigating factors.[27] As I discuss in the next chapter, together with changes in sentencing practices, the development of an adversarial criminal process from the start of the 1700s profoundly altered the dynamics of the criminal trial—but the significance of an accused's plea remained.

Conceptual Interdependency and Connection to the Substantive Law

Up to the end of the eighteenth century, unfitness to plead and infancy were part of a fluid mental incapacity terrain, marked by both conceptual interdependency and connection between what would later be discrete procedural doctrines and the substantive criminal law. Taking unfitness to plead first, as it developed out of procedural formalities in the early modern era, unfitness to plead exhibited a connection to the substantive law via the informal law of insanity. Reflecting the then conjoined nature of criminal liability and capacity at trial, a clear distinction between factors affecting an individual at the time of the trial and factors affecting liability was unknown in this period. As conveyed by the use of the same term for both conditions, there was no conceptual distinction between 'insanity' as it related to conviction (an insanity plea) and 'insanity' as it related to the time of the trial (insanity on arraignment). The relevant difference between the two lay not on the conceptual level but in the time at which the defendant's insanity became apparent. Less obvious insanity might appear only at trial.[28] Thus, the informal insanity plea was connected with the informal process of excusing an individual from trial: insanity at the time of the offence and insanity on arraignment represented two different points in time at which the individual might be judged to be insane, where insanity was a broad, minimally disaggregated concept.

The trial of Susannah Milesent for the theft of a petticoat in 1794 provides an illustration of the conceptual interdependency of insanity at the time of the offence and insanity on arraignment. The trial had been put off for two sessions 'on account of [the defendant] appearing insane'. When Milesent was tried, a prison nurse testified that, while in gaol, the defendant had broken windows, 'made use of very bad expressions', and taken off her clothes. Another witness testified:

---

[26] See, for example, *OBP*, John Smith, 5 April 1676 (t16760405-3), and for a later example, *OBP*, William Burrams, 13 January 1796 (t17970113-97).

[27] Langbein *The Origins of the Adversary Criminal Trial* 36, 20; see also Beattie *Crime and the Courts in England* 336.

[28] According to Roger Smith, historically, 'insanity' could be raised at any stage between arrest and execution of sentence (90). When a person showed extremely abnormal conduct, it was likely that insanity would be raised early on: R Smith *Trial by Medicine: Insanity and Responsibility in Victorian Trials* (Edinburgh: Edinburgh University Press, 1981) 90.

I am servant to Mr Priestly.
> Q. Have you known this woman ever since she has been in gaol?
> Q. What has been her conduct? -... in a kind of mad way.
> Q. What have you known her to do?—I saw her break windows of the ward she was in...
> ...
> Q. Upon your oath, what is your opinion? Do you think she is a mad woman, or a woman in her senses?—I did not think her to be a woman in her senses.
> Q. Do you take her to be a mad woman? I do.[29]

The jury found Susannah Milesent 'deranged and not in a sound mind'. This verdict may seem like an informal insanity verdict but, significantly, the defendant's insanity had only appeared at trial—there was no suggestion that, at the time of stealing the petticoat (to be 'wedded', 'because mine is a nasty old one'), the defendant had been deranged.[30]

Beyond the conceptual interdependency with insanity, the law then known as insanity on arraignment also serves to reveal something about the significance of the conduct of the (potentially unfit) accused in criminal process in this period. Here, an accused's conduct—encompassing the acts comprising the offence, but also the conduct surrounding the offence and his or her demeanour in court—had a thick significance, extending beyond that now commonly accorded to the *actus reus* of an offence. As I discuss in relation to evidence and proof of insanity, and also as part of my 'manifest madness' analysis, evaluation of an individual's conduct was made not so much via deduction of his or her mental processes from his or her behaviour, but on the basis that the behaviour constituted the 'mad' condition.[31] Thus, in the testimony advanced in the trial of Susannah Milesent, although there is a reference to the defendant's 'senses', the emphasis is clearly on her conduct (and particularly on her conduct in the time since the offence). This record suggests that, in this era, when a 'mad' individual was charged with a criminal offence, his or her conduct was more than a threshold issue in the legal evaluation process.

Over and above the significance of the (potentially unfit) accused's conduct for legal evaluation, conduct was significant in another respect. In this period, legal historians have thought of the developing law on unfitness as characterized by a strict approach.[32] In my thinking, the embryonic principles that applied to excusing or exempting particular individuals from trial have a different significance. This may be illustrated with reference to Matthew Hale's *The History of the Pleas of the Crown*, referred to above. According to Hale, 'a man' who becomes 'absolutely mad' before arraignment 'ought not by law to be arraigned during such his phrenzy,

---

[29] *OBP*, Susannah Milesent, 11 November 1794 (t17941111-1).

[30] The Old Bailey record does not indicate what if any order was made in relation to Susannah Milesent. Like the practice of disposing of certain individuals who successfully raised an informal insanity plea, it is likely that disposal of defendants who were 'mute by visitation of God' was an informal, discretionary, and individualized matter, affected by variables such as social position, financial resources, and family support.

[31] See Chapter 6 for a historical discussion in the context of insanity; see also Chapter 3 regarding 'manifest madness'.

[32] For instance, Walker argues that an accused had to be 'very disordered indeed' to have his or her trial postponed: see Walker *Crime and Insanity in England (Vol 1)* 222.

but be remitted to prison until that incapacity be removed'.[33] Hale's directives have been interpreted to suggest that his use of the term 'absolute' indicates the need for total or profound incapacity if an individual was to be given a reprieve from trial. My own assessment of the historical development of the law on unfitness to plead suggests an alternative view on these statements. In a way that parallels my suggestion about the 'wild beast' insanity test for insanity at the time of the offence (which I make in Chapter 5), Hale's reference to the 'absolute' character of the 'madness' that exempted a defendant from trial was more of a requirement of form than of degree or extent. According to this analysis, the requirement that the accused be 'absolutely mad' may have meant that his or her 'madness' had to be obvious or manifest, rather than extreme in the sense of total or profound, in order to excuse him or her from trial. This reinterpretation is subtle but important because it suggests that the emphasis in excusing individual defendants from trial was on behaviour or conduct rather than on the particulars of his or her disorder, an aspect of the development of the law that, as a result of beliefs about its apparent strictness, has not been given due attention.[34]

The conceptual interdependence with insanity, and the connection between the procedural and the substantive law, extended to infancy. In the context of what were largely undifferentiated ideas about incapacity, legal tests drew on then prevalent Judeo-Christian teachings and beliefs, according to which both children and the insane were thought to have impaired ability to understand 'good and evil'.[35] This terminology appeared in cases involving young defendants and those raising an informal insanity plea. A good example is provided by the trial record of the proceedings against three children for theft in 1787, where the Court opined:

... [i]deots, lunaticks, and persons non compos mentis, are not answerable for crimes that they commit; in the same way, a child that is of so tender years as to be alike incapable of distinguishing good from evil, and of knowing the moral consequences of its actions, is not capable, in point of law, of committing a crime.[36]

The conceptual connections between infancy and insanity (and unfitness in its nascent state), reflected genuine and deep interdependence among conceptions of incapacity. While these connections have now come to be treated typically as a mere analogy, when the perspective is expanded to encompass historical

---

[33] Matthew Hale, *Historia placitorum coronae* [30]. The standard Hale articulated applied to capital offences rather than misdemeanours: see Walker *Crime and Insanity in England (Vol 1)* 222.

[34] See Chapter 3 for a discussion of the thick significance of a 'mad' defendant's conduct in legal evaluation and adjudication.

[35] See A Platt and B L Diamond 'The Origins of the "Right and Wrong" Test of Criminal Responsibility and its Subsequent Development in the United States: An Historical Survey' (1966) 53 *California Law Review* 1227. See also discussion in *R v JTB* [2009] 2 Cr App R 500.

[36] *OBP*, John Tirey, William Tirey, James Tirey, 23 May 1787 (t17870523–30). The 'good and evil' test was used in the murder trial of Earl Ferrers in 1760 (*R v Ferrers* (1760) 19 St Tr 885) and in the trial of Daniel M'Naghten in 1843. See Chapters 5 and 6 for discussion.

Formalization of Unfitness to Plead and Infancy I: Dangerousness and Disposal

From the start of the nineteenth century, it is possible to track the formalization of law and practice concerning unfitness to plead and infancy. Starting from this point, I divide the process of formalization of these provisions into three stages. Within the first stage of formalization, parts of the mental incapacity terrain took on sharper definition and the sort of incapacity connoted by unfitness on the one hand and infancy on the other came to be clearly distinguished. In this first stage, broadly corresponding with the 1800s, the process of formalization was driven by concerns with dangerousness and disposal, and these concerns generated a deep dynamic of inclusion, according to which the scope of the doctrines was drawn broadly. The concern with dangerousness and disposal would be replaced by more humanitarian concerns such as fairness to the defendant in the second stage of formalization, but, here again, the result was a dynamic of inclusion, whereby both unfitness to plead and infancy were defined broadly.

'Now sane or not':[38] Insanity on Arraignment

In its first stage, the formalization of the law on unfitness occurred in two steps. The Criminal Lunatics Act 1800 represented the first step in the process.[39] This Act was triggered by the trial of James Hadfield, tried for high treason after attempting to shoot King George III.[40] Hadfield was acquitted 'as being under the influence of insanity' and detained under the civil law of vagrancy (rather than the criminal law).[41] Section 2 of the Criminal Lunatics Act applied to those found to be insane at the time of the trial:

If any person indicted for any offence shall be insane, and shall upon arraignment be found to be by a jury lawfully empanelled for that purpose, so that such person cannot be tried on indictment...it shall be lawful for the Court...to direct such finding to be recorded,

---

[37] In criminal law scholarship, the conceptual connections between insanity and infancy are reflected in Michael Moore's argument that insanity, intoxication, and infancy all belong in the category of 'status excuse': see M S Moore 'Causation and the Excuses' (1985) 73 *California Law Review* 1091, 1098. See also Maher 'Age and Criminal Responsibility' 493.
[38] *Rex v Pritchard* (1836) 7 C & P 303, 304 per Baron Alderson.
[39] 39 & 40 Geo. 3, c.94. This Act was subtitled 'An Act for the Safe Custody of Insane Persons Charged with Offences'.
[40] *R v Hadfield* (1800) 27 St Tr 1281. I discuss this case in more detail in Chapter 5.
[41] See M J Wiener *Reconstructing the Criminal: Culture, Law and Policy in England, 1830–1914* (Cambridge: CUP, 1990) 84; R Moran 'The Origin of Insanity as a Special Verdict: The Trial for Treason of James Hadfield' (1985) 19(3) *Law and Society Review* 487, 511.

and thereupon to order such person to be kept in strict custody until his Majesty's pleasure shall be known.[42]

The Criminal Lunatics Act 1800 did not define what constituted insanity on arraignment, just as it did not define insanity for the purposes of conviction, and it employed the same term ('insanity') to refer to insanity on arraignment and to insanity for the purposes of conviction. This suggests that each reference connoted the same broad and multifarious phenomena,[43] and that the distinction between the two continued to lie at the point in time at which the individual's condition became apparent.[44] Like Section 1 of the Act, which applied to individuals found to be insane at the time of the alleged offence, Section 2 was primarily concerned with disposal. Through this statutory provision, it became possible to detain those individuals found to be insane on arraignment indefinitely. Individuals could be detained in whatever manner the Crown saw fit, which, in practice, meant prison. In relation to both insanity on arraignment, and insanity for the purposes of conviction, the backdrop of the development of the law was the spectre of capital punishment, which, when humanitarian concerns became more prominent, contributed to the expansive approach taken to the scope of unfitness to plead.[45]

At this point, the meanings given to incapacity for the purposes of unfitness continued to revolve around insanity, which was a loose, broad, and moralized notion, defined by extra-legal norms. The social meanings of incapacity, then as now, were complex, and I discuss these meanings in more detail in the context of the law on insanity in the next chapter. Here, I suggest that what would come to be called unfitness—a legal creation which encompassed physical and mental impairments—was an omnibus notion, encompassing a range of incapacities, and defined by a range of social, religious, cultural, and other norms bearing on incapacity. In the absence of elaborated legal concepts of incapacity, ordinary people's ideas about 'madness and lunacy' provided the animating framework for ascriptions of insanity on arraignment (and insanity for the purposes of conviction).[46] In this era,

---

[42] Section 2 of the 1800 Act had a broad reach as it applied to those charged with 'any offence', meaning that it covered offences of treason, murder, felony, and misdemeanor: see Walker *Crime and Insanity in England (Vol 1)* 80, 224. The enhanced profile that individuals who could not be tried enjoyed by the end of the eighteenth century, and concern about their disposal, helps to account for the exclusion of a specific provision on unfitness in this Act.

[43] Thus, although Duff is now right to state that an unfit defendant is not exempt from trial merely because he or she would have been eligible for an insanity verdict in the early decades of the nineteenth century, this claim could not have been made with confidence. R A Duff *Trials and Punishments* (Cambridge: CUP, 1986) 30.

[44] As Walker suggests, this would have been contingent, depending 'partly on the judgment of individual doctors, partly on the extent to which his state of mind had improved or deteriorated between the crime and the trial, and partly on the strictness of the court': see Walker *Crime and Insanity in England (Vol 1)* 85.

[45] Like insanity for the purposes of conviction, insanity for the purposes of trial prevented defendants who had been charged with capital offences from being executed as defendants found unfit were rarely remitted for trial: see *Crime and Insanity in England (Vol 1)* 229.

[46] A R Poole suggests that a definition was not needed in the 1800 Act and the statutory reference to defendants who were 'insane on arraignment' would have been taken to refer to 'madness and lunacy': A R Poole 'Standing Mute and Fitness to Plead' [1968] *Criminal Law Review* 6; see also Grubin 'What Constitutes Fitness to Plead?' 752.

'madness' was considered readily intelligible to people without expert knowledge, who, observing the behaviour of others, inside court and beyond it, could be confident about their ability to know 'madness' when they saw it. At this time, ordinary people were considered competent to testify to an individual's 'mad' condition and it was against common meanings of 'madness' that legal evaluation and adjudication practices occurred.[47]

In the second step comprising the first stage of the formalization of unfitness to plead, unfitness came to be given greater definition as a legal construct, and, in this process, to take on a more elaborated and more technical character. The 1836 decision of *Pritchard* contained a sustained judicial discussion of insanity on arraignment, and put flesh on the bones of the law on unfitness, providing what would become the criteria for a finding that an individual was unfit.[48] Pritchard, who was 'deaf and dumb', was charged with bestiality, which was strictly, although not in practice, a capital offence.[49] The jury found Pritchard 'mute by the visitation of God' but able to plead. By a sign, Pritchard entered a plea of not guilty. Baron Alderson ordered the jury to try the question of whether he was 'now sane or not':

> There are three points to be inquired into:—First, whether the prisoner is mute of malice or not; secondly, whether he can plead to the indictment or not; thirdly whether he is of sufficient intellect to comprehend the course of the proceedings on the trial so as to make a proper defence—to know that he might challenge any of you to whom he may object—and to comprehend the details of the evidence.[50]

The three criteria for a finding of unfitness set out in *Pritchard*, encompassing issues of communication ('whether he can plead to the indictment or not') and comprehension ('whether he is of sufficient intellect to comprehend the proceedings'), form the basis of the current law, which I discuss below.

The technical explication of insanity on arraignment in the decision of *Pritchard*, and the almost contemporaneous development of a formal insanity doctrine in the *M'Naghten Rules*, wrought a conceptual cleavage between these two parts of the criminal law. In this process, the law on unfitness became stricter, and insanity for purposes of 'insanity on arraignment' came to be 'only tangentially related to insanity for purposes of liability'.[51] The concern with dangerousness that underpinned the 1800 Act was to subsist in each area of law. While some procedural points of connection between unfitness to plead and the insanity doctrine remain,

---

[47] See further Chapters 5 and 6.
[48] *Rex v Pritchard* (1836) 7 C & P 303. *Pritchard* followed soon after *Rex v Dyson* (1831) 7 C & P 305, which also included a discussion of unfitness. Dyson was regarded as 'deaf and dumb', and Justice Parke directed the jury to determine whether the defendant was 'sane or not', instructing them using the words of Hale: if the defendant did not have 'intelligence enough to understand the nature of the proceedings against her, they ought to find her not sane' (306). The jury returned a verdict that Dyson was 'not sane' and the Court ordered Dyson to be kept in strict custody as under the 1800 Act.
[49] Smith *Trial by Medicine* 93.
[50] *Rex v Pritchard* (1836) 7 C & P 303, 304. Pritchard was found 'not capable of taking his trial' and was confined 'in prison during his Majesty's pleasure'.
[51] C Emmins 'Unfitness to Plead: Thoughts Prompted by Glenn Pearson's Case' [1986] *Criminal Law Review* 604, 606; see also Walker *Crime and Insanity in England (Vol 1)* 224–5.

unfitness to plead formalized in a markedly more technical way than insanity, according to which unfitness has become a discrete procedural provision.

Infancy: the Social Seeds of Change

Doctrines and practices relating to young defendants were also formalizing over the 1800s. This was a gradual process. While the idea of an absolute presumption against responsibility for children aged seven and below, and a rebuttable presumption for those under 14, had taken root in legal commentary, these rules were not necessarily reflective of the practical operation of the law. Indeed, Martin Wiener suggests that the special status of a child under 14 years was usually ignored.[52] The *Old Bailey Proceedings* suggest that there was no precisely formulated test for the ideas about the criminal responsibility of children, with courts referring to 'the difference between falsehood and truth' and 'right and wrong', for instance.[53] In terms of proving if a particular young person had 'guilty knowledge', although in *Smith* in 1845, Justice Erle directed the jury that such 'knowledge' cannot be presumed from the 'mere commission' of the act,[54] it is not clear that this restriction on the means of proof would have been generally followed. Beyond this, age ('tender years', 'youth') continued to be a basis for mercy in some instances, and interacted with other factors such as mental state ('a weak mind'), poverty ('distressing circumstances'), intoxication, the influence of others ('bad companionship'), and good character in mitigating sentences.[55]

The general picture of the treatment of child offenders during this century is bleak. Wiener suggests that during the first half of the century, juveniles were treated as being 'even *more* liable to sanctions than earlier'.[56] During this period, children were subject to imprisonment, transportation, and execution for criminal behaviour. This was a period of fear about juvenile delinquency, a fear which intersected with concerns about victimization and economic crises. As historians point out, children's crimes were those of poverty—stealing, vagrancy, or beg-

---

[52] See Wiener *Reconstructing the Criminal* 50–2 for discussion.

[53] *OBP*, William Newton Allnutt, 13 December 1847 (t18471213-290) (a trial in which a 'medical man' testified that the 12-year-old prisoner was suffering from 'partial insanity' the effect of which was to prevent him from distinguishing right from wrong).

[54] *Reg v Smith* (Sidney) (1845) 1 Cox CC 260. See also *R v Kershaw* (1902) 18 TLR 357 and *CC (A Minor) v DPP* [1996] 1 Cr App R 375. It seems possible that *Reg v Smith* actually represented a change in legal practice at the time, just as *Woolmington* is widely regarded to have changed the law on burdens of proof while professing to uphold it (see Chapter 6 for discussion of this decision). In any case, there seems to have been some residual uncertainty about this prohibition on considering the facts themselves in serious cases. As recently as 1988, in *R v Coulburn* (1988) 87 Cr App R 309, the Court of Appeal appeared to rely on what the child defendant knew about sticking a knife into the victim (315–16). The House of Lords subsequently cautioned that that decision could not provide authority for the general proposition that 'the facts may be left to speak for themselves if the offence is serious enough': see *C (A Minor) v DPP* [1996] AC 1, 9 per Laws J.

[55] An example of the role of good character is provided by the trial of *OBP*, John Peter Mayaffree, 26 February 1746 (t17460226-36). The trial record states that 'The Jury on Account of his Excellent Character and tender Years, recommended him to his Majesty's Mercy'.

[56] Wiener *Reconstructing the Criminal* 51.

ging.[57] Reforms in the legal treatment of child offenders were instituted from mid-century. The Juvenile Offenders Acts of 1847 and 1850 provided that whipping and flogging could be used as alternatives to prison, and made provision for the separate arraignment and disposition of boys and girls aged less than 14 years.[58] The Reformatory Schools (Youthful Offenders Act) 1854 provided for segregation in prison by age, with those aged under 16 years sent to a reformatory after serving a sentence.[59] In the last decades of the century, greater flexibility in sentencing was introduced, but a separate court system for juveniles was not created until 1908.

The broader legal context for these developments was the formalization of the criminal trial process more generally, which coincided with the development of an administrative structure for dealing with insane and unfit individuals.[60] Developments in the first half of the 1800s occurred against the backdrop of the growing opposition to the breadth of capital punishment, which arose in the later eighteenth and early nineteenth centuries, and which led prosecutors, judges, and juries to attempt to restrict the scope of the death penalty and resulted in a reduction and reorganization of the number of capital statutes from 1827.[61] Over the course of the nineteenth century, a number of reforms to criminal procedure significantly affected the structure of criminal trials.[62] The primary aim of the various reforms to criminal trials was to expedite the criminal process, with concern about the rights of the accused merely a secondary consideration.[63] In addition, this period saw a significant expansion of summary jurisdiction, and a series of Acts which, for the first time set out a detailed uniform procedure for magistrates to follow.[64] As Wiener writes, these developments in criminal process significantly altered the structure of the criminal trial, moving it towards 'a more restrained, rule-governed, predictable, depersonalized process'.[65]

---

[57] See for instance, G S Frost *Victorian Childhoods* (Westport, CT: Praeger Publishers, 2009) 133, and ch. 6 more generally.
[58] See *Victorian Childhoods* 133.
[59] Reformatory Schools (Youthful Offenders) Act 1854 (17 Vict, c 86); Frost *Victorian Childhoods* 136.
[60] See Chapter 6 on insanity and automatism.
[61] See Langbein *The Origins of the Adversary Criminal Trial* 334–6; L Farmer 'Reconstructing the English Codification Debate: The Criminal Law Commissioners, 1833–45' (2000) 18(2) *Law and History Review* 397, 406.
[62] The reform of the criminal trial was a plank in a large raft of reforms, which extended to the criminal law and prisons, and which were themselves a part of reform of government, aiming at 'tackling corrupt practices and modernizing political and legal institutions': see Farmer 'Reconstructing the English Codification Debate' 403.
[63] 'Reconstructing the English Codification Debate' 413. These reforms included the introduction of defence counsel in felony trials (Prisoners' Counsel Act 1836 (6 & 7 Will IV c.114)), the creation of public prosecutors (Prosecution of Offences Act 1879 (42 & 43 Vict. c.22)), and the introduction of a limited appeal system in criminal cases (Crown Cases Act 1848 (11 & 12 Vict c.43)) and the defendant's right to give evidence at the end of the century (Criminal Evidence Act 1898). See D J A Cairns *Advocacy and the Making of the Adversarial Criminal Trial, 1800–1865* (Oxford: Clarendon Press, 1998) 169–76; C Emsley *Crime and Society in England 1750–1900* (Harlow: Pearson Longman, 2005) 183–211.
[64] Wiener *Reconstructing the Criminal* 66–7. On the development of summary jurisdiction, see Farmer *Criminal Law, Tradition and Legal Order*.
[65] *Reconstructing the Criminal* 65.

Combined with the enhanced social profile of crime, these developments pushed juvenile delinquency into prominence as a focus for social and political concern, and prompted the development of an administrative structure for young offenders. Reformatories, mentioned above, were part of this new administrative structure. As Wiener argues, the early Victorian era saw a 'new optimism' about reforming juveniles, onto which was overlaid a 'new acknowledgement of juvenile weakness and need for special help' by mid-century.[66] Based on a paternalistic approach to young offenders, whereby crime was depicted as a symptom of underlying problems, this era saw particular dispositions for young offenders (such as 'Borstal training') and separate prisons (such as Parkhurst, which opened in 1838), and, after 1850, new privately run reformatory schools.[67] These institutions and approaches represented attempts to reform wayward children (albeit through discipline and regimen, in keeping with the prevailing ethos of the period), and reflected a more generalized and diffused social concern about the so-called 'perishing' or 'dangerous classes'. By the end of the Victorian era, the criminal justice system was moving to deal with the young as 'a distinct category of lessened responsibility'.[68] This presaged the changing social concerns that would come to drive the formalization of infancy (and unfitness to plead) in the subsequent era.

These changing social concerns rested on what Wiener labels 'the emerging sentimentalization of childhood' that took place over this period.[69] Changing wages, living standards, patterns of education and the 'new model childhoods' that were part of the 'ideal of domesticity', combined to link childhood to ideas of innocence and vulnerability and fostered the idea that children were in need of welfare and protection.[70] The higher social profile of childhood in the nineteenth century, and the emergence of ideas of childhood as a distinct stage of the development of the person, as well as the appearance of a specialist or expert knowledge on youth facilitated these developments. Yet, even as childhood was becoming the subject of specific meanings, connections to existing ideas of incapacity—around disability and femininity—persisted, in that young people, 'lunatics', and women were regarded as problematic in the context of Victorian insistence on 'personal responsibility and self-mastery'.[71] While the incapacity associated with unfitness to plead continued to connote mental impairment and

---

[66] *Reconstructing the Criminal* 131, 135.
[67] See *Reconstructing the Criminal* 133–5 for discussion.
[68] *Reconstructing the Criminal* 294 and, more broadly, 285–94.
[69] *Reconstructing the Criminal* 51.
[70] See Frost *Victorian Childhoods* ch. 7. Frost argues that these changes amounted to an expansion of the time in which children could be children. See also H Cunningham *The Children of the Poor* (London: Blackwell, 1991). Cunningham argues that the theory of 'recapitulation', a belief that all children proceeded through the stages of civilization, helped erode distinctions between rich and poor (97), fostering an idea that childhood for all children should be marked by freedom.
[71] Wiener *Reconstructing the Criminal* 131. As Wiener writes about juveniles, 'their guilt (like that of lunatics) was more questionable than that of adult offenders, although (also like lunatics) they seemed more ruled by impulse and thus in the long run even more of a social danger' (131). For a discussion of gender, 'madness' and crime in the context of infanticide, see my Chapter 8.

disability, childhood gradually came to be accorded a *sui generis* notion of difference that did not reduce to incapacity.

Formalization of Unfitness to Plead and Infancy II: Fairness and Special Treatment

The next stage in the formalization of unfitness to plead and infancy corresponded with the period of the twentieth century up to the mid 1990s. Reviewing this period, it is possible to detect a change in the concerns underpinning the dynamic of inclusion that was shaping formalization. In this period, a deep dynamic of inclusion continued to drive the formalization of the law on unfitness to plead and infancy, but, now, more humanitarian concerns with fairness to defendants and a sense of the appropriateness of special treatment for some emerged to intersect with subsisting concerns about dangerousness. In this period, it is the combination of these concerns that accounts for the dynamic of inclusion, and thus the continuation of an expansive approach to unfitness to plead and infancy.

'With reference to the Question whether the Prisoner can or cannot be Tried upon the Indictment':[72] Unfitness to Plead

The first unfitness case to go to the new Court of Criminal Appeal, *Governor of Stafford Prison ex parte Emery*, usefully illustrates both these emerging and subsisting concerns driving a dynamic of inclusion. In *Emery*, the Court upheld the 'strict custody' order imposed on Emery, a 'deaf mute', who had been charged with a felony. Emery was unable to write or communicate via sign language. On appeal, Emery's counsel argued that, because the jury had found Emery incapable of pleading 'by reason of his inability to communicate with and be communicated with by others', it would be 'a straining of [the] language [of the verdict] to construe the finding as one of insanity'.[73] The Court rejected this argument, stating:

> It might work great injustice in many cases to put a prisoner against whom such a finding was recorded upon his trial as if he were perfectly sane, and if he was found guilty to punish him as an ordinary criminal; or it might be the cause of much mischief if he were found not guilty and allowed to go free.[74]

---

[72] *Rex v Governor of Stafford Prison ex parte Emery* [1909] 2 KB 81, 86 per Lord Alverstone.
[73] *Rex v Governor of Stafford Prison ex parte Emery* [1909] 2 KB 81, 83.
[74] *Rex v Governor of Stafford Prison ex parte Emery* [1909] 2 KB 81, 84. Lord Alverstone referred with approval to the decisions of *Dyson* and *Pritchard* and stated that the word 'insane' in Section 2 of the 1800 Act ought to be construed 'with reference to the question whether the prisoner can or cannot be tried upon the indictment' (86). Lord Alverstone justified this expansive approach by claiming that it was 'in accordance with reason and common sense' (84–5). The broad approach of the court in *Emery* to insanity for the purposes of unfitness was cited with approval by the Court of Criminal Appeal in *Podola* in 1960 (*R v Podola* [1960] 1 QB 325, 356).

This reasoning exposes the nuances of the dynamic of inclusion as it played out in relation to unfit defendants: in addition to a concern about dangerousness, concern about fairness to the defendant had emerged to inform the law. The currents of sympathy and concern about fairness were channelled through a sense of the beneficence of legal processes dealing with unfit defendants. The decision in *Emery* adopted an expansive approach to insanity for the purposes of insanity on arraignment and confirmed that it encompassed disabilities relating to communication as well as comprehension.

The formalization of unfitness was advanced by the Court of Appeal decision of *Podola* in 1960,[75] and the Criminal Procedure (Insanity) Act 1964, which repealed the Criminal Lunatics Act 1800. Taken together, this decision and this Act significantly firmed up the law relating to unfitness. The *Podola* Court concluded that the burden of proving unfitness lay with the defence.[76] In relation to the standard of proof for unfitness, it now became clear that, if the defence raises the issue, the standard of proof is on the balance of probabilities; if the issue is raised by the prosecution, the standard of proof is beyond reasonable doubt.[77] The Criminal Procedure (Insanity) Act 1964 followed the Criminal Law Revision Committee (CLRC)'s report, *Criminal Procedure (Insanity)*, which reviewed the law on unfitness to plead and made a number of recommendations for reform to the law.[78] The recommendations of the CLRC's Report that were incorporated into the 1964 Act gave the judge discretion to postpone the trial of unfitness until the close of the prosecution argument, permitting the defence to submit a 'no case to answer'

---

[75] *R v Podola* [1960] 1 QB 325.
[76] *R v Podola* [1960] 1 QB 325. Before it was resolved in *Podola*, the question of the burden of proof for unfitness to plead had vacillated considerably. The burden of proving a defendant fit to plead was held to lie with the prosecution in *R v Davies* (1853) 3 C & K 328 (see also *R v Sharp* [1960] 1 QB 357). In *Podola*, Chief Justice Lord Parker stated that the correct approach was that the burden of proving unfitness lay on the defence—an approach which had been taken in *Reg v Turton* (1854) 6 Cox 395 (see also *R v Rivett* (1950) 34 Cr App R 87)—and that *Davies* and its progeny were wrongly decided (351).
[77] *R v Podola* [1960] 1 QB 325, 350; *Robertson* [1968] 1 WLR 1767, 1773. The evidential issue of the burden and standard of proof that applied to the unfitness to plead issue was before the Court in *Sharp* (*R v Sharp* [1960] 1 QB 357). In this case, the Court decided that, as unfitness was a preliminary issue, 'it would be right for the prosecution to put its evidence before the court and to begin' (360 per Justice Salmon). This issue came to the Court of Criminal Appeal in the same year in *Podola*, where the Court held that *Sharp* was wrongly decided. In *Podola*, the Court held that the burden of proof on the issue of the defendant's unfitness lay with the defence, and that the standard of proof is the balance of probabilities (350).
[78] Criminal Law Revision Committee, *Criminal Procedure (Insanity)* (Cmnd 2149, 1963). The CLRC recommended that the question of a defendant's ability to plead continue to be determined by a jury because of the 'great public importance of the issue from the point of view of the accused and of the public' (para 15). The CLRC noted the problem that certain defendants may be entitled to an acquittal, although it may not be possible to try them because of their disability (para 18). With this in mind, the Committee recommended that the court have discretion as to whether the question of fitness should be addressed when raised, or postponed until any time up to the opening of the defence case (para 24, 28). Neither the CLRC Report nor the 1964 Act addressed the substantive issue of the reach of the law on unfitness, perhaps on the basis that, as the CLRC Report stated, the criteria of unfitness were 'well established'. As a result, the criteria for determining whether a defendant was unfit to plead continued to be governed by the Criminal Lunatics Act 1800 and the cases decided under it.

motion which, if successful, meant that the defendant would be acquitted.[79] The Act codified the common practice that either the prosecution or defence may raise the issue of the defendant's unfitness.[80] The Act also provided that the court must make an order that the unfit individual be admitted to hospital to be discharged at the discretion of the Home Secretary (who also had discretion to remit the defendant for trial at a later date).[81] This order meant that an unfit accused could be detained without the Crown proving whether he or she had committed the offence charged.[82] Further, because the consequence of a finding of unfitness was indefinite hospitalization, an unfit person could be detained for a longer period of time than if he or she had pleaded or been found guilty and sentenced to a jail term.[83]

Although criticism of the 1964 Act followed soon after its passage, the law was not reformed until 1991. The Criminal Procedure (Insanity and Unfitness to Plead) Act 1991 incorporated some of the changes to the law recommended by the Butler Committee in its 1975 review of the 1964 Act and its operation.[84] The 1991 Act represented an effort to increase the use of unfitness to plead. As the Butler Committee had recommended, the 1991 Act amended the 1964 Act to introduce a procedure for a 'trial of the facts' to follow a finding of unfitness. A 'trial of the facts'—which the Butler Committee had suggested should extend to cover the *actus reus* and *mens rea* of the offence charged—was to determine whether the defendant had 'done the act or made the omission charged as the offence'. The outcome of such a 'trial' was not to count as a conviction and could not be followed by punishment.[85] Again, per the Butler Committee recommendations, the 1991 Act also introduced a requirement that expert evidence from two medical practitioners support a finding of unfitness.[86] These legislative reforms did not represent all of the Butler Committee's recommendations, however. The 1991 Act omitted to enact the recommendation that a finding of unfitness be made by a judge alone

---

[79] Section 4(2). This also resolved earlier inconsistency in the case law discussions of the point in the proceedings in which the issue of unfitness could be raised. In *Roberts* (*R v Roberts* [1954] 2 QB 329), Justice Devlin held that the issue of the defendant's fitness could either be raised at the start of the trial, or it could be postponed until the end of the prosecution case. *Roberts* was not followed in *Benyon* (*R v Benyon* [1957] 2 QB 111), where the Court held that the issue of fitness must be dealt with as a preliminary issue. In that case, Justice Byrne relied on Hale's *History of the Pleas of the Crown*, the Criminal Lunatics Act 1800 and the nineteenth-century decision of *Berry* (*R v Berry* (1876) 1 QBD 447).

[80] Section 4. The judge must raise the issue of unfitness if he or she believes it to be an issue and it has not been raised by either party: *R v Podola* [1960] 1 QB 325, 349–50 per Lord Parker.

[81] Sections 5(1) and 5(4).

[82] As Duff writes, the Act treated the unfit defendant as if he or she was guilty: see Duff *Trials and Punishments* 33.

[83] The prospect of indefinite detention in hospital meant that, unless the defendant was charged with a serious offence, defence counsel had little incentive to initiate an inquiry into unfitness: see *R v H* [2003] UKHL 1, [8]; R D Mackay 'The Decline of Disability in Relation to the Trial' [1991] *Criminal Law Review* 87, 88; G Kearns and R D Mackay 'The Trial of the Facts and Unfitness to Plead' [1997] *Criminal Law Review* 644, 645.

[84] United Kingdom *Report of the Committee on Mentally Abnormal Offenders* (Cmnd 6244, 1975) ('Butler Report').

[85] Butler Report paras 10.24–10.25 and 1991 Act, s 4A.

[86] 1991 Act, s 4(6) and Butler Report para 10.41.

unless the defence requested a jury determination.[87] Instead, the 1991 Act provided that a 'trial of the facts' was to be heard by a jury empanelled specifically for that purpose and that the jury must be 'satisfied' that the defendant 'did the act or made the omission charged against him as the offence'.[88] Although there is empirical data to indicate that a 'trial of the facts' does not always follow a finding of unfitness, where it does, the majority of unfit individuals are found to have done the act.[89] I discuss the 'trial of the facts' procedure again below.

Like changes to the process, the introduction in the 1991 Act of a range of disposal options for those found unfit to plead (as well as for those found not guilty on the grounds of insanity) was designed to increase the use of unfitness to plead provisions.[90] Reflecting both the perceived problems flowing from lack of flexibility in the 1964 Act and an increasing differentiation within the category of unfit individuals, the 1991 Act provided that a Crown court could issue a hospital order with or without restriction, a supervision order, and an absolute discharge.[91] In relation to remission of unfit defendants, the Home Secretary retains the power to remit unfit defendants for trial in all instances except those in which the defendant was subject to a hospital order without restrictions.[92] Initially, these disposal options did not apply where the defendant had been charged with an offence for which the sentence was 'fixed by law' (that is, murder, to which a mandatory

---

[87] The Committee labelled the part played by the jury an anachronism, and noted that juries are not normally involved in the decision as to 'whether the trial should proceed' (Butler Report para 10.22). The Butler Committee had recommended that judges should have the power to decide the question of unfitness, whether the medical evidence is unanimous or disputed, unless the defence desire that the question go to the jury (para 10.20).

[88] Section 4A(2). The requirement of jury decision-making has recently been altered by the Domestic Violence Crime and Victims Act 2004, which I discuss below.

[89] See R D Mackay 'Unfitness to Plead—Data on Formal Findings from 2002 to 2008', Appendix C, Law Commission *Unfitness to Plead: A Consultation Paper* (Law Com No 197, 2010) and R D Mackay, B J Mitchell and L Howe 'A Continued Upturn in Unfitness to Plead—More Disability in Relation to the Trial Under the 1991 Act' [2007] *Criminal Law Review* 530.

[90] For the range of disposal options, see 1991 Act, s 5(2) and Butler Report para 10.29.

[91] Criminal Procedure (Insanity and Unfitness to Plead) Act 1991, s 5, as amended by Domestic Violence, Crime and Victims Act 2004, s 24. Of these disposal options, empirical studies suggest that hospital based disposals are most common: see Mackay 'Unfitness to Plead– Data on Formal Findings from 2002 to 2008' (Law Com No 197, 2010). When compared with disposals following successful insanity defences (where the courts have the same set of options), community based disposals are less common where a defendant has been found unfit to plead (Mackay, Mitchell and Howe 'A Continued Upturn in Unfitness to Plead' 544; R D Mackay and G Kearns 'An Upturn in Unfitness to Plead? Disability in Relation to the Trial Under the 1991 Act' [2000] *Criminal Law Review* 532, 545). It is likely that this reflects the fact that more defendants who are unfit at the time of the trial will need hospital treatment than those who were insane at the time of the offence (Mackay and Kearns 'An Upturn in Unfitness to Plead?' 545) and also the likelihood that the unfitness provision operates to capture severe species of disorder.

[92] 1991 Act, Sch 1, para 4(2). Although it has always been possible to remit a defendant to court to determine if he or she has become fit to plead, before 1982, it was Home Office policy to remit defendants for trial only in exceptional circumstances. In the decade before the passage of the 1991 Act, the Home Office altered its policy on the remission of defendants found unfit to plead. In the years since 1982, when the policy changed, nearly half of the number found unfit to plead in England and Wales have been remitted to trial. Of this group, the majority was found guilty: see D Grubin 'Regaining Unfitness to Plead: Patients found Unfit to Plead who Return for Trial' (1992) 2(2) *Journal of Forensic Psychiatry* 140, 142–5.

penalty of life applies), where the only option available to a court was a hospital order. This situation was remedied with the Domestic Violence, Crime and Victims Act 2004, which removed the underused option of a guardianship order and provided that, where the sentence for an offence is 'fixed by law', the courts have power to order a hospital order only if the necessary medical criteria are satisfied.[93] Although findings of unfitness have increased in the years since the passage of the 1991 Act,[94] they remain uncommon.[95] The low numbers of finding of unfitness have led R M Mackay to conclude that 'the law is markedly unsuccessful in fulfilling what should be a protective function for the mentally disordered'.[96]

This stage in the formalization of unfitness to plead brought with it an enhanced reliance on expert psychiatric and psychological knowledges of incapacity. The Criminal Procedure (Insanity and Unfitness to Plead) Act 1991 mandated the use of expert medical evidence in relation to unfitness to plead (and the insanity plea). The Atkin Committee on Insanity and Crime,[97] the Royal Commission on Capital Punishment,[98] and the Butler Committee,[99] had all recommended that expert

---

[93] Domestic Violence, Crime and Victims Act 2004, s 24. The 2004 Act also seems to have addressed the compatibility with Article 5(1)(e) of the Human Rights Act 1998 that arises because the court's only interest in an inquiry into unfitness is into 'the accused's ability to engage in the proceedings, not his mental state more generally': see *R v Grant* [2002] QB 1030 and D Tausz and D C Omerod 'Fitness to Plead: Whether Defendant Found Unfit to Plead Permitted to put before Jury Defences of Lack of Intent and Provocation' [2002] *Criminal Law Review* 403, 405. In connecting its reference to 'hospital order' to the same term in the Mental Health Act 1983, the Domestic Violence, Crime and Victims Act 2004 changed the law to provide that there must be medical evidence which justifies hospitalization if this is ordered by the court: s 24.

[94] In research commissioned for the Law Commission, Mackay found that, between 2002 and 2008, the annual average number of findings of unfitness exceeded 100 for the first time: Mackay 'Unfitness to Plead– Data on Formal Findings from 2002 to 2008' (*Unfitness to Plead: A Consultation Paper* Law Com No 197, 2010). Older research by Mackay and colleagues found that, between 1997 and 2001, there was an average of 45 findings of unfitness to plead per year: see Mackay, Mitchell and Howe 'A Continued Upturn in Unfitness to Plead' 530. As Mackay and colleagues suggest, this increase may be attributed to the introduction of a range of disposals for unfit defendants (532; see also Mackay and Kearns 'An Upturn in Unfitness to Plead?' 546).

[95] As several commentators suggest, this may be because, historically, there was little incentive to raise the issue when a successful finding of unfitness resulted in indefinite hospitalization. See, for example, P Fennell 'The Criminal Procedure (Insanity and Unfitness to Plead) Act 1991' (1992) 55 *Modern Law Review* 547, 547; Mackay 'The Decline of Disability in Relation to the Trial' 88. With judges also cognizant of indefinite hospitalization, it is possible that, as Mackay has suggested, the low numbers of defendants found unfit to plead before the 1991 Act may also have been a result of courts avoiding the law on unfitness and using their powers under the Mental Health Act 1983 to remand certain mentally disordered defendants in hospital (Mackay 'The Decline of Disability in Relation to the Trial' 96).

[96] Mackay *Mental Condition Defences* 245.

[97] *Committee on Insanity and Crime* ('Atkin Committee') (Cm 2005, 1923) 9, 21.

[98] United Kingdom, Royal Commission on Capital Punishment 1949–1953 Report (Cmd Paper 8932, 1953) para 225.

[99] The Butler Committee reasoned that, in practice, expert evidence is usually adduced (Butler Report para 10.41). The Committee seemed to be motivated to make such evidence mandatory because of the weighty consequences of a finding of unfitness: under the 1964 Act, both a finding of unfitness and a successful insanity defence resulted in the indefinite hospitalization of defendants. Concerns to this effect were also evident is the decision of the European Court of Human Rights in *Winterwerp v The Netherlands* ((1979) 2 EHRR 387). In relation to the claim that Winterwerp's right to liberty under Article 5 of the European Convention on Human Rights was violated after he was committed to a psychiatric hospital via an emergency procedure, the European Court stated that a

evidence from two medical practitioners be required to support a finding of unfitness (and insanity). The historical situation seems to have been that anyone with knowledge about the individual related to his or her unfitness could raise the issue in court.[100] Seemingly reflective of established practice in the mid-twentieth century, the Court in *Dashwood* stated that when a defendant may be unfit, 'the court acts in such a case on information conveyed to it from any quarter', including the defendant, his or her advisors, or the prosecution or an independent person.[101] These rules continue to govern the way in which unfitness may be raised, even as formally adduced expert evidence has come to be more prominent in the law. In current practice, it is likely that unfitness would be raised by the defence, prosecution, or the judge, as opposed to an independent person. With expert evidence now mandatory, empirical studies indicate that, as a matter of practice, such evidence is crucial to the outcome of an inquiry into unfitness.[102]

Stretching above its practical significance, expert evidence of unfitness has a broader if more nebulous significance in legal practices. As Don Grubin writes, being unfit to plead is not a psychiatric condition[103]—but legal reliance on expert medical evidence makes the unfit individual the subject of specialist language and knowledge and assists in rendering unfitness a technical and discrete issue.[104] In addition, and running parallel to the practical and more discursive role of expert evidence and expert knowledge, lay knowledge of 'madness' remains significant in the law on unfitness (although it could no longer be described as providing the animating framework for findings of unfitness as in the earlier eras). As I discuss in detail

---

decision to detain people of 'unsound mind' should be made on 'objective medical expertise' and that the relevant mental disorder 'must be of a kind or degree warranting compulsory confinement' [39].

[100] As John Beattie suggests in relation to this period, juries would gather evidence from 'those in court who had any dealings with the prisoner—magistrates, jailers and if there happened to be a doctor in the court he might be asked to examine the prisoner': see *Crime and the Courts in England* 337.

[101] *Rex v Dashwood* [1943] KB 1, 4; see also Walker *Crime and Insanity in England (Vol 1)* 231; Criminal Law Revision Committee *Criminal Procedure (Insanity)* (Cmnd 2149, 1963) para 15; *R v H* [2003] UKHL 1, [4].

[102] D Grubin 'Unfit to Plead in England and Wales, 1976–1988 A Survey' (1991) 158 *British Journal of Psychiatry* 540, 545; B J Winnick 'Reforming Incompetency to Stand Trial and Plead Guilty: A Restated Proposal and a Response to Professor Bonnie' (1995) 85(3) *Journal of Criminal Law and Criminology* 571, 620. However, there also appear to be problems with the use of expert evidence in this context. Perhaps in part because unfitness to plead does not have the profile of the insanity defence, there seems to be some uncertainty about the criteria for a finding of unfitness: see E P Larkin and P J Collins 'Fitness to Plead and Psychiatric Reports' (1989) 29(1) *Medicine, Science and the Law* 26, 26. In their study, Larkin and Collins examined pre-trial psychiatric reports and found that only about one third of them included a statement about unfitness to plead and supported this statement with reference to the legal criteria for such a finding (30). Similarly, Mackay and Kearns found that only a minority of pre-trial reports they examined explicitly addressed the criteria for a finding of unfitness ('An Upturn in Unfitness to Plead?' 538). There also seems to be some confusion between the criteria for a finding of unfitness to plead and the ingredients of the insanity defence, with some experts in Grubin's study commenting on whether the defendant could distinguish between right and wrong: see Grubin 'Unfit to Plead in England and Wales' 540. As Grubin suggests, it is possible that those found unfit to plead are little different from 'the majority of mentally disturbed defendants who come before the courts every year' (545).

[103] Grubin 'Unfit to Plead in England and Wales' 548.

[104] I discuss the significance of expert evidence in this respect in relation to diminished responsibility: see Chapter 9.

in relation to insanity, legal actors—including judges, prosecution, and defence counsel—rely on lay knowledge of unfitness although this interacts with their expert legal knowledge of criminal process.[105] As a result, the role of lay knowledge of mental incapacity in criminal processes does not begin and end with lay adjudication. Even though the 2004 reforms to the way unfitness to plead is decided (which I discuss below) have meant unfitness is decided by a judge rather than a jury, this does not mean lay knowledge has been eclipsed. In this respect, it is interesting that, as was recently reaffirmed, it is still open to the judge, in the exercise of his or her discretion, to reject the evidence of unfitness, if raised after the trial has commenced, on the basis that his or her observations of the defendant in court are inconsistent with a claim to unfitness.[106]

In its second stage, the formalization of the law of unfitness to plead occurred on two tracks, with the higher courts on one track and summary proceedings on the other. Neither the 1964 Act nor the 1991 Act addressed the issue of the procedure for dealing with unfit defendants in the summary jurisdiction, as both related only to trials on indictment. Magistrates continue to rely on the civil law as it provides a proxy structure to deal with unfitness to plead in summary jurisdiction.[107] This situation has been the subject of long-standing criticism.[108] Although arguably originally the result of historical happenstance,[109] the continuation of a two-track formalization of the law on unfitness to plead exposes an abiding concern with dangerousness, which continues to inform the development of this area of criminal law. The distinction between magistrates' courts and higher courts broadly maps onto a distinction between less serious and more serious offences (with more serious

---

[105] See further Chapter 6.
[106] See *R v Habib Ghulam* [2010] 1 WLR 891, 895, 897.
[107] Under the *Mental Health Act* 1983, magistrates can make a hospital or guardianship order where an individual has been convicted of an offence punishable with imprisonment (s 37(1)) or where a defendant has been charged with such an offence (s 37(3)); see also N Walker and S McCabe *Crime and Insanity in England (Vol 2): New Solutions and New Problems* (Edinburgh: Edinburgh University Press, 1973) 107. Under the Mental Health Act 1983, s 37(3) the power of magistrates' courts over defendants who had not been convicted extended only to those who were 'mentally ill' or 'severely subnormal', meaning that defendants with communication difficulties were not covered and had to rely on the discretionary powers of magistrates to dismiss the case: see Emmins 'Unfitness to Plead' 611. These defendants may now be caught by the provision because the Mental Health Act 2007 has amended the 1983 Act to remove different categories of mental disorder, replacing them with one definition of mental disorder as 'any disorder or disability of the mind' (Mental Health Act 2007, s 1 amending Mental Health Act 1983). The Butler Committee had recommended that the power to determine unfitness be extended to magistrates courts (para 10.35).
[108] Most recently, see Law Commission *Unfitness to Plead: A Consultation Paper* (Law Com No 197, 2010) Chapter 8. The Law Commission identifies the problems with the approach to unfitness in magistrates' courts and youth courts, but refrains from making particular recommendations in the Consultation Paper in advance of feedback from consultees. See also Butler Report para 10.35; and Walker and McCabe *Crime and Insanity in England (Vol 2)* 107.
[109] Walker and McCabe suggest that, at the end of the nineteenth century, the Home Office advocated a practice of dismissing charges against certain defendants and encouraged magistrates 'to use their civil powers of committal to lunatic asylums' in petty cases (Walker and McCabe *Crime and Insanity in England (Vol 2)* 105. The legacy of this practice is that, in the current era, magistrates cannot try an issue of unfitness to plead, nor commit it to the Crown Court for it to be tried (*R v Lincoln (Kesteven) Justices, ex parte O'Connor* [1983] 1 WLR 335; see also S White 'The Criminal Procedure (Insanity and Unfitness to Plead) Act' [1992] *Criminal Law Review* 4, 13).

offences broadly connoting more dangerous offenders): as the process of finding that an individual is not amenable to an ordinary trial is more formalized in the latter, the part played by dangerousness in sustaining this two-track system becomes clear.

Protection from 'the full force of the criminal law':[110] Infancy

In the period of the twentieth century up to the mid 1990s, the criminal law relating to young offenders also continued a process of formalization. As was the case with unfitness to plead, a deep dynamic of inclusion continued to drive this process of formalization, but more humanitarian concerns with welfare and special treatment interacted with concerns carried over from the previous era. This stage of formalization represented the crest of the expansionist approach to the law of infancy, which has come to be more narrowly circumscribed in the current era.

The second stage of the formalization of infancy unfolded on both the level of law and practice. A separate court system was created by the Children's Act 1908.[111] Juvenile courts, which operate as specialized magistrates' courts, adopt modified procedures including a 'finding of guilt' rather than a conviction.[112] It was in this stage of formalization that the age of criminal responsibility was set at its current level—10 years.[113] The mid-century point coincided with the peak of a welfare or treatment-oriented approach to young offenders, which was part of a broader optimism about rehabilitation of offenders.[114] For instance, if it had been implemented in full, the Children and Young Persons Act 1969 would have raised

---

[110] *C (A Minor) v Director of Public Prosecutions* [1996] AC 1, 36.

[111] This Act provided that the most serious offences committed by children were to be tried in Crown courts, by a judge and jury. The 1908 Act included special measures for children charged with murder (ss 103, 104), and similar special measures were included in the Children and Young Persons Act 1933 (s 53(1)), applying to offenders aged 14 to 17 who were charged with attempted murder, manslaughter, or wounding with intent. This provision was amended again in the Criminal Justice Act 1961 to allow children charged with offences for which the maximum period of imprisonment was 14 years or more to be tried in the Crown courts.

[112] See Bottoms and Dignan 'Youth Justice in Great Britain' 82–3. Under the Criminal Justice Act 1991, a child aged 12 to 14 cannot be sentenced to custody unless he or she is a 'persistent offender', although a custodial sentencing option is available for those aged 15 and over. For a useful overview of procedures relating to young offenders, see C Ball 'Youth Justice? Half a Century of Responses to Youth Offending' [2004] *Criminal Law Review* 28. Ball tracks the cumulative erosion in the welfare-oriented, special treatment of young offenders over the second half of the twentieth century, realized in part on the back of the separation of criminal process from the civil process of care proceedings in the early 1990s. See L Gelsthorpe 'Recent Changes in Youth Justice Policy in England and Wales' in E Weijers and A Duff (eds) *Punishing Juveniles: Principle and Critique* (Oxford: Hart, 2002) 45–66. For a discussion of the Scottish system of Children's Hearings, see Bottoms and Dignan 'Youth Justice in Great Britain' 44–76.

[113] The age of criminal responsibility had been raised to eight in the Children and Young Persons Act 1933 (23 & 24 Geo.5 c.12) after the *Report of the Departmental Committee on the Treatment of the Young Offender (The Molony Committee Report)* (Cmd 2831, 1927). The age was raised to 10 years by Children and Young Persons Act 1963, s 16. The age of criminal responsibility in Scotland was recently raised to 12: see Criminal Procedure (Scotland) Act 1995, s 41A, as amended by Criminal Justice and Licensing (Scotland) Act 2010.

[114] See D Garland *The Culture of Control: Crime and Social Order in Contemporary Society* (Oxford: OUP, 2001).

the age of criminal responsibility to 14.[115] The formalization of the criminal law threshold for criminal responsibility—at a particular chronological age—had thinned out the legal approach to young offenders,[116] but the rules related to *doli incapax* protected the child from 'the full force of the criminal law'.[117] The revocation of indeterminate sentences for young people convicted of criminal offences also occurred in this period—rather late in the formalization of the criminal process pertaining to young people.[118] The indeterminate sentence of 'detention at Her Majesty's pleasure' remains for young offenders convicted of murder.[119]

During this period, the now revoked law of *doli incapax* for those aged 10–14 years, which continued to be governed by the common law, provided a legal halfway house for those who found themselves above the threshold age of criminal responsibility but were not so mature as to be treated like any adult.[120] The law of *doli incapax* for children aged 10–14 years, which is generally referred to as a rebuttable presumption (by way of contrast with the conclusive presumption of *doli incapax* for those aged under 10 years), was not solely a procedural doctrine. As it involved a preliminary or circumscribed inquiry into the capacities of a child defendant, it seems to have occupied an uneasy middle ground between procedure

---

[115] It was implemented in part after a change of government. See Gelsthorpe 'Recent Changes in Youth Justice Policy in England and Wales' 45, 49–51.

[116] As Ashworth points out, age can only be an imperfect guide to something like maturity: see A Ashworth 'Child Defendants and the Doctrines of Criminal Law' in J Chalmers, F Leverick and L Farmer (eds) *Essays in Criminal Law in Honour of Sir Gerald Gordon* (Vol 8, Edinburgh Studies in Law, 2010) 29.

[117] *C (A Minor) v DPP* [1996] AC 1 [58]. This is in contrast to the way the civil rules on competency have developed: in order to empower decision-making, rules about incompetency have been narrowly circumscribed. For a comparison of civil and criminal norms regarding the responsibility of young people, see B Lyons 'Dying to be Responsible: Adolescence, Autonomy and Responsibility' (2010) 30(2) *Legal Studies* 257.

[118] In relation to young people, the Criminal Justice Act 1982 replaced indeterminate sentences of Borstal training with determinate sentences of Youth Custody. For discussion, see C Ball 'Young Offenders and the Youth Court' [1992] *Criminal Law Review* 277.

[119] Children and Young Persons Act 1933, s 53(1). This sentence is in lieu of a life sentence, as would apply to an adult convicted of murder (Criminal Justice Act 2003, Sch 21). The case of the murder of James Bulger ushered in a change in government policy in this area. Until this point, the Home Secretary, in consultation with the trial judge and the Lord Chief Justice, had decided the tariff for adult mandatory life sentences and juveniles sentenced to 'detention during Her Majesty's pleasure'. In the case of Thompson and Venables, and in the context of intense public concern, the tariff had been set at 15 years, with no review for 12 years. In *R v Secretary of State for the Home Department, ex parte Doody* (1994) 1 AC 57, the Court of Appeal upheld a Divisional Court decision requiring the Home Secretary to review regularly the period of detention of children and young people. The policy was changed and withstood a human rights challenge on the basis of Article 3 in the European Court of Human Rights: see *T v The United Kingdom* (Application No 24724/94); *V v The United Kingdom* (Application No 24888/94). For discussion, see D Haydon and P Scraton '"Condemn a Little More, Understand a Little Less": The Political Context and Rights Implications of the Domestic and European Rules in the Venables-Thompson Case' (2000) 27(3) *Journal of Law and Society* 416.

[120] In addition, the scope of defences such as duress to take into account the age of the defendant represents a further way in which age acts as a protective factor in the criminal law context. For discussion, see Ashworth 'Child Defendants and the Doctrines of Criminal Law' 35–43.

and substance (which was perhaps an ingredient in its demise). Before it was abolished, *doli incapax* for those aged 10–14 years provided an additional, preliminary hurdle for the prosecution to overcome in trying these children. Children who were considered to be insufficiently mature to appreciate that their actions were 'seriously wrong' (a phraseology which, from the first decades of the twentieth century, gradually superseded earlier formulations referencing the discretion to 'discern between good and evil'[121]) were not able to be tried or convicted. The child who had capacity would be treated like any other offender (although specific sentencing laws as well as a separate court system apply to children and age continues to be available as a basis for clemency in sentencing). In determining whether children were *doli incapax*, the standard of proof was the criminal standard, and it was necessary to rebut this presumption before proceeding to prove the elements of the offence, the *actus reus* and *mens rea*. It was for the prosecution to rebut the presumption of *doli incapax*.[122] It was generally accepted that the closer in age the child to full responsibility, the easier to rebut the presumption.[123] Some evidence suggests that the presumption was ignored, and, when it was considered, not difficult to rebut.[124] Although it was customary to refer to the now revoked law of *doli incapax* as a presumption, it was also a defence, and, as such, the law meant that a defendant could respond to criminal charges with an argument that he or she lacked an appreciation that the relevant conduct was 'seriously wrong' and should be found not guilty on this basis.[125]

As elsewhere on the mental incapacity terrain, the conduct comprising the offence committed by a child for the purposes of the rebuttable presumption of *doli incapax* had an enhanced or thick significance, beyond the significance generally accorded to the *actus reus*—as a threshold issue. This is usefully illustrated by reference to the evidence needed to rebut the now-defunct presumption of *doli incapax*, which supports my argument in two ways. On the one hand, the prohibition on relying on the acts comprising the offence to rebut the presumption means that evidence over and above that relating to the *actus reus* was required to rebut the presumption. In this respect, the presumption may be contrasted with the presumption of innocence, which may be rebutted by evidence of the acts comprising the offence. This requirement of evidence over and above the *actus reus* demands consideration of the defendant's conduct around the offence. On the other hand,

---

[121] See *C (A Minor) v DPP* [1996] AC 1, 18. The phrase 'seriously wrong' was used by the Court in *R v Gorrie* (1918) 83 JP 136 and adopted by the Divisional Court in *JM (A Minor) v Runeckles* (1984) 79 Cr App R 255.

[122] *R v Kershaw* (1902) 18 TLR 357. In a way that echoes the justification for the reverse burden of proof in insanity, an argument that the burden of disproving knowledge of wrongness should be on the defence has been mounted by Glanville Williams on the basis that whether a child knew something was wrong was peculiarly within the child's knowledge: see G Williams 'The Criminal Responsibility of Children' [1954] *Criminal Law Review* 493, 499–500.

[123] *R v Coulburn* (1988) 87 Cr App R 309; *A v DPP* [1997] 1 Cr App R 27, 32. For discussion, see Crofts *The Criminal Responsibility of Children and Young Persons*.

[124] See S Bandalli 'Abolition of the Presumption of Doli Incapax and the Criminalisation of Children' (1998) 37(2) *The Howard Journal* 114.

[125] See *DPP v P* [2008] 1 WLR 1005.

and somewhat paradoxically, the second way in which evidence required to rebut the presumption supports my claim about the thick significance of the defendant's conduct relates to the way in which the prosecution appear to have been slicing the elements of the offence and associated actions—rather finely, enabling the latter to be taken into account despite the prohibition on considering 'mere commission' of the act. In addition to relying on the evidence of teachers, psychologists, and others who had had contact with the child, the prosecution could use the circumstances surrounding the act to rebut the presumption of *doli incapax*. As the Court stated in *A v DPP*, '[c]onsideration of conduct closely associated with the act is permitted for the purpose of deciding whether guilty knowledge is proved'.[126] 'Conduct closely associated with the act' included lying when confronted by the police at the scene,[127] and running away and hiding,[128] each of which are closely connected to the offence element itself.[129] Both the formal requirement of evidence over and above the *actus reus*, and the fine slicing of elements of the offence and associated actions effectively enhance the role for the young defendant's conduct in the legal process. As this discussion suggests, a young defendant's conduct holds greater significance than is typically accorded to the *actus reus*.

By the close of this period, the welfare or treatment-oriented approach to young offenders had been gradually eroded, and, alongside the dynamic of inclusion, a dynamic of exclusion has come to structure this area of the mental incapacity terrain. By contrast with previous eras, a familiar concern with the dangerousness of young offenders, for instance, now feeds a dynamic of exclusion, according to which the scope of the law of infancy has come to be more circumscribed. This dynamic now operates alongside a dynamic of inclusion. Across the criminal justice system, contradictory constructions of childhood and childhood offending pertain, producing a dense matrix of welfare-based and punitive approaches to offending by children. For instance, in the light of changing expert knowledge about childhood and adolescence, and in the context of the politicization of child offending, the age of criminal responsibility has been criticized—both for being too high and for being too low.[130] The erosion of special procedures for infancy has been referred to as the 'adultification' of youth justice.[131] An example of this process of 'adultification' is the advent of anti-social behaviour

---

[126] *A v DPP* [1997] 1 Cr App R 27, 34.
[127] *L (A Minor) v DPP* [1996] 2 Cr App R 501.
[128] *JM (A Minor) v Runeckles* (1984) 79 Cr App R 255.
[129] It is interesting to note that the significance of the *actus reus* of the offence with which a young person has been charged has spilled over from non-exculpatory doctrines into the sphere of criminal offences. The Sexual Offences Act 2003 provides that a person under 18 commits an offence if he does anything that would be an offence if he were aged 18 (s 13). Francis Bennion has argued that this offence rests on the mistaken assumption that only the *actus reus* is significant when a young person is alleged to have committed a serious offence, referring to this as a 'defective deeming' provision: see F Bennion 'Mens Rea and Defendants Below the Age of Discretion' [2009] *Criminal Law Review* 757.
[130] See for discussion H Keating 'The Responsibility of Children in the Criminal Law' [2007] *Child and Family Law Quarterly* 183. Keating argues that children are held to be responsible at the age of 10 to make them responsible rather than as an acknowledgment that they are responsible at this point.
[131] See J Fionda 'Youth and Justice', in J Fionda (ed) *Legal Concepts of Childhood* (Oxford: Hart, 2001).

orders, which have undercut the practical significance of the age of criminal responsibility, as these orders mean that children under 10 may be exposed to quasi-criminal proceedings. These mixed approaches to infancy arguably represent a subset of broader social ambiguity in the meanings of childhood.[132]

Formalization of Unfitness to Plead and Infancy III: the Rise of a Dynamic of Exclusion

In the years since the mid 1990s, unfitness to plead and infancy have continued a process of formalization. However, this process has come to be structured in part by a dynamic of exclusion, which has fostered a more circumscribed approach to the doctrines, and which now operates alongside a dynamic of inclusion. In relation to infancy, even in the absence of a change to the age of criminal responsibility, it is possible to detect the rise of a dynamic of exclusion, as a result of which the space beyond the bounds of criminal responsibility has been circumscribed. This is evidenced in the abolition of *doli incapax* for children aged over 10 years. Evidence of the rise of a dynamic of exclusion is also apparent in the law on unfitness to plead. As I discuss below, the concerns driving the dynamic of exclusion are those, like fairness to the defendant, familiar from the preceding period, but, by contrast with the preceding period, they are now being listed in support of a more circumscribed approach to unfitness.

A 'modern outlook'?:[133] the Abolition of *Doli Incapax* for Children 10–14 Years

In the decision that prompted the legislative intervention abolishing *doli incapax* for children aged over 10 years, the House of Lords roundly critiqued the law but held that it was too firmly embedded in the common law to be abrogated by judicial means.[134] In *C v DPP*, the House of Lords expressed support for a 'modern outlook', echoing the Divisional Court, which had heard the matter before it, and which had labelled the rule of *doli incapax* 'perverse' on the basis that 'it tends to absolve from criminal responsibility the very children most likely to commit criminal acts'.[135] The Divisional Court noted that it was no part of the general law that a defendant should be proved to appreciate that his or her act was 'seriously

---

[132] See for discussion, G Douglas 'The Child's Right to Make Mistakes: Criminal Responsibility and the Immature Minor' in G Douglas and L Sebba (eds) *Children's Rights and Traditional Values* (Aldershot: Ashgate, 1998) 264–87.
[133] *C (A Minor) v DPP* [1996] AC 1, 36 per Lord Lowry.
[134] See *C (A Minor) v DPP* [1996] AC 1.
[135] *C (A Minor) v DPP* [1996] AC 1, 11, referring to the judgment of Laws J in the Divisional Court in *C v DPP* [1994] 3 WLR 888. Both Courts drew on a critique of *doli incapax* mounted by Glanville Williams: G Williams 'The Criminal Responsibility of Children'.

wrong', a stipulation that was itself 'conceptually obscure'.[136] These and other criticisms of *doli incapax* had been aired in antecedent government reports.[137] After *C v DPP*, Parliament legislated to abolish *doli incapax* in the Crime and Disorder Act 1998.[138] Subsequent decisions interpreted this Act to have abolished both the presumption and the defence of *doli incapax* as it applied to children aged over 10 years.[139] As a result of this change in the law, the distinction between children aged 10 and over and children aged 14 years and over has been removed.[140] With the removal of what had been a 'protection from the full force of the law' for young defendants, and without a change in the age of criminal responsibility, the merciful space accorded to youth was circumscribed. Concern for the welfare of young people, familiar from the preceding era, was feeding a dynamic of exclusion, which was now driving the formalization of the law.

As well as evidencing the rise of a dynamic of exclusion—according to which the scope of infancy is defined more narrowly—the final stages of the life of *doli incapax* for those aged 10–14 years reveals the conceptual ambiguity that surrounds youth offending. This relates to the meanings accorded to the abnormality of youth via the criminal law. In cataloguing the undesirable aspects of *doli incapax* for childrenaged over 10 years, the House of Lords pointed out that the doctrine worked in such a way that meant all children aged 10 to 13 were presumed to lack understanding until they were proved to be of normal mental development. This apparent illogicality masks a deeper, conceptual ambiguity about the kind of difference or abnormality connoted by infancy in criminal law. To me, there seems

---

[136] *C (A Minor) v DPP* [1996] AC 1, 9 referring to the judgment of Laws J in the Divisional Court in *C v DPP* [1994] 3 WLR 888.

[137] See Home Office *Tackling Youth Crime, Reforming Youth Justice: A Consultation Paper* (London, Home Office, 1997) and Home Office *No More Excuses—A New Approach to Tackling Youth Crime in England and Wales* (Cmd 3809, 1997).

[138] Crime and Disorder Act 1998, s 34. Unlike earlier proposals to abolish *doli incapax*, such as that of the Report of the Ingleby Committee on Children and Young Persons (Cmd 1191, 1960) and the Law Commission's draft criminal code (*Codification of the Criminal Law: A Report to the Law Commission* (Law Com No 143, 1985)), the legislation did not hook this change to the law to an increase in the age of criminal responsibility.

[139] See *JTB* [2009] 2 Cr App R 500. The House of Lords decision ran against *obiter* comments by Smith LJ in *DPP v P* [2008] 1 WLR 1005 that the statute had left the defence of *doli incapax* in place. In *JTB*, the House of Lords ruled that the defence had existed separately from the presumption (*contra* the Court of Appeal) but reasoned that the mischief that the statutory provision was designed to remedy was such that Parliament intended to abolish both. For discussion, see T Crofts 'Catching Up with Europe: Taking the Age of Criminal Responsibility Seriously in England' (2000) 17(4) *European Journal of Crime, Criminal Law and Criminal Justice* 267.

[140] Irrespective of the age of the criminal responsibility, all defendants should have sufficient understanding to comprehend the proceedings. See *T v United Kingdom* (2000) 30 EHRR 121, *V v United Kingdom* (2000) EHRR 121, *SC v United Kingdom* (2004) 40 EHRR 10 and *DPP v P* [2008] 1 WLR 1005. In concluding that the trial of Thompson and Venables had breached the right to a fair trial under Article 6 of the Convention, the European Court of Human Rights stated that a criminal trial of a young child should be conducted 'in such a way as to reduce as far as possible his or her feelings of intimidation and inhibition' (*T v United Kingdom* (2000) 30 EHRR 121 [85]). This ruling prompted changes in Crown Court trials of children charged with serious offences: see H Keating 'Reckless Children?' [2007] *Criminal Law Review* 546. It is notable that, although the applicant in *SC* had been found fit to plead, the Court still found that there had been a breach of Article 6, which indicates that effective participation requires more than the cognitive capacities currently assessed via the test for unfitness.

to be a slippage between the notion of offending by children (a category based on the type of offender) and the notion of childhood offending (a category based on the type of offence). According to the first notion, the relevant difference or abnormality is age, while, according to the second notion, the relevant difference relates to the type of offence committed. The conceptual slippage between 'crimes committed by children' and 'childhood crimes' is revealed in the case of children who commit serious offences. They are vulnerable to the exhaustion of mercy: at this end of the offence spectrum, the special status granted to children seems to wear out. This is perhaps best illustrated by the treatment the two 10-year-old killers of Jamie Bulger, a high-profile offence which was met with a punitive social and legal response (of which the changes chronicled here are a part).[141] This type of case exposes the kind of abnormality connoted by infancy as unstable, liable to description as either a time-limited stage in human development, or as an indelible stamp of dangerous difference. With the abolition of *doli incapax* for children over 10 years, what is now an apparently sharp distinction between the period of non-responsibility and the moment of criminal responsibility masks this ambiguity about youth offending. This ambiguity about youth offending is arguably a product of a broader ambiguity in social attitudes and beliefs about childhood,[142] although, it is notable that a parallel conceptual ambiguity can also be detected elsewhere on the mental incapacity terrain.[143]

'To speed things along and tidy things up':[144] Unfitness to Plead in the Current Era

Like infancy, the formalization of unfitness to plead has continued into the current era. And, also like infancy, this process has come to be structured in part by a

---

[141] The case ushered in a raft of reforms to juvenile justice. See for discussion M Freeman 'The James Bulger Tragedy: Childish Innocence and the Construction of Guilt' in A McGillivray (ed) *Governing Childhood* (Dartmouth: Aldershot, 1997) 115–34.

[142] David Archard argues that Western philosophical approaches to children coalesce around an idea of the child as an 'unfinished human', defined in terms of what it lacks—rationality, freedom, and moral responsibility. But the influence of developmental psychology on social views of childhood, according to which the period of childhood is marked by distinct states that correspond to particular sets of abilities and skills, subverts any straightforward idea of an absence of adult capacities: see D Archard 'Philosophical Perspectives on Childhood' in J Fionda (ed) *Legal Concepts of Childhood* (Oxford: Hart, 2001) 43–6.

[143] In 2006, the Law Commission for England and Wales proposed a reformulated doctrine of diminished responsibility, which would have provided a partial defence where a defendant was unable to understand the nature of his or her conduct, or where he or she was unable to form a rational judgment or his or her self-control was 'substantially impaired by an abnormality of mental functioning arising from a recognised medical condition', or developmental immaturity for a defendant under 18, where that abnormality or developmental immaturity 'provides an explanation for the defendant's [homicidal] conduct' (*Murder, Manslaughter, and Infanticide* (Law Com No 304, 2006) para 5.112). The part of this proposal that related to 'developmental immaturity' was not included in the new diminished responsibility provision contained in Coroners and Justice Act 2009, s 52, and parliamentary debate suggests that the slipperiness of a notion of 'normal immaturity' scuppered such a protective exclusion: see HL Deb 30 June 2009, vol 712, col 185–8.

[144] *Hansard* (HL), vol 658, col 1413 (11 March 2004), debating the recent changes to the way in which unfitness to plead is decided, which I discuss below.

dynamic of exclusion, which has fostered a more circumscribed approach to unfitness to plead, and which now operates alongside a dynamic of inclusion. Again, the concerns driving the dynamic of exclusion are familiar from the preceding period, but, now, they have come to generate a more circumscribed approach to unfitness.

(i) The 'Trial of the Facts'

Over recent years, the scope of a 'trial of the facts' has been determined by a series of decisions passed by appellate courts. Beneath the technicality of judicial discussion, it is possible to detect evidence of both a dynamic of inclusion and a dynamic of exclusion operating here. As discussed above, a 'trial of the facts' was included in Section 4A of the Criminal Procedure (Insanity and Unfitness to Plead) Act 1991. This change rendered unfitness a more specialized and complex legal provision (while leaving the criteria for a finding of unfitness intact). Judicial determination of the scope of a 'trial of the facts' has focused on the meaning of the phrase, 'the act'. When first invited to consider the phrase in *Egan*, the Court of Appeal concluded that an inquiry into whether a defendant 'did the act' required the prosecution to prove 'all the necessary ingredients' of the offence.[145] The *Egan* interpretation was criticized on the basis that it contravened parliamentary intention.[146] Shortly after *Egan* was handed down, a differently constituted Court of Appeal had the opportunity to revisit the question of the proper interpretation of 'did the act or made the omission charged' in the 1991 Act. In *Attorney General's Reference (No 3 of 1998)*, the Court of Appeal concluded that, as the language of the 1991 Act borrowed that of the Trial of Lunatics Act 1883, the phrase carried the same meaning as it did in the 1883 statute.[147] When it came to decide on the scope of a 'trial of the facts' in *Antoine*, the House of Lords elected to follow *Attorney*

---

[145] *R v Egan* [1998] 1 Cr App R 121, 125. As a result of this interpretation, the question of whether the defendant 'did the act' extended to encompass the *mens rea* as well as the *actus reus* of the offence with which the defendant had been charged. This interpretation of the phrase 'did the act or made the omission charged' accorded with the recommendation of the Butler Report para 10.24.

[146] Support for this position was drawn from the parliamentary debate about the Bill that became the 1991 Act. In the House of Commons, the Member for Ryedale, who proposed the Bill, stated that it would provide for the court to 'look only at the facts of the case', not at 'the intentions of the accused' (*Hansard* (HC), vol 186, col 1272 (1 March 1991)). According to the Member for Ryedale, 'it would be meaningless to try to form an impression of the motives of someone, who, because of his mental condition, is unfit to plead' (*Hansard* (HC), vol 186, col 1272 (1 March 1991)). The Minister of State for the Home Office, John Patten, concurred, stating that 'it would be unrealistic and even contradictory where a person is unfit to be tried properly because of his mental state, that the trial of the facts should nevertheless have to consider that very aspect': *Hansard* (HC) vol 186, col 1280 (1 March 1991).

[147] *Attorney General's Reference (No 3 of 1998)* [2000] QB 401, 410. This case concerned the Trial of Lunatics Act 1883 (46 & 47 Vict. c.38), s 2(1) which provided that insane defendants who 'did the act or made the omission charged' as an offence would be subject to a special verdict of guilty but insane. Unlike the Criminal Lunatics Act 1800, which referred to 'offence', the 1883 Act referred to 'act' and 'omission'. This led the Court to hold that, for the purposes of a 'trial of the facts', the Crown need only prove that the defendant had done the *actus reus* of the offence—apart from insanity, the defendant's *mens rea* was irrelevant (at 411).

General's Reference (No 3 of 1998) rather than *Egan*.[148] In relation to the meaning of the term 'act', the House of Lords concluded that statutory use of the phrase 'act or omission' rather than 'offence' in Section 4A(2) indicated that Parliament had made it clear that the jury was not to consider the mental elements of an offence.[149] The House of Lords reasoned that Section 4A strikes a balance 'between the need to protect a defendant who has, in fact, done nothing wrong, and is unfit to plead' and 'the need to protect the public' in distinguishing between 'a person who has not carried out the *actus reus* of the crime charged against him and a person who has carried out an act (or made an omission) which would constitute a crime if done (or made) with the requisite *mens rea*'.[150]

Most recently, the two issues left outstanding by *Antoine* have been resolved. The first, resolved in the decision of *Grant*, related to the availability of the partial defence of provocation in a 'trial of the facts'. The Court of Appeal concluded that provocation is not available to a defendant who has been found unfit to plead.[151] The second issue that remained after *Antoine* concerned participatory liability. That issue arose in *Martin*, in which the defendant was charged with several offences arising from a stabbing.[152] The defendant was found unfit to plead and, on a 'trial of the facts', was found to have done the act. On appeal, the Court of Appeal upheld the trial judge's directions to the effect that the jury could find that the defendant did the act if he either stabbed the victim or if he took part in what he 'knew' at the time to be a knife attack, concluding that reference to what the defendant 'knew' was not an inappropriate reference to the state of mind of the defendant.[153]

Reflective of the larger forces influencing the development of criminal law and procedure in the current era, and following the implementation of the European Convention on Human Rights 1950 into domestic law via the Human Rights Act 1998, a 'trial of the facts' has also been measured against human rights norms. The

---

[148] *R v Antoine* [2001] 1 AC 340. Antoine had been charged with murder and, at trial, the defence had attempted to raise the defence of diminished responsibility. When the defendant was found unfit to plead, the trial judge held that diminished responsibility could not be raised in a 'trial of the facts'. The House of Lords upheld the first instance decision.

[149] *R v Antoine* [2001] 1 AC 340, 375 per Lord Hutton.

[150] *R v Antoine* [2001] 1 AC 340, 375–6 per Lord Hutton. The reasoning of the House of Lords in *Antoine*, and the Court of Appeal in *Attorney General's Reference (No 3 of 1998)*, precludes an unfit defendant charged with murder from relying on the defence of diminished responsibility because this defence arises only where all the elements of the offence have been made out (*Antoine* 368). As a result of these two decisions, the only kind of defences an unfit defendant can rely on in a 'trial of the facts' are defences of accident, mistake, or self-defence. In *Antoine*, Lord Hutton acknowledged that even these defences 'almost invariably involve some consideration of the mental state of the defendant' (376). To address this 'difficulty', Lord Hutton stated that, where there is 'objective evidence' of accident, mistake, or self-defence, 'the jury should not find that the defendant did the "act" unless satisfied beyond reasonable doubt on all the evidence that the prosecution has negatived that defence' (376).

[151] *R v Grant* [2002] QB 1030. The Court concluded that any consideration of provocation necessitated an examination of the defendant's state of mind, which was precluded by s 4A(2) of the 1991 Act (1048).

[152] *R v Martin* [2003] 2 Cr App R 322.

[153] *R v Martin* [2003] 2 Cr App R 322, 339, 338.

issue of the compatibility of a 'trial of the facts' with human rights norms has been considered by the Court of Appeal on more than one occasion and by the House of Lords in *R v H*.[154] In these decisions, the courts concluded that Article 6, the right to a fair trial, was not engaged because proceedings under Sections 4, 4A and 5 of the 1991 Act (*R v H* considered Section 4A only) did not involve a criminal charge within the meaning of Article 6.[155] Regarding Article 5, the right to liberty and security, the Court in *Grant* held that it was reasonable that mandatory hospitalization (which I discussed above) follow a finding that the defendant, who was charged with murder, had done the act but was under a disability so as to be unfit to be tried.[156]

The gradual process by which the scope of a 'trial of the facts' has been determined evidences concern with both the dangerousness of the unfit individual and fairness to him or her. These two concerns are referenced in a statement about the purpose of a 'trial of the facts' recently made by the Court of Appeal:

> The purpose of such a hearing is to try to arrive as nearly as possible at the same result as if there had been a trial, the dual objectives being that, if it could not have been proved after a full trial that the person in question did the acts alleged, he should be acquitted, but, if it could be proved, he should be eligible to be detained under the protectionary powers.[157]

By contrast with previous eras, the familiar concerns with the dangerousness of the defendant and fairness to him or her no longer point in the same direction. Rather, they are currently pitched to compete with each other, meaning that the law on a 'trial of the facts' demands a balance between them. This balancing process occurs across both a dynamic of inclusion (according to which concern with dangerousness drives an expansive approach to unfitness) and a dynamic of exclusion (according to which the law of unfitness should not be drawn too widely, so as to too readily deny an individual who has been charged with an offence an ordinary trial).

There is a final point to note regarding a 'trial of the facts'. Reflecting the intimate connection between *actus reus* and *mens rea* as a matter of practice if not theory, and as the cases indicate, it has proved difficult to neatly quarantine issues to be dealt with in a 'trial of the facts' as required per Section 4A. In its 2010 Consultation Paper on unfitness to plead, the Law Commission recognized that limiting Section 4A to the external elements of an offence had proved problematic, but, also noted that, on the other side, 'requiring the prosecution to prove all

---

[154] *R v H* [2003] UKHL 1; see also *R v Grant* [2002] QB 1030, *M (Edward) & Ors* [2002] 1 Cr App R 25.
[155] *R v Grant* [2002] QB 1030, 1049; *R v H* [2003] UKHL 1 [18].
[156] *R v Grant* [2002] QB 1030 1049.
[157] *R v B, W, S, H and W* [2009] 1 Cr App R 261, 271. For a normative argument about a 'trial of the facts', see Duff *Trials and Punishments*. Duff argues that the judicial inquiry into the facts of a particular case after a finding of unfitness serves an 'instrumental purpose—to decide what should be done with the disordered defendant' (122). For Duff, proving that the defendant committed the offence serves 'the evidential role of a predictor of future danger' and 'the justificatory role of a precondition' for the particular disposal of the defendant (122).

elements of the offence could, without more, be detrimental to public safety'.[158] The Law Commission canvassed a range of options to deal with the 'trial of the facts' issue, and proposed replacing it with a two-step procedure. According to this proposal, there would be a procedure whereby the jury considers evidence on all elements of the offence, leading to three possible outcomes—that the accused did the act and there are no grounds for acquittal, an outright acquittal, or a special verdict (such as 'not guilty by reason of insanity').[159] As the Commission acknowledged, this procedure would have some of the qualities of a trial because, if implemented, it would involve the option of a qualified acquittal, but it would not result in a conviction.[160]

(ii) A Decision of the Judge Alone

The process of deciding unfitness is now dominated by professional actors. As per the Criminal Lunatics Act 1800, until 2004, a jury decided whether a defendant was unfit to plead (the 'trial of the issue'). As a result of the Domestic Violence, Crime and Victims Act 2004, juries no longer have a role in deciding whether a defendant is unfit to plead, although a jury is empanelled for a 'trial of the facts' following a finding of unfitness.[161] The 2001 *Review of the Criminal Courts of England and Wales* (the Auld Report) advocated a change in the law in this respect.[162] The change from jury to judge decision-making on the issue of unfitness reflects institutional pressures to save on the length and cost of trials. The Auld Report's express concerns with the efficiency of the criminal trial process seem to have motivated the legislature to reform how unfitness is decided.[163] Making

---

[158] Law Commission *Unfitness to Plead: A Consultation Paper*, (Law Com No 197, 2010) para 6.128.

[159] *Unfitness to Plead: A Consultation Paper* para 6.130. The Law Commission recommended that, if the accused is acquitted, provision should be made for a judge to hold a further hearing (to be held at the discretion of the judge on the application of any party or the representative of any party to the proceedings) to determine whether or not the acquittal is because of mental disorder existing at the time of the offence: 6.140, 6.152.

[160] *Unfitness to Plead: A Consultation Paper* para 6.132–6.133.

[161] *Domestic Violence, Crime and Victims Act* 2004, s 22, which provided that a judge is to make determinations on the question of unfitness. If a defendant is found unfit to plead by a judge, a jury is empanelled for the purposes of a 'trial of the facts'. Even prior to the passage of this Act, empirical studies of the role of the jury in proceedings on unfitness concluded that it was 'somewhat formalistic' on the basis there was usually no dispute between the prosecution and defence as to a defendant's unfitness (Mackay, Mitchell and Howe 'A Continued Upturn in Unfitness to Plead' 534; Mackay and Kearns 'An Upturn in Unfitness to Plead?' 536).

[162] *Review of the Criminal Courts of England and Wales* (Auld Report) (London, Home Office, 2001). The report concluded that the jury procedure for determining unfitness is cumbersome, especially if the issue of unfitness is raised on arraignment as it requires empanelling two juries: one for the 'trial of the issue', and one for the 'trial of the facts' (para 213). The Review concluded that it was 'difficult to see' what a jury contributed to the determination of unfitness that a judge could not also contribute (para 213).

[163] The parliamentary debates about the reform proposal reveal government concern that finding a defendant unfit to plead was a 'very cumbersome and very complex procedure which is not necessary' (*Hansard* (HL), vol 658, col 1413 (11 March 2004)). Having been questioned directly about whether the amendment was not just an attempt to 'speed things along and tidy things up' at the expense of public involvement in the criminal process (*Hansard* (HL), vol 658, col 1413 (11 March 2004)),

Dynamics of Inclusion and Exclusion: Unfitness to Plead and Infancy 99

the issue of unfitness one for a judge alone cements the current position of unfitness as a discrete procedural issue relating to the question of whether the trial will go forward, and represents the most recent step in the process of formalization.

(iii) The Criteria for a Finding of Unfitness

The criteria for a finding of unfitness look set to be the last bastion to fall along the formalization trajectory. The strong procedural profile of unfitness to plead as a discrete, technical provision has diverted focus away from the substantive content of the provision—the criteria for a finding of unfitness—which had received little judicial or other attention until recent years. This strong procedural profile has meant that, while legislative-driven change has reformed the way in which unfitness is decided and proved, the legal test for unfitness continues to be governed by the common law. The criteria were unaffected by the 1964 and 1991 Acts and thus have remained unaltered since the decision of *Pritchard*.[164] As outlined above, the criteria for a finding of unfitness are 'whether the prisoner is mute by malice or not', 'whether he can plead to the indictment or not', and 'whether he is of sufficient intellect to comprehend the course of the proceedings on the trial so as to make a proper defence'.[165] While a variety of medical conditions has formed the basis of findings that defendants are unfit,[166] it is widely recognized that the *Pritchard*

Baroness Scotland replied that the requirement that a judge give reasons for his or her decision would make the decision about unfitness more transparent than if decided by a jury: *Hansard* (HL), vol 658, col 1414 (11 March 2004)).

[164] *Pritchard* was upheld by the Court of Criminal Appeal in *R v Robertson* [1968] 1 WLR 1767; *M* [2003] EWCA Crim 3452. Prior to the 1964 Act, the CLRC had commented that 'what constitutes unfitness to plead is, in general, well established' and had not recommend any changes in the criteria for unfitness to plead: Criminal Law Revision Committee, *Criminal Procedure (Insanity)* (Cmd 2149, 1963). Similarly, in its review, the Butler Committee had concluded that the criteria for unfitness to plead 'work well': para 10.3. The Committee did recommend that the reference to the ability to challenge jurors be omitted from the criteria for a finding of 'disability in relation to trial' (the language of the Report) and that two further criteria be added to those laid down in *Pritchard*—that the defendant be able to give adequate instructions to his or her legal advisors and that he or she be able to plead 'with understanding' to the indictment (Butler Report para 10.3)—but this reformulation did not constitute a substantive change to the common law: see Grubin 'What Constitutes Fitness to Plead?' 748, 754; Mackay *Mental Condition Defences* 244.

[165] *Pritchard* 304. Formally, these criteria are cumulative and each one must be satisfied for a defendant to be fit to plead: see Mackay, Mitchell and Howe 'Yet More Facts about the Insanity Defence' 536. In practice, however, it seems that the *Pritchard* criteria tend to be paraphrased, which suggests that there is in effect a composite standard for unfitness. In his direction on unfitness in *Sharp* (*R v Sharp* [1960] 1 QB 357), Justice Salmon stated that the jury must be satisfied that the defendant was 'fit to communicate with his advisors' and that he was able to understand the trial process (360). In *Friend* (*R v Friend* [1997] 1 WLR 1433), Lord Justice Otton referred to the *Pritchard* criteria and summarized them to the effect that 'the test of unfitness is whether the defendant will be able to comprehend the course of the proceedings so as to make a proper defence' (1441).

[166] Intellectual disability (*R v Burles* [1970] 2 WLR 597; *R v Grant* [2002] QB 1030; *R v Martin* [2003] 2 Cr App R 322), mental illness (*R v Antoine* [2001] 1 AC 340) and situations where the defendant is 'deaf and dumb' (*R v Berry*; *Rex v Dyson* (1831) 7 C & P 305; *R v Roberts* [1954] 2 QB 329) have given rise to findings of unfitness. Neither amnesia about the offence (*R v Podola* [1960] 1 QB 325) nor a form of hysteria (which left the defendant unable to communicate except in writing) (*R v Holman* (Unreported) CA, 27 April 1994) can ground a finding of unfitness to plead.

criteria set a high threshold for a defendant to be found unfit to plead. In relation to comprehension, for instance, the criteria are restricted to defects of cognition.[167] As R M Mackay argues, on the current law, a defendant will be fit even if he or she has only a 'rudimentary' understanding of the trial process.[168]

Motivated by a desire to reform the law in accordance with 'modern psychiatric thinking and with the modern trial process', the Law Commission's 2010 Consultation Paper on unfitness to plead contained a proposal that unfitness be determined by a broad test that assesses whether the accused has decision-making capacity for trial.[169] Modelled on the civil law of capacity, this test would take into account all the requirements for meaningful participation in the criminal proceedings, bearing in mind the spectrum of decisions an individual may need to make.[170] According to the Commission's proposal, in determining the defendant's decision-making capacity, it would be incumbent on the judge to take account of the complexity of the particular proceedings and gravity of the outcome for the defendant.[171] In this respect, the Law Commission proposal straddled what were two distinct strands of reform proposals: the first strand of reform proposal advocated the enhancement and further elaboration of the *Pritchard* criteria for a finding of unfitness to plead,[172] and the second strand of reform proposal advocated a flexible, open-textured approach that would allow judges to determine

---

[167] As a result, delusions, mood disorders and other features common to mental illness, and potentially relevant to a defendant's understanding of the trial process, are strictly excluded from the parameters of the legal inquiry: see Grubin 'What Constitutes Fitness to Plead?' 753.
[168] Mackay *Mental Condition Defences* 245.
[169] See Law Commission *Unfitness to Plead: A Consultation Paper* (Law Com No 197, 2010) paras 1.15 and 3.41 for discussion. At the time of writing, the proposals have not been incorporated into legislation.
[170] Law Commission *Unfitness to Plead: A Consultation Paper* (Law Com No 197, 2010) paras 3.41, 3.99. The Commission's proposal draws on the Mental Capacity Act 2005 which provides that a person is unable to make a decision for him or herself if he or she is unable to understand the information relevant to the decision, retain that information, use or weigh it as part of the process of making the decision or communicate the decision (s 3(1)). The Act also provides that a person is not to be treated as unable to make a decision 'unless all practicable steps to help him to do so have been taken without success' (s 1(3)). Reform in the direction of the civil law standard has also been proposed by the Scottish Law Commission, which reasoned that a test of 'effective participation' in criminal trials would meet European Convention on Human Rights standards on a fair trial (European Convention on Human Rights 2004 para 4.30).
[171] The Commission specified that, in particular, the judge should take account of how important any disability is likely to be in the context of the decision the accused must make in the context of the trial which he or she faces (*Unfitness to Plead: A Consultation Paper* (Law Com No 197, 2010) para 3.101).
[172] R M Mackay, among others, had suggested that the criteria should be expanded so as to amount to a test of 'decisional competence', a broader notion than the current test which, as discussed above, refers to the defendant's ability to understand the trial proceedings, challenge jurors, and instruct lawyers (R D Mackay 'Mentally Abnormal Offenders: Disposal and Criminal Responsibility Issues' in M McConville and G Wilson (eds) *The Handbook of the Criminal Justice Process* (Oxford: OUP, 2002) 732; see also R D Mackay 'On Being Insane in Jersey: Part 3—The Case of Attorney General v O'Driscoll' [2004] *Criminal Law Review* 291, 292–5 and Mackay *Mental Condition Defences* 244–6 and Scottish Law Commission *Report on Insanity and Diminished Responsibility* (Edinburgh, 2004) paras 4.11–4.19.

unfitness to plead in the context of each case.[173] In accordance with the common law, this new decision-making capacity test would not require that any decision the accused makes be rational or wise.[174]

As with the most recent developments in the law of unfitness to plead, these proposed changes reveal the presence of both dynamics of inclusion and exclusion. The Law Commission's proposal to introduce a broad test that assesses whether the accused has decision-making capacity for trial represents a continuation of the dynamic of inclusion, by which the scope of unfitness is defined broadly, in that the Law Commission made its proposals on the basis that the new test would expand the scope of the law and anticipated that it would increase findings of unfitness, if implemented.[175] But there are several factors to indicate that a dynamic of exclusion, working in the other direction, to circumscribe unfitness, is now in play in this area as well. First, the Commission made a case for their proposal on the basis that it is appropriately *limited* to an assessment of an individual's ability to make particular decisions, and does not, for instance, 'necessarily reduce a person to being "unfit" simply because of a low cognitive ability or learning disability'.[176] Second, and concurrent with their proposals for a new test for unfitness, the Law Commission advocated increasing the use of 'special measures' (such as giving evidence via live video link) in ordinary trials to minimize the 'exclusion' of 'vulnerable defendants'.[177] Reflecting on the jurisprudence of the European Court of Human Rights (which has developed largely in relation to child defendants), as well as domestic case law, the Law Commission proposed that the decision-making capacity of those who are potentially unfit should be assessed with a view to ascertaining whether an accused could undergo a trial or plead guilty with the assistance of special measures or reasonable adjustments. The Commission noted that taking the availability of 'special measures' into account in the new test for unfitness is likely to increase the prospect that some defendants currently found

---

[173] Those advocating flexibility in the criteria for unfitness hold that the meaning of unfitness to plead is dependent on the context in which the defendant finds him or herself. (Freckelton 'Rationality and Flexibility in Assessment of Fitness to Stand Trial' 48; Winnick 'Reforming Incompetency to Stand Trial and Plead Guilty' 590). The standard to be applied in determining unfitness should thus depend on the seriousness and complexity of the charges, the relationship between the defendant and his or her lawyers and the communication skills of his or her lawyers, among other factors (Freckelton 'Rationality and Flexibility in Assessment of Fitness to Stand Trial' 48). Winnick labels this a 'sliding-scale approach to competency' ('Reforming Incompetency to Stand Trial and Plead Guilty' 592).
[174] Law Commission *Unfitness to Plead: A Consultation Paper* (Law Com No 197, 2010) para 3.57. It has long been clear that the legal question of a defendant's fitness to plead does not correspond to his or her ability to act in his or her own best interests (*R v Robertson* [1968] 1 WLR 1767; *R v M* [2003] EWCA Crim 3452). In *Robertson*, the Court of Appeal allowed an appeal from a murder trial where a defendant, who was representing himself, was found unfit. The Court of Appeal concluded that, as the trial judge had directed the jury with reference to the defendant's ability to make a 'proper' defence, the jury may have erroneously thought that a defendant who could not act in his or her best interests was unfit (1773).
[175] Law Commission *Unfitness to Plead: A Consultation Paper* (Law Com No 197, 2010) para 3.37.
[176] *Unfitness to Plead: A Consultation Paper* para 3.42.
[177] *Unfitness to Plead: A Consultation Paper* para 2.105. See also T P Rogers et al 'Fitness to Plead and Competence to Stand Trial: a Systematic Review of the Constructs and their Application' (2008) 19(4) *Journal of Forensic Psychiatry and Psychology* 576.

unfit will be able to stand trial.[178] This suggests that, even in the context of flexible disposal options for an unfit individual, the imperative to try the individual wherever possible enjoys an enhanced prominence. This reflects the growing human rights influence on this area of law, and the importance of a trial and a conviction in advance of a custodial order,[179] which is feeding into a dynamic of exclusion here.

Through a process of formalization, unfitness to plead and infancy now take technical and distinct legal form, although each traces their origins to the same broad set of morally evaluative principles and practices which rested on largely undifferentiated ideas of incapacity. While the process of formalization continues in the current era, the deep dynamics that are shaping it have altered over time: the process of formalization was shaped by a deep dynamic of inclusion—whereby the scope of these mental incapacity doctrines was drawn broadly—but, recently, has also come to be structured by a dynamic of exclusion, whereby the scope of the doctrines is more circumscribed. At base, both doctrines encapsulate the notion that a defendant should be the subject, rather than the object, of criminal process. As such, both infancy and unfitness to plead have symbolic significance in the criminal justice system. Although obscured by the prevailing technicality and precision of the relevant legal forms, infancy and unfitness to plead concern both a defendant's understanding of, and participation in, criminal proceedings, and the reach of the criminal law, and, together, engage the normative dimension of criminal process.

---

[178] Law Commission *Unfitness to Plead: A Consultation Paper* paras 4.27 and 4.25.
[179] See *Moyle v R* [2008] EWCA Crim 3059 [38]. The Court stated that delusions—as to the Court's powers of sentence, its objectivity, and the evil influences thought to be present in the proceedings—did not necessarily require a finding that the person is unable to give instructions and to understand the proceedings [38].

5
Incapacity and Disability: the Exculpatory Doctrines of Insanity and Automatism

This chapter and Chapter 6 cover a part of criminal law that is now traversed by the two exculpatory mental incapacity doctrines of insanity and automatism (also known as insane automatism and non-insane automatism respectively). As is well known, the law on insanity is governed by the *M'Naghten Rules*, which were drafted in 1843.[1] A discrete doctrine of automatism appeared only in the 1950s.[2] Until this point, insanity and what would come to be called automatism coexisted in a way that was not sharply delineated, and, in this chapter (and the following), I examine insanity and automatism side by side, an approach which reveals the significance of legal concern with dangerousness. It was this concern that forced a cleavage between insanity and automatism, which eventually hardened into two distinct doctrines. Concern with dangerousness continues to inform the relationship between insanity and automatism, and appreciating its role here assists in understanding this part of the mental incapacity terrain.

In broad brush strokes, the first of the two main arguments advanced in this chapter is that when a loose, broad, and partially moralized notion of incapacity—defined largely by extra-legal norms—pertained as a foundation for exculpation, claims now falling within the parameters of both insanity and automatism were accommodated within an informal insanity doctrine and under a flexible criminal process. This obviated the need for a specific exculpatory doctrine of automatism. Even once a formal doctrine of insanity developed in the first half of the nineteenth century, some claims to exculpation that now fall within the bounds of automatism were accommodated by the breadth of insanity. Gradually, however, as mental incapacity came to be the subject of expert medical knowledge—a change that took place as much beyond as within criminal law—this broad notion of incapacity ossified into a narrower notion of disability, fostering a more circumscribed approach to insanity. It was in this context that a discrete automatism doctrine

---

[1] *M'Naghten* (1843) 10 Cl & Fin 200. The spelling of M'Naghten is disputed (see B L Diamond 'On the Spelling of Daniel M'Naghten's Name' in D J West and A Walk (eds) *Daniel McNaughton: His Trial and the Aftermath* (Ashford: Gaskell Books, 1977) 86–90 and R Moran *Knowing Right from Wrong: The Insanity Defense of Daniel McNaughtan* (New York: The Free Press, 1981) xi–xiii for discussion). I adopt a common variant of the spelling of M'Naghten.

[2] A reference to a discrete doctrine of automatism first appeared in the 1951 decision of *Harrison-Owen*: *R v Harrison-Owen* [1951] 2 All ER 726.

appeared in the second half of the twentieth century. By way of contrast with other mental incapacity doctrines, but reflecting the persistence of a broad, moralized notion of incapacity in this part of the mental incapacity terrain, automatism is delimited via a tripartite construction which tracks the lines of non-culpability, catching a miscellaneous collection of cases in which individuals share little more than an absence of blameworthiness.

The second main argument of this chapter relates to the meanings given to those individuals seeking to rely on exculpatory insanity in and through legal processes. In brief, individuals pleading insanity have been constructed as dangerous, a construction which has been a driving force for most of the developments regarding the insanity doctrine. Reflecting the rise of expert psychiatric and psychological knowledge of mental incapacity, the notion of dangerousness has become a less moralized and more medicalized one in the recent history of insanity—interpolating with the more technical notion of risk in recent decades. The construction of insane defendants as dangerous forged an intimate and durable connection between the law of insanity and the issue of disposal. As this reference to disposal suggests, the close corollary of the argument made here about the meanings given to exculpatory 'madness' in criminal law is the evidentiary and procedural aspects of the way such 'madness' becomes known and is proved for evaluation and adjudication purposes. The evidentiary and procedural dimensions of exculpatory 'madness' form the focus of Chapter 6.

Of Unsound Minds and Wild Beasts: Insanity before *M'Naghten*

In his seminal work on mental incapacity, Nigel Walker traces the earliest recorded acquittal on the basis of insanity ('the felon was of unsound mind') to 1505.[3] At some point during the early modern period, for reasons that are unclear, it became regular practice to acquit the insane defendant rather than leave him or her to be pardoned by the King.[4] Although the absence of sources renders the picture of exculpatory insanity at this point somewhat unclear, it is generally accepted that an informal practice of excusing an insane defendant from trial long preceded the appearance of a formal insanity doctrine.[5] At the time of the earliest recorded acquittal based on insanity, there seems to have been no substantial elaboration of

---

[3] N Walker *Crime and Insanity in England (Vol 1: The Historical Perspective)* (Edinburgh: Edinburgh University Press, 1968) 25–6. Walker suggests that, as trial by ordeal was replaced with trial by jury in the medieval era, insane individuals charged with serious offences (such as homicide) became likely to be tried and, if convicted, left to the royal prerogative of mercy.

[4] See Walker *Crime and Insanity in England (Vol 1)* 25.

[5] See, eg, Walker *Crime and Insanity in England (Vol 1)* 19. According to this informal practice, and in the context of private investigation and prosecution, the insane individual's family would provide compensation to the victim or his or her family and look after the insane person (Walker *Crime and Insanity in England (Vol 1)* 26). On the system of private investigation and prosecution, see P King 'Decision-Makers and Decision-Making in the English Criminal Law 1750–1800' (1984) 27(1) *Historical Journal* 25, 27; J H Langbein *The Origins of the Adversary Criminal Trial* (Oxford: OUP, 2003) 10–13.

the meaning of a phrase like 'unsound mind' or any particular procedural structure for adjudicating claims to insanity. Although insanity was a somewhat disaggregated notion in the early modern era, with, for example, a recognized distinction between intellectual disability and insanity,[6] overall, it was a broad and loose concept, and, under these conditions, some states—including those that might now form the basis of an automatism plea, such as physical injury to the head prior to an offence of violence—fell within the bounds of exculpatory insanity.

The capacity of informal criminal processes to accommodate insane individuals remained large, even as criminal process underwent significant changes associated with the rise of adversarial criminal procedure in the period over the eighteenth century. As mentioned in the previous chapter, together with changes in sentencing practices, developments in criminal procedure profoundly affected legal practices. Over time, the accelerating involvement of lawyers meant that judges came to perform the more limited role of 'umpire and trial manager', while juries came to play an 'increasingly constructive' role.[7] If an individual was convicted, a range of sentencing options meant that a capital offence did not necessarily mean execution: some defendants raising informal insanity pleas were given partial verdicts, a 'largely jury administered scheme of mitigation' that enabled jurors to temper the harshness of the law.[8] Some features of criminal process remained largely unchanged over the 1700s. Prosecutions continued to be brought by victims and what would now be called pre-trial process remained 'chancy' and 'largely informal', in Keith Smith's words, and the way in which insane defendants were dealt with varied widely.[9] At the start of the century, as at the end, if an insane individual was acquitted, no particular disposal was mandated, and what happened to the defendant varied according to his or her personal circumstances.[10]

---

[6] See Walker *Crime and Insanity in England (Vol 1)* 27–8, 36.
[7] K J M Smith *Lawyers, Legislators and Theorists: Developments in English Criminal Jurisprudence 1800–1957* (Oxford: Clarendon Press, 1998) 44–5.
[8] M J Wiener *Reconstructing the Criminal: Culture, Law and Policy in England, 1830–1914* (Cambridge: CUP, 1990) 59; see also King 'Decision-Makers and Decision-Making' 37; D Rabin *Identity, Crime and Legal Responsibility in Eighteenth Century England* (Basingstoke: Palgrave Macmillan, 2004) 31; Langbein *The Origins of the Adversary Criminal Trial* 58; J M Beattie *Crime and the Courts in England 1660–1800* (Oxford: OUP, 1986) 530; D Hay 'Property, Authority and the Criminal Law' in D Hay, P Linebaugh, J G Rule, E P Thompson and C Winslow (eds) *Albion's Fatal Tress: Crime and Society in Eighteenth Century England* (London: Allen Lane, 1975) 17–63. If an insane defendant was convicted after the passage of the Transportation Act 1718 (4 Geo. I c.11), he or she faced the possibility of imprisonment or transportation to America or Australia from 1719, a development that 'widened the discretionary powers of the judge and jury in the face of the increasing number of capital statutes' that were passed in this era: see Rabin *Identity, Crime and Legal Responsibility* 35; see also P King *Crime, Justice and Discretion in England 1740–1820* (Oxford: OUP, 2000) 355.
[9] Smith *Lawyers, Legislators and Theorists* 42. As Dana Rabin writes, 'constant negotiation shaped the decision to prosecute, the gathering of evidence, the testimony given, the judge and jury reception of the information at trial, and the judge's decision to recommend for or against a royal pardon' (*Identity, Crime and Legal Responsibility* 25). In this context, as Rabin plausibly suggests, some matters involving insane defendants—particularly those related to minor offences—would have been among those not to come to trial (*Identity, Crime and Legal Responsibility* 24).
[10] Historical studies indicate that some individuals were discharged into the care of relatives, or private asylums, while those who were poor or who seemed to constitute a continuing danger were

It was in this dynamic procedural and punishment context that the first famous insanity case appeared—that of Edward Arnold in 1724.[11] Arnold was charged with maliciously shooting at a prominent local member of the aristocracy, Lord Onslow, under the recently enacted Black Act.[12] Arnold pleaded that he did not know what he was doing and did not intend any harm. Evidence adduced at trial by Arnold's family and the local community indicated that Arnold was given to 'irrational antics and minor acts of violence and damage', but evidence led by the prosecution about the preparation of the offence suggested that Arnold could 'form a steady and resolute design'.[13] In his directions to the jury, Justice Tracy stated:

When a man is guilty of a great offence, it must be very plain and clear before a man is allowed such an exemption... it must be a man that is totally deprived of his understanding and memory, and doth not know what he is doing, no more than an infant, than a brute, or a wild beast [in order to avoid punishment].[14]

Although sometimes taken to indicate the strictness of informal insanity at this time, what has come to be known as the 'wild beast' insanity test was more of an informal standard than a 'precise formula' for assessing lack of intent.[15] For this reason, the 'wild beast' insanity test does not conclusively indicate that, by this point in time, 'partial insanity'—the kind of insanity that affected an individual in some respects but not others—was fatal to any claim to exculpation or that lack of reason (as opposed to lack of control) was the preferred basis for exculpatory insanity.

Over and above the issue of the strictness of the informal insanity law at this point, the 'wild beast' test is significant in another way. Viewed in light of the informal criminal processes then prevailing, the 'wild beast' insanity test appears significant for what it suggests about the relevance of the formal qualities of exculpatory 'madness', and the ways in which it was proved, for legal purposes. Paralleling my reading of Matthew Hale's reference to the 'absolute' character of the 'madness' associated with unfitness to plea (which I discuss in Chapter 4), the

---

detained in gaol: see Beattie *Crime and the Courts in England* 84; Walker *Crime and Insanity in England (Vol 1)* 42–3.

[11] *Edward Arnold* (1724) 16 St Tr 695.

[12] (1723) 9 Geo. 1 c.22. See generally Hay 'Property, Authority and the Criminal Law' 17–63.

[13] See Walker *Crime and Insanity in England (Vol 1)* 55 and R Moran 'The Origin of Insanity as a Special Verdict: The Trial for Treason of James Hadfield' (1985) 19(3) *Law and Society Review* 487, 502 respectively.

[14] Extracted in Walker *Crime and Insanity in England (Vol 1)* 56. Arnold was convicted but, as a result of Lord Onslow's intercession, he was imprisoned rather than executed. See T Maeder *Crime and Madness: The Origins and Evolution of the Insanity Defense* (New York: Harper and Row, 1985) 11; Walker *Crime and Insanity in England (Vol 1)* 57.

[15] J P Eigen 'Delusion's Odyssey: Charting the Course of Victorian Forensic Psychiatry' (2004) 27 (5) *International Journal of Law and Psychiatry* 395, 398. Several scholars have interpreted this test to indicate that only total madness or a complete lack of memory and understanding would suffice for an insanity acquittal at this time (see for example Moran 'The Origin of Insanity as a Special Verdict' 488). Yet, the variability of insanity cases in this era militates against such generalizations. As a result, the judge's directions to the jury should be interpreted in their context: as Beattie has argued, because of the status of the victim, the court clearly pressed hard to defeat the insanity doctrine in *Arnold's Case* (Beattie *Crime and the Courts in England* 85).

'wild beast' insanity test is more of a requirement of form than of degree or extent. Given the norms of proof then prevailing, Justice Tracy's direction that insanity must be 'very plain and clear' is as significant as his direction on the deprivation of understanding and memory. The conduct of an insane defendant had a particular significance in the criminal courtroom: exculpation of a defendant claiming insanity was made not so much via a deduction of his or her internal mental processes from his or her behaviour but on the basis that that behaviour constituted a 'mad' condition.[16] Further, Arnold's insanity was regarded as evident in his conduct beyond the act comprising the offence.[17] I take up the issue of evidence and proof of insanity in the next chapter.

The 'wild beast' test was not the only formulation of insanity in this era. The *Old Bailey Proceedings* indicate that a myriad of references were made to describe states that fell within the bounds of insanity. The brief references to a defendant's 'distracted Gestures', 'the Oddness of his Behaviour', or 'violent phrensies of mind'[18] contained in the trial records of the *OBPs* were designed to tap into ordinary people's understanding of 'madness'. An example of the role of ordinary people's testimony about incapacity, is provided by the trial of Benjamin Allen on a charge of the theft of books and paper in 1768. After stating that he knew 'nothing at all of it' and explaining that he was asked to carry a bundle by a gentleman, four of Allen's acquaintances spoke on his behalf, one of whom said he had looked 'upon him to be insane' and another said that Allen was subject to fits which 'had disordered him in his head very much'.[19] Allen was given a partial verdict and sentenced to be whipped. As these extracts suggest, and as Roy Porter argues, in this era, 'madness was an extremely broad sociocultural category, with many manifestations and meanings' and 'meanings of madness multiplied within lay culture, describing individuals, acts and situations out of the ordinary'.[20] As it was part of common knowledge, ordinary people without specialist knowledge were regarded as competent to detect and evaluate 'madness'. I discuss the relevance of social meanings of 'madness' in Chapter 6.

Each of the expressions employed to capture insanity was partly prescriptive and partly descriptive of an abnormal mental state: at this juncture, exculpatory insanity had not yet undergone any sustained conceptual elaboration in criminal law. Individuals articulated claims to exculpation on the basis of insanity alongside a range of other claims. References to defendants 'acting like a crazed Person, for a

---

[16] See Chapter 3 for a discussion of the formal qualities of 'madness' per my 'manifest madness' analysis.

[17] As Walker points out, at trial, evidence was adduced about Arnold's conduct when he was in prison after the offence. Walker argues that 'thus the way was paved' for the subsequent introduction of medical witnesses 'who had examined the accused after his crime': see *Crime and Insanity in England (Vol 1)* 55–6.

[18] See *OBP*, Thomas Draper, 17 May 1727 (t17270517-12); *OBP*, William Barnelly, 9 July 1729 (t17290709-64); and *OBP*, Richard Greenwood, 29 April 1767 (t17670429-50) respectively.

[19] *OBP*, Benjamin Allen, 24 February 1768 (t17680224-73).

[20] R Porter *Mind-Forg'd Manacles: A History of Madness in England from the Restoration to the Regency* (London: Athlone Press, 1987) x, 29.

Week of 10 Days before the Time when the Murther was committed'[21] and evaluative statements to the effect that the defendant was a 'Lunatick',[22] or 'out of his senses'[23] or a 'Distracted Person'[24] intermingled with references to character, age, and other factors. As Dana Rabin argues, like other 'pleas of mental distress', insanity was raised by individuals in order to persuade the judge and the jury that their crime was 'committed without criminal intent'.[25] During this period, the 'thin doctrine of capacity as a condition for criminal responsibility'[26] that was a feature of the exculpatory criminal trial (which I discuss in Chapter 4) was only gradually being replaced by a more robust subjective concept of criminal fault.[27] In this context, references to potentially exculpatory mental states (such as 'unable to tell good from evil') were designed to challenge the authenticity of the manifest meaning of a defendant's acts as criminal.

Facilitated by the fact that, at this time, there was little 'refinement' of matters such as 'levels of mental culpability and recognition of defences involving incapacity or the actor's freedom and choice of action',[28] claims of mental abnormality and volitional incapacity—now divided by the boundary between insanity and automatism—coexisted alongside each other, and, indeed, were bound up together in some cases. Given the breadth of 'madness' as a sociocultural category, it is likely that individuals such as those who could point to both external and internal causes of incapacitous conduct fell within the bounds of socially defined 'madness'.[29] Mindful of the need for caution in searching for prototypical automatism cases,[30] those *OBP* trial records which refer to an external cause may be tentatively regarded as informal claims to exculpation on the basis of automatism. The record of William Walker's trial for the murder of his wife in 1784 provides a good example of what may be thought of as an informal automatism claim.[31] Walker stabbed his wife with a knife. There was no evidence of discord between the defendant and his wife, and several witnesses testified that they did not think

---

[21] *OBP*, Coustantine Mac-Yennis, 26 February 1724 (t17240226–78).
[22] *OBP*, Edward Bromfield, 9 September 1696 (t16960909–27).
[23] *OBP*, Francis David Stirn, 10 September 1760 (t17600910–19).
[24] *OBP*, Henry Clifford, 13 January 1688 (t16880113–30).
[25] Rabin *Identity, Crime and Legal Responsibility* 1–2.
[26] N Lacey 'Responsibility and Modernity in Criminal Law' (2001) 9(3) *Journal of Political Philosophy* 249, 261.
[27] In George Fletcher's terminology, this was the era of 'manifest criminality', whereby liability for an offence rested on the presumption that the defendant's act manifested his or her 'criminal purpose'. See G P Fletcher *Rethinking Criminal Law* (New York: OUP, 2000) 232.
[28] Smith *Lawyers, Legislators and Theorists* 43.
[29] As discussed in Chapter 8 in relation to infanticide, these social meanings had particular gender inflections, which impacted on the ways in which women's claims to exculpatory 'madness' were articulated and received by courts.
[30] The brevity of the *OBP*s records and the informality of claims to exculpation in this era meant that factors which would later be important, such as the cause of incapacity (internal or external), were sometimes left unidentified. It is also likely that, as Nigel Walker argues in relation to the nineteenth century, some charges brought against defendants who engaged in what would now be called automatistic conduct were rejected by the grand jury and did not come to trial: see *Crime and Insanity in England (Vol 1)* 167.
[31] *OBP*, William Walker, 21 April 1784 (t17840421–13).

Walker was 'mad'. The judge seemed confounded by the facts, and commented that it was 'one of the most extraordinary cases I ever met with'. By way of defence, William Walker simply stated 'I am not sensible as I did kill my wife, and please you my Lord'. In his summing up, the judge stated that something 'singular and extraordinary' must have happened to Walker in the days before the killing to disturb him from his 'orderly state', effectively imputing an external cause to the defendant, and Walker was found not guilty on the basis of insanity.

The *OBP*s also contain records of cases in which an external cause operated together with an internal cause. A good example of this type of case is the trial of Richard Montgomery in 1727. In that case, an apothecary deposed that he had administered medicines to the defendant 'to remove his Indisposition' the day before the alleged offences (theft and robbery) took place.[32] The defendant's 'extravagant Expressions', evidence that 'Lunacy ran in the Blood of the Family' and the fact that one of the offences took place in plain view of people coming from church, were possibly behind the jury verdict that the defendant was *non compos mentis*. As this verdict indicates, the informal insanity law was sufficiently capacious to capture both internal and external causes of incapacity.

The Cleaving Apart of Insanity and Automatism

Concern with dangerousness forced the cleaving apart of insanity and what would come to be called automatism. This cleaving apart was initially prompted by another famous insanity trial, that of James Hadfield for high treason in 1800. Hadfield had attempted to shoot King George III, believing that this act would ensure that he himself would be killed but the world would be saved.[33] As special privileges accompanied treason trials, Hadfield was entitled to assistance from counsel in the preparation of evidence and the examination and cross-examination of witnesses.[34] His counsel, Thomas Erskine, argued that, rather than 'total deprivation of memory and understanding', 'delusion was the inseparable companion of real insanity'.[35] A doctor from Bethlem examined Hadfield and stated in court that 'when any question is put to him which relates to the subject of his lunacy, he answers irrationally'.[36] The Justices interrupted Erskine's defence and the Attorney-General confirmed that he did not want to challenge the evidence. Hadfield was acquitted and, in accordance with the practice that had prevailed since the early modern era, the jury gave both their verdict and its factual basis: '[w]e find the prisoner Not Guilty; he being under the influence of insanity at the time the act was committed'.[37]

---

[32] *OBP*, Richard Montgomery, 30 August 1727 (t17270830–29).
[33] *R v Hadfield* (1800) 27 St Tr 1281 (*Hadfield's Case*).
[34] See Langbein *The Origins of the Adversary Criminal Trial* 84–5, 97–102.
[35] Extracted in Walker *Crime and Insanity in England (Vol 1)* 77.
[36] Extracted in Walker *Crime and Insanity in England (Vol 1)* 76.
[37] Extracted in Moran 'The Origin of Insanity as a Special Verdict' 510. Hadfield was sent to Newgate prison.

The uncertainty attending Hadfield's disposal led Parliament to pass the Criminal Lunatics Act 1800, an Act which contained the first fissures of a crevice between insanity and automatism, and represented the first step in the formalization of insanity (and insanity on arraignment/unfitness to plead). Section 1 of this Act provided:

That in all cases... of any person charged with treason, murder, or felony, that such person was insane at the time of the commission of such offence, and such person shall be acquitted, the jury shall be required to find specially whether such person was insane at the time of the commission of such offence, and to declare whether such person was acquitted by them on account of such insanity; and if they shall find that such person was insane at the time of the committing such offence, the court before whom such trial shall be had, shall order such person to be kept in strict custody, in such place and in such manner as to the court shall seem fit, until his Majesty's pleasure shall be known.[38]

While the Act did not define insanity for legal purposes, it fundamentally altered the procedural context in which claims to exculpation on the basis of insanity were made. As a result of the 1800 Act, it was no longer open to the jury simply to acquit the insane defendant.[39] The Act also brought the detention of insane defendants into the criminal law, providing the court with power to keep such individuals in custody.[40]

As the 1800 Act suggests, this first step in the cleaving apart of insanity and automatism—and along the path to the formalization of the law on insanity—was something of a backdoor development, as it concerned the disposal of individuals

---

[38] Criminal Lunatics Act 1800, s 1, which was subtitled 'An Act for the Safe Custody of Insane Persons Charged with Offences' (39 & 40 Geo. III c. 94). The provision in the Act that a defendant found 'not guilty on account of insanity' would be detained 'in strict custody... until His Majesty's pleasure be known' maintained the tradition that the King embodied the justice and mercy of the realm: see Moran 'The Origin of Insanity as a Special Verdict' 515. The 1800 Act was to apply retrospectively, so as to include Hadfield: Walker *Crime and Insanity in England (Vol 1)* 78. Unlike the provision relating to insanity on arraignment, also contained in the 1800 Act, the insanity provision applied only to offences of treason, murder, or felony, not to misdemeanours, perhaps as the result of an assumption that the insanity doctrine applied only to capital offences: Walker *Crime and Insanity in England (Vol 1)* 80. The Insane Prisoners Act 1840 (3 & 4 Vict. c. 54) introduced the special verdict of 'not guilty by reason of insanity' for misdemeanours.

[39] Walker *Crime and Insanity in England (Vol 1)* 78. Rupert Cross argues that a distinction between insanity and automatism has been implicit in the criminal law since this Act, with the distinction between insanity and automatism marking the difference between indefinite detention and a complete acquittal (R Cross, 'Reflections on Bratty's Case' [1962] *Law Quarterly Review* 236, 238). But it is important to note that the parameters of as yet emergent categories of insanity and automatism were by no means fixed and that exculpation on the basis of what might now be called automatism remained informal and variable, achieved in the absence of a discrete doctrine until the second half of the twentieth century.

[40] Although it had been possible to detain insane defendants before 1800, the Act introduced a 'more systematic means of containing them within a voluntarist legal system' (Wiener *Reconstructing the Criminal* 85). As Wiener argues, this procedure offered a 'middle path' between humanity and security: it was an alternative to conviction and punishment, and also provided 'new legal means to incarcerate an offender' (*Reconstructing the Criminal* 85). While in theory, defendants such as Hadfield could be released if they were no longer a danger to themselves or others, in practice, the period of confinement was life (Moran 'The Origin of Insanity as a Special Verdict' 515). The effect of the passage of the 1800 Act was that an individual did not have to be convicted of a crime in order to be confined under the criminal law (Moran 'The Origin of Insanity as a Special Verdict' 517).

acquitted on the basis of insanity, rather than the law itself. The link established in the Criminal Lunatics Act 1800 between a successful insanity plea, a particular trial verdict (the special verdict) and indefinite detention would prove to be an enduring feature of exculpatory insanity.[41] Even after indefinite detention fell away, and other disposal options were made available to courts, the link between a successful insanity plea and the special verdict has remained, conjoining the issue of criminal non-responsibility and disposal in a way that is unique in criminal law. The special verdict forms part of the distinctive procedural frame governing insanity claims, and I discuss this in the next chapter.

The concern with disposal that was evident in the passage of the Criminal Lunatics Act 1800 reflected a particular attitude to insane individuals charged with criminal offences: that they were dangerous. It was this construction of insane defendants which legitimated the indefinite detention that followed a successful insanity doctrine. This construction of insane defendants as dangerous has been remarkably durable: with the exception of the most recent developments relating to the disposal of insane defendants, it has been the driving force behind the insanity doctrine since 1800.[42] In *Sullivan*, Lord Diplock stated that 'the purpose of the legislation relating to the defence of insanity, ever since its origin in 1800, has been to protect society against recurrence of the dangerous conduct'.[43] The construction of insane defendants as dangerous has concentrated the attention of judges and law reformers on issues relating to disposal, issues which have dominated discussions of the law of insanity. This concern with dangerousness has been rearticulated in recent decades as a concern with risk—a less overtly moralized and more technical concept—that I discuss below.

At the turn of the nineteenth century, with the contours of the fault element of criminal offences and its relationship to exculpatory insanity yet to be explicated, the insane defendant's conduct formed the basis on which he or she was constructed as dangerous. An insane accused's conduct—including the acts comprising the offence, but also the conduct surrounding the offence—had a thick significance, extending beyond that now commonly accorded to the *actus reus* of an

---

[41] In the Trial of Lunatics Act 1883, the special verdict was repackaged as 'guilty but insane', thus technically altering the form of the special verdict from an acquittal to a conviction (see Moran 'The Origin of Insanity as a Special Verdict' 519). However, although the special verdict was briefly regarded as a conviction—from the decision in *Ireland* (*R v Ireland* (1910) 9 Cr App R. 139) until that decision was overturned in *Felstead* (*R v Felstead* [1914] AC 534)—the special verdict has always effectively been an acquittal, evidenced by the fact that the defendant could not appeal against it (Moran 'The Origin of Insanity as a Special Verdict' 519; S White *What Queen Victoria Saw: Roderick Maclean and the Trial of Lunatics Act, 1883* (Chichester: Barry Rose Law, 2000) 68). It was only after the passage of the Criminal Procedure (Insanity) Act 1964 that a special verdict accrued a right of appeal (s 2). The Criminal Procedure (Insanity) Act 1964 also returned the form of the special verdict to 'not guilty by reason of insanity' (s 1), a change which had been recommended by the inter-war *Committee on Insanity and Crime (the Atkin Committee)* (*Report of the Committee on Insanity and Crime* (Cmd 2005, 1924), 11–12) and United Kingdom Royal Commission on Capital Punishment 1949–1953 Report (Cmnd 8932, 1953) para 456).
[42] See R Moran 'The Punitive Uses of the Insanity Defence: The Trial for Treason of Edward Oxford (1840)' (1986) (9) *International Journal of Law and Psychiatry* 171, 189; see also E Colvin 'Exculpatory Defences in Criminal Law' (1990) 10 *Oxford Journal of Legal Studies* 381, 386.
[43] *R v Sullivan* [1984] 1 AC 156, 172.

offence. As I discuss in relation to evidence and proof of insanity, and also as part of my 'manifest madness' analysis, evaluation of an individual's conduct was made not so much via deduction of his or her mental processes from his or her behaviour, but on the basis that the behaviour constituted the 'mad' condition.[44] This emphasis on the manifest meaning of the individual's conduct would produce a strange side-effect: the seriousness of the offence with which the defendant was charged affected both the law and process under which he or she was processed. I discuss this in the final section of this chapter.

In the decades following the passage of the Criminal Lunatics Act 1800, changes in the broader social and political context in which insanity trials took place reinforced this abiding concern with the dangerousness of individuals raising insanity at trial. The final decades of the eighteenth century had been marked by a growing public awareness of the social problem posed by the insane, generated by a developing interest in the phenomenon of insanity and a sense of what Martin Wiener calls 'moral unease' in subjecting 'madmen to criminal sanctions,' as well as a heightened concern with social order.[45] The rise of insanity as a social problem at this point drew public attention to the criminally insane who, in Wiener's words, 'kept now bumping up against the more ubiquitous law and against similarly expanding standards of respectability'.[46] The first decades of the 1800s featured significant parliamentary and public debate about the ineffectiveness of the criminal law and its ability to properly take into account different levels of moral culpability.[47] Concurrently, as Wiener suggests, public interest in crime, 'both popular and serious', was growing.[48] Wiener argues that, because crime was a metaphor of disorder and loss of control, criminal laws came to occupy 'cultural high ground', and to be a central plank of the Victorian discourse of moralization.[49] Insane defendants were positioned at the confluence of these broad social currents relating to criminality, the effectiveness of the criminal justice system and morality, which pushed the law on insanity into prominence.

The first decades of the nineteenth century were also marked by the rise of the psychiatric profession, embodying an expert knowledge of 'madness'. The appearance of an expert knowledge about 'madness' in the nineteenth century significantly altered the knowledge context and the evidentiary and procedural practices

---

[44] See Chapter 6 for a historical discussion in the context of insanity; see also Chapter 3 regarding 'manifest madness'.

[45] Wiener *Reconstructing the Criminal* 84. The growing public awareness of insanity was evident in the enactment of vagrancy legislation, such as the Vagrancy Act 1744 ('An Act...relating to Rogues, Vagabonds etc...') (17 Geo. II c.5), which meant that the insane could be held under civil laws (see Walker *Crime and Insanity in England (Vol 1)* 70). Public awareness of insanity was also evidenced in, and heightened by, the voluntary subscription hospitals and asylums for the insane that appeared in the second half of the eighteenth century (see W F Bynum 'Rationales for Therapy in British Psychiatry 1780–1835' in A Scull (ed) *Madhouses, Mad-Doctors and Madmen: The Social History of Psychiatry in the Victorian Era* (London: Athlone Press, 1981) 40–4; Walker *Crime and Insanity in England (Vol 1)* 70).

[46] Wiener *Reconstructing the Criminal* 83–4.

[47] See Smith *Lawyers, Legislators and Theorists* 56–8.

[48] See Wiener *Reconstructing the Criminal* 15, and, more generally, 14–26.

[49] *Reconstructing the Criminal* 47–8.

governing exculpatory 'madness'. In this period, specialist knowledge about 'madness' was considerably contested and conflicted. As exemplified by the new notion of 'moral insanity', developing psychiatric knowledge emphasized individual will and emotions, as opposed to intellect.[50] The notion of 'moral insanity' denoted 'primarily an alienation of feelings, of natural sentiments', and 'spoke to the impulsive nature of the will, which drove the afflicted person into motiveless, revolting activity': according to Joel Eigen, it thus addressed the issue of criminal liability directly.[51] 'Moral insanity' and other diagnostic entities would be significant in the development of the law of insanity and other mental incapacity doctrines such as infanticide in the subsequent decades. This changing knowledge context—discussed in detail in Chapter 6—contained the germ of the changing foundation of the law of insanity—from a broader and looser idea of incapacity, to a narrower and more technical, and eventually more medicalized, idea of disability.

A 'fierce and fearful delusion': Daniel M'Naghten and the Creation of the *M'Naghten Rules*

In 1843, Daniel M'Naghten, aiming to shoot the Prime Minister, shot and killed his private secretary, Edward Drummond. M'Naghten was charged with willful murder and pleaded not guilty. At trial, the Solicitor General, referring to *Arnold's Case* and *Hadfield's Case*, stated that M'Naghten could not be excused on the grounds of insanity if he had 'that degree of intellect which enabled him to know and distinguish between right and wrong'.[52] Alexander Cockburn, M'Naghten's counsel, argued that, although M'Naghten had done the act, he should not be held responsible for it because the 'fierce and fearful delusion' that he was being persecuted subsisted at the time of the killing and meant that he was unable to control his actions.[53] Witnesses for the prosecution and defence included lay people who had known the prisoner in Glasgow and London, and several medical experts, including Dr Monro, who was the Superintendent of Bethlem. After hearing the medical witnesses, Chief Justice Tindal stopped the proceedings and remarked that 'the whole of the medical evidence is on one side'.[54] The jury found M'Naghten

---

[50] *Reconstructing the Criminal* 26; J P Eigen *Witnessing Insanity: Madness and Mad Doctors in the English Court* (New Haven: Yale University Press, 1995) 79; see also M J Clark '"Morbid Introspection," Unsoundness of Mind, and British Psychological Medicine c.1830–1900' in W F Bynum, R Porter, and M Shepherd (eds) *The Anatomy of Madness: Essays in the History of Psychiatry* (London: Routledge, 1988) 83–4; N Rafter 'The Unrepentant Horse-Slasher: Moral Insanity and the Origins of Criminological Thought' (2004) 42(4) *Criminology* 979, 993–9; H Rimke and A Hunt 'From Sinners to Degenerates: The Medicalization of Morality in the Nineteenth Century' (2002) 15(1) *History of the Human Sciences* 59, 70–3.
[51] Eigen *Witnessing Insanity* 78–80.
[52] *M'Naghten* (1843) 10 Cl & Fin 200, extracted in West and Walk (eds) *Daniel McNaughton* 16.
[53] Extracted in Moran *Knowing Right from Wrong* 1. The passage of the Prisoners' Counsel Act 1836 meant that M'Naghten's defence counsel could address the jury.
[54] Extracted in West and Walk (eds) *Daniel McNaughton* 72.

'not guilty by reason of insanity'. This outcome was highly controversial, with Queen Victoria and others expressing concern that the verdict was unduly lenient.

The *M'Naghten Rules* were formulated in response to five questions put to 15 judges of the Queen's Bench by the House of Lords, when, subsequently, they were called to appear to defend the *M'Naghten* decision. The now famous judicial statement drafted in response to the questions from the Lords provided in part:

[T]he jurors ought to be told in all cases that every man is to be presumed sane, and to possess a sufficient degree of reason to be responsible for his crimes, until the contrary be proved to their satisfaction; and that to establish a defence on the ground of insanity it must be clearly proved that at the time of the committing of the act, the party accused was labouring under such a defect of reason, from a disease of the mind, as not to know the nature and quality of the act he was doing, or, if he did know it, that he did not know he was doing wrong.[55]

The *M'Naghten Rules* form the current law on insanity in England and Wales, and I provide a detailed analysis of them in the next section of this chapter. While the *Rules* themselves have been of primary interest to legal scholars, the way in which they were created has been at least as significant as their content. The unique character of the *Rules*—a judicial formulation, developed independently of a specific trial, and in a legislative context—has earned them the label 'judicial legislation',[56] and served to entrench them in the criminal law of England and Wales.

The *M'Naghten Rules* triggered rather than settled debate about the insanity doctrine in the years after 1843. The scope of the insanity doctrine, its purpose (to exculpate those who were not morally accountable or those who could not be deterred) and its basis (in cognitive or volitional disorder) were the subjects of discussion by legal and political commentators. As Keith Smith suggests, the debate about *M'Naghten* insanity turned on two issues: the meaning of 'wrong' (whether according to 'the laws of God or man') and what came to be called 'irresistible impulse' (the extent to which the law accommodated or ought to accommodate volitional incapacity).[57] While the insanity doctrine was the subject of discussion on the part of judges and commentators, there was no significant conceptual

---

[55] *M'Naghten* (1843) 10 Cl & Fin 200, 210. This statement forms the core of the *M'Naghten Rules* but the Queen's Bench judges also responded to questions about the significance of delusions on the part of defendants claiming insanity and the role of medical evidence where it is given by someone who has not seen the defendant before trial. These parts of the judges' response were not the focus of judicial or other attention after they were drafted and are no longer considered authoritative: see Walker *Crime and Insanity in England (Vol 1)* 100; T Ward 'A Terrible Responsibility: Murder and the Insanity Defence in England 1908–1939' (2002) 25 *International Journal of Law and Psychiatry* 361, 374.

[56] D J A Cairns *Advocacy and the Making of the Adversarial Criminal Trial, 1800–1865* (Oxford: Clarendon Press, 1998) 178.

[57] Smith *Lawyers, Legislators and Theorists* 223–5. As Smith chronicles, in relation to the first issue, opinions as to the meaning of the wrongness element of the *Rules* varied from knowledge of illegality to the broader notion of knowledge of moral wrongfulness. In relation to volitional incapacity or irresistible impulse, the fact that the *Rules* did not expressly allow for exculpation on the basis of impairment of volitional power, came to produce a 'steadily accumulating body of medical and, later, legal literature' that supported the view that the insanity doctrine was too narrowly conceived. See also Walker *Crime and Insanity in England (Vol 1)* 105; Wiener *Reconstructing the Criminal* 270 and

development of ideas of criminal non-responsibility at this time. In Smith's words, 'fundamental structural questions' concerning the relationship between defences and *mens rea* or voluntariness 'remained quite beyond express judicial interest'.[58] Debate over the meaning of wrongness and the status of 'irresistible impulse' continued into the twentieth century when, as I discuss below, the Court of Criminal Appeal adjudicated both issues.

In part because of what Smith labels judicial 'failure to articulate the theoretical basis upon which the defence rested',[59] and as a result of the intervention of expert medical professionals in trials involving insanity, the operation of the law in the decades after *M'Naghten* was more flexible than its technical construction suggested.[60] Thus, while the *M'Naghten Rules* have been interpreted as a limitation on the scope of exculpatory insanity,[61] the conceptual indeterminacy and the operational flexibility of criminal process provided some scope to accommodate claims for exculpation that would now fall within the bounds of automatism. Some support for this argument about the capacity of the newly formalized insanity doctrine is provided by Eigen in his study of criminal trials from the Victorian era. Eigen argues that, in this period, a diverse population of 'mentally wayward' defendants sought exculpation on the basis of their abnormal mental states. Against the background of a burgeoning expert psychiatric knowledge, and popular interest in mesmerism, various defendants presented the court with an array of afflictions such as 'unconsciousness', mental 'absence', amnesia, and impulse that departed qualitatively from 'delusion, delirium and mania', the mainstays of insanity.[62] Eigen suggests that 'unconsciousness' was 'originally employed as a synonym for lack of awareness' but gradually expanded to 'a state of mental life inaccessible to the waking person', covering 'the truly unknown features of a prisoner's affect'.[63] This period seems to mark the beginning of the significance of unconsciousness for what would later be known as automatism.[64]

M J Wiener *Men of Blood: Violence, Manliness and Criminal Justice in Victorian England* (Cambridge: CUP, 2004) 280.

[58] Smith *Lawyers, Legislators and Theorists* 257–8.
[59] *Lawyers, Legislators and Theorists* 223.
[60] Several commentators take this view. See, eg Wiener *Reconstructing the Criminal* 275.
[61] See, for example, J P Eigen, 'Lesion of the Will: Medical Resolve and Criminal Responsibility in Victorian Insanity Trials' (1999) 33(2) *Law and Society Review* 425, 438–9; R D Mackay *Mental Condition Defences in the Criminal Law* (Oxford: Clarendon Press, 1995) 95; Smith *Lawyers, Legislators and Theorists* 220. In Keith Smith's words, the *M'Naghten Rules* constituted 'a synthesized "restatement" of earlier case-law, while asserting more strongly a narrow knowledge or cognitive basis of the defence, and, by implication, denying the relevance of ineffective volitional control' (*Lawyers, Legislators and Theorists* 220).
[62] J P Eigen 'Sense and Sensibility: Fateful Splitting in the Victorian Insanity Trial' in R A Melikan (ed) *Domestic and International Trials 1700–2000: The Trial In History Volume II* (Manchester; Manchester University Press, 2003) 9.
[63] 'Sense and Sensibility' 167.
[64] It was in the context of these cases that a defendant's actions were first described as 'automatic': see 'Sense and Sensibility' 144–6. Several of the defendants identified by Eigen were granted insanity defences while others had their charges dismissed or received directed acquittals on miscellaneous grounds or miscellaneous verdicts such as 'not guilty on the grounds of unconsciousness' ('Sense and

A narrower idea of disability as a basis for insanity was emerging during this era—invoked for instance in the use of terms such as 'disease' and 'defect' in the *M'Naghten Rules*—but a lingering, moralized notion of incapacity subsisted as a basis for the insanity plea. Conditions of the late Victorian era combined to emphasize a moralized idea of abnormality as a foundation for exculpation (even as this foundation was itself gradually becoming a more medicalized concept—as a result of the rise of expert medical knowledge of 'madness'). In the wider cultural and political frame, the late Victorian era was characterized by an emphasis on personal responsibility, which Roger Smith refers to as an 'individualized form of conformity with the social order'.[65] The aim of engaging the law as an instrument of moralization pushed the notion of a subjective test for criminal liability to the fore as a defendant's 'powers of reason and self-government' were subjected to new scrutiny.[66] As a result, Wiener argues that defences that classed the defendant as abnormal were more palatable than those that positioned the defendant on a continuum with non-criminal individuals.[67] For this reason, Wiener claims that the insanity plea rose to prominence while other pleas, such as intoxication, declined. According to Wiener, 'the gradually broadening recognition of mental unsoundness' presented less of a challenge than intoxication or provocation because it meant that excused defendants were not likely to be returned to society and 'it did not offer a competing vision of "normal" behaviour to that of the Victorian judiciary and Home Office'.[68] The effect of these changed conditions was such that, by the end of the era, the prominence of the insanity doctrine had outstripped its practical role and raised it to a position of symbolic importance in the criminal law.

Insanity As We Know It: the *M'Naghten Rules*

The *M'Naghten Rules* represent the current law on insanity in England and Wales. Their importance in the context of insanity and, more broadly, across the mental

---

Sensibility' 138–9, 145). The place of insanity verdicts in these cases attests to the continuing flexibility and capaciousness of the insanity doctrine in the decades after *M'Naghten*.

[65] R Smith *Trial by Medicine: Insanity and Responsibility in Victorian Trials* (Edinburgh: Edinburgh University Press, 1981) 164; see also N Lacey 'In Search of the Responsible Subject: History, Philosophy and Social Sciences in Criminal Law Theory' (2001) 64(3) *Modern Law Review* 350, 365; Wiener *Reconstructing the Criminal* 91. This emphasis on personal responsibility raised the profile of those, such as the criminally insane, who could not attain it. Criminal and, to a lesser extent, civil law, was used as an instrument for fostering 'self-disciplining and gratification-deferring personalities in the population at large' (Wiener *Reconstructing the Criminal* 91). Significantly, the principle of individual responsibility which came to stand at the centre of the law was as much aspirational as actual (*Reconstructing the Criminal* 54).

[66] *Reconstructing the Criminal* 84.

[67] In Wiener's words, 'if ordinary men were now expected to master their passions, then the only successful path to avoid a guilty plea was likely that of showing the prisoner to be not ordinary': see M J Wiener 'Judges and Jurors: Courtroom Tensions in Murder Trials and the Law of Criminal Responsibility in Nineteenth Century England' (1999) 17 *Law and History Review* 467, 504.

[68] Wiener *Men of Blood* 287. The idea of a distinctive and confined class of defendants who lay outside the bounds of humanity could be 'readily reconciled' with Victorian expectations of personal self-discipline (*Men of Blood* 287).

The Exculpatory Doctrines of Insanity and Automatism

incapacity terrain, is such that they warrant a detailed discussion, which I offer in this section. There are three limbs to the current insanity doctrine, and I discuss each in turn.

(i) 'defect of reason'

The first limb of *M'Naghten* insanity, 'defect of reason', is both a cause and an effect: it must cause an individual not to know the 'nature and quality' of the act, or, alternatively, that it was 'wrong', and it must be an effect of a 'disease of the mind'. The requirement that a defendant seeking to make an insanity plea must suffer from a 'defect of reason' has been narrowly interpreted such that 'defect of reason' denotes cognitive defects. In *Kemp*, Lord Devlin distinguished between defects of reason caused by 'diseased' minds and those caused by merely 'untrained' minds, stating that:

> A defect of reason is by itself enough to make the act irrational and therefore normally to exclude responsibility in law. But the Rule was not intended to apply to defects of reason caused simply by brutish stupidity without rational power.[69]

Although a 'defect of reason' need not be permanent, a defendant must be 'deprived of the power of reasoning' at the time of his or her act—it is not enough that a defendant be 'momentarily absentminded or confused'.[70] The effect of interpreting 'defect of reason' in *M'Naghten* to denote cognitive defects has been to exclude defects of conation, the psychological processes of desire and volition. The narrow, cognitive component of *M'Naghten* has been the focus of much of the criticism directed at the insanity doctrine.[71] However, some of the heat of these criticisms of *M'Naghten* dissipated with the introduction of diminished responsibility (which encompasses volitional incapacity).[72]

(ii) 'disease of the mind'

The 'disease of the mind' limb of *M'Naghten* insanity forms the core of the doctrine, providing a discrete and ostensibly scientific basis for the exculpation that flows from a successful plea. Judicial interpretation of 'disease of the mind'— around the idea of an internal as opposed to external cause—has not only set the scope of insanity, but also determined the dividing line between insanity and automatism. The meaning of the phrase 'disease of the mind' was first subject to

---

[69] *R v Kemp* [1957] 1 QB 399, 408.
[70] *R v Clarke* (1972) 56 Cr App R 225, 228.
[71] As the Butler Committee noted in 1975, this component of the insanity doctrine excludes many individuals, such as those with mood disorders, who can only be described as 'mad' (United Kingdom, *Report of the Committee on Mentally Abnormal Offenders* (Cmnd 6244, 1975) ('Butler Report') para 18.6; see also S Dell, 'Wanted: An Insanity Defence that Can be Used' [1983] *Criminal Law Review* 431). For the Butler Committee, the 'main defect' of *M'Naghten* insanity lay in the fact that it relies on a 'now obsolete belief in the pre-eminent role of reason in controlling social behaviour' (para 18.6).
[72] See *R v Byrne* [1960] 2 QB 396 and Chapter 9.

judicial discussion in the first instance decision of *Kemp*, in which Justice Devlin stated that the phrase refers to 'the mental faculties of memory, reason and understanding' and was intended to be a limitation on the scope of 'defect of reason'.[73] A 'disease of the mind' may be organic or functional, permanent or 'transitory or intermittent' as long as it pertains at the time the defendant acts.[74] In *Bratty v Attorney-General for Northern Ireland*, Lord Denning stated that 'disease of the mind' includes but is not limited to the major mental disorders as identified by psychiatrists and other medical professionals.[75] What constitutes a 'disease of the mind' is a question of law for the judge and a range of conditions have been held to constitute diseases of the mind for the purposes of the insanity doctrine.[76]

The broad approach to 'disease of the mind'—as a 'disease which affects the proper functioning of the mind'[77]—has led to the odd situation where some physical disorders, such as hyperglycaemia, sleepwalking, and epilepsy, fall within the ambit of 'disease of the mind' and thus within the bounds of insanity for criminal law purposes.[78] In *Burgess*, which concerned sleepwalking, the Court of Appeal favoured expert evidence to the effect that the defendant was in a 'hysterical dissociative state' when the offence occurred, which was defined as a state 'in which, for psychological reasons, such as being overwhelmed by his emotions, the person's brain works in a different way'.[79] Thus, as Burgess suffered from 'an abnormality or disorder, albeit transitory, due to an internal factor', the only option open to him was insanity.[80] The inclusion of physical disorders within the scope of the insanity doctrine is the product of the organization of exculpatory mental incapacity doctrines according to the source of the defendant's incapacity (his or her disability).[81]

---

[73] *R v Kemp* [1957] 1 QB 399, 407. In *Kemp*, the Court brought arteriosclerosis within the bounds of 'disease of the mind' on the basis that 'hardening of the arteries is a disease which is shown on the evidence to be capable of affecting the mind in such a way as to cause a defect, temporarily or permanently, of its reasoning, understanding and so on' (408 per Justice Devlin).

[74] *R v Kemp* [1957] 1 QB 399, 406–7 per Lord Devlin; *R v Sullivan* [1984] 1 AC 156, 172 per Lord Diplock.

[75] *Bratty v Attorney-General for Northern Ireland* [1963] AC 386, 412. Bratty, who was charged with the murder of a woman he strangled with a stocking, testified that he had a 'terrible feeling' and that a 'sort of blackness' came over him at the time of the offence (extracted in *Bratty* 388) and his counsel adduced evidence of psychomotor epilepsy.

[76] These include alcoholism (*DPP v Beard* [1920] AC 479 at 501; *Attorney-General for Northern Ireland v Gallagher* [1963] AC 349), arteriosclerosis (*R v Kemp* [1957] 1 QB 399), hyperglycaemia (*R v Hennessy* [1989] 1 WLR 287), psychomotor epilepsy (referred to in *Bratty v Attorney-General for Northern Ireland* [1963] AC 386, 403 per Lord Kilmuir), and sleepwalking (*R v Burgess* [1991] 2 QB 92).

[77] *R v Hennessy* [1989] 1 WLR 287, 292.

[78] Re hyperglycaemia, see *R v Hennessy* [1989] 1 WLR 287; re sleepwalking, see *R v Burgess* [1991] 2 QB 92; re epilepsy, see *R v Sullivan* [1984] 1 AC 156.

[79] *R v Burgess* [1991] 2 QB 92, 101.

[80] *R v Burgess* [1991] 2 QB 92, 101.

[81] See T H Jones 'Insanity, Automatism and the Burden of Proof on the Accused' (1995) 111 *Law Quarterly Review* 475, 498; see also E Lederman 'Non-Insane and Insane Automatism: Reducing the Significance of a Problematic Distinction' (1985) 34 *International and Comparative Law Quarterly* 819, 824; P Robinson *Structure and Function in Criminal Law* (New York: Clarendon Press, 1997) 92–4. I discuss the significance of a disability-based system in Chapter 2.

In addition to consideration of the effect of a particular condition on an individual's 'mental faculties of memory, reason and understanding', whether mental disorder is prone to recur affects the categorization of a particular condition as a 'disease of the mind'. Like disposal, this consequentialist consideration is underpinned by a concern with dangerousness. In a comment implying a causal relationship between mental incapacity and violence, Lord Denning stated in *Bratty* that 'any mental disorder which has manifested itself in violence and is prone to recur is a disease of the mind'.[82] In *Burgess*, the Court of Appeal stated that, although the low probability of recurrence does not mean a condition is not a 'disease of the mind', 'if there is a danger of recurrence that may be an added reason for categorising the condition as a disease of the mind'.[83] This approach relies on a perceived causal relationship between mental disorders and violence such that consideration of the likelihood of recurrence can be appended to more materialist concerns with the effect on 'the mental faculties of memory, reason and understanding' of organic or functional disorders. This naturalized or taken-for-granted relationship between violence and mental disorder legitimates the broad scope of 'disease of the mind' for the purposes of the insanity doctrine.

As this approach to 'disease of the mind' makes clear, concern with dangerous individuals is driving the way in which the boundary of the insanity doctrine is drawn.[84] As Lord Denning stated in *Bratty*, an involuntary act by a person suffering from a 'disease of the mind' does not give rise to an unqualified acquittal because 'that would mean that he would be let out to do it again'.[85] Similarly, in *Hill v Baxter* Justice Devlin stated that 'if there is some temporary loss of consciousness arising accidentally, it is reasonable to hope that it will not be repeated and that it is safe to let an acquitted man go entirely free' but 'if disease is present, the same thing may happen again, and therefore, since 1800, the law has provided that persons acquitted on this ground should be subject to restraint'.[86] As I discuss in the next section of this chapter, the 'disease of the mind' requirement marks the boundary between insanity and automatism, and thus the boundary between the special verdict and an ordinary acquittal, and a broad approach to 'disease of the mind' has ensured a narrow scope for automatism. The effect of the judicial interpretation of 'disease of the mind' is to exclude those individuals whose incapacity ('defect of reason') is the result of an external as opposed to an internal cause. The presence of an external trigger, such as a diabetic's injection of insulin, means that an

---

[82] *Bratty v Attorney-General for Northern Ireland* [1963] AC 386, 412.
[83] *R v Burgess* [1991] 2 QB 92, 99.
[84] As a number of writers have argued, the absence of a disposal power under the automatism doctrine has resulted in a broad approach to the phrase 'disease of the mind': see, for example, Cross, 'Reflections on Bratty's Case' 239; Mackay *Mental Condition Defences* 58; A Norrie *Crime, Reason and History: A Critical Introduction to Criminal Law* (London: Butterworths, 2001) 182.
[85] *Bratty v Attorney-General for Northern Ireland* [1963] AC 386, 410.
[86] *Hill v Baxter* [1958] 1 QB 277, 285–6; see also *R v Sullivan* [1984] 1 AC 156, 172 per Lord Diplock. As Norrie concludes, 'a broad definition of mental disease opens up the possibilities for the court to order a form of social control where the alternative, under a finding of non-insane automatism, is that the accused walks free' (*Crime, Reason and History* 182).

individual can rely on automatism.[87] As R D Mackay argues, the scope of the phrase 'disease of the mind' has ensured that most states of automatism (where that term is used descriptively) fall within the bounds of insanity and thus result in special verdicts as opposed to acquittals.[88]

(iii) Knowledge of the 'nature and quality' of the Act or that it was Wrong

The third limb of *M'Naghten* insanity specifies two ways in which a 'defect of reason' must affect an individual if he or she is seeking to rely on the insanity doctrine: it must affect either his or her knowledge of the 'nature and quality' of the act, or his or her knowledge that it was 'wrong'. The third limb of *M'Naghten* insanity has been accorded a narrow scope and has been criticized on the basis that it restricts the exculpatory potential of the doctrine.[89] In relation to the 'nature and quality' of the act requirement, it is likely that the *M'Naghten* judges regarded this phrase as 'too clear to need explanation',[90] and it has only been subject to limited judicial attention in the twentieth century. The phrase has been interpreted to refer to the physical circumstances and consequences of the defendant's act.[91] The effect of this interpretation of the 'nature and quality' requirement is to exclude consideration of the defendant's appreciation of the 'moral or social nature of his act'.[92] As a result of this approach, under *M'Naghten* strictly interpreted, the content of a defendant's delusions will be determinative of whether he or she fits within *The Rules*.[93]

By contrast with the reference to the 'nature and quality' of the act, the meaning of the reference to knowledge of wrongness in the *M'Naghten Rules* has been the subject of significant debate, beginning in the decades after *M'Naghten*. Over the twentieth century, wrongness for the purposes of *M'Naghten* has come to be given a narrow scope, and, in this respect, the law of insanity evidences the rise of a technical conception of criminal responsibility in the late modern era.[94] In 1916, the Court of Criminal Appeal adjudicated the issue of the meaning of wrongness in the decision of *Codère*. In that decision, Lord Reading CJ stated that, for *M'Naghten* insanity, 'the standard to be applied is whether according to the

---

[87] See, for example, *Quick* [1973] 57 Cr App R 72.
[88] Mackay *Mental Condition Defences* 98; see also Norrie *Crime, Reason and History* 182.
[89] As R D Mackay writes, the effect of the narrow approach to the first and the third limb of *M'Naghten* is 'to exclude the vast majority of mentally disordered persons from the realm of the insanity doctrine, as inevitably in most cases they will know what they are doing and that the offence they are committing is legally wrong' (*Mental Condition Defences* 100).
[90] Walker *Crime and Insanity in England (Vol 1)* 101.
[91] *R v Codère* (1916) 12 Cr App R 21, 26–7.
[92] A E Gotlieb 'Intention, and Knowing the Nature and Quality of an Act' (1956) 19(3) *Modern Law Review* 270, 272.
[93] See Norrie *Crime, Reason and History* 180–1. To fit within *M'Naghten*, a defendant's delusions must be directly related to their criminal act (*Crime, Reason and History* 181).
[94] See Lacey 'Responsibility and Modernity in Criminal Law' 267–8 for discussion.

ordinary standard adopted by reasonable men the act was right or wrong'.[95] This interpretation meant *M'Naghten* wrongness was a moral standard. However, since this decision, the courts have moved to a narrower interpretation of 'wrongness' that equates it with 'legal wrong'. In *Windle* in 1952, the House of Lords concluded that 'wrongness' had always meant contrary to law. Lord Goddard CJ stated that:

> Courts of law can only distinguish between that which is in accordance with the law and that which is contrary to law ... the law cannot embark on the question, and it would be an unfortunate thing if it were left to juries to consider whether some particular act was morally right or wrong.[96]

The decision in *Windle* means that wrongness in *M'Naghten* connotes legal wrongness.[97] Mirroring other developments in the jurisprudence relating to mental incapacity doctrines, the reasoning in *Windle* indicates that a more formal and technical as opposed to moral-evaluative standard for exculpatory insanity is considered preferable in the current era.

This third limb of *M'Naghten* provides the clue to understanding the different ways in which insanity may exculpate an individual. Although the usual way in which the insanity doctrine is assumed to function is to negative the *mens rea* element required for an offence,[98] this is only a partial account of *M'Naghten* insanity. The relationship between insanity and *mens rea* is not so straightforward: insanity may negative *mens rea*, but it does not reduce to a denial of *mens rea*.[99] As several commentators have pointed out, knowledge of the wrongness of an act is not an application of the ordinary rules of *mens rea*.[100] An individual may have the *mens rea* for an offence, and yet, as a result of a defect of reason resulting from a disease of the mind, he or she may not know that the act was wrong. Thus, the insanity doctrine actually operates in two ways: it either negates an element of the offence (*mens rea*) or it has a more global impact, exculpating an individual although he or she performed the *actus reus* with the requisite *mens rea*.[101]

---

[95] *R v Codère* (1916) 12 Cr App R 21, 27.
[96] *R v Windle* [1952] 2 QB 826, 833.
[97] In a persuasive argument based on nineteenth-century English authorities, the High Court of Australia concluded that, *contra Codère* and *Windle*, the notion of 'wrong' employed in *M'Naghten* was the same as 'right and wrong' or 'good and evil' (*R v Stapleton* (1952) 86 CLR 358, 369). In England and Wales, there is some indication that wrongness is interpreted more flexibly in practice (Mackay *Mental Condition Defences* 104; T Ward 'Magistrates, Insanity and the Common Law' [1997] *Criminal Law Review* 796, 803).
[98] See, for example, Butler Report para 18.22. For instance, Glanville Williams argues that the *M'Naghten* test amounts to 'little more than an assertion that the defendant cannot be convicted without the necessary mental element' (G Williams *Textbook of Criminal Law* (London: Stevens, 1978) 593). This argument is supported by the fact that the insanity doctrine is available only to offences with a *mens rea* element: *DPP v H* [1997] 1 WLR 1406, 1409.
[99] As Celia Wells points out, the proposition that insanity negatives *mens rea* is true only where *mens rea* refers to a subjective mental element (C Wells 'Whither Insanity?' [1983] *Criminal Law Review* 787, 794).
[100] See A Ashworth *Principles of Criminal Law* (Oxford: OUP, 2009) 143–4; J C Smith 'Insanity—Available as a Defence in Summary Trials' [1997] *Criminal Law Review* 129, 133; Ward 'Magistrates, Insanity and the Common Law' 802.
[101] See Colvin 'Exculpatory Defences in Criminal Law' 394; P Robinson 'Criminal Law Defences: A Systematic Analysis' (1982) 82 *Columbia Law Review* 199, 205. This idea about the more global

The Appearance of a Discrete Automatism Doctrine and the Rise of Disability as a Basis for Insanity

In this section, I pick up the historical story again, to chart the appearance of a discrete automatism doctrine, and the rise of disability as a basis for insanity. There were three developments in the law of insanity in the first half of the twentieth century that prepared the ground for the appearance of a discrete automatism doctrine (and indirectly contributed to the rise to prominence of a narrow idea of disability, as a basis for exculpatory insanity). The first development related to the scope of the insanity doctrine, which was hollowed out by two distinct changes to mental incapacity more broadly. These changes reflected the ongoing formalization of the doctrines across the terrain of mental incapacity. With the passage of the Infanticide Acts 1922 and 1938, all killings of newborn children by their mothers were taken outside the reach of the law of murder and the law of insanity.[102] In addition, the House of Lords decision in *Beard's Case*, considering the effect of intoxication on an individual charged with a criminal offence, dismissed the *M'Naghten* test as irrelevant to such an issue. The Court concluded that insanity and intoxication are distinct, and that it is 'inconvenient to use the same language in charging juries in relation to different defences'.[103] The reasoning of the House of Lords here hints at the rise of a technical conception of insanity, according to which it was a more circumscribed notion with precise meaning, rather than a more nebulous notion connoting incapacity in a general way.

The second relevant development in the first half of the twentieth century related to the enhanced profile of the *actus reus* component of criminal offences. In the House of Lords decision in *Woolmington*, in addition to their famous comments on the burden of proof, the judges made reference to a requirement that an offence consist of a voluntary act on the part of the defendant. The House of Lords stated that, when dealing with a murder charge, the Crown must prove 'death as a result of the voluntary act of the accused' as well as malice on the part of the defendant.[104] The decision in *Woolmington* does not elaborate on what has come to be called the voluntary act requirement. However, in approving of the earlier decision of *Davies*, which held that there is no onus on the defendant to prove that the act alleged was accidental where intent was an element of the offence,[105] it seems that the reference to a voluntary act in *Woolmington* connoted non-accidental or deliberate. It was on top of these ideas about voluntariness that a discrete automatism doctrine would later develop.

---

impact of mental incapacity on a particular individual connects to my discussion of the formal qualities of 'madness' on the mental incapacity terrain: see Chapter 3.

[102] See further Chapter 8 on infanticide.
[103] *DPP v Beard* [1920] AC 479, 506 per Lord Birkenhead. See further Chapter 7 on intoxication.
[104] *Woolmington v DPP* [1935] All ER 1, 8 per Lord Sankey. The *Woolmington* Court also stated that the persuasive burden of proof of insanity lay with the defendant. I discuss this in Chapter 6 on evidence and proof of exculpatory incapacity.
[105] *R v Davies* [1913] 1 KB 573.

Around the same time as the decision in *Woolmington* was handed down, judicial and legislative discussion of *M'Naghten* insanity combined to definitively exclude what was termed 'irresistible impulse' or 'uncontrollable impulse' from the reach of insanity. The definitive exclusion of 'irresistible impulse' was the third of the three developments preparing the ground for the appearance of automatism. As a disorder of volition, 'irresistible impulse' had haunted the development and operation of the law of insanity throughout the nineteenth century (in ideas of 'moral insanity', for example). In 1923, the Committee on Insanity and Crime (the Atkin Committee), which had been convened to advise on reform of the law on insanity, proposed a new defence of 'irresistible impulse', which Tony Ward argues was designed to 'provide a legal justification for verdicts which were reached by juries under the existing [*M'Naghten*] *Rules*'.[106] At the same time, in *Kopsch*, the Court of Criminal Appeal decisively rejected the proposition that irresistible impulse fell within the bounds of the insanity doctrine. The Court referred to 'uncontrollable impulse' as a 'fantastic theory', which, if it were to become part of the criminal law, would be 'merely subversive'.[107]

Taken together, the hollowing out of insanity, the *Woolmington* decision, and the definitive exclusion of 'irresistible impulse' from the insanity doctrine amplified the importance of voluntariness, will, or consciousness for criminal responsibility and shrank the official space provided for exculpation where these elements were absent. This effect came to be felt in the second half of the twentieth century. By the 1950s, when the first reference to a discrete automatism doctrine appeared in the case law, the *M'Naghten Rules* had been conclusively drawn to exclude volitional impairment, and diminished responsibility, which encompasses volitional impairment, had not yet been introduced into the English and Welsh law.[108] The development of a discrete doctrine of automatism at this point represented a judicial response to the restricted scope of insanity and the formalization of other mental incapacity doctrines, onto which was overlaid a growing sense of the inappropriateness of the label insanity, with its increasingly technical connotations, for all claims of exculpatory 'madness'.

The appearance of a discrete doctrine of automatism marked a reconfiguration of the merciful space around exculpatory mental incapacity. This reconfiguration has gone largely unremarked. In part because the appearance of a discrete doctrine of

---

[106] T Ward 'Law, Common Sense and the Authority of Science: Expert Witnesses and Criminal Insanity in England, CA 1840–1940' (1997) 6(3) *Social and Legal Studies* 343, 354; see also Smith *Lawyers, Legislators and Theorists* 323; T Ward 'The Sad Subject of Infanticide: Law, Medicine and Child Murder 1860–1938' (1999) 8(2) *Social and Legal Studies* 163, 168. The Atkin Committee was broadly supportive of the *M'Naghten* formulation of insanity, concluding that *M'Naghten* was 'in substance, sound', but proposed explicitly encompassing irresistible impulse as a basis for exculpation (United Kingdom *Report of the Committee on Insanity and Crime* (Cmd 2005, 1924), 7–8). The subsequent Criminal Responsibility (Trials) Bill 1924, which proposed enlarging the *M'Naghten Rules* to include defendants 'wholly incapable of resisting the impulse to do the act', was defeated. See for discussion Smith *Lawyers, Legislators and Theorists* 323; T Ward 'A Terrible Responsibility' 372.

[107] *R v Kopsch* (1925) 19 Cr App Rep 50, 51–2 per Lord Hewart.

[108] Homicide Act 1957, s 2, as amended by the Coroners and Justice Act 2009; *R v Byrne* [1960] 2 QB 396. See Chapter 9 for discussion.

automatism was depicted as merely a matter of making explicit what had always been implicit in this area of criminal law, and because the significance of the formal legal development was obscured by the descriptive use of the label automatism (evident in terms such as 'insane automatism' in place of insanity and 'self-induced automatism' in place of intoxication), the novelty of the new contours of the terrain of mental incapacity seems to have been regarded as more a matter of nomenclature than substance. The general understanding, more implicit than explicit, seems to have been that the formal change marked more faithful adherence to the organization of mental incapacity doctrines along the lines of the cause of incapacitated conduct.[109] But, what is as significant is the way in which this change quarantined the broad, moralized notion of incapacity that underpins the doctrine of automatism. I return to this point about the basis of automatism in the next section of the chapter.

At the same time as the terrain of mental incapacity was undergoing reconfiguration to produce a discrete automatism doctrine, broader social developments, extending well beyond the bounds of the criminal law, were coming to have a profound although largely taken-for-granted effect on the law of insanity. This effect—the rise of a notion of disability as a basis for insanity, definitively displacing the broader and more moralized notion of incapacity—was generated by the rising social profile of psychiatry and psychology as forms of expert knowledge. The post-war era was something of a high-water mark of faith in the transformative potential of this type of knowledge and, relatedly, in the rehabilitative ideal that suffused the criminal justice field at the time.[110] It was in this era that such knowledges took on mass influence. It was in the 1950s and 1960s, when economic, social, and cultural developments combined to forge a focus on individual authenticity, self-determination, and self-expression—in short, a psychological way of thinking—to spread among the populations of societies such as those of England and Wales.[111] Under these changed social conditions, insanity for criminal law purposes, which had already come to be more narrowly drawn, attracted a more medicalized meaning, a change which seems to have had progressively greater impact up to the current era.

In the absence of change to the *M'Naghten Rules*, it is necessary to look beyond the 'law on the books' for support for my suggestion that these extra-legal developments had a profound impact on exculpatory insanity in the second half of the twentieth century. Some evidence can be gleaned from the difference between the first and second generations of reform recommendations regarding *M'Naghten* insanity, issued in the 1950s and 1970s, respectively. The first generation of reform

---

[109] See Mackay *Mental Condition Defences* 97 for discussion of the need for a distinction between what he refers to as insane and non-insane automatism.

[110] In David Garland's analysis, this era marked the 'most vigorous' developments in penal-welfare strategies: see D Garland *The Culture of Control: Crime and Social Order in Contemporary Society* (Oxford: OUP, 2001) 34, and more generally. For a discussion of these broader social developments on the treatment of 'madness' in prison, see T Seddon *Punishment and Madness: Governing Prisoners with Mental Health Problems* (London: Routledge, 2007) 33–9.

[111] See generally N Rose *Governing the Soul: The Shaping of the Private Self* (London: Free Association Press, 1999); N Rose *Inventing our Selves: Psychology, Power, and Personhood* (Cambridge: CUP, 1996).

proposals is represented by the Royal Commission on Capital Punishment. In its 1953 Report, the Commission recommended that the jury should be directed to determine whether 'at the time of the act the accused was suffering from a disease of the mind (or mental deficiency) to such a degree that he ought not to be held responsible'.[112] As Smith argues, this proposal rested on the belief that 'responsibility was essentially a subjective, ethical question, making the relationship between insanity and criminal responsibility inherently incapable of precise definition'.[113] Alongside such a belief, this proposal also exudes a confidence about the broad acceptability of an overtly moralized insanity law. By the time of the second generation of reform recommendations, the overtly-moralized basis for exculpation via insanity had become less palatable. In 1975, the Butler Committee proposed a new special verdict, 'not guilty on evidence of mental disorder', which was to be more closely linked to medical concepts and indeed to medical evidence.[114] The contrast between these proposals indicates that, even in the absence of change to the *M'Naghten Rules*, insanity came to be thought of as grounded in a more medicalized notion of disability. This change in the grounding of exculpation on the basis of insanity is also evident in changes to practices of evidence and procedure governing insanity, which are canvassed in Chapter 6.

The Persistence of Incapacity: the Requirements of the Doctrine of Automatism

As a discrete doctrine, automatism now occupies an area that had been taken up by a capacious informal insanity law operating under a flexible criminal process. When compared with insanity, automatism rests on a broader and more overtly moralized notion of incapacity, as opposed to a narrower, more technical, and medicalized notion of disability. The doctrine of automatism has been defined according to three components, and I structure my discussion of the law around them.

---

[112] United Kingdom Royal Commission on Capital Punishment 1949–1953 Report (Cmd 8932, 1953) para 333.
[113] Smith *Lawyers, Legislators and Theorists* 327. While this approach was 'supremely pragmatic' (and perhaps captures jury practice), it unnerved a number of commentators (including a minority of members of the Commission) who argued against the Commission's proposal and 'little if any support emerged for the Report's proposal': see *Lawyers, Legislators and Theorists* 327–8.
[114] Aiming to 'avoid the use of medical terms about which there may be disputed interpretations or whose meaning may change with the years' (Butler Report para 18.17), the reformulated defence would have been comprised of two parts: (a) did the defendant know what he or she was doing?; or (b) was he or she suffering from 'severe mental illness or severe subnormality' at the time of the act? 'Severe subnormality' was to be defined as in the Mental Health Act 1959 to refer to 'a state of arrested or incomplete development of mind' (Butler Report para 18.30). 'Severe mental illness' was to be defined to encompass significant impairment of intellectual functions, mood, thinking, perception and delusional beliefs (Butler Report para 18.35). The language of the proposed new verdict—'severe mental illness or severe subnormality'—would have meant that, in practice, expert witnesses would have decided the availability of insanity (Mackay *Mental Condition Defences* 137), and unlike the Committee's proposals on disposal of insane defendants (Butler Report paras 18.42–18.45), which were implemented in the Criminal Procedure (Insanity and Unfitness to Plead) Act 1991, the proposals about the substance of insanity were not implemented.

(i) 'Total destruction of voluntary control'

To make out a plea of automatism, a defendant must suffer a 'total destruction of voluntary control'.[115] This must have the effect that the defendant does not understand the nature and quality of his or her act.[116] In a line of cases concerning driving offences, the courts have concluded that anything short of 'total destruction of voluntary control', such as impaired or reduced control, is insufficient for exculpation on the basis of automatism. Because nothing short of involuntariness or unconsciousness is sufficient for automatism, it does not exculpate individuals who are only partially incapacitated. Although it has been recognized that consciousness and control over action are matters of degree,[117] automatism in England and Wales does not (at least formally) countenance anything short of a 'total destruction of voluntary control'. The requirement of total loss of control has a profound effect, significantly restricting the availability of automatism.[118] In addition, over and above the practical effect of this requirement, because the automatism doctrine is available only to those defendants who are *un*conscious or acting *in*voluntarily, automatistic defendants are able to be constructed as abnormal (a difference of kind, as opposed to a difference of degree), even if their abnormality is only transient.[119]

There is ambiguity about whether automatistic incapacity centres on involuntariness or unconsciousness or whether it may be either. The former approach emphasizes the effect of the relevant external factor on action or *actus reus*, and the latter emphasizes its effect on mental state or *mens rea*. The case law on automatism furnishes evidence of each approach to the meaning of automatistic incapacity. On the one hand, some of the judicial and academic discussions of automatism suggest that it is defined by the presence of involuntary conduct.[120] On the other hand,

---

[115] *Attorney-General's Reference (No 2 of 1992)* [1994] QB 91, 105 per Lord Taylor of Gosforth.

[116] *R v Hennessy* [1989] 1 WLR 287, 291; see also S Prevezer 'Automatism and Involuntary Conduct' [1958] *Criminal Law Review* 440, 440–1.

[117] In *Isitt*, Lawton LJ stated that 'it is a matter of human experience that the mind does not always operate in top gear. There may be some difficulty in functioning': *R v Isitt* (1978) 67 Cr App R 44, 48. For discussion, see N Morris 'Somnambulistic Homicide: Ghosts, Spiders and North Koreans' (1951) 5 *Res Judicatae* 29, 32; see also N Levy and T Bayne 'Doing without Deliberation: Automatism, Automaticity and Moral Accountability' (2004) 16(3) *International Review of Psychiatry* 209.

[118] In *Watmore v Jenkins*, the defendant was charged with dangerous driving following a hypoglycaemic episode and acquitted. His acquittal was overturned on appeal on the basis that he had not suffered a 'complete destruction of voluntary control' ([1962] 2 QB 572,587). In *Broome v Perkins* (*Broome v Perkins* (1987) 85 Cr App R 321), the Court concluded that automatism was unavailable because, at certain stages of the journey, 'the defendant's mind was controlling his limbs and that thus he was driving' (333). Likewise, in *Attorney-General's Reference (No 2 of 1992)* [1994] QB 91, the defendant, who adduced expert evidence that he was in a condition of 'driving without awareness', was not able to rely on a defence of automatism because he had merely 'reduced' control (105).

[119] I take up this issue of differences of degree versus differences of kind in the context of diminished responsibility: see Chapter 9.

[120] See, for example, *R v Harrison-Owen* [1951] 2 All ER 726; *Attorney-General's Reference (No 2 of 1992)* [1994] QB 91; S Yeo 'Clarifying Automatism' (2002) 25 *International Journal of Law and Psychiatry* 445, 446. The early definition of automatism offered in *Watmore v Jenkins* (*Watmore v Jenkins* [1962] 2 QB 572) reflects this approach to the doctrine. In that case, Winn J opined that

some discussions about automatism centre on unconsciousness.[121] It is possible that ambiguity about the meaning of acting in a state of automatism is unavoidable because, as Glanville Williams suggests in relation to epilepsy, the distinction between impairment of consciousness and impairment of self-control is a fine one.[122] Indeed, alongside discussions of automatism as either involuntariness or unconsciousness, there are a number of comments encompassing both ideas. In perhaps the most famous definition of automatism, Viscount Kilmuir defined automatism as:

> connoting the state of a person who, though capable of action, is not conscious of what he is doing. ... It means unconscious, involuntary action and it is a defense because the mind does not go with what is being done.[123]

Overall, the ambiguity about the kind of incapacity that forms the basis of automatism indicates that the doctrine operates primarily through the principle of non-culpability. If, in Paul Robinson's words, nearly any disability may give rise to the 'involuntariness defence' because the resulting 'dysfunction is apparently sufficiently gross that it establishes its own abnormality',[124] the question of whether it entails involuntariness or unconsciousness or either is not crucial to its coherence.

The significance of the ambiguity about whether automatistic incapacity centres on involuntariness or unconsciousness lies in the way in which automatism relates to the elements of the offence. *Contra* arguments that automatism goes to either the *actus reus* or the *mens rea*, the most precise way to conceptualize the relationship between the automatism doctrine and the elements of a criminal offence is that it relates to both *actus reus* and *mens rea*. Automatism is a claim of incapacity that has both a physical and a mental dimension. As Norval Morris writes, when pleading automatism, the defendant is claiming that the mental element of the *actus reus* (voluntariness) is lacking or, alternatively, that the physical element of the *mens rea* (consciousness) is lacking.[125] Thus, as Andrew Ashworth suggests, although 'one way of rationalizing' automatism is to maintain that it 'negates the *actus reus*, since

---

automatism was 'a modern catch-phrase which the courts have not accepted as connoting any wider or looser concept than involuntary movement of the body or limbs of a person' (586).

[121] See, for example, *R v Stripp* (1979) 69 Cr App R 318, 323 per Ormrod LJ. For discussion, see I D Elliott 'Automatism and Trial by Jury' (1967–1968) 6 *Melbourne University Law Review* 53, 60; P Fairall 'Automatism' (1981) 5 *Criminal Law Journal* 335, 335 and P Fairall 'Voluntariness, Automatism and Insanity: Reflections on Falconer' (1993) 17 *Criminal Law Journal* 81; B McSherry, 'Epilepsy, Automatism and Culpable Driving' (2002) 21 *Medicine and the Law* 133; G Williams, *Textbook of Criminal Law* (London: Stevens, 1978) 608–9. In *Charlson* (*R v Charlson* [1955] 1 WLR 317), Barry J compared the defendant's case with that of an epileptic: 'the actions of an epileptic are automatic and unconscious, and his will and his consciousness are not applied to what he is doing; he is not in control of his actions' (320).

[122] Williams *Textbook of Criminal Law* 611.

[123] *Bratty v Attorney-General for Northern Ireland* [1960] AC 386, 401, quoting the Court of Criminal Appeal judgment in *Bratty*. Similarly, in *R v Sullivan* [1984] 1 AC 156, 173 Lord Diplock referred to actions which were 'unconscious and thus "involuntary" in the legal sense of that term'.

[124] Robinson *Structure and Function in Criminal Law* 85–6.

[125] Morris 'Somnambulistic Homicide' 30; see also S Prevezer 'Automatism and Involuntary Conduct' 445.

it shows that the conduct or omission was not the result of the defendant *acting* but of something *happening to* the defendant', automatism is actually a broader claim, more a denial of authorship.[126] On this basis, it is clear that there is something of a disjunction between the voluntary act requirement of an offence and the exculpatory doctrine of automatism. The act requirement (voluntariness) is an offence doctrine (which excludes mere thoughts from the reach of the criminal law and triggers the special rules that ground liability for omissions), while involuntariness is more accurately conceptualized as an exculpatory doctrine, functioning to ensure that certain actors who have caused harm are not liable on the basis that they cannot control their conduct.[127] The idea that automatism entails a broad claim along the lines of a 'denial of authorship' hints at the more global way in which incapacity affects particular individuals.[128]

(ii) Internal/External Factor Distinction

If an individual suffers a 'total destruction of voluntary control', it must also be the result of an external factor if he or she is to come within the bounds of the automatism doctrine. A range of external factors has grounded claims to automatism.[129] As Lord Denning cautioned in *Bratty v Attorney-General for Northern Ireland*, 'it is not every involuntary act which leads to a complete acquittal'.[130] If an individual's behaviour is the result of an internal factor, that is, it arises from a 'disease of the mind', he or she will only be able to rely on the insanity doctrine. As mentioned above, the principle that the existence of an internal cause precludes reliance on the automatism doctrine was developed in the first instance decision of *Kemp*, and confirmed by the House of Lords in *Bratty*.[131] In *Bratty*, the House of Lords stated that because, in that case, the only basis for the allegedly unconscious act was a 'disease of the mind' (in that case, arising from psychomotor epilepsy),

---

[126] See Ashworth *Principles of Criminal Law* 88–90.
[127] See Robinson *Structure and Function in Criminal Law* 31–6: see also W Wilson *Criminal Law: Doctrine and Theory* 2nd edn (London: Longman, 2003) 227. This disjuncture between the voluntariness requirement and exculpatory automatism has been regarded as something of a paradox in criminal law. Norrie argues that the criminal law employs a 'narrow physical conception of the nature of involuntariness' for the purposes of the law of *actus reus* which 'squeezes out subjective excuses' derived from broader moral bases (*Crime, Reason and History* 110). But, Norrie argues, consideration of prior fault as required by the automatism doctrine has the effect of 're-moralising' involuntariness for the purposes of exculpation, ensuring 'convictions in situations where the judges believe that control must be affirmed, and application of the technical test might secure an acquittal' (*Crime, Reason and History* 111). Norrie concludes that the 'structural dynamic of excluding and re-admitting substantive moral issues' lies at the root of the modern criminal law (*Crime, Reason and History* 58).
[128] I discuss this point about the more global impact of mental incapacity on particular individuals in my analysis of the formal qualities of 'madness' on the mental incapacity terrain: see Chapter 3.
[129] These include cerebral concussion (*Bratty v Attorney-General for Northern Ireland* [1960] AC 386, 414 per Lord Denning), a blow from a stone or an attack from a swarm of bees (referred to in *Hill v Baxter* [1958] 1 QB 277, 283 per Lord Goddard), hypoglycaemia (*R v Quick* [1973] 57 Cr App R 722; *R v Budd* [1962] Crim LR 49; *R v Bingham* [1991] Crim LR 433) and dissociation (per the Canadian decision of *R v Rabey* (1980) 15 CR (3d) 225; *R v T* [1990] Crim LR 256).
[130] *Bratty v Attorney-General for Northern Ireland* [1963] AC 386, 410.
[131] See *R v Kemp* [1957] 1 QB 399 and *Bratty v Attorney-General for Northern Ireland* [1963] AC 386.

'there can be no room for the alternative defence of automatism'.[132] If, however, an individual can legitimately rely on both an internal and an external cause for his or her automatistic behaviour, he or she is entitled to raise both automatism and insanity.[133]

Although the internal/external distinction, built on the M'Naghten requirement of a 'disease of the mind', is an 'intellectually tidy arrangement',[134] it is an artificial approach to exculpatory mental incapacity producing arbitrary results. The use of the internal/external factor distinction to mark the boundary between automatism and insanity has led to the odd situation where a diabetic individual can fall into one or other category, depending on the level of insulin in his or her blood. If a diabetic commits an offence when he or she has too little insulin (high blood sugar or hyperglycaemia), he or she will only be able to rely on insanity, not automatism, because diabetes is regarded as an internal factor.[135] On the other hand, if a diabetic defendant commits an offence when he or she has an excess of insulin in their bloodstream (low blood-sugar or hypoglycaemia), he or she will be able to rely on the defence of automatism because the injection of insulin will amount to an external factor.[136]

In addition to the arbitrary results produced by the internal/external factor distinction, and despite its apparent technicality, there is no clear or necessary line between internal and external causes.[137] This is demonstrated by the change in the status of sleepwalking defendants. In England and Wales, sleepwalking, or somnambulism, was regarded as a condition that gave rise to automatism until the

---

[132] *Bratty v Attorney-General for Northern Ireland* [1963] AC 386, 404 per Lord Kilmuir; see also at 410 per Lord Denning.

[133] *R v Roach* [2001] EWCA Crim 2698). In *Roach*, the Court stated that 'the legal definition of automatism allows for the fact that, if external factors are operative upon an underlying condition which would not otherwise produce a state of automatism, then a defence of (non-insane) automatism should be left to the jury' ([28] per Potter LJ). This rule allowing an individual to raise both automatism and insanity is subject to the rules of evidence and procedure governing exculpatory incapacity. See Chapter 6.

[134] E Baker 'Human Rights, M'Naghten and the 1991 Act' [1994] *Criminal Law Review* 84, 89.

[135] In *R v Hennessy* [1989] 1 WLR 287, the defendant was charged with one count of theft (of a car) and one count of driving while disqualified. Hennessy claimed that he was in a state of automatism at the time of the offences, admitting that he had failed to take his insulin for 'two or three days' before he committed the offences. The Court of Appeal upheld Hennessy's convictions and the ruling of the trial judge that his state of mind was caused by a disease (diabetes) and so the defence of automatism was not available.

[136] *R v Quick* [1973] 57 Cr App R 722; *R v Bingham* [1991] Crim LR 433. Quick, an insulin-dependent diabetic who was charged with assault occasioning actual bodily harm, claimed that he was hypoglycaemic at the time of the assault because he had taken insulin but had not eaten much food. On appeal, the Court of Appeal ruled that the defence of automatism should have been left to the jury because a 'malfunctioning of the mind of transitory effect caused by the application to the body of some external factor such as violence, drugs [such as insulin], including anaesthetics, alcohol and hypnotic influences cannot fairly be said to be due to disease' as is required for the 'disease of the mind' element of the *M'Naghten Rules* (922 per Lord Justice Lawton).

[137] This has been widely recognized: see for instance M Goode 'On Subjectivity and Objectivity in Denial of Responsibility: Reflections on Reading Radford' (1987) 11 *Criminal Law Journal* 131, 141; J Edwards 'Automatism and Criminal Responsibility' (1958) 21 *Modern Law Review* 375, 377; R F Schopp *Automatism, Insanity and the Psychology of Criminal Responsibility* (Cambridge: CUP, 1991) 83–4.

decision of *Burgess* in 1991, when it was held to be a 'disease of the mind', thus giving rise to insanity.[138] Burgess appealed his conviction for wounding with intent to cause grievous bodily harm (inflicted on a friend) on the basis that he was sleepwalking during the events that comprised the offence and should have been able to rely on automatism. The Court of Appeal dismissed the appeal, concluding that, on the evidence, the defendant's condition was properly characterized by the trial judge as a 'disease of the mind'.[139] Beyond the issue of its spurious technicality, and its arbitrary results, the internal/external factor distinction has also been criticized because it has no basis in expert medical knowledge. As the Butler Committee stated, the 'sharp divide' between insanity and automatism is 'unknown to medical science'.[140]

For the purposes of automatism, external factors are limited to physical or tangible causes. As mentioned above, in *Burgess*, the defendant argued that he was in an automatistic state when the events comprising the offence took place. In concluding that there were no external factors operating on the defendant at the time of the offence, the Court of Appeal commented that 'the possible disappointment or frustration caused by unrequited love is not to be equated with something such as concussion'.[141] Similarly, in *Hennessy*, the defendant was unsuccessful in arguing that stress, anxiety, and depression were external factors for the purposes of automatism. There, the Court of Appeal concluded that stress, anxiety, and depression may be 'the result of the operation of external factors' but are not 'in themselves separately or together external factors of the kind capable in law of causing or contributing to a state of automatism'.[142] A justification for the restriction of external factors to physical factors is proffered by the Court in *Hennessy* which concluded that factors such as stress and anxiety were prone to recur and lacked 'the feature of novelty or accident which is the basis of the distinction drawn by Lord Diplock in Reg. v Sullivan'.[143]

As this use of the 'feature of novelty or accident' to prop up the restriction of the category of external factors suggests, concern with dangerousness has driven the process of drawing a line between internal and external factors. A number of commentators make this point.[144] The plea of automatism, arising from an external

---

[138] *R v Tolson* (1889) 23 QBD 168; *Bratty v Attorney-General for Northern Ireland* [1963] AC 386, 409 per Lord Denning and at 415 per Lord Morris.
[139] *R v Burgess* [1991] 2 QB 92, 101 per Lord Lane CJ; see R D Mackay and B J Mitchell 'Sleepwalking, Automatism and Insanity' [2006] *Criminal Law Review* 901 for discussion.
[140] Butler Report para 18.22; see also I Ebrahim et al 'Violence, Sleepwalking and the Criminal Law: Part 1: The Medical Aspects' [2005] *Criminal Law Review* 601, 603; P Fenwick, 'Somnambulism and the Law: A Review' (1987) 5(3) *Behaviourial Sciences and the Law* 343, 350 and P Fenwick 'Epilepsy, Automatism and the English Law' (1997) 16 *Medicine and the Law* 349, 351. The distinction drawn by Lawton LJ in *Quick* between hypoglycaemia and hyperglycaemia has been described as 'medically naïve' (C Howard and P T D'Orban 'Violence in Sleep: Medico-Legal Issues and Two Case Reports' (1987) 17 *Psychological Medicine* 915, 923).
[141] *R v Burgess* [1991] 2 QB 92, 98 per Lord Lane CJ.
[142] *R v Hennessy* [1989] 1 WLR 287, 294.
[143] *R v Hennessy* [1989] 1 WLR 287, 294.
[144] See, for example, Lederman 'Non-Insane and Insane Automatism' 824; Mackay *Mental Condition Defences* 41, 58; Schopp *Automatism, Insanity* 81–3; W Wilson et al 'Violence, Sleepwalking

factor, marks out an individual who is less dangerous (or not dangerous at all) when compared with an insane defendant. An external cause, such as an excess of insulin caused by an injection, or a concussion caused by a head injury, is 'externally demonstrable'[145] and constructed as non-replicable or one-off and can therefore safely fall within the scope of automatism. The relevance of a concern with dangerousness to the courts is neatly captured by Justice Devlin who stated that 'if there is some temporary loss of consciousness arising accidentally, it is reasonable to hope that it will not be repeated and that it is safe to let an acquitted man go entirely free'.[146]

(iii) **Prior Fault**

Even if an individual suffers a 'total destruction of voluntary control' and it is the result of an external factor, he or she will only be able to rely on automatism if he or she is not in any way to blame for the automatistic state. This third and final component of automatism circumscribes exculpatory involuntariness along moral culpability lines (and ensures the scope of the doctrine lies in judicial hands).[147] The effect of this component of automatism has been felt chiefly in relation those cases of automatistic behaviour caused by intoxication (via alcohol or drugs), which have been hived off and dealt with via the law of intoxication (which is also known as 'self-induced automatism'), an area of law marked by a palpable moral condemnation of intoxicated offending.[148] Beyond quarantining automatistic behaviour caused by alcohol or drugs from that caused by other factors, the requirement that an automatistic individual evidence no prior fault has the potential to disqualify other individuals who might seek to claim exculpation on the basis of automatism. Some suggestion to this effect was given by the Court in *Bailey*, where the defendant had taken insulin but neglected to eat as his doctor had directed. The Court of Appeal held that an automatism plea was open to the defendant,

---

and the Criminal Law: Part 2: The Legal Aspects' [2005] *Criminal Law Review* 614, 617. As these commentators explain, policy concerns have meant that the automatism doctrine, which results in a complete acquittal, has been narrowly drawn, while the insanity doctrine requirement of a 'disease of the mind' has been expansively drawn, ensuring that dangerous defendants are caught by the latter and subject to the disposal powers attached to the special verdict.

[145] Goode 'On Subjectivity and Objectivity' 143.
[146] *Hill v Baxter* [1958] 1 QB 277, 285.
[147] As a normative matter, this position has been advocated by several commentators: see, for example, S Kadish 'Excusing Crime' [1987] *California Law Review* 257, 266–7, 286–9. It has also been suggested that the restriction around prior fault should apply to insanity: see E W Mitchell *Self-Made Madness: Rethinking Illness and Criminal Responsibility* (Aldershot: Ashgate, 2003).
[148] In *Bratty v Attorney-General for Northern Ireland* [1963] AC 386, the House of Lords stated that the automatism doctrine must be viewed as separate and distinct from the plea of voluntary intoxication (414 per Lord Denning; see also *R v Lipman* [1970] 1 QB 152). The jurisprudence on intoxicated offending is marked by the idea that a defendant is culpable for voluntary intoxication. In *Majewski* (*DPP v Majewski* [1977] AC 443), Lord Edmund-Davies contrasted cases of voluntary intoxication by drugs or alcohol with those excuses in which 'the actor is wholly free from fault in relation to the onset of a mental state' (487). Further, the idea that the defendant is at fault for becoming intoxicated in the first place is one of the rationales for the particular rules comprising the law on intoxicated offending (see, for example, *R v Hardie* (1985) 80 Cr App R 157, 162 per Parker LJ). See further Chapter 7.

had he raised sufficient evidence of it.[149] According to the Court, the relevant question is 'whether the prosecution has proved the necessary element of recklessness'.[150] This comment suggests that the courts might engage in a general inquiry into the defendant's prior fault in determining whether he or she may make use of the law of automatism.

The no prior fault requirement for automatism is typically hidden in the definition of voluntariness. As only certain types of conduct (those for which the defendant is not at fault) will be regarded as 'involuntary', the descriptive aspect of automatism (was a defendant in a state of automatism?) obscures its moral-evaluative aspect (does he or she deserve to be held liable for the offence?). But it is this broad moral-evaluative aspect of the doctrine that forms its core, and marks automatism out on the mental incapacity terrain. As I discuss in Chapter 2, unlike other mental incapacity doctrines, automatism does not prescribe a particular disability as a baseline for exculpation.[151] This moral-evaluative aspect of automatism accounts for what Robinson calls the 'special role' of the 'involuntariness defence' in the system of 'excuse defences'.[152] Robinson's conceptualization of automatism suggests that the fact that the doctrine tracks lines of moral culpability is justified on the basis of the shortcomings of other 'excuse defences'. In recognizing the 'catch-all' character of automatism, Robinson's account of the doctrine as a companion to other doctrines pinpoints the valuable flexibility encoded in exculpation which is independent of a particular disability. Robinson suggests that, in practice, 'the absence of a disability requirement has the collateral effect of broadening the defence to cases beyond instances of complete lack of volition'; but, for Robinson, if something less than a 'total lack of volition' forms the basis for a successful plea, this may be justified because it represents 'a proper result in cases of blamelessness that otherwise would be denied a defence'.[153]

---

[149] *R v Bailey* [1983] 1 WLR 760. Bailey was charged with wounding with intent to cause grievous bodily harm under the Offences Against the Person Act 1861. At first instance, the recorder directed the jury that self-induced incapacity could not form the basis of an automatism doctrine and the defendant was convicted. On the basis that 'there may be material distinctions between a man who consumes alcohol or takes dangerous drugs and one who fails to take sufficient food after insulin', the Court held that Bailey's self-induced automatism (or intoxication) could be taken into account in relation to any offence, not just a 'specific intent' offence: *R v Bailey* [1983] 1 WLR 760, 764–5 per Lord Griffiths.

[150] *R v Bailey* [1983] 1 WLR 760, 765.

[151] See further Chapter 2.

[152] According to Robinson, this special role is that of a 'catch-all excuse', which may be used when the defendant's control is 'impaired by a disability other than one of those recognized in the traditional excuse defences', such as insanity and intoxication (Robinson *Structure and Function in Criminal Law* 166). This means that the function of the defence is to ensure that certain actors who have caused harm are not liable on the basis that they cannot control their conduct (*Structure and Function in Criminal Law* 31, 36; see also Kadish 'Excusing Crime' 259). Robinson argues that no particular cause is stipulated for a defence of involuntariness because 'total lack of volition is an obvious and convincing ground for exculpation' (*Structure and Function in Criminal Law* 166).

[153] *Structure and Function in Criminal Law* 167. Where a defendant has raised an issue of impaired capacity at the time of the offence, but for some reason this is insufficient to ground a defence of automatism, it may be taken into account on sentence. This has been important in cases involving driving offences (see, for example, *Broome v Perkins* (1987) 85 Cr App R 321). In the Court of Appeal decision of *R v Isitt* (1978) 67 Cr App R 44, the Court considered an appeal from a dangerous driving

Automatism's grounding in a broad moralized notion of incapacity injects flexibility into the mental incapacity domain. Some suggestion of the value of this flexibility is provided by the 1990 Court of Appeal decision of *R v T*. T was charged with robbery and assault occasioning actual bodily harm. On arrest, T stated that she had been raped three days before the offence. At trial, she adduced medical evidence that she was suffering post-traumatic stress disorder and had been in a dissociative state at the time of her offences. The Court held that rape could constitute an external factor and thus that automatism was open to T.[154] The Court of Appeal decision is most accurately explained as a response to T's sympathetic situation as a survivor of rape. In other circumstances, it might not be sufficient for a defendant seeking to rely on automatism to be in a 'dream', as was found to be the case in this instance.[155] Thus, even though, as Lord Justice Lawton put it in *Quick*, it is only 'those in desperate need of some kind of a defence' that enter the 'quagmire of law' that is automatism,[156] the more moralized automatism doctrine provides welcome flexibility on the mental incapacity terrain.

On the Eve of Reform?

As discussed above, a concern with dangerousness has been a driving force for most of the developments regarding the insanity doctrine, including the cleaving apart of insanity and automatism from within a capacious informal insanity law. The durable legacy of a concern with dangerousness also accounts for a further unusual aspect of the law of insanity: it was not clear until recently that the insanity doctrine is available to defendants tried summarily. The Criminal Lunatics Act 1800 had restricted the special verdict to offences of treason, murder, and felony, and, despite its extension to misdemeanours via the 1840 Act, it was generally assumed that the insanity doctrine was unavailable in magistrates' courts.[157] However, in the 1997 decision of *R v Horseferry Road Magistrates ex parte K*, the Court concluded that the

---

conviction. Isitt had a hysterical fugue while driving. As discussed above, the Court of Appeal upheld his conviction because, 'physically at any rate', he had been driving the van, so he was precluded from relying on automatism. The Court noted that, although the psychiatric evidence did not amount to a defence, it might be relevant by way of mitigation (49).

[154] *R v T* [1990] Crim LR 256. The prosecution had argued that post-traumatic stress disorder was a 'disease of the mind' and the only defence open to T was insanity. In response to this argument, the Court stated that post-traumatic stress involving a normal person was not a 'disease of the mind' (257). The prosecution had also argued that T's ability to open the pen knife, which was used during the course of the robbery, demonstrated that she had retained partial control over her actions. The Court concluded that T was acting as though she was in a 'dream' (257). The prosecution's arguments might be thought to have defeated T's argument on one of two grounds: the external factor requirement and/or the 'total loss of self-control' requirement of the automatism defence.

[155] The Court of Appeal's decision is in contrast with the driving offences decisions, referred to above, in which anything short of 'total loss of self-control' was fatal to a claim for exculpation via the automatism defence.

[156] *Quick* (1973) 57 Cr App R 722, 734.

[157] The Butler Committee worked on this assumption but recommended extending the defence to magistrates' courts (para 18.19). This recommendation was not implemented.

1800 Act had not removed the common law doctrine of insanity from summary trials and thus, that a defendant could raise insanity in a summary case when charged with an 'appropriate charge'.[158] The uncertainty over exactly what constituted an 'appropriate charge' was resolved when the Queen's Bench Division concluded that insanity is only available in magistrates' courts where an individual has been charged with an offence containing a *mens rea* element.[159]

Like the problem itself, the extant solution to the question of the reach of the insanity doctrine betrays an abiding concern with dangerousness. With trials on indictment, and now trials on indictment plus summary offences with a *mens rea* element, broadly corresponding to serious criminal offences, a concern with dangerousness seems to account for the extension of the insanity doctrine only so far. But, with both a burgeoning number of summary offences and the advent of the Human Rights Act influencing criminal evidence and procedure in recent years, this two-track system (which also applies to unfitness to plead) is under some pressure. In addition, greater social and cultural awareness of mental disorder, and enhanced lay familiarity with the psychiatric lexicon, raises questions about the ongoing utility of the label insanity for a plea based on a broad range of conditions (including physical conditions such as epilepsy). Indeed, the uncertainty about the availability of insanity across the spectrum of criminal offences, compliance with the European Convention on Human Rights, and the use of the 'outdated' label insanity are each specifically identified as factors warranting a review of the law of insanity, which is part of the Tenth Programme of Law Reform.[160] Given the trajectory travelled by insanity to this point in time, it seems reasonable to expect that any reformulation of the law would closely tether the doctrine to its now solid grounding in a medicalized notion of disability.

Beyond the issue of the specific formulation of an insanity doctrine, over recent decades, dangerousness has been rearticulated as a concern with risk, a less overtly moralized and more technocratic concept. But this concern with risk has nonetheless reinscribed the significance of the backdoor concern with the disposal of insane individuals that has driven the insanity doctrine for so long. Described in various ways—as a set of technologies, or a way of thinking about interactions between individuals and collectivities, for instance—risk captures a broad social development affecting the myriad of ways in which responsibility is understood and

---

[158] *R v Horseferry Road Magistrates ex parte K* [1997] QB 23, 46.
[159] *DPP v H* [1997] 1 WLR 1406, 1409. If a (potentially) insane defendant appearing in a magistrate's court is charged with a strict liability offence, he or she may receive an ordinary acquittal. Alternatively, the defendant may be subject to an inquiry into his or her unfitness and, if the defendant is found to have 'done the act or made the omission charged', magistrates have discretion to make a hospital or guardianship order (Mental Health Act 1983, s 37(3)).
[160] See <http://www.justice.gov.uk/lawcommission/areas/insanity.htm> (last accessed 9 September 2011), and 10th Programme of Law Reform, Law Commission No 311 (London, 2008), available at <http://www.justice.gov.uk/lawcommission/publications/programmes-law-reform.htm> (last accessed 9 September 2011). In foreshadowing its review of insanity, the Law Commission specifically identified the inappropriateness of the label 'insanity' for intellectual and physical disorders such as epilepsy.

assigned to states, agencies, families, and individuals in the era of late modernity.[161] By contrast with dangerousness, risk is more amenable to quantification, and seems less speculative. This new concern with risk now pervades criminal justice practices, impacting on the development of criminal offences,[162] for instance, and is reflected in the rise of preventative detention, the eponymous practice of 'risk assessment' and testing, and the advent of a discrete label for certain offenders—'dangerous and severe personality disorder'—which is an administrative rather than medical label.[163] Psychiatric knowledge, practices, and professionals have been harnessed to the task of addressing risk, with, according to Nikolas Rose, a 'logic of prediction' supplanting a 'logic of diagnosis'.[164] Under these conditions, the consequentialist dimension of the law of insanity takes on a new lease of life, effectively revitalizing a concern with disposal that had been sustained for so long by concern with dangerousness.

---

[161] See for discussion, P O'Malley *Risk, Uncertainty and Government* (London: Glasshouse Press, 2004) and other work by the same author.
[162] See for discussion, L Zedner 'Pre-crime and Post-criminology?' (2007) 11(2) *Theoretical Criminology* 261–81 and V Tadros 'Crimes and Security' (2008) 71(6) *Modern Law Review* 940–70.
[163] See J Peay *Mental Health and Crime* (London: Routledge, 2010) 175–86.
[164] See N Rose *Powers of Freedom: Reframing Political Thought* (Cambridge: CUP, 1999) 261 and 260–3 more generally.

6
Knowing and Proving Exculpatory Mental Incapacity

This chapter provides the epistemological analogue to the analysis of the substantive law contained in the previous chapter. As suggested in Chapter 5, a loose, broad, and partially moralized notion of incapacity as a foundation for exculpation via insanity gradually ossified into a narrower notion of disability, a development which fostered a more circumscribed approach to insanity. This development eventually produced a discrete automatism doctrine, an exculpatory doctrine that continues to be grounded in a broad moralized notion of incapacity. As foreshadowed in Chapter 5, the process by which insanity came to be the subject of expert medical knowledge—a change that took place as much beyond as within criminal law—was crucial to these developments, which also impacted at the level of evidence and proof. This chapter examines the evidentiary and procedural rules that govern the way in which claims to exculpatory mental incapacity are made in court. While the focus is specifically on exculpatory mental incapacity—the part of the terrain of mental incapacity now traversed by the doctrines of automatism and insanity—this chapter may be read alongside my 'manifest madness' analysis, which pertains to the terrain of mental incapacity as a whole.[1]

This chapter presents two main arguments. The first concerns types of knowledge of exculpatory mental incapacity. Here, I aim to shift away from the overly general, binary story told about the rise of one type of knowledge (expert or specialized medical knowledge), at the expense of another, (non-specialized) knowledge. Examining the history of informal insanity reveals the role played by ordinary people, and what may be called common knowledge of 'madness', in animating legal evaluations of exculpatory 'madness'. Coinciding with the formalization of insanity into its modern form, in the *M'Naghten Rules*, evidence from medical experts came to be significant in trials involving claims to exculpation on the basis of mental incapacity. However, as I discuss below, this expert knowledge about 'madness' (now predominantly psychiatric and psychological knowledge) did not come to cover the field of knowledge practices in criminal law. This type of knowledge continues to share the field with lay knowledge of mental incapacity, which appeared at the same time as expert knowledge was carved out from common

[1] See Chapter 3.

knowledge.² In this chapter, I suggest that recognizing the different dimensions of expert knowledge of 'madness'—the prudential as well as ontological—helps to account for the ways in which space remains for lay knowledge of mental incapacity in legal practices.

The second of the two main arguments advanced in this chapter concerns the rules of evidence and procedure that structure claims of exculpatory mental incapacity. The rules of evidence and procedure relating to automatism can be contra-distinguished from those relating to insanity, usefully throwing each into relief. The bulk of the rules related to insanity crystallized from practices in the era of the 'reconstructive' criminal trial and this accounts in part for their distinctiveness. These rules governing insanity are oriented in such a way as to make the court a 'witness to the truth'.³ They reflect what are assumed to be common interests in identifying an individual as 'mad' and subjecting him or her to a particular disposal. By contrast, the appearance of a discrete automatism doctrine in the second half of the twentieth century coincides with a version of the adversarial criminal trial concerned with due process and the effective management of criminal cases, and, as a result, the rules of evidence and procedure governing automatism reflect this orientation of criminal process.

The Naturalization of 'Madness' and the Role of Common Knowledge of 'Madness'

The early modern era was marked by a broad movement from what Joel Eigen calls 'religio-astrologic conceptions of madness' to 'scientific-organic perspectives'.⁴ At the beginning of this era, the Christian worldview dominated and 'madness' was viewed as 'the wages of vice or sin'.⁵ As Roy Porter argues, the decline of the religious view of 'madness' via the 'massive naturalization of the understanding of insanity' paved the way for 'emergent secular and social mappings of madness', according to which insanity could be viewed 'naturalistically, historically and socially'.⁶ This change happened gradually, with elements of the earlier religious

---

² As I suggest in Chapter 3, what marks out the terrain of mental incapacity in criminal law is not the presence of one particular type of knowledge, but the interaction between different types of knowledge—expert and non-expert knowledge.
³ A Duff et al *The Trial on Trial (Vol 3): Towards a Normative Theory of the Criminal Trial* (Oxford: Hart, 2007) 47.
⁴ J P Eigen *Witnessing Insanity: Madness and Mad Doctors in the English Court* (New Haven: Yale University Press, 1995) 5. This movement was part of a broader transformation which had major epistemological implications: for a discussion in the context of theology and natural sciences, see L Dalston 'Marvelous Facts and Miraculous Evidence in Early Modern Europe' (1991) 18 *Critical Inquiry* 93.
⁵ R Porter *Mind-Forg'd Manacles: A History of Madness in England from the Restoration to the Regency* (London: Athlone Press, 1987) 43; see also D Rabin *Identity, Crime and Legal Responsibility in Eighteenth Century England* (New York: Palgrave Macmillan, 2004) 15.
⁶ *Mind-Forg'd Manacles* 108, 81.

view still detectable in law and culture beyond the end of the early modern era.[7] Within this period of significant change and wide diversity in social and cultural attitudes to 'madness', and in Porter's words, there was a 'genuinely widespread' belief that 'the essence of madness was to be visible, and known by its appearance'.[8] In the legal context, this belief formed a discrete but significant kernel of continuity over time; as I discuss in Chapter 3, this feature of 'madness' continues to be significant at the point of intersection with crime, colouring the way in which 'madness' is given meaning in criminal law practices.[9]

Alongside changes in social attitudes to 'madness', notions of evidence and proof for legal purposes were also changing over the early modern era. The decline of 'the ordeal' and the rise of jury trials in the medieval era corresponded with changing epistemological practices. 'The ordeal' had been accompanied by a complex evidentiary apparatus, including practices of proof such as *peine forte et dure*.[10] In its place, a practice of trial by jury developed, which exhibited an epistemological and practical reliance on the situated knowledge of the jurors. The role of the judge in this context was 'quasi-prosecutorial', involving, for instance, examination of what jurors knew.[11] This was the era of the 'self-informing' jury: with jurors initially drawn from the accused's local community, they were expected to bring knowledge of both the facts and the accused to the trial.[12] For the purposes of adjudication, relevant considerations included the character, reputation, and standing of the accused in his or her community. Under these conditions, expertise was introduced into legal processes via the use of so-called 'special juries' (such as juries of matrons, empanelled to determine if a woman was pregnant), which were advisors to the decision-makers or, sometimes, the decision-makers themselves.[13] As Antony Duff and colleagues argue, the trial process at this point was an inquiry, and the verdict reached expressed 'a complex social and moral judgment of both the incident and the defendant himself rather than a weighing of the evidence'.[14]

---

[7] This is evident for instance in the treatment of witches. For discussion, see O Davies *Witchcraft, Magic and Culture, 1736–1951* (Manchester: Manchester University Press, 1999).
[8] Porter *Mind-Forg'd Manacles* 35.
[9] See further Chapter 3, where, under the 'manifest madness' label, I analyse the mental incapacity terrain as marked by two topographical features, one ontological and one epistemological.
[10] It has been suggested that 'trial by ordeal' was not strictly a proof outcome, as in proof of facts: rather, it was an adjudication outcome in that it marked the termination of a dispute: see H L Ho 'The Legitimacy of Medieval Proof' (2003–04) 19(2) *Journal of Law and Religion* 259. See also A Duff et al *The Trial on Trial (Vol 3)* 22–5.
[11] See A Duff et al *The Trial on Trial (Vol 3)* 26.
[12] See T A Green 'A Retrospective on the Criminal Trial Jury, 1200–1800' in J Cockburn and T A Green (eds) *Twelve Good Men and True: The Criminal Trial Jury 1200–1800* (Princeton: Princeton University Press, 1988) 358–400; D Kerlman 'Was the Jury Ever Self-Informing?' in M Mulholland and B Pullan (eds) *Judicial Trials in England and Europe 1200–1700* (Manchester: Manchester University Press, 2003) 58–80.
[13] For an overview, see J C Oldham 'The Origins of the Special Jury' (1983) 50 *University of Chicago Law Review* 137 and S Landsman 'Of Witches, Madmen and Products Liability: An Historical Survey of the Use of Expert Testimony' (1995) 13 *Behavioral Sciences and the Law* 131, 134–8. Regarding the 'jury of matrons', see J C Oldham 'On Pleading the Belly: A History of The Jury of Matrons' (1985) 6 *Criminal Justice History* 1.
[14] A Duff et al *The Trial on Trial (Vol 3)* 27.

What is typically called the 'altercation' criminal trial gradually emerged out of the trial process as inquiry. In epistemological terms, the 'altercation' criminal trial was something of a hybrid. As Barbara Shapiro argues, both criminal and civil trials in the early modern era incorporated older ideas as well as emerging professional epistemological assumptions and patterns of thought relating to proof.[15] The criminal trial centred on the idea that the direct confrontation of the accused with his or her charge was the best means of discovering the truth of the allegation.[16] As the presence of witnesses in court became more commonplace over the sixteenth century, the role of jurors was increasingly restricted to evaluating the evidence presented to them, and something of an inchoate distinction between witnesses and jurors developed. Jurors might still have known personally the facts at issue or acquired knowledge outside the court, but their role was more akin to that of 'judges of the fact', to use the contemporary expression.[17] At this time, a distinction between 'fact' and 'law' developed, with 'fact' denoting particular events, deeds, or actions that were perceived by the senses.[18] Jurors—those of the 'middling sort' of society—were required to reach a 'moral certainty' in relation to their verdicts, a degree of conviction that formed the basis for the development of a standard of proof.[19] Over the sixteenth and seventeenth centuries, the idea that facts of human action could be established with a high degree of certitude by witness testimony, and that ordinary, independent persons have sufficient ability to evaluate that testimony for truth value, took on a broader cultural acceptability.[20]

---

[15] For instance, the older device of oaths, grounded in earlier beliefs about conscience and governed by fear of divine sanction, was retained while newer criteria for assessing witnesses (such as the exclusion from civil trials of witnesses with financial interests) were introduced. Witnesses could provide evidence of what they had seen or heard and courts could rely on documents that recorded actions or rights to supplement such evidence: see B Shapiro *A Culture of Fact, England, 1550–1720* (Ithaca: Cornell University Press, 2000) 12–13. As Dear argues, the truth could be accepted by others on the basis of personal and institutional authority: see P Dear, 'The Meanings of Experience' in K Park and L Dalston (eds) *The Cambridge History of Science Vol 3 Early Modern Science* (Cambridge: CUP, 2006) 106–31.
[16] A Duff et al *The Trial on Trial (Vol 3)* 31–2.
[17] See B Shapiro 'The Concept of "Fact": Legal Origins and Cultural Diffusion' (1994) 26(2) *Albion: A Quarterly Journal Concerned with British Studies* 230. The idea of 'matter of fact' did not admit of mere probability that something was true: see P Dear 'From Truth to Disinterestedness' (1992) 22(4) *Social Studies of Science* 619, 627.
[18] See Dear 'From Truth to Disinterestedness' 620–1. A 'matter of fact' was a social as well as epistemological category, with the social status of witnesses a relevant factor in the production of truth. Indeed, assumptions about reliable witness testimony roughly corresponded to the existing social hierarchy, with factors such as gender, status and reputation, and property-holding affecting witness credibility: see Shapiro *A Culture of Fact* 14–17.
[19] In general, see A Duff et al *The Trial on Trial (Vol 3)* 29–40. In relation to the 'middling sort', see C Herrup *The Common Peace* (Cambridge: CUP, 1987) 2. Regarding the notion of a 'moral certainty', as Peter Dear argues, a 'moral certainty' (as opposed to physical or metaphysical certainty) was 'guaranteed by prudent and truthful men', rather than by the possibility of independent confirmation: see P Dear 'From Truth to Disinterestedness' 624. Dear charts the ways in which, over the seventeenth century, objectivity came to be attached to disinterestedness rather than truth, and the way in which it thus affected experimental philosophy.
[20] B Shapiro 'The Concept of "Fact"' 252. Shapiro argues that this lesson about impartiality drawn from the English legal system was transferred to other ventures, such as scientific practice, which were seeking methods to truthfully ascertain matters of fact and to give observed and experimentally derived

As a result of these developments, even after the jury ceased to be 'self-informing', the epistemological authority of ordinary people in the criminal trial context remained significant.

The role of the testimony given by ordinary people about 'madness' should be understood against this background. With 'madness' 'entrenched in a common cultural consciousness', to use Porter's words,[21] it was the subject of what I call common knowledge.[22] By this I mean that, while 'madness' was protean, it was known and understood by ordinary people in the absence of specialist knowledge or particular insights. As Porter puts it, 'the mad and the sad were extremely familiar figures in the early modern physical and mental landscapes', and 'talking about madness—even talking *authoritatively* about it—was not traditionally the preserve of any profession'.[23] For these purposes, common knowledge of 'madness' was part of a broader knowledge landscape, encompassing knowledge of a defendant's character, family, and social status, each of which might have been an ingredient in any particular decision about whether to bring him or her to trial and then in the trial verdict. Flowing from the way in which crime was identified, and initially investigated, ordinary people played a significant role in criminal process.[24] Family members, neighbours, apprentices, and publicans, gave evidence identifying and evaluating conduct as 'mad'. As Porter argues, in insanity cases at this time, 'what counted was the community perception—witnesses, friends, family, magistrate and jury'.[25] As the distinction between witnesses and jurors hardened, the role of ordinary people as witnesses to and evaluators of 'madness' came to be distinct from and separate to the role of jurors in the trial process, but both sets of individuals were regarded as competent to detect and evaluate 'mad' conditions.

In the absence of sophisticated legal tests for exculpatory insanity, common knowledge formed an animating framework for decisions about mental incapacity. In this era, a variety of different formulations of exculpatory insanity coexisted, of which the 'wild beast' test is the best known. Each of these was as much descriptive as prescriptive of insanity. As I suggested in the previous chapter, the combination of a capacious informal insanity law and informal criminal processes in the early modern era resulted in a wide scope for exculpation on the basis of incapacity. The brief references to 'madness' in the *Old Bailey Proceedings* were designed to tap into common knowledge of 'madness'. In the record of Philip Parker's trial for murder

---

natural matters of fact, for instance, the status of knowledge. Shapiro regards the 'peculiar faith' of the English in the ability of lay people to ascertain the truth as a cultural matter (233).

[21] Porter *Mind-Forg'd Manacles* 19.

[22] See Chapter 3. In his work on 'manifest criminality', George Fletcher refers to 'general knowledge, on which judgments of criminality depended (G P Fletcher *Rethinking Criminal Law* (Oxford: OUP, 2000) 82. Nicola Lacey refers to 'local knowledge': N Lacey 'Responsibility and Modernity in Criminal Law' (2001) 9(3) *Journal of Political Philosophy* 249, 265.

[23] Porter *Mind-Forg'd Manacles* 14, 18.

[24] See for discussion Herrup *The Common Peace* ch. 3.

[25] Porter *Mind-Forg'd Manacles* 38. For a discussion of the idea of community in the early modern era, see P Withington *Society in Early Modern England: The Vernacular Origins of Some Powerful Ideas* (Cambridge: Polity Press, 2010).

in 1708, evidence was adduced that, at the time of the offence, 'the prisoner talk'd very extravagantly, and had all the symptoms of lunacy upon him'. The jury concluded that the killing was 'purely the effect of distraction' and Parker was acquitted.[26] Similarly, when Alice Hall was tried for the murder of two women in 1709, evidence that she had been 'for a considerable time Distracted, and fancied she was Damn'd, that she was a Spirit, and not a Woman; and sometimes was so very Outrageous that she was chain'd in her Bed' seems to have been behind the jury's decision to acquit her on the basis that she was 'under great disorder of Mind when she committed the Fact'.[27] Of course, not all claims to insanity were successful. In one of the famous insanity trials of the period, held in 1760, Earl Ferrers testified that he suffered from occasional insanity and is recorded as saying that, at the time he killed his steward, 'I did not know what I was about', but to no avail: Ferrers was convicted and executed.[28]

'Madness' in this era was 'read off' an individual's conduct. In Porter's words, 'there were indeed inner as well as outer truths, but outward signs encoded inner realities'.[29] This aspect of the way in which 'madness' was made known was linked to the interdependence of the conceptual and the evidentiary (an interdependence which I suggest remains at the point of intersection of 'madness' and crime[30]). In relation to insanity for criminal law purposes, conduct had a thick significance—a defendant's conduct in gaol, his or her demeanour in court and history of behaviour, as well as the acts comprising the offence, were enlisted in the process of assessing whether an individual would be able to avoid punishment. Thus, as I suggest in Chapter 5 in relation to *Arnold's Case*, Judge Tracy's direction that it must be 'very plain and clear' when a man is excused from punishment on the basis of his lack of 'understanding and memory' is as much about the form as the content of 'madness'. 'Madness' was both known and tangible. This idea about the way 'madness' was known is usefully summed up by a lay witness in another *OBPs* trial, that of Thomas Reed, who stated that 'he look'd upon him [Reed] as a craz'd man'.[31]

The record of the trial of Thomas Nash for the murder of his wife in 1727, in which Nash made a case for incapacity based on an external cause, usefully illustrates the ways in which 'madness' was 'read off' an individual's conduct. The trial record reads in part:

Eleanor Susmith depos'd. That she had known him for some Years to be a very Crazy Person, not taking his natural Rest, but magotting and rambling like a Mad-man.

---

[26] *OBP*, Philip Parker, 8 December 1708 (t17081208-34).
[27] *OBP*, Alice Hall, 17 January 1709 (t17090117-19).
[28] *R v Ferrers* (1760) 19 St Tr 885, extracted in Rabin *Identity, Crime and Legal Responsibility* 22. See also D Hay 'Property, Authority and the Criminal Law' in D Hay, P Linebaugh, J G Rule, E P Thompson and C Winslow (eds), *Albion's Fatal Tress: Crime and Society in Eighteenth Century England* (London: Allen Lane, 1975) 33–4.
[29] Porter *Mind-Forg'd Manacles* 35.
[30] See Chapter 3. See also A Loughnan '"In a Kind of Mad Way": A Historical Perspective on Evidence and Proof of Mental Incapacity' (2011) 35(3) *Melbourne University Law Review* 1047.
[31] *OBP*, Thomas Reed, 4 December 1723 (t17231204-20).

Mr. Page further depos'd. That at Times he was besides himself, especially at Spring and Fall, when he was seldom in a Capacity to follow Business.
...
Mr. Watson further depos'd. That he had known him 13 Years, and that he would sometimes go to his Neighbours Houses and demand such Things as he had occasion for, but where he met with Opposition he came no more, and only tyrannized over them that feared him; . . . he had formerly been a Soldier for fourteen Years, during which Time he had received several dangerous Wounds in the Head, and has still several Marks to shew, which makes it probable those Wound's might weaken his Intellectuals.[32]

The evidence that the head wounds Nash had received in war made it 'probable that those Wound's might weaken his Intellectuals', and other evidence about his 'magotting and rambling' behaviour seems to have convinced the jury, who returned a verdict that the accused was *non compos mentis*. This verdict indicates that, at this time, the scope of the informal insanity law was wide enough to encompass both external and internal causes of incapacity.

The idea that 'madness' could be 'read off' an individual's conduct provided an element of continuity as the fact-finding contours of insanity trials underwent significant change over the eighteenth century. These changes were preceded by a period in which, up to 1700, criminal trial process was changing such that 'truth was becoming internal to the trial procedure'.[33] Ushered in by the special rules that applied to treason trials following the Treason Trials Act 1696, criminal trial process developed protections for the defendant which paved the way for the development of the adversarial trial. Changes from 1700 were associated with the rise of the adversarial trial process. The nascent regularization of prosecution and the gradual entry of lawyers (defence counsel began to participate in criminal trials from the 1730s, although they were limited to gathering and adducing evidence, and examining and cross-examining witnesses, and could not address the jury[34]) combined to shift the focus from the defendant him or herself to those who spoke about or on behalf of him or her.[35] These changes corresponded to changing ideas about proof: the reconfiguration of the criminal trial meant that it became a 'contest between two cases', based on the presentation of evidence, and the dynamic came to be one of testing the prosecution case.[36] However, as 'madness' continued to be understood as generally known and tangible, there were significant

---

[32] *OBP*, Thomas Nash, 12 April 1727 (t17270412–21).

[33] See A Duff et al *The Trial on Trial (Vol 3)* 40.

[34] Defendants' right to a full legal defence in felony trials was only formally realized with the Prisoners Counsel Act 1836. Defendants did not gain the right to give evidence at trial until the end of the nineteenth century: Criminal Evidence Act 1898. See D J A Cairns *Advocacy and the Making of the Adversarial Criminal Trial, 1800–1865* (Oxford: Clarendon Press, 1998) 169–76; C Emsley *Crime and Society in England 1750–1900* (London: Pearson Longman, 2005) 183–211.

[35] This has been referred to as the 'silencing' of the defendant in the adversarial criminal trial. For a discussion by way of contrast with the inquisitorial system, see J Hodgson 'Conceptions of the Trial in Inquisitorial and Adversarial Procedure' in A Duff et al *The Trial on Trial (Vol 2): Judgment and Calling to Account* (Oxford: Hart, 2006) 223, 235–9. See also A Duff et al *The Trial on Trial (Vol 3)* 203–13.

[36] A Duff et al *The Trial on Trial (Vol 3)* 44.

continuities over this time between what counted as proof of 'madness'—both within and beyond the bounds of the courtroom. I return to this point below.

'As a medical man, I have no hesitation in saying so':[37] Expert Knowledges of 'Madness'

The backdrop to the appearance of an expert knowledge of 'madness' was the radical cultural and social transformation of the scientific revolution. In a complex set of developments that played out from the sixteenth century onwards, older ideas (of 'humours' and 'vapours', for instance) that had held sway gave way to newer ideas based on 'micromechanism and microstructures of ailment and body'.[38] What was called 'the new philosophy'—what is now called science—opposed both classical and medieval traditions.[39] The scientific revolution prepared the ground for the modern organization of knowledge. The Enlightenment of the eighteenth century marked the restructuring of knowledge, leading to its increasingly formal organization, moves that were prompted by a perceived need for knowledge to be 'systematic, professional, useful and co-operative'.[40] This change produced the types of knowledge that would be closely associated with the political, social, and cultural changes grouped together under the umbrella of modernity.[41] Expert medical knowledge (itself an omnibus term) occupied a special place in this respect, becoming bound up in the way in which both society and self, and individuals' relations with each other, came to be conceptualized.[42]

The development of a specialist or elite knowledge about mental states grew out of these larger changes in the knowledge landscape, and altered the epistemological profile of 'madness' well beyond the bounds of criminal law and process. Although

---

[37] OBP, William Newton Allnutt, 13 December 1847 (t18471213–290).

[38] See S Shapin *Never Pure: Historical Studies of Science as if it was Produced by People with Bodies, Situated in Time Space, Culture and Society, and Struggling for Credibility and Authority* (Baltimore: Johns Hopkins University Press, 2010) 293, and more generally, his ch. 13. As Shapin notes, while the humanist movement associated with the Renaissance was intended as a revival of the classical tradition, the scientific revolution of the seventeenth century was self-consciously a process of intellectual innovation.

[39] Opposition to 'the new philosophy' in universities led to the creation of 'scientific societies', such as the Royal Society of London (established in 1660), existing outside their boundaries: see P Burke *A Social History of Knowledge: From Gutenberg to Diderot* (Cambridge: Polity Press, 2000) 38–44.

[40] *A Social History of Knowledge* 46, and, more generally, 44–9.

[41] See A Giddens *Modernity and Self-Identity: Self and Society in the Late Modern Age* (Berkeley: Stanford University Press, 1991) and *The Consequences of Modernity* (Cambridge: Polity Press, 1990).

[42] See generally N Rose 'Medicine, History and the Present' in C Jones and R Porter (eds) *Reassessing Foucault: Power, Medicine and the Body* (London: Routledge, 1994). As Mary Poovey argues, efforts to represent and conceptualize the population of Britain as an aggregate and to delineate a social sphere, distinct from a political and economic domain date from this period: see M Poovey *Making A Social Body: British Cultural Formation 1830–1864* (Chicago: University of Chicago Press, 1995) ch. 1. In this process, medicine has been implicated in the ways in which society came into existence, representing the first positive knowledge to be taken as expertise: see Rose 'Medicine, History and the Present' 56.

the rise of an expert knowledge of 'madness' reached a critical point in the nineteenth century, when it came to have an effect on criminal law processes such as those relating to exculpatory mental incapacity, it can be traced back to the eighteenth century.[43] As Nikolas Rose writes, from the last decades of the 1700s onwards, phrenology, criminal anthropology, and other 'sciences of the soul' appeared, reflecting a growing social demand for 'vocabularies for the managing of human difference'.[44] These emerging disciplines began to address broad questions about the interaction of mind and body in a way that would have a significant impact on criminal law principles and practices.[45] As Nicola Lacey argues, the development of this type of knowledge formed the basis for the 'factualisation' of *mens rea*, an ingredient in the rise to dominance of a subjectivist concept of fault in criminal law.[46]

From the first decades of the nineteenth century, a growing number of individuals, including hospital physicians, surgeons, visiting and consulting physicians, gaol medical attendants, and asylum superintendants and their assistant medical officers, laid claim to a specialist knowledge of 'madness'. 'Alienists', a loose and heterogeneous body of individuals with a variety of beliefs, practices, and varying claims to authority and credibility, formed part of this group. At this time, specialist knowledge about 'madness' was considerably contested and conflicted. A myriad of ideas about 'madness' (revealed in clinical concepts such as 'moral insanity', 'lesion of the will' and 'monomania') competed for space, with a range of individuals claiming authority over 'lunacy'. The dynamic character of the field reflected the dynamism of the broader arena of expert medical knowledge, which was undergoing significant reorganization during this time.[47] This was itself part of a profound reorganization of elite knowledges that took place over the nineteenth century. This development encompassed new objects of knowledge, and spawned new specializations and new intellectual cum social groups or 'knowledge associations'.[48] These new specializations and associations were marked by permeable

---

[43] See T Forbes *Surgeons at the Bailey: English Forensic Medicine to 1878* (New Haven: Yale University Press, 1985).

[44] N Rose *Powers of Freedom: Reframing Political Thought* (Cambridge: CUP, 1999) 138, and, more generally, ch. 12. For Rose, these 'psy' knowledges, are bound up in the form of political power, and in the relations between self and others and state.

[45] See generally J P Eigen *Unconscious Crime: Mental Absence and Criminal Responsibility in Victorian London* (Baltimore: Johns Hopkins University Press, 2003).

[46] See Lacey 'Responsibility and Modernity in Criminal Law' 268. The 'factualisation' of *mens rea* was a prerequisite for subsequent doctrinal requirements like a requirement of 'abnormality of mind' in diminished responsibility: see Chapter 9.

[47] By the end of the 1800s, this reorganization would result in a professional cohesion that was buttressed by a core body of licensing, recognized educational institutions, and learned societies. See generally C Lawrence *Medicine in the Making of Modern Britain* (London: Routledge, 1994) and 'Incommunicable Knowledge: Science, Technology and the Clinical Art in Britain 1850–1914' (1986) 20(4) *Journal of Contemporary History* 503. It has been suggested that the combination of a collective desire to expand medical knowledge, and the rise of an administrative rationality that augured for the governance of large populations through classifications prompted the acceptance of specialisms in medicine in the last decades of the century: see G Weisz 'The Emergence of Medical Specialization in the Nineteenth Century' (2003) 77 *Bulletin of Historical Medicine* 536, 572–4.

[48] The new 'knowledge associations' marked the professionalization of groups such as natural scientists, surgeons, and 'alienists'. For discussion, see M Daunton 'Introduction' in M Daunton (ed) *The Organisation of Knowledge in Victorian Britain* (Oxford: OUP, 2005) 1–27.

intellectual and social borders, and disagreement and debate meant that their particular configuration was in flux over the course of the century.[49]

The constitution of this specialist knowledge of 'madness' as expertise for criminal legal purposes is a distinct dimension of the rise of scientific and medical knowledge of 'madness'. By the time the *M'Naghten Rules* were formulated in 1843, courtroom testimony given by those claiming expertise in 'madness' was becoming more common.[50] While defendants' neighbours and relatives continued to provide evidence of what Eigen calls 'manifest distraction', as they had in the seventeenth and eighteenth centuries,[51] testimony from alienists and other experts was gradually becoming more important. 'Mad doctors' had given evidence in court before *M'Naghten*, but their involvement and profile increased in the second half of the nineteenth century. This development is sometimes interpreted as evidence of a 'turf war', and narrated as a strategy on the part of medical experts to enhance professional reputation,[52] although, as Eigen and others have argued, the entry of alienists to the courtroom would not have been possible without 'at least passive acquiescence of the bench'.[53]

Mindful that the greater preponderance of experts in London may have skewed the picture somewhat, the *OBPs* can be enlisted to bear out this claim about the rising profile of expert medical professionals in the criminal context. 'Alienists' and others make several appearances at the Old Bailey, and particular individuals, such as John and Thomas Monro, father and son physicians at Bethlehem Hospital, and Gilbert McMurdo, surgeon at Newgate gaol, achieved notoriety as medical witnesses. Evidence from the *OBPs* suggests that experts were asked to address a variety

---

[49] For a discussion in the context of medical knowledge, see W F Bynum *Science and the Practice of Medicine in the Nineteenth Century* (Cambridge: CUP, 1994).

[50] See generally, J P Eigen '"An Inducement to Morbid Minds": Politics and Madness in the Victorian Courtroom' in M D Dubber and L Farmer (eds) *Modern Histories of Crime and Punishment* (Berkeley: Stanford University Press, 2007) 66–87.

[51] J P Eigen 'Delusion's Odyssey: Charting the Course of Victorian Forensic Psychiatry' (2004) 27 (5) *International Journal of Law and Psychiatry* 395, 399.

[52] For instance, Roger Smith pits the 'voluntarist' discourse of law against the 'determinist' discourse of medicine (R Smith *Trial by Medicine: Insanity and Responsibility in Victorian Trials* (Edinburgh: Edinburgh University Press, 1981) 3) and argues that a strident conflict characterized the encounter between an 'established criminal administration' and the newly emerging profession of psychiatry in the nineteenth century (*Trial by Medicine* 168). According to Smith, the 'vehemence' of this conflict has died away in the current era because 'psychiatry has become a profession' and because courts are using 'deferential language and accepting extra-judicial medical institutions' ((*Trial by Medicine* 169). See also P Bartlett 'Legal Madness in the Nineteenth Century' (2001) 14(1) *Social History of Medicine* 107, 110.

[53] J P Eigen and G Andoll 'From Mad-Doctor to Forensic Witness: The Evolution of Early English Court Psychiatry' (1986) *International Journal of Law and Psychiatry* 159, 169; see also Eigen 'Delusion's Odyssey' 411; T Ward 'Observers, Advisors, or Authorities? Experts, Juries and Criminal Responsibility in Historical Perspective' (2001) 12 *Journal of Forensic Psychiatry* 105, 110. In addition, as Martin Wiener argues, accounts of such conflict neglect the extent to which Victorian psychiatry and law shared concerns, in relation to the control of impulses, for example: see M J Wiener *Reconstructing the Criminal: Culture, Law and Policy in England, 1830–1914* (Cambridge: CUP, 1990) 84. In relation to the current era, Norrie argues that, crucially, law and psychiatry share the 'individuation of social problems', meaning that they have 'more in common as co-workers at the coal face of social order than their ideological disagreements' would suggest (A Norrie *Crime, Reason and History: A Critical Introduction to Criminal Law* (London: Butterworths, 2001) 195).

of issues relating to claims for exculpation on the basis of insanity, including issues of causation, effect, and prognosis, as well as what would now be referred to as the 'ultimate issue'—whether an individual's insanity plea should be granted (which I discuss below). In part reflecting the still emergent nature of elite knowledge of 'madness', the multiplicity of theories and beliefs that enjoyed some currency, and the still moralized as opposed to medicalized character of 'madness', medical witnesses were able to include various matters, such as domestic violence, poverty, and other stressors, in their clinical considerations.[54] At the same time as this witness testimony was becoming more important, and as the terms of the *M'Naghten Rules* themselves suggest, terms and references from the medical lexicon were making a mark on the development of legal tests for criminal responsibility.[55]

The enhanced legal profile of expert evidence on insanity brought with it greater scrutiny of experts, and robust questioning about the bases on which they reached conclusions. The expanding role of lawyers in the criminal trial meant that the power lay with them and the emphasis was on examination and cross-examination. My examination of the *OBPs* suggests that experts were frequently questioned on the basis of their beliefs, the relationship between insane conditions and the alleged offence and the causes of insanity, among other matters. This reflected both the increasing demand for certainty as well as the restrictions placed on defence counsel, who were not permitted to address the jury directly.[56] The changing demands on experts help to account for the presence, in the trial records, of generalized statements about mad conditions, and some evidence of restriction on the scope of the testimony of experts who had not seen the prisoner (to general questions such as 'What are the symptoms of insanity? In what way do you judge such a symptom to be one of insanity or the reverse?'[57]), which are present in the *OBPs* from this period.[58] These types of questions featured in some of the trials

---

[54] For instance, *OBP*, John Francis, 26 November 1849 (t18491126–41) (in which Alexander John Sutherland, a physician, stated 'Yes, I should think that if he was really mad in 1846 because he expected to be transported, it would not be at all improbable that if he expected to be transported in 1849, it would produce a temporary state of madness'). I discuss this point about the capaciousness of 'clinical' assessments in relation to infanticide in Chapter 8. Here, it is useful to note that, by the end of the nineteenth century, while rules had hardened to exclude certain social considerations from general inquiries into criminal liability, the open-textured nature of medical diagnoses facilitated their inclusion in relation to insanity. See Norrie *Crime, Reason and History* 191.

[55] As I discuss in Chapter 5, reliance on expert medical evidence did not resolve broader disputes about the scope and purpose of the insanity doctrine, which continued over the course of the nineteenth century. For example, the difficulty of distinguishing between an 'irresistible impulse' and an impulse that was merely unresisted beset the law on insanity until 'irresistible impulse' was brought within the doctrine of diminished responsibility after it was introduced by statute in 1957: see *R v Byrne* [1960] 2 QB 396.

[56] See S Landsman 'One Hundred Tears of Rectitude: Medical Witnesses at the Old Bailey, 1717–1817' (1998) 16(3) *Law and History Review* 445.

[57] See *OBP*, John Francis, 26 November 1849 (t18491126–41) (in which the judge restricted the scope of the questions that could be put to the expert witness). See also my Chapter 3 for a discussion of the relevance of expert testimony on the general nature of the mental condition suffered by the defendant.

[58] This period is also notable for a growing awareness of the different status of experts who saw the defendant close to the time of the offence, and those who had not seen him or her until closer to the trial, or, indeed at the trial. For instance, in Mary Ann Hunt's trial for murder (*OBP*, Mary Ann Hunt,

subsequent to the *M'Naghten* decision, suggesting the progressive way in which the boundaries of expert testimony outlined in the *M'Naghten Rules* were worked out.

Bearing in mind the way in which adversarial criminal procedures were developing during this time, from my study of the *OBPs*, one particular aspect of expert medical evidence on insanity stands out—its largely non-partisan flavour. The *OBPs* trial records convey a palpable sense of the baseline acceptability or non-contentious nature of this evidence underlying the specific issue of a particular individual and charge. This palpable baseline acceptability hints at the broader social caché enjoyed by medical knowledge in the nineteenth century. A number of trial records feature more than one expert medical witness and there appears to have been significant cross-referencing among experts (for instance, 'I agree with Dr Bucknill that loss in business, hereditary taint, and habitual drinking, and a blow to the head, would be likely to create insanity'[59]). This cross-referencing stretched across the still porous boundary between expert and lay person, encompassing the latter's witness evidence about an individual's mad condition. On hearing testimony from lay witnesses like parents, siblings, the owners of licensed establishments, fellow soldiers, co-workers and the like, medical witnesses testified about insanity in the family ('madness is notoriously hereditary'[60]), antecedent injuries ('there is a very distinct mark on the upper part of his head ... that injury would affect the brain at the time very decidedly'[61]), and conduct at the time leading up to the offence ('It is only confirmatory of the opinion I had formed, that he was not in a sound state'[62]). The totality of the evidence sustained conclusions such as 'I have heard a great deal more about him to-day than before—the general' [sic] evidence is that his mind is deranged'.[63] This cross-referencing—among experts and between experts and non-experts, between the time of the offence (and even before this) and the time of the trial—produced a complex blend of the particular and the general and offered a critical weight to expert evaluation of 'madness' in a particular instance.

While experts came to be called by both prosecution and defence, the idea that their evidence was partisan seemed not to have been a concern for Old Bailey judges, up to and including the Victorian era. Three sets of factors account for the non-partisan flavour of the expert medical testimony relating to insanity. The first of these relates to the nature of expert medical knowledge itself and the role of 'medical men'. As a species of scientific knowledge, medical knowledge had (and has) powerful rhetorical claims to truth, accuracy, and impartiality, the significance of which I discuss in

16 August 1847 (t18470816–1797)), after the issue was raised by defence counsel, the Court referred to *M'Naghten* in admitting an additional expert medical professional, who was present in Court, to testify to the defendant's sanity ('I have attended to the evidence in the case since my arrival here ... [the witness statements] do not, in my judgment, indicate any unsoundness in the prisoner').

[59] *OBP*, James Sweetland, 28 June 1880 (t18800628–423).
[60] *OBP*, William Tuchet, 21 October 1844 (t18441021–2396).
[61] *OBP*, William Parker, 12 January 1874 (t18740112–123).
[62] *OBP*, Charles Broadfoot Westron, 4 February 1856 (t18560204–263).
[63] *OBP*, John Cuthbert, 25 October 1875 (t18751025–588).

Chapter 3.[64] Further, as professional boundaries around the practice of 'alienists' were still emergent, the connections between types of medical expert meant that all traded on the standing of experts more familiar with the criminal courtroom, such as surgeons. The non-partisan flavour of expert testimony on insanity also reflects the heritage of the involvement of 'medical men' in coronial inquiries (which continue to be oriented in a way that marks them out from other legal practices[65]) and was in part a product of the way in which experts came to be involved in insanity cases—through treatment, or observation once the individual came to be in some form of institution.[66] As Carole Jones notes, up to this point, the state was the main client of those individuals who made up the body of medical experts.[67] It is possible that any whiff of bias this produced was countered by the fact that, where such expert witnesses gave evidence that an individual was insane, it worked to the advantage of the defendant.

The second set of factors relates to the scope of the insanity doctrine at this time: it was loose and broad such that medical experts testified to matters other than those relating to insanity as we would now view it, from the vantage point of the current era. Even after the formulation of insanity in the *M'Naghten Rules*, insanity remained capacious, incorporating claims that would later fall into the category of automatism. The *OBPs* indicate that expert medical witnesses gave evidence in relation to what would now be conceptualized as automatism claims.[68] More generally, it appears that experts were enlisted to explain what might appear to be motiveless or unconscious conduct.[69] The scope of insanity was significant because it meant that testimony was not restricted to clinical diagnoses, in a strict sense, enabling expert medical witnesses to gain legitimacy on the basis of broad, non-technical judgments. Nonetheless, the practice of introducing expert evidence under a broad and loose insanity doctrine contributed to the change in the basis of the doctrine, which would gradually narrow its scope. As I suggest in Chapter 5,

---

[64] See my 'manifest madness' analysis in Chapter 3. For a discussion of the particular workings of expert medical evidence in a trial taking place in the Victorian era, see G Edmond 'The Law-Set: The Legal-Scientific Production of Medical Propriety' (2001) 26(2) *Science, Technology and Human Values* 191–226.

[65] On the historical practice of the coroners' inquests, and their gradual recasting as medical tribunals over the course of the nineteenth century, see I Burney *Bodies of Evidence: Medicine and the Politics of the English Inquest, 1830–1926* (Baltimore: Johns Hopkins University Press, 2000).

[66] Regarding the period 1717–1817, see Landsman 'One Hundred Tears of Rectitude' 445.

[67] C Jones *Expert Witnesses: Science, Medicine and the Practice of Law* (Oxford: Clarendon Press, 1994) 22. Stephen Landsman argues that the role of medical witnesses was often 'that of quasi-official inquirers' called into the case by public officials such as magistrates and coroners: see Landsman 'One Hundred Tears of Rectitude' 453.

[68] An example is provided by William Crouch's trial for the murder of his wife (*OBP*, William Crouch, 6 May 1844 (t18440506–1363)), in which the defendant argued he was in a state of concussion from a blow to the head. Several experts testified about concussion and head wounds, one of whom stated that 'it was not at all a serious wound'. Crouch was convicted and sentenced to death.

[69] For instance, *OBP*, James Huggins, 7 July 1851 (t18510707–1502) (in which John Conolly, a physician to the Asylum at Hanwell is recorded as saying 'if a man who appeared to be fond of his wife for many years, beat her frequently and violently, I should strongly suspect that he was mad'). See Eigen 'An Inducement to Morbid Minds' 66–87.

and in part as a result of the rise of an expert medical knowledge of 'madness', insanity has come to be grounded in a circumscribed notion of disability (as opposed to a broader, looser notion of incapacity), while the now stand-alone doctrine of automatism continues to be founded in a broad, moralized notion of incapacity.

The features of the particular mode of criminal trial into which medical experts and others were introduced furnishes the final set of factors that accounts for the non-partisan flavour of expert medical evidence on 'madness'. As Duff and colleagues argue, this was the era of the 'reconstructive trial', a distinctive stage in the development of the adversarial trial. This stage was marked out by a fuller exploration of issues of guilt, intention and evidence at trial than had previously been the practice. Duff and colleagues pinpoint the passage of the Prisoners' Counsel Act 1836 as marking the beginning of this era.[70] As these authors argue, in this mode, the trial is concerned with the 'reconstruction of past events, in order to make the court witness to the truth of the events and so test the guilt of the accused person'.[71] This mode of trial was premised on a number of reforms to criminal procedure that took place from the first decades of the century and significantly affected the structure of criminal trials.[72] By the end of the century, and by its end, trials were significantly longer, and, reflecting police control of prosecution processes, featured an increased number of witnesses.[73] As Duff and colleagues write, scientific and medical witnesses played a key part in this reconstructive trial process, and their increasingly common appearance in court for both prosecution and defence hardened the distinction between fact and opinion, a distinction which would come to form the basis of the formalized evidentiary rules relating to expert testimony.[74] The non-partisan flavour of expert medical testimony I have been discussing coincided with the crystallization of the rules of evidence and procedure governing the fact-finding process in insanity cases at this juncture. This has meant that these rules have retained a feel of the reconstructive trial, and are oriented to making the court a witness to the truth in a way that helps to

---

[70] A Duff et al *The Trial on Trial (Vol 3)* 46–7. This year also saw the passage of the Medical Witnesses Act, which meant that medical witness at coronial inquests were to be paid.

[71] *The Trial on Trial (Vol 3)* 47. See also L Farmer 'Arthur and Oscar (and Sherlock): The Reconstructive Trial and the "Hermeneutics of Suspicion"' (2007) 5(1) *International Commentary on Evidence* 1.

[72] These reforms, which continued over the century, included the introduction of defence counsel in felony trials (Prisoners' Counsel Act 1836 (6 & 7 Will IV c.114)), the creation of public prosecutors (Prosecution of Offences Act 1879 (42 & 43 Vict. c.22)), and the introduction of a limited appeal system in criminal cases (Crown Cases Act 1848 (11 & 12 Vict. c.43)) and the defendant's right to give evidence at the end of the century (Criminal Evidence Act 1898). See generally Cairns *Advocacy and the Making of the Adversarial Criminal Trial* 169–76; Emsley *Crime and Society* 183–211.

[73] As Lindsay Farmer observes, the primary aim of the various reforms to criminal trial process was to expedite the criminal process with concern about the rights of the accused merely a secondary consideration: see L Farmer 'Reconstructing the English Codification Debate: The Criminal Law Commissioners, 1833–45' (2000) 18(2) *Law and History Review* 397, 413. For a discussion of the significance of the development of a sizable summary jurisdiction, which also occurred over this period, see L Farmer *Criminal Law, Tradition and Legal Order: Crime and the Genius of Scots Law 1747 to the Present* (Cambridge: CUP, 1997).

[74] See L Farmer 'Arthur and Oscar (and Sherlock)' 51, and, regarding expert evidence more generally, see M Redmayne *Expert Evidence and Criminal Justice* (Oxford: OUP, 2001).

account for their distinctiveness in the criminal law of the current era. I discuss these rules below.

'I have seen a great many insane persons, and I should put him down as such':[75] the Significance of Prudential Knowledge and the Ongoing Role of Lay Knowledge

The story of expert medical evidence of insanity—the strategic selection of particular individuals, certain kinds of evidence, and distinct scientific techniques for use as expertise in criminal processes—is complex. Here, by way of contribution to our understanding of this area of criminal process, I wish to comment on the particular issue of the place of expert knowledge of 'madness' alongside non-expert knowledge in the criminal law context. Growing legal reliance on expert medical evidence of insanity and the development of specialist knowledges of 'madness' might be thought to herald the end of a role for common knowledge in ascriptions of non-responsibility based on insanity. Certainly, broadly, it is incontrovertible that, with the rise of expert medical knowledge about insanity, the significance of ordinary peoples' testimony about an individual's insane condition declined and the significance—both practical and symbolic—of expert witness evidence increased. But, while acknowledging the growing significance of expert medical knowledge of insanity, it is important to recognize that this expert knowledge shared the knowledge field with non-expert knowledge of mental incapacity. Before the development of an expert knowledge of insanity, the knowledge of ordinary people had been common, and I referred to common knowledge above. The rise of an expert knowledge of 'madness', however, meant that the knowledge of ordinary people was reconstituted, and, as I discuss in Chapter 3, I refer to this type of knowledge as 'lay' in order to highlight that it is defined as non-expert. This type of knowledge plays a role in legal practices along with expert knowledge of insanity.

A sense of the shared knowledge field relating to insanity in criminal law can be gleaned from the gradual way in which expert knowledge cleaved apart from the broader body of common knowledge relating to insanity. There are two aspects to this point: first, knowledge of insanity and second, evidence about insane conditions. Regarding knowledge of insanity, it is clear that, as Porter argues, the development of expert medical knowledge of insanity 'emerged on the basis of 'natural beliefs' about madness already well entrenched within common culture'.[76] This meant that there was significant overlap between lay and expert knowledge of insanity, and that, at least initially, expert knowledge was as much moralized as medicalized.[77] While the fit between lay and 'specialist' knowledge of insanity

---

[75] *OBP*, Robert Pate, 8 July 1850 (t18500708-1300).
[76] Porter *Mind-Forg'd Manacles* 33.
[77] Some evidence for the ongoing significance of lay knowledge as a framework for understanding insanity outside the bounds of the criminal law may be found in Akihito Suzuki's study of the care of

loosened over time, even by the mid-Victorian era professional medical discourse had not separated itself from common moral discourse.[78] Regarding evidence about insane conditions, it is important not to overstate the change wrought to the criminal trial by expert evidence about insanity. At least initially, the role of medical witnesses was an extension of their role as neighbour or friend; like other witnesses, experts, such as prison doctors, were likely to be familiar with defendants, and did not stress their expertise.[79] As Tony Ward argues, experts built upon common sense views and relied on 'widely recognized signs of madness' in their diagnosis and testimony.[80]

Even once expert knowledge of insanity cleaved apart from common knowledge (producing a lay knowledge of insanity), it continued to share the criminal law field with other types of knowledge. To gain an appreciation of how this worked, it is necessary to think carefully about the precise significance of expert knowledge of exculpatory mental incapacity, and here, I suggest a slight recasting of the usual story told about the rise of expert knowledge of 'madness' for criminal law purposes. As I mention in Chapter 3, the development of an expertise on 'madness' entailed a large scale movement from a situation in which 'madness' was generally 'known' and 'visible', to a situation in which it was only 'visible and legible to the trained eye'.[81] In general, this development has been narrated primarily in terms of its ontological significance, with experts claiming to give meaning to 'madness'. However, in terms of understanding the way in which specialist knowledge was received in the legal arena, and the way in which expert testimony was evaluated, the situation was more nuanced that this general story would suggest. When the quantum of experience of insanity is taken into account, it becomes clear that it is not so much that insanity became 'hidden' in the legal context, but rather that sheer volume of exposure to it became more important. That is, prudential knowledge of insanity rose to the fore, according a certain type of knowledge of insanity a distinctive authority.

To explain how this recasting is significant, it is first necessary to distinguish between prudential and ontological types of expertise, as different dimensions of expert knowledge. In the context of the development of expertise about dietetic medicine at the end of the seventeenth and beginning of the eighteenth centuries,

---

the insane at home. In an account of what he calls 'domestic psychiatry', Akihito Suzuki examines the attitudes and beliefs of those nineteenth-century middle and upper class families who cared for an insane member at home. He argues that lay frameworks formed an important lens for understanding madness. In Suzuki's words, rather than depend on the 'dictates of learned medicine, laypersons employed their own cultural framework to understand, treat and cope with the madness of their family members' (93): see A Suzuki *Madness at Home: The Psychiatrist, the Patient, and the Family in England 1820–1860* (Berkeley: University of California Press, 2006).

[78] Wiener *Reconstructing the Criminal* 123. Shapin's words about the vocabulary of dietetic culture—that it was the subject of 'joint ownership' by doctors and patients—seem apposite here: see Shapin *Never Pure* 289.

[79] Eigen and Andoll 'From Mad-Doctor to Forensic Witness' 168.

[80] T Ward 'Law, Common Sense and the Authority of Science: Expert Witnesses and Criminal Insanity in England, CA. 1840–1940' (1997) 6(3) *Social and Legal Studies* 343, 353.

[81] Rose *Powers of Freedom* 138, and, more generally, ch. 12.

Steven Shapin suggests that prudential expertise, accumulated experience and judgment informed by that experience, is analytically distinct from ontological expertise, which refers to the type of expertise claimed on the basis of special knowledge about underlying or hidden structures of the world or the domain in question.[82] As Shapin notes, prudential expertise is not necessarily based on 'knowledge of underlying processes reckoned qualitatively different from, or superior in kind to, lay knowledge'.[83] In addition, even ontological expertise has to be presented (in Shapin's context, to patients) in a way that allows possessors of this knowledge to capitalize on their knowledge.[84] This analysis of the different dimensions of specialist medical knowledge is germane to expert medical knowledge of insanity, and, indeed, takes on a particular significance in the nineteenth century, when the increasingly prominent courtroom profile of expert medical professionals of all stripes coincided with the rise to prominence of statistical studies.[85] Viewed from the perspective of the legal process, this analysis raises a question about the distinct significance of prudential expertise in relation to insanity, which risks being subsumed beneath ontological expertise in understanding the significance of expert knowledges of 'madness' for criminal law purposes.

Reflecting on the prudential dimensions of expert medical knowledge of insanity, it appears that there are good reasons to take this dimension of expertise seriously when thinking about criminal law knowledge practices. What we see from examination of the *OBPs* is that the medical experts giving evidence in insanity trials reinforced their authority by way of reference to prudential expertise, to the expertise of experience. The following two records from the *OBPs* included questions that elicited responses referencing the expert's authority in these terms.[86] For instance, Edward Oxford's trial for treason records the following exchange between the barrister for the Crown and an expert witness:

Q. Why could not any person form an opinion whether a person was sane or insane from the circumstances which have been referred to? A. Because it seems to require a careful

---

[82] Shapin *Never Pure* 311. This type of expertise was not new in the seventeenth and early eighteenth centuries, but the mechanical ideas of the scientific revolution gave it new bases for cultural authority (312).

[83] *Never Pure* 310–11. Shapin discusses this distinction in relation to the kinds of expertise that might be claimed by 'empirics' and 'rational physicians' (although he notes that neither these categories of expertise nor associated professional communities were mutually exclusive).

[84] For Shapin, even as scientific language (for example of 'particles' and 'blood vessels') began to separate from everyday language, this ontological knowledge had to be displayed in a way that permitted physicians to capitalize on their expertise: see *Never Pure* 312.

[85] As Ian Hacking argues, during the nineteenth century, following the rise of probability in the years to 1850, notions of normalcy and deviations from the norm came into existence—it became possible to class individuals in new ways, producing knowledge that was harnessed for new means of social control. I Hacking *The Taming of Chance* (Cambridge: CUP, 1990). Hacking chronicles the ways in which, buttressed by statistical information gathered—on suicides etc—for the purposes of social control, it became possible to define new classes of people, to conceptualize society in new ways and to speak of 'laws of probability'.

[86] Other trials could be referenced here: see, for instance, *OBP*, Ann Cornish Vyse, 7 July 1862 (t18620707-745) and *OBP*, John Selby Watson, 8 January 1872 (t18720108-117).

comparison of particular cases, more likely to be looked to by medical men, who are especially experienced in cases of unsound mind.[87]

Similarly, in the trial record of James Huggins' trial for damage to property in 1850, Sir Alexander Morrison, a physician at Bethlehem Hospital, testified:

My attention has been directed for a great many years to persons of unsound mind—I have had the management, and charge of lunatics at Bethlehem Hospital for about seventeen years—I have had opportunities from my experience of paying attention to the subject of insanity—I have not had an interview with the prisoner—I have heard the whole of the evidence which has been given in court to-day on the part of the prosecution and defence.[88]

These exemplary extracts suggest the importance of experts' quantum of experience with insanity (in the latter case, apparently more important than an interview with the prisoner), which interacted with other factors influencing the evaluation of expertise such as the social status of the relevant expert.

The rise of a prudential expertise about insanity was premised on particular institutional conditions. These particular institutional conditions revolved around the designated spaces for the insane. Although asylums had appeared towards the end of the 1700s, it was only in the 1800s that they became the predominant way of managing and treating the insane.[89] This development was significant in that it both reflected and enhanced the social profile of the insane, and regulated the handling of the insane in new ways.[90] For my purposes in discussing the dimensions of expertise about 'madness', asylums have a particular significance because they created the institutional and organizational conditions for the development of prudential knowledge of 'madness'. As Rose argues, these sorts of spaces provided the conditions for the 'statisticalization and normalization of diseases', creating a space in which any one case is located 'within a field structured by norms'.[91]

The asylum movement ushered in a situation in which 'state apparatus assumed a much greater role in the handling of insanity'.[92] The enhanced role of the state spilled over from the civil administrative sphere into the criminal sphere. The second half of the nineteenth century saw the rise of an elaborate administrative framework for insanity and an affiliated change in the processing of the insane and the criminally insane. The Insane Prisoners Act 1840 provided that if two justices

---

[87] *OBP*, Edward Oxford, 6 July 1840 (t18400706–1877). For detailed discussion of this case, see J P Eigen '"I answer as a physician": Opinion as Fact in pre-McNaughtan Insanity Trials' in M Clark and C Crawford (eds) *Legal Medicine in History* (Cambridge: CUP, 1994) 184–91.

[88] *OBP*, James Huggins, 7 July 1851 (t18510707–1502).

[89] See generally A Scull *Museums of Madness: The Social Organization of Insanity in Nineteenth-Century England* (London: Allen Lane, 1979), but, for a critical account of the historiography on the asylum movement, and a discussion of the care of the insane outside the bounds of the asylum, see Suzuki, *Madness at Home* Introduction.

[90] As Andrew Scull argues, asylums ensured that the insane were a prominent feature of the social landscape: see A Scull 'The Insanity of Place' (2004) 15(4) *History of Psychiatry* 417, 427. These asylums are now somewhat notorious for the ways in which they were open to the public: see Porter *Mind-Forg'd Manacles* 36–7.

[91] Rose 'Medicine, History and the Present' 60.

[92] A Scull 'The Social History of Psychiatry in the Victorian Era' in A Scull (ed) *Madhouses, Mad-Doctors and Madmen: The Social History of Psychiatry in the Victorian Era* (London: Athlone, 1981) 6.

of the peace certified that a prisoner was insane, either before or after trial, he or she could be transferred to an asylum.[93] Under the Insane Prisoners (Amendment) Act 1864,[94] the Home Office instituted its own medical examination of those who had been charged with capital offences and, when insanity was found, the defendants were removed to Broadmoor, which opened in 1863, or, later, to other mental hospitals.[95] With the passage of the Criminal Lunatics Act 1884, the Home Secretary was obliged to order an examination of the defendant in certain circumstances.[96] These changes to the administrative frame surrounding the insanity doctrine seem to have had an effect on the number of offenders who made the plea.[97]

The significance of the prudential dimension of expert knowledge about 'madness' as it relates to criminal law practices has not been fully appreciated. Scholars have emphasized the significance of ontological expertise over prudential expertise. But the latter seems to have been equally significant in understanding the patterns of proof of 'madness' in criminal process leading into the current era. This prudential dimension of expert knowledge was a distinctively modern inflection on knowledge of 'madness': what became relevant was knowledge of a class of people. These references to a quantum of experience, possible because of the institutionalization of the insane, expose the means by which expert knowledge of insanity acquired a distinctive basis of authority, and thus indicates one of the ways in which such knowledge was legitimated. In addition, the significance of this prudential dimension of expert knowledge of 'madness' was such that it meant that a space remained, within the legal context, and for the purposes of evaluation and adjudication, for lay or non-expert knowledge of 'madness'. The assessment of the particular condition of an individual, at a specified moment in time (the issue when claims of exculpatory 'madness' are made) was not and is not the exclusive jurisdiction of this type of knowledge. As I discuss in the next section, the role of lay knowledge is evident in the persistence of lay evaluation processes, and in the role of legal actors, who are lay for the purposes of knowledge of mental incapacity, meaning that expert knowledge continues to share the field with non-expert knowledge of 'madness'. When viewed in light of recent emphasis on safeguarding the domain of lay evaluation of insanity, which I discuss below, it seems that something of the blend of the general and the particular, referred to above in

---

[93] See N Walker *Crime and Insanity in England (Vol 1: The Historical Perspective)* (Edinburgh: Edinburgh University Press, 1968) 204.
[94] 27 & 28 Vict. c.29.
[95] See M J Wiener *Men of Blood: Violence, Manliness and Criminal Justice in Victorian England* (Cambridge: CUP, 2004) 281–2.
[96] 47 & 48 Vict. c.64. Walker argues that, by this time, the narrowness of the *M'Naghten Rules* was beginning to be appreciated, and the Home Secretary's power to look beyond them was welcome: see *Crime and Insanity in England (Vol 1)* 210.
[97] Referring to the national statistics for murder, Walker identifies an 'upward trend' in the success of the plea in the last decades of the 1800s (*Crime and Insanity in England (Vol 1)* 85–6). In Wiener's study, the proportion of offenders charged with murder who were certified as criminal lunatics increased markedly between 1857 and 1890 (Wiener *Reconstructing the Criminal* 272; see also M J Wiener *Men of Blood: Violence, Manliness and Criminal Justice in Victorian England* (Cambridge: CUP, 2004) 284).

relation to cross-referencing among experts, and between experts and non-experts, seems to have persisted, albeit in a different guise.

Knowing More Than They Can Say: Experts (and Non-Experts) in the Current Era

In the period since the rise to prominence of expert medical knowledge of insanity in the nineteenth century, both legal processes and extra-legal conditions relating to expertise have changed significantly. With the contemporaneous formalization of rules of evidence and procedure, an expert has come to be clearly differentiated from any other witness on the basis that he or she can give evidence of opinion on a question facing the court.[98] Both formal and informal privileges attach to the distinct status of expert witnesses.[99] More broadly, the proliferation of forms of knowledge falling within the broad category of scientific knowledge means that a dense matrix of individuals, methods, institutions, practices, and authority structures form the backdrop to legal reliance on expert evidence concerning matters such as insanity.[100] Stretching beyond the confines of criminal law and process, the social and cultural status of expert knowledge has undergone a profound change, which is connected with the social, cultural, and political transformation from modernity to late modernity. Indeed, a changed attitude to expertise has been depicted as paradigmatic of this transformation. While this complex story is beyond the scope of this book, it is useful to note that, broadly, the transformation is characterized as one from automatic trust in experts, to self-conscious or calculated trust.[101]

Against this larger frame, legal knowledge practices related to insanity continue to feature a mix of expert and non-expert knowledges and the involvement of expert and non-expert knowers. The significance of the mix of different types of knowledge on the mental incapacity terrain has been analysed in terms of the legitimization of criminal responsibility practices. For instance, Tony Ward has referred to the 'dual authority of science and lay consensus', which he argues underpins mental

---

[98] In addition, an expert is not generally compellable (that is, required to be present in court) and can be paid. For discussion, see P Alldridge 'Forensic Science and Expert Evidence' (1994) 21(1) *Journal of Law and Society* 136.

[99] The practical dimension of the expert's status in the criminal courtroom is his or her 'social capital'. See M Lynch 'Circumscribing Expertise: Membership Categories in Courtroom Testimony' in S Jasanoff (ed) *States of Knowledge: The Co-production of Science and Social Order* (London: Routledge, 2004) for discussion.

[100] Given this, a strong case has been made for the close sociological study of experts and expertise in law: see G Edmond and D Mercer 'Experts and Expertise in Legal and Regulatory Settings' in G Edmond (ed) *Expertise in Regulation and Law* (Aldershot: Ashgate, 2004) 1–31.

[101] See Giddens *Modernity and Self-Identity* and *Consequences of Modernity*. Over this period, scientific knowledge has been subject to large scale demystification and deconstruction. Science studies scholars have argued that science (and technology) no longer stand far above common knowledge, a situation that has been contrasted with the high-water mark of scientific infallibility, the post-war era: see H Collins and R Evans *Rethinking Expertise* (Chicago: University of Chicago Press, 2007).

incapacity doctrines such as insanity and diminished responsibility historically.[102] To me, the conviction that both expert and non-expert knowledge is crucial to this part of criminal law also applies in the current era. In my analysis, the broad continuity in knowledge practices related to exculpatory 'madness' (now divided across two doctrines, insanity and automatism) suggests that, under altered extra-legal conditions, it continues to be a combination of types of knowledge of mental incapacity that provides a robust basis for adjudication and evaluation of claims to exculpatory 'madness'.

In relation to the expert component of this mix of knowledges, the role of this type of knowledge is in part practical. Expert knowledge, in the form of expert evidence, helps to back up an individual's claim to exculpatory 'madness'. The rules about the basis on which verdicts may be handed down evidences this role for expert knowledge in proof of exculpatory insanity. While expert medical evidence gradually became a common feature of insanity trials over the course of the nineteenth and twentieth centuries, it was only recently that expert evidence was mandated.[103] The Criminal Procedure (Insanity and Unfitness to Plead) Act 1991 introduced a requirement that no jury is entitled to find insanity without evidence from two or more registered medical practitioners.[104] By contrast, but in keeping with its grounding in a broader, more moralized notion of incapacity (as opposed to a more technical notion of disability), there is no requirement that expert evidence be adduced in support of an automatism claim. There are, however, a number of judicial comments suggesting that expert evidence plays a significant role in cases in which it is raised. In relation to automatism, the significance of expert evidence lies in part in overcoming the 'presumption of mental capacity'.[105] In *Bratty*, Lord

---

[102] Ward 'Observers, Advisors, or Authorities?' 105.

[103] There is no requirement at common law that medical evidence be adduced in relation to a plea of insanity: *Rex v North* (1937) 1 *Criminal Law Journal* 84. Given that a formalized insanity doctrine has existed since 1843, and expert medical evidence had been introduced in court even earlier, it is notable that the statutory evidence requirement comes very late on in the development of the law on evidence and procedure that governs insanity claims.

[104] Section 1(1) of the Act requires 'written or oral evidence of two or more registered medical practitioners at least one of whom is duly certified' before the jury may deliver a special verdict. This requirement had been suggested in the Butler Report (para 18.37). Commentators have offered different explanations for its inclusion in Section 1(1) in the 1991 Act. These explanations include that it was introduced in order to promote consistency between the criminal law and the civil law (P Fennell 'The Criminal Procedure (Insanity and Unfitness to Plead) Act 1991' (1992) 55 *Modern Law Review* 547, 549); to alleviate judicial anxiety about 'the corrupt and/or unreliable medical expert' (T H Jones 'Insanity, Automatism and the Burden of Proof on the Accused' (1995) 111 *Law Quarterly Review* 475, 510); or to satisfy the European Convention on Human Rights (E Baker 'Human Rights, M'Naghten and the 1991 Act' [1994] *Criminal Law Review* 84, 86). Parliamentary discussion at the time the 1991 Act was introduced sheds little light on the legislative motivation for the evidence provision. Discussion of the Bill indicates that the provision seemed to be uncontroversial. The private member who proposed the Bill stated that Section 1 was an 'important' component of the Bill, which gave 'statutory backing to the *M'Naghten Rules*' (HC Deb 19 April 1991, vol 186, col 727). Given that the Bill left the substantive insanity doctrine unaltered, and the fact that the *M'Naghten Rules* do not require expert medical evidence, it is hard to see how this is the case.

[105] R D Mackay 'Mentally Abnormal Offenders: Disposal and Criminal Responsibility Issues' in M McConville and G Wilson (eds) *The Handbook of the Criminal Justice Process* (Oxford: OUP, 2002) 464. It has also been suggested that expert evidence plays a role in filtering out spurious claims to

Denning stated that, in displacing the presumption of mental capacity, 'the evidence of the man himself will rarely be sufficient unless it is supported by medical evidence which points to the cause of mental incapacity'.[106]

The line between the admissibility and non-admissibility of expert evidence—whether it be evidence concerning mental state at the time of the offence, or to support particular defence pleas, or going to the reliability of an individual's evidence[107]—demarcates the distinction between normality and abnormality. The rationale for expert evidence is that it addresses matters lying beyond the competence of the jury to evaluate. This role for expert medical evidence of incapacity has been invoked, for instance, in relation to automatism. In *Hill v Baxter*, Justice Devlin stated:

> I do not doubt that there are genuine cases of automatism and the like, but I do not see how the layman can safely attempt without the help of some medical or scientific evidence to distinguish the genuine from the fraudulent.[108]

This rationale is premised on the opinion doctrine, which itself is a feature of the modern law of evidence. Expert evidence is an exception to the prohibition on opinion evidence.[109]

---

exculpation based on automatism. As several commentators have pointed out, the cases that form the mainstay of automatism litigation are those in which the defendant performs apparently purposeful criminal actions (I D Elliott, 'Automatism and Trial by Jury' (1967–1968) 6 *Melbourne University Law Review* 53, 53; R D Mackay *Mental Condition Defences in the Criminal Law* (Oxford: Clarendon Press, 1995) 68; Walker *Crime and Insanity in England (Vol 1)* 165). A defendant's ability to perform complex and perhaps violent actions either involuntarily or unconsciously may be greeted with disbelief (R Cartwright 'Sleepwalking Violence: A Sleep Disorder, a Legal Dilemma and a Psychological Challenge' (2004) 161 *American Journal of Psychiatry* 1149, 1149). The evidence given by medical, psychiatric and psychological experts about the cause of a state of automatism (such as diabetes in *Quick* or dissociation in *Burgess*) or, perhaps whether a particular defendant suffered a 'total loss of self-control', would seem to provide support for the plausibility of a claim to automatism.

[106] *Bratty*, 413. Similarly, in *Stripp*, the Court concluded that the appellant's evidence that he had hit his head and suffered concussion was, in the absence of medical evidence, insufficient to provide a foundation for automatism: *R v Stripp* (1979) 69 Cr App R 318, 323.

[107] See *Chard* (1971) 56 Cr App R 268; *Turner* [1975] QB 834; and *Pinfold and Mackenney* [2004] 2 Cr App R 5 respectively. For discussion, see I Dennis, *The Law of Evidence* 4th edn (London: Sweet and Maxwell, 2010) 887–93. In relation to proof of mental incapacity in particular, see A Colman and R D Mackay 'Excluding Expert Evidence: A Tale of Ordinary Folk and Common Experience' [1991] *Criminal Law Review* 800 and R D Mackay and A Colman 'Equivocal Rulings on Expert Psychological and Psychiatric Evidence: Turning a Muddle into a Nonsense' [1996] *Criminal Law Review* 88.

[108] See *Hill v Baxter* [1958] 1 QB 277, 285. Another illustration of this rationale is provided by the decision of the Court in *Smith* where the Court of Appeal stated that 'this type of automatism—sleepwalking—call it what you like, is not something, we think, which is within the realm of the ordinary juryman's experience': *R v Smith* [1979] 1 WLR 1445, 1451.

[109] At least in theory, the expert is not able to give evidence on the 'ultimate issue', which is for the jury to decide. In *Holmes* ([1953] 2 All ER 324), the Court of Criminal Appeal approved a cross-examination in which the psychiatric expert was asked if the defendant knew the nature of his act and that it was wrong. It has been recognized that the 'ultimate issue' rule has been applied unevenly, and there is some suggestion that it is being abandoned by courts: see Dennis *The Law of Evidence* 903–7. See also B J Mitchell 'Putting Diminished Responsibility Law into Practice: A Forensic Psychiatric Perspective' (1997) 8(3) *Journal of Forensic Psychiatry* 620 regarding expert evidence of diminished responsibility.

In addition to this practical role for expert evidence and expert knowledge, it has an additional, more discursive significance: expert evidence assists in constructing the defendant as abnormal by making his or her condition the subject of specialist language of pathology. This role for expert evidence can be detected in relation to insanity (for instance, in connecting intoxication to the disease of alcoholism). This role for expert knowledge seems particularly significant in automatism cases because consciousness or voluntariness are matters of degree, and expert evidence plays a part in drawing a line at the point at which what might be (merely) a difference of degree becomes a difference of kind: the use of expert evidence to provide 'credible support'[110] for an automatism claim, for instance, provides a way of drawing a line at the point of abnormality. The process of drawing a line entails a reconstruction that ensures that the more slippery idea of a quantitative difference (impaired consciousness or voluntariness) is made to resemble a firmer qualitative difference (unconsciousness or involuntariness), and it is this kind of difference which is the basis of exculpation via the automatism doctrine.[111]

Turning now to the lay or non-expert component of this mix of knowledges covering the field of exculpatory 'madness', and here too, this type of knowledge also plays a role in proof of insanity and automatism. Again, as is the case for expert knowledge, this role is multifaceted, but, with the rise of expertise about 'madness', it can no longer be said to provide an animating framework for decisions about exculpatory incapacity. The role of lay knowledge is easiest to detect in relation to lay evaluation practices (archetypally, the role of a jury in a serious criminal trial). In relation to automatism, the question of whether a defendant was in fact acting in a state of automatism is a question of fact for the jury,[112] although the effect of the tight circumscription of automatism (via the tripartite requirements of a 'total loss of voluntary control', the external/internal factor distinction, and no prior fault), as well as the 'presumption of mental capacity', effectively limit the role of the jury because the circumstances in which the plea can be made are rare. The role of lay evaluation is wider when it comes to insanity. By contrast with other criminal law exculpatory doctrines, which are widely open to defence pleas, it is not possible for the prosecution to accept a plea of 'not guilty by reason of insanity' since the issue must go to a jury.[113] This requirement has a symbolic

---

[110] *Bratty*, 414.
[111] I discuss this issue of differences of kind versus differences of degree in the context of a discussion of diminished responsibility: see Chapter 9.
[112] *R v Harrison-Owen* [1951] 2 All ER 726.
[113] *R v Crown Court at Maidstone ex parte London Borough of Harrow* [2000] 1 Cr App R 117 at 123; see also S Dell 'Wanted: An Insanity Defence that Can be Used' [1983] *Criminal Law Review* 431, 431. The *M'Naghten* rules included the requirement that the issue of insanity go to the jury, and thus, like the reverse burden of proof, its durability may be explained as a consequence of the 'quasi-legislative status' of the *Rules*: see Dennis *The Law of Evidence* 459. The Butler Committee recommended that the prosecution be allowed to accept a plea (Butler Report para 18.50). However, this recommendation has not been implemented. This feature of the *M'Naghten Rules* has put the practical advantages of a plea option, canvassed by the Court in *Cox* in relation to the defence of diminished responsibility, beyond the reach of the insanity doctrine. See *R v Cox* [1968] 1 WLR 308 and Chapter 9.

significance, as the jury must be seen to approve the insanity plea. The practical significance of the requirement that insanity go to the jury has, however, been questioned.[114] But even acknowledging researchers' claims about the greater importance of expert medical evidence in insanity trials, it should be recalled that this evidence may lead jurors to 'reconsider their interpretations' but 'it does not compel them to abandon their own sense of what is plausible'.[115]

Beyond the specific role of lay jurors in the evaluation of insanity and automatism cases, lay knowledge has a broader if more diffused role in relation to exculpatory 'madness'. This becomes apparent if, as I suggest in Chapter 3, it is recognized that legal actors—judges, prosecutors, and defence counsel—have lay knowledge when it comes to mental incapacity. This status as lay in relation to mental incapacity is not to deny legal actors their status as experts regarding legal practices and processes: rather, it is to acknowledge that, as Antony Giddens argues, in the current era, 'all experts are themselves lay people most of the time'.[116] It is my suggestion that, in relation to matters involving claims to exculpation on the basis of mental incapacity, legal expertise is mixed up with lay knowledge or non-expertise. Approached this way, the role of lay knowledge of mental incapacity extends beyond lay evaluation, because legal actors employ such knowledge of mental incapacity in the execution of their roles. This is significant because, even if lay people have come to have a circumscribed role in the procedure relating to insanity, this does not entail a correspondingly minor role for the knowledge of 'madness' possessed by ordinary people. This type of knowledge continues to inform legal practices around mental incapacity. I take up this point again in Chapter 7.

Proving Exculpatory 'Madness': Reconstruction and Due Process

The final aspect of knowing and proving exculpatory mental incapacity to examine is the rules of evidence and procedure governing claims of 'madness'. The crystallization of procedural and evidentiary practices relating to exculpatory 'madness'

---

[114] In empirical studies of the operation of the insanity doctrine since the passage of the Criminal Procedure (Insanity and Unfitness to Plead) Act 1991, several commentators have observed that, in a number of trials, juries were directed to return a special verdict or presented with a situation where all parties, and all expert evidence, supported the special verdict (R D Mackay, B J Mitchell and L Howe 'Yet More Facts about the Insanity Defence' [2006] *Criminal Law Review* 399, 404; R D Mackay and G Kearns 'More Fact(s) About the Insanity Defence' [1999] *Criminal Law Review* 714, 721). Some of this research concludes that expert medical evidence is of primary importance in relation to the outcome of an insanity trial: Mackay and Kearns 'More Fact(s) About the Insanity Defence' 721. It appears that, in certain instances, the requirement that the issue of insanity go to the jury may be a mere formality. Of course, in other instances, the existence of the requirement that the defence go to the jury means that there is potential for an independent determination on the question of the defendant's insanity. Nonetheless, this research suggests that caution is needed in assessing the requirement that the insanity doctrine go to the jury so as not to overstate its significance.

[115] T Ward 'English Law's Epistemology of Expert Testimony' (2006) 33(4) *Journal of Law and Society* 572, 585.

[116] See Giddens *Modernity and Self-Identity* 138, and, more generally, ch. 4.

160   *Manifest Madness: Mental Incapacity in Criminal Law*

occurred in two broad stages. In the first, the conditions of the 'reconstructive' criminal trial prevailed, and both this and the non-partisan flavour of expert evidence of insanity pertaining at the time, informed the distinctive rules that govern claims to insanity. By the second stage, coinciding with the appearance of a discrete automatism doctrine, the adversarial trial had come to be oriented around an idea of due process, and the defendant viewed in part as a suspect.[117] As a result of these different sets of conditions, the evidentiary and procedural rules that developed to govern automatism claims stand in contrast with those of insanity. I structure my discussion of these rules along the lines of a comparison between those applying to insanity and those applying to automatism.

The 'Presumption of Sanity' and the 'Presumption of Mental Capacity'

Presumptions have a prominent role in structuring proof of mental incapacity. It has been said that presumptions are rules of law, not rules of evidence—and their purpose is a practical one as they assign tasks in the courtroom (between, say, prosecution and defence counsel)—but they connote particular epistemological positions.[118] The two presumptions governing exculpatory mental incapacity—the 'presumption of sanity' and the 'presumption of mental incapacity'—are predicated on an idea of what it is regarded as reasonable to believe about 'madness'. The significance of the presumptions is two-fold: they work to construct the individual relying on the doctrine as exceptional, and they limit the scope of the doctrines by screening out weaker cases. Taken together, this means that the presumptions have a circumscribing effect on the law of insanity and automatism.[119]

The *M'Naghten Rules* refer to the 'presumption of sanity', stating that 'jurors ought to be told in all cases that every man is to be presumed sane, and to possess a sufficient degree of reason to be responsible for his crimes, until the contrary be proved to their satisfaction'.[120] In order to structure the relationship between insanity and automatism, the courts have relied on what Lord Denning called the 'presumption of mental capacity', whereby 'a man's act is presumed to be voluntary unless there is evidence from which it can reasonably be inferred that it was involuntary'.[121] The 'presumption of mental capacity' is different from the

---

[117] See A Duff et al *The Trial on Trial (Vol 3)* 50–3.
[118] As H L Ho puts it, presumptions deal with the question 'what to do', rather than 'what (it is reasonable for one) to believe': see H L Ho *A Philosophy of Evidence Law* (Oxford: OUP, 2008) 97. But, it has been suggested that a presumption indicates that there are good grounds for believing a particular claim, although these grounds are somewhat incomplete. See R Hall 'Presuming' 11(42) *The Philosophical Quarterly* (1961) 10.
[119] Moreover, whether the defendant is making a claim of automatism or one of insanity is a question of law for the judge (see *Bratty* 412 per Lord Denning), which can be interpreted as another circumscribing aspect of these presumptions.
[120] Extracted in R Moran *Knowing Right from Wrong: The Insanity Defense of Daniel McNaughtan* (New York: The Free Press, 1981) 173. See also *OBP*, Charles O'Donnell, 20 November 1876 (t18761120-27).
[121] *Bratty* 413. 'Normally', the presumption of mental capacity is sufficient to prove that the defendant acted 'consciously and voluntarily': *Bratty* 407 per Viscount Kilmuir.

'presumption of sanity', as the former does not place a legal burden on the defence.[122] It does, however, require the defence to raise a 'proper foundation' for an automatism claim.[123] Once a 'proper foundation' for the plea has been laid, the trial judge must determine whether, as a question of law, the condition alleged by the defendant is non-insane automatism, as opposed to insanity.[124]

A close look at *Bratty v Attorney-General for Northern Ireland* illustrates the significance of presumptions in circumscribing the scope of exculpatory mental incapacity. At trial, the defence put forward three arguments in the alternative: first, that Bratty was in a state of automatism due to psychomotor epilepsy; second, that his mental condition was such that he was not capable of forming intent to murder and should be liable only for manslaughter; and, third, that he was insane within the meaning of the *M'Naghten Rules*. The trial judge left insanity to the jury, but not automatism or lack of *mens rea*. Bratty was convicted and appealed. The House of Lords dismissed the appeal. The issue of the defendant's *mens rea* was given very little consideration. The Lords concluded that, as the jury must have found the defendant sane and responsible at the time of the killing because he was convicted, there were no grounds for the view that he lacked the intent to kill or commit grievous bodily harm. As this case suggests, however, claims that a defendant did not form the requisite *mens rea*, and claims that he or she was in a state of automatism (and could not form the *mens rea*) may be difficult to untangle in a particular case. But the presumption attached to automatism ensures that it is hard to argue that the prosecution has not made out one of the elements of the offence in cases such as *Bratty*—the defendant is in effect directed into a mental incapacity claim. A concern that an acquittal could too readily flow from a claim by the defendant to have been in a state of automatism at the time of the offence is detectable between the lines in the *Bratty* decision: a 'presumption of mental capacity' provides an evidential barrier to thin claims for exculpation on the basis of automatism.

---

[122] *Bratty* 413 per Lord Denning.
[123] *Bratty* 413; *R v Budd* [1962] Crim LR 49; *Burgess* 96 per Lord Lane. A 'proper foundation' has been interpreted 'to come very close to saying that there must be a *prima facie* case raised by the defence': *R v Stripp* (1979) 69 Cr App R 318 at 322 per Lord Justice Ormrod.
[124] *Watmore v Jenkins* [1962] 2 QB 572 586; *Broome v Perkins* (1987) 85 Cr App R 321 at 331; *R v Burgess* 96 per Lord Lane. If the condition amounts to (non-insane) automatism, the doctrine will be left with the jury. If the condition amounts to insanity (on the basis that it arises from a 'disease of the mind'), the doctrine of insanity will be left with the jury. Thus, if, as was the case in *Bratty*, the evidence that the defendant was acting in an automatistic state was held to be consistent only with an insanity doctrine because it was caused by a 'disease of the mind', the judge need not leave automatism to the jury. As I D Elliot argues, this means that there is a possibility that the jury will find that the elements of *M'Naghten* insanity have not been proved on the balance of probabilities and convict the defendant, although they are not satisfied that the defendant acted consciously (Elliott 'Automatism and Trial by Jury' 64–5). As Elliot concludes, a defendant who is convicted in these circumstances has been denied the protection of the decision in *Woolmington* as the prosecution has been absolved of its obligation to prove the elements of the offence ('Automatism and Trial by Jury' 65–6; see also P Fairall 'Automatism' (1981) 5 *Criminal Law Journal* 335, 339).

Raising Insanity or Automatism

Either the defence or the prosecution can raise the issue of an individual's insanity. The original position at common law was that only the defence could raise insanity,[125] but in the mid-twentieth century, the rule was reinterpreted retrospectively. In *Bratty*, the House of Lords held that, if the defendant adduces evidence of mental disorder to deny the requisite *mens rea* for an offence, the prosecution may adduce similar evidence in order to secure a special verdict rather than an acquittal.[126] Further, as a result of the decision in *Bratty*, the judge may direct the jury on the issue of insanity even if it has not been raised by the defence or the prosecution.[127] By contrast, the general rule is that automatism may only be raised by the defence. If the defence raises automatism, it will be open to the prosecution to raise insanity because the defendant's state of mind has been put in issue.[128] The rule about the defence raising automatism arguably reflects the fact that, if successful, it results in an unqualified acquittal. In this respect, automatism stands in contrast to the insanity doctrine, unfitness to plead, and infanticide. But, it is similar to common law defences, such as self-defence, which may only be raised by the defendant.

The rule about raising automatism may be understood through the general lens of due process, according to which the trial is now oriented to the efficient processing of criminal cases.[129] Under these conditions, it makes sense to leave the question of automatism to the defence. The rule about raising insanity demands a different explanation. The rule about raising insanity may be interpreted as a device to ensure that potentially dangerous defendants are not granted ordinary acquittals on the grounds that they did not form the requisite *mens rea* due to mental abnormality—the rule ensures that the defendant cannot achieve an acquittal with evidence of mental incapacity and avoid the disposals that are triggered by a

---

[125] *Rex v Smith* (1910) 6 Cr App R 19. It is possible that the genesis of this original common law position lay in the medieval court practice of acquitting insane defendants, referred to above. Even after this practice ended, and insane defendants had to rely on the royal prerogative to escape punishment, the fact that the insanity doctrine resulted in an acquittal may have meant it was only in the interests of the defence to raise the issue, ensuring the procedural rule about raising insanity remained in place.

[126] *Bratty* 411–12. In addition, if the defence raises diminished responsibility, the prosecution is entitled to raise evidence tending to prove insanity (Criminal Procedure (Insanity) Act 1964, s 6, overruling *R v Price* [1963] 2 QB 1). If the prosecution raises insanity, it bears the burden of proving insanity beyond all reasonable doubt (*Podola* [1960] 1 QB 325; *Grant* [1960] Crim LR 424).

[127] In that case, Lord Denning cited with approval the decision of *Kemp*, in which Justice Devlin stated that judges are entitled to raise insanity of their own accord (*R v Kemp* [1957] 1 QB 399, cited in *Bratty* at 412).

[128] When the defence has raised automatism, the prosecution may counter with insanity so that, if the defendant suffers from a 'disease of the mind', he or she will not receive a complete acquittal but will be subject to the disposal options flowing from a special verdict: *Bratty* 411 per Lord Denning; *Kemp*, 408 per Justice Devlin. In this respect, automatism has a parallel with diminished responsibility, which, if raised by the defence, may be met with prosecution evidence of insanity: see Chapter 5 on automatism and Chapter 9 on diminished responsibility.

[129] A Duff et al *The Trial on Trial (Vol 3)* 50.

successful insanity plea.[130] Alongside this concern with dangerousness, the rule is premised on a distinctive basis—the idea that all parties have both the interest and the capacity to signal the presence of an insane defendant in the courtroom, and in avoiding the general verdict (an acquittal or conviction) that would otherwise follow. To me, viewed in this light, the rule echoes the concerns of the older 'reconstructive' criminal trial process, suggesting that the court continues to be a 'witness to the truth' of insanity.[131]

The Burden of Proof: Legal or Evidentiary

The *M'Naghten Rules* provide that the legal burden of proving insanity lies with the defence. The 'presumption of sanity' means that, unless the issue of insanity is raised by the prosecution, as discussed above, the defence must prove the defendant's insanity to the balance of probabilities standard.[132] By contrast, after an initial period of uncertainty,[133] in *Bratty*, the House of Lords held that, unlike insanity, the defence need only raise evidence of automatism, rather than prove it to a legal standard. Thus, if sufficient evidence of automatism is raised by the defence, the prosecution bears the burden of proving beyond reasonable doubt that the defendant was not acting in an automatistic state.[134] The rule that an evidential burden is borne by the defence in relation to automatism has been interpreted as a means of safeguarding the defence from abuse via bogus claims.[135]

In its famous decision on burdens of proof, the House of Lords in *Woolmington* stated that it is the duty of the prosecution to prove the guilt of the prisoner, but classed the insanity doctrine as an exception to this principle, stating that it was one situation in which 'it is incumbent upon the accused to prove his innocence'.[136] The Court gave no explanation as to why insanity was considered an exception to the general rule. Rather, the House stated:

---

[130] This interpretation of the rule has been adopted by a number of commentators. See, for example, J Monahan 'Abolish the Insanity Defense? Not Yet' (1973) 26 *Rutgers Law Review* 719, 727; G Williams *Textbook of Criminal Law* (London: Stevens, 1978) 596.
[131] A Duff et al *The Trial on Trial (Vol 3)* 47.
[132] *R v Soderman* (1935) AC 462; *R v Carr-Briant* [1943] KB 607.
[133] The issue of the burden and standard of proof was not addressed in *Harrison-Owen, Charlson*, or *Kemp* and specifically reserved in *Hill v Baxter* (285). In *Hill v Baxter*, Justice Devlin stated, *obiter*, that 'as automatism is akin to insanity in law there would be great practical advantage if the burden of proof was the same in both cases' (285). Despite Justice Devlin's comment, when determined, the burden and standard of proof in insanity and automatism differ.
[134] *Bratty* 408 per Viscount Kilmuir; see also *R v Burns* (1973) 58 Cr App R 364 at 374. In refusing to follow the earlier suggestion in *Hill v Baxter* and impose a reverse burden for automatism, the Court in *Bratty* was mindful of the principle of *Woolmington*, 'that it is for the prosecution to prove every element of the offence charged': 407 per Viscount Kilmuir; 416 per Lord Morris of Borth-y-Gest.
[135] R D Mackay argues that the burden of proof represents a 'controlling factor' in automatism, allowing the courts to distinguish between genuine and fraudulent cases (Mackay *Mental Condition Defences* 35).
[136] *Woolmington v DPP* 8.

M'Naghten's case stands by itself. It is the famous pronouncement on the law bearing on the question of insanity in cases of murder. It is quite exceptional and has nothing to do with the present circumstances. In *M'Naghten's* case the onus is definitely and exceptionally placed upon the accused to establish such a defence... It is not necessary to refer to *M'Naghten's* case again in this judgment for it has nothing to do with it.[137]

As a result of the decision in *Woolmington*, the insanity doctrine became an 'anomaly' in the common law.[138] What is referred to as the reverse burden of proof marks the insanity doctrine out from other common law doctrines: where a burden on the defence exists elsewhere in the common law, it is an evidentiary one (as in duress and self-defence).

The traditional explanation for the anomalous burden of proof for insanity gestures towards a diffused concern with the 'provability' of exculpatory incapacity—it rests on the idea some facts are peculiarly within the provenance of the defendant, resulting in a perceived difficulty in proving abnormal mental states. According to this idea, inferences about an insane defendant's mental state cannot be made with the confidence with which inferences about the mental state of non-insane defendants may be made.[139] Reasoning based on this concern is found in Lord Woolf's comment that the burden of proof in insanity is reversed because 'proof of the commission of any offence requires the existence of a guilty mind and the ability to prove this depends on courts being able to rely on the presumption of mental capacity in the absence of evidence to the contrary'.[140] Relatedly, the reverse burden of proof has also been explained as a result of concern with feigned insanity. The concern here is that juries might be duped by fabricated claims of insanity. Smith has suggested that 'fear of fakery', coupled with anxiety about the 'indeterminacy' of criminal responsibility, aggravates 'uncertainty over the level of moral, cognitive, and volitional capacity necessary to incur criminal liability'.[141] Smith's argument does not explain how the reverse burden in particular came to be conceived of as a solution to that indeterminacy, and, overall, the traditional explanation for the anomalous burden of proof for insanity is not entirely persuasive.

My own reading of the reverse burden is two-part, seeking to account separately for the placement of the burden on the defence in the *M'Naghten Rules*, and the burden remaining on the defence, even as a contemporary anomaly. The burden of proof was placed on the defence at the time of *M'Naghten* in 1843 because, in this era, such a burden was not anomalous, but rather an instance of the general

---

[137] *Woolmington v DPP* 5.
[138] Jones 'Insanity, Automatism' 477. For a critical discussion of the reverse burden in insanity, see E Colvin 'Exculpatory Doctrines in Criminal Law' (1990) 10 *Oxford Journal of Legal Studies* 381; for an analysis of the 'peculiar knowledge' doctrine, see A Stumer *The Presumption of Innocence* (Oxford: Hart, 2010) 172–6.
[139] P W Ferguson 'Reverse Burdens of Proof' (2004) 22 *Scots Law Times* 133, 138.
[140] *R v Lambert* [2002] QB 1112, 1122; see also *Hill v Baxter* 282.
[141] K J M Smith *Lawyers, Legislators and Theorists: Developments in English Criminal Jurisprudence 1800–1957* (Oxford: Clarendon Press, 1998) 95.

practices of English courts.[142] On this reading, the reverse burden was originally one instance of a general rule that something like a nascent burden of proof for all defences rested on the defence.[143] This explanation fits with the account of *Woolmington* that regards it as altering rather than affirming the law on burdens of proof.[144] Why, then, was insanity left behind when, after *Woolmington*, burdens of proof became 'progressively more favourable' to defendants?[145] Here, successive failures to reform the *M'Naghten* insanity doctrine must bear a significant portion of the responsibility. Beyond this, it seems to me that the effect of older ideas about the court as a 'witness to the truth' of insanity can still be felt here. When viewed in light of continuities around the substantive significance of a defendant's conduct in insanity cases,[146] the idea of a heavier burden on the defendant than is otherwise placed on him or her via the common law seems to reflect the stamp of the distinctive 'reconstructive' criminal trial process.

The Special Verdict or the General Verdict

A verdict of 'not guilty' following a successful automatism plea is an ordinary acquittal. This means that it is a typical full defence.[147] By contrast, if the jury finds the

---

[142] G P Fletcher 'Two Kinds of Legal Rules: A Comparative Study of Burden-of-Persuasion Practices in Criminal Cases' (1968) 77 *Yale Law Journal* 880, 902. Fletcher argues that the reverse burden reflects the criminal law's debt to 'private litigation', to use his term for the civil (as opposed to criminal) law (Fletcher 'Two Kinds of Legal Rules' 917; see also Jones 'Insanity, Automatism' 478). According to Fletcher, reflecting the norms of private litigation, criminal law conceptualized the prosecution and defence as two equal parties, each with 'duties to persuade' on the issues in the case ('Two Kinds of Legal Rules' 899). Thus, the burden of proof fell on the defence for denials of the relevant facts (as opposed to affirmative statements of the facts): a plea of insanity was such a denial ('Two Kinds of Legal Rules' 899).

[143] Jones 'Insanity, Automatism' 477–8. For this reason, Jones suggests that the *M'Naghten* judges may have been applying to insanity what they understood as a general rule ('Insanity, Automatism' 477).

[144] Fletcher 'Two Kinds of Legal Rules' 903. As Ian Dennis suggests, in altering the law, the Court in *Woolmington* may have been unwilling to challenge *M'Naghten* because of its 'quasi-legislative status' (Dennis *The Law of Evidence* 459; see also Cairns *Advocacy and the Making of the Adversarial Criminal Trial* 178).

[145] Fletcher 'Two Kinds of Legal Rules' 890.

[146] The ongoing significance of a defendant's conduct over time may have blunted both pragmatic and normative arguments that the prosecution should bear the burden of disproving a defendant's insanity (beyond all reasonable doubt). For instance, Morse's claim that 'no substantial injustice to the defendant will result from placing the persuasion burden on the defendant because, when legal insanity is truly present under a narrow test of insanity, most cases will be quite clear' (S J Morse 'Excusing the Crazy: The Insanity Defence Reconsidered' (1985) 58 *Southern California Law Review* 777, 825), is based on the premise that abnormality is evident or obvious. See A Loughnan, '"Manifest Madness": Towards A New Approach to the Insanity Defence' (2007) 70(3) *Modern Law Review* 379. See also Chapter 3.

[147] Because a verdict of 'not guilty' on the basis of automatism results in an ordinary acquittal, which cannot be distinguished from other 'not guilty' verdicts, there is no empirical data available about the use of the automatism defence in England and Wales. In the absence of statistical data, there is, however, some suggestion that automatism is not a popular defence (see, eg Mackay *Mental Condition Defences* 67). Why is the automatism defence unpopular? As Mackay notes, the explanation lies in part in the restricted parameters of the defence which means that only a select group of defendants fall within its bounds (*Mental Condition Defences* 67). In addition, it is possible that those defendants who are eligible to raise automatism are unwilling to do so because, by putting their

defendant insane, the result is the special verdict, 'not guilty by reason of mental disorder'. As I discuss in Chapter 5, the Criminal Lunatics Act 1800 provided that, where a 'person was insane at the time of the commission' of a felony offence, he was to be acquitted and 'the jury shall be required to find specially whether such person was insane at the time of the commission of such offence', after which the court 'shall order such person to be kept in strict custody'. In contrast to a general verdict ('guilty' or 'not guilty'), the special verdict includes a statement of the factual basis on which the verdict has been reached.

The longstanding and intimate connection between the insanity doctrine and the special verdict has been explained as the result of a policy concern with marking out those defendants who are to be subject to the special coercive powers of the state from those who are either to be acquitted or convicted through the normal processes of the criminal law. In this light, and reflecting the interaction of social welfare and policy concerns and the principles of criminal liability in this area of the law, the special verdict is a unique device by which the detention of insane defendants in the interests of social protection was brought within the bounds of the criminal law.[148] It is clear that the special verdict is both premised on and signals that the insane defendant is dangerous, a construction that has proved remarkably durable, as I discuss in Chapter 5. As George Fletcher puts it, 'a finding of insanity answers the question: is the accused sufficiently dangerous to be justifiably committed?'[149] An additional dimension of the special verdict is illuminated by Paul Robinson's analysis: according to Robinson, the special verdict avoids any 'potential for misapprehension' about why the defendant has been exculpated, ensuring that the interests of 'condemnation and general deterrence' remain intact.[150]

---

mental state in issue, they may face a special verdict if the insanity doctrine is raised by the prosecution. This is perhaps a weaker argument since the Criminal Procedure (Insanity and Unfitness to Plead) Act 1991 introduced a range of disposal options to follow a special verdict. Another possible explanation for the unpopularity of automatism is uncertainty about how a jury would receive an automatism plea. It is possible that claims by defendants that they are engaged in purposeful, complex, and violent behaviour while in automatistic states are regarded as implausible; see Cartwright 'Sleepwalking Violence' 1149). Arguably, the strength of this explanation for the unpopularity of automatism would vary according to the cause of a particular defendant's automatistic actions (and perhaps also the nature of the offence with which he or she is charged).

[148] See, for example, Jones 'Insanity, Automatism' 515; Colvin 'Exculpatory Defences in Criminal Law' 392; Mackay *Mental Condition Defences* 73, 90–2.

[149] Fletcher 'Two Kinds of Legal Rules' 920. According to Walker, the special verdict pays lip-service to the idea that the insane defendant is innocent but avoids the danger of treating him or her as such: see *Crime and Insanity in England (Vol 1)* 81.

[150] Robinson suggests that it may be because of this 'potential for misapprehension' that the insanity doctrine takes the form of a special verdict ('not guilty by reason of insanity') and concludes that more 'excuse defences' should take this form: see P Robinson 'Criminal Law Defences: A Systematic Analysis' [1982] 82(2) *Columbia Law Review* 199, 247; see also G Williams 'The Theory of Excuses' [1982] *Criminal Law Review* 732, 741. As part of his wider analysis of 'disability excuses', Robinson argues that the 'disability requirement' of the defence, whereby the defendant must have a particular abnormality (insanity) at the time of the offence, 'serves to distinguish the defendant from the general population' ('Criminal Law Defences' 226; see also P Robinson *Structure and Function in Criminal Law* (Oxford: Clarendon Press, 1997) 84). Distinguishing the defendant from the general population is essential because, according to Robinson, 'excuses have a great potential for undercutting

Some commentators have advocated the possibility of reforming the law to introduce a special verdict to follow a successful automatism plea. This law reform proposal has two variants, an older and a newer variant. In its older variant, in order to foster an expanded scope of automatism, some commentators have argued that a set of disposal options should be available in cases of automatism. Citing historical precedent for conditional acquittals, Walker argues that 'the logical course would have been to ask for legislation to allow the court to insist on precautions in such cases [as *Charlson*]'.[151] The modern variant of this proposed reform, advocated by R M Mackay (among others) involves extending the special verdict to automatism. This would preserve automatism as a legal entity but provide some control over automatistic defendants considered to be dangerous.[152] Neither conditional acquittals nor an extension of the special verdict disposal options is on the current law reform agenda. An alternative law reform proposal, although one also motivated by concern with disposals of dangerous defendants, would alter the boundary between the insanity and automatism doctrines.[153]

Disposal or No Disposal

Reflecting concerns with dangerousness that marked the development of the insanity doctrine itself, and procedural features such as the special verdict, for all but the recent decades of a formal insanity law, there has only been one disposal option following a successful insanity plea: indefinite detention. As a result of the Criminal Procedure (Insanity) Act 1964, the outcome of an insanity verdict became hospitalization.[154] The Criminal Procedure (Insanity and Unfitness to Plead) Act 1991 amended the law to introduce a range of disposals to follow an

---

the condemnation and general deterrence of the harmful conduct' which is the subject of the offence ('Criminal Law Defences' 246). For Robinson, because an excuse is based on 'subjective criteria' like mental illness, and not on approval or tolerance of the act, the reason for an acquittal will only be clear to those who are aware of what evidence was adduced at trial ('Criminal Law Defences' 246).

[151] Walker *Crime and Insanity in England (Vol 1)* 175. Other commentators have suggested that an acquittal with certain conditions would be appropriate for defendants, such as diabetics, seeking to rely on automatism (G Maher, J Pearson and B Frier 'Diabetes Mellitus and Criminal Responsibility' (1984) 24 (2) *Medicine, Science and Law* 95, 100). The legal basis for such conditional acquittals is not clear (R D Mackay 'The Automatism Defence—What Price Rejection?' (1983) 34(1) *Northern Ireland Legal Quarterly* 81, 85).

[152] See R D Mackay 'Craziness and Codification—Revising the Automatism and Insanity Defences' in I Dennis (ed) *Criminal Law and Justice* (London: Sweet and Maxwell, 1987) 116–18.

[153] The Butler Committee advocated this approach. In order to extend the special verdict to cases which would otherwise receive a complete acquittal, the Butler Committee proposed retaining the (non-insane) automatism defence, but redefining the boundary between insane and non-insane automatism (paras 18.20, 18.25). The Committee proposed that (non-insane) automatism be restricted to 'transient states not related to other forms of mental disorder arising solely as a consequence of' the consumption of drugs or alcohol or physical injury (para 18.23). The Committee proposed that all other cases of what was regarded as (non-insane) automatism would fall within the bounds of the special verdict, which the Committee relabelled as 'not guilty on evidence of mental disorder' (para 18.22). This proposal would have ensured that most defendants who commit offences while in states of automatism would be formally acquitted but subject to a disposal order by the court.

[154] Criminal Procedure (Insanity) Act 1964, s 5.

insanity verdict.[155] These disposal options did not initially apply where the defendant had been charged with an offence for which the sentence is 'fixed by law'.[156] But the Domestic Violence, Crime and Victims Act 2004 (which removed guardianship orders as one of the disposal options) provided that, where the sentence for an offence is 'fixed by law', the courts have power to order a hospital order only if the necessary medical criteria are satisfied.[157] Post the 2004 Act, the disposal of insane defendants is more flexible than it has been since 1800.

Statutory reforms to provide for a range of disposal options can be readily interpreted as a response to fairness and human rights concerns about indefinite hospitalization. The criticisms of indefinite detention under the 1964 Act were legion: it possibly meant longer detention than the defendant would face had he or she been convicted of the offence and may not have been an appropriate response to the condition which gave rise to the insanity plea.[158] These considerations meant that there was little reason for defence counsel to make a plea of insanity except in those cases where the defendant was charged with a serious offence (something which has arguably skewed popular understanding of the operation of the law of insanity). Even after the 1991 Act was passed, concerns remained about the lawfulness of indefinite hospitalization imposed on individuals charged with murder but found 'not guilty by reason of insanity', which were only addressed in 2004.[159] Underscoring specific concerns with the human rights of insane individuals appears to be a different attitude on the part of legislators and others to the criminally insane. These recent reforms to the disposal of insane defendants represent something of a decoupling of insanity and dangerousness, although, reflecting the rise of concerns with risk (which I discuss in Chapter 5), some sort of disposal still follows a successful insanity plea.

To conclude this discussion of evidence and proof of exculpatory 'madness', it is appropriate to refer to the empirical profile of both insanity and automatism. These emprical profiles serve to highlight the way in which the symbolic significance of these doctrines outstretches their practical role in the criminal law. Empirical research indicates that findings of 'not guilty by reason of insanity' have increased since the passage of the 1991 Act, although overall rates of success in raising

---

[155] With the passage of the 1991 Act, Crown courts could issue: a hospital admission order; a guardianship order; a supervision order; or an order for absolute discharge (s 5(2)(b)(iii)).

[156] Section 5(3)) (that is, murder, to which a mandatory penalty of life applies)—in that case, the only option open to the court was a hospital order,

[157] Domestic Violence, Crime and Victims Act 2004, s 24; see also Mackay, Mitchell and Howe 'Yet More Facts' 408. The most recent empirical research available covers the operation of the insanity doctrine between 1997 and 2001, thus encompassing the reforms introduced in the 1991 Act (but not the 2004 Act). According to a study conducted by Mackay, Mitchell and Howe, just over half the total number of special verdicts resulted in community-based orders, such as hospital admission orders and supervision and treatment orders (Mackay, Mitchell and Howe 'Yet More Facts' 407).

[158] E Griew 'Let's Implement Butler on Mental Disorder and Crime!' [1984] *Current Legal Problems* 47, 49–50.

[159] See P J Sutherland and C A Gearty 'Insanity and the European Court of Human Rights' [1991] *Criminal Law Review* 418 for discussion.

Knowing and Proving Exculpatory Mental Incapacity 169

insanity remain low.[160] Mackay and colleagues suggest that this increase is due to the flexibility in disposal orders introduced in the Act, concluding that the Act has removed disincentives for pleading insanity.[161] Several writers note that the number of defendants with mental illnesses is significantly higher than the insanity doctrine figures suggest.[162] There seem to be three explanations, which, together, provide a persuasive explanation for the low numbers of individuals successfully relying on the insanity doctrine. First, defendants who raise insanity might instead be found unfit to plead, or, if they have been charged with murder, may rely on diminished responsibility rather than insanity.[163] A second explanation is that even after reforms to introduce of a range of disposal options, the prospect of a hospital order or other disposal may seem unattractive. A third explanation for the low number of defendants utilizing the insanity doctrine is the limited reach of the *M'Naghten* doctrine,[164] although, as several commentators note, the insanity doctrine has a more flexible application in practice than is apparent on the face of the law.[165]

---

[160] There is no statistical information about the number of defendants who raise the insanity doctrine, but the number of defendants who raise it successfully is low. A recent study, found 116 special verdicts in the 10 years to 2001 (Mackay, Mitchell and Howe 'Yet More Facts' 400). In the first five years after the passage of the Criminal Procedure (Insanity and Unfitness to Plead) Act 1991, there were a total of 44 special verdicts returned (Mackay and Kearns 'More Fact(s) About the Insanity Defence' 716). As there were just 52 special verdicts returned between 1975 and 1989 (Mackay *Mental Condition Defences* 102), these figures indicate that findings of 'not guilty by reason of insanity' have increased since the passage of the 1991 Act.

[161] Mackay, Mitchell and Howe 'Yet More Facts' 400. Elsewhere, Mackay suggests that the 1991 Act represents a shift towards restoration of the defence as one of practical importance (*Mental Condition Defences* 73).

[162] See, for example, Dell 'Wanted' 434. It is widely acknowledged that the majority of mentally disordered offenders are processed through the ordinary procedures of guilty pleas, trials, and plea bargains (see, for example, Griew 'Let's Implement Butler' 48).

[163] Mackay *Mental Condition Defences* 181; Walker *Crime and Insanity in England (Vol 1)* 160. In relation to diminished responsibility, some commentators have suggested that defendants choose to plead guilty to manslaughter rather than risk the stigma of a special verdict and the indefinite detention order (Butler Report para 18.9; Dell 'Wanted' 433). If defendants who might raise the insanity doctrine are instead relying on other defences, they are losing the right to a trial (through unfitness to plead provisions) or receiving a conviction rather than an acquittal (in the case of diminished responsibility).

[164] The contemporary insanity doctrine is widely recognized as overly narrow (Butler Report para 18.7; K W M Fulford 'Value, Action, Mental Illness and the Law' in S Shute, J Gardner and J Horder (eds) *Action and Value in the Criminal Law* (Oxford: Clarendon Press, 1993) 300; Griew 'Let's Implement Butler' 48). With its restricted base in cognitive impairment, the *M'Naghten* insanity doctrine excludes many defendants who, although they do not come within the *Rules*, are nevertheless so disordered that they should not be held responsible for their actions (Butler Report para 18.5; Dell 'Wanted' 433).

[165] See, for example, T Ward 'A Terrible Responsibility: Murder and the Insanity Defence in England 1908–1939' (2002) 25 *International Journal of Law and Psychiatry* 361, 361. The practical operation of the insanity doctrine has been depicted as a 'benevolent conspiracy between psychiatrists and the court' that widens the scope of the *Rules* (Williams *Textbook of Criminal Law* 599). Empirical research suggests that, in practice, the *M'Naghten* insanity test seems to have a wider reach than a strict reading of *M'Naghten* would suggest. In particular, the 'wrongness' limb of the *M'Naghten* test is more important in practice than its technical construction would suggest. Mackay's empirical study found that 'wrongness' is the limb most commonly used to secure a special verdict (R D Mackay 'Fact and Fiction About the Insanity Defence' [1990] *Criminal Law Review* 247, 250). Mackay and Gerry Kearns argue that the 'wrongness' limb of the *M'Naghten Rules* is frequently used by psychiatrists in a broad, common sense way, to cover both legal and moral wrong, in a way that effectively expands the scope of the *M'Naghten Rules* (Mackay and Kearns 'More Fact(s) About the Insanity Defence' 722–3).

If the law of insanity is to be reformed following the Law Commission's current programme of reform (which I canvass in Chapter 5),[166] it seems reasonable to expect that it might be with a view to increasing the numbers of individuals successfully raising insanity.

---

[166] See <http://www.justice.gov.uk/lawcommission/areas/insanity.htm> (last accessed 9 September 2011), and 10th Programme of Law Reform, Law Commission No 311 (London, 2008), available at <http://www.justice.gov.uk/lawcommission/publications/programmes-law-reform.htm> (last accessed 9 September 2011).

PART III

7
'Since the days of Noah':[1] the Law of Intoxicated Offending

The rules about how intoxication affects criminal liability are rather notorious for their complexity and technicality. The rules determine when evidence of an individual's intoxication—by alcohol or any other drug—can be introduced in court to raise reasonable doubt as to whether he or she formed the mental element or *mens rea* of the offence. When such evidence can be introduced is determined by two factors: how the person became intoxicated and the kind of criminal offence they are alleged to have committed. In relation to the way in which the person became intoxicated, a distinction is drawn between self-induced, voluntary, or advertent intoxication, and involuntary or inadvertent intoxication. As I discuss below, involuntary intoxication is admissible as evidence across the board of criminal offences. By contrast, the legal approach to voluntary intoxication—the type of intoxication at issue in the majority of cases—varies according to the type of offence with which an individual is charged, with evidence of it admissible only in relation to some offences.

The first of the two main arguments advanced in this chapter relates to lay or non-expert knowledge of intoxication. While, as a result of a process of formalization, technical and complex rules appear to dominate criminal law practices relating to intoxicated offending, they continue to depend on lay or non-expert knowledge of intoxication. Like lay knowledge of mental incapacity more broadly, and as I discuss in Chapters 3 and 6, the development of a lay knowledge of intoxication was the product of the development of an expert knowledge about intoxication. At the same time as a set of expert knowledges about alcohol, and its effects, appeared in the nineteenth century, a body of lay knowledge about intoxication was created. This knowledge now shares the field with expert knowledge, and, as elsewhere on the mental incapacity terrain, continues to play a role in criminal law doctrines and practices concerning mental incapacity. Regarding lay knowledge of intoxication in particular, in the current era, I suggest that this type of knowledge plays a three-fold part in the criminal law on intoxicated offending—broadly, to block particular arguments about what is known and not known about intoxication.

The second of the two main arguments advanced in this chapter relates to the meanings given to intoxicated offending via legal doctrines and practices. Stretching

---

[1] *R v Lawrence* [1981] 2 WLR 524, 530 per Lord Hailsham.

above its technical form, the law on intoxicated offending can be seen to be Janus-faced. That is, the law encodes two different sets of meanings related to intoxication—intoxication as exculpatory abnormality and as morally culpable conduct—which are suspended in a fine balance in criminal law and process. The formalization of informal practices relating to intoxicated offending over the nineteenth century, and continuing into the twentieth century, marked the formation of a distinct legal entity of intoxication recognizable in the current era. As a result of this process of formalization, intoxication ceased to be an informal plea for exculpation, and came to be most accurately conceptualized as a 'doctrine of imputation', and, on my account of the mental incapacity terrain, a non-exculpatory mental incapacity doctrine.[2] But even after its formal structure and role in criminal law solidified, the law on intoxicated offending continues to countenance two different conceptualizations of intoxication, which accounts in part for the controversy surrounding this part of the criminal law.

The Emergence of an Informal Intoxication Plea

It is not possible to be precise about how, if at all, intoxication affected liability in the early modern era. The unrefined nature of liability structures, and the dominance of capital punishment, meant that there was no distinction between considerations of liability on the one hand and punishment on the other.[3] This precluded the fine-tuning of liability in the way that would have been required if intoxication was to operate as either a mitigating or an aggravating factor. There are, however, dicta to the effect that drunken offending was condemned by judges. In the first reported case on intoxication, *Reniger v Feogossa*, decided in 1551, the Court stated that a person who kills another shall not be 'privileged' if he [sic] was drunk when he acted, and actually 'deserves double punishment, because he has doubly offended, viz. in being drunk to the evil example of others, and in committing the crime of homicide'.[4] Similarly, in *Beverley's Case*, the Court stated that the defendant's 'drunkenness does not extenuate his act or offence nor turn it to his avail, but it is a great offence in itself'.[5] Given the unelaborated liability

---

[2] As I discuss in Chapter 2, although sometimes labelled an excuse or a defence, these rules work to impute liability to an individual, and I refer to the intoxication doctrine or law, or the law of intoxicated offending here.
[3] As John Langbein argues, sentencing decisions and the procedure for determining guilt were collapsed into each other, as both were part of the one procedure: J H Langbein *The Origins of the Adversary Criminal Trial* (Oxford: OUP, 2003) 48, 57–60. Further, with the widespread use of capital punishment, there were many offences for which there was no distinction between conviction and punishment, although the royal prerogative of mercy meant that some defendants sentenced to death would not be hanged: Langbein *The Origins of the Adversary Criminal Trial* 60.
[4] *Reniger v Feogossa* (1551) 75 ER 1, 31 extracted in *DPP v Beard* [1920] 1 AC 479, 494; see also J Hall 'Intoxication and Criminal Responsibility' (1944) 57(7) *Harvard Law Journal* 1045, 1046.
[5] *Beverley's Case* (1603) 4 Co Rep 123, (1550) 1 Plowd 1, 19, extracted in D McCord 'The English and American History of Voluntary Intoxication to Negate Mens Rea' (1990) 11 *Journal of Legal History* 372, 374. Referring to *Reniger v Feogossa* and *Beverley's Case*, one commentator has argued that they may be interpreted to indicate that, in addition to being no defence at common law, intoxication was an aggravating factor: see McCord 'The English and American History' 373; see also *DPP v Beard*

structures that pertained at this time, it is most accurate to think of the dicta from these cases as in large part moral evaluative judgments.

Over the seventeenth and eighteenth centuries, there were significant changes in both the patterns of alcohol consumption, and the social meanings given to alcohol, each of which affected legal processes concerning intoxicated individuals. At the start of this period, consumption of ales and wine was restricted to the few who could afford it; by the end of the period, distilled spirits were cheap and widely available.[6] Over the same time, drunkenness became a public sight and alcoholism came to be understood as a social problem.[7] In terms of attitudes to intoxication, over the 1600s and 1700s, while older ideas about drunkenness, sin, and crime persisted, new ideas about intoxication as a threat to the social order appeared.[8] At the beginning of this era, drunkenness was viewed as a failure of self-control on the part of the individual. As Dana Rabin writes, seventeenth-century writers placed drunkenness 'prominently on the slippery slope from minor sin to heinous crime'.[9] However, partly as a result of the 'phenomenon of mass and lethal intoxication', drunkenness came to be understood not simply as weakness of the will, but as a 'tyranny of habits', which threatened to engulf the personality.[10]

The changing social profile of intoxication produced a change in legal practices related to intoxicated offending. Although intoxication did not constitute a formal defence to a criminal charge, as the writings of contemporary legal commentators such as Matthew Hale make clear, in practice, the rule disallowing intoxication as an excuse was disregarded.[11] Those individuals raising intoxication in arguing for acquittal, mitigation, or pardon—legal categories which had indistinct conceptual

---

[1920] AC 479, 494 per Lord Birkenhead. However, this argument seems untenable as there is no evidence that the allegedly aggravating effect of intoxication had any practical effect on liability or sentence (R U Singh 'History of the Defence of Drunkenness in English Criminal Law' (1933) 49 *Law Quarterly Review* 528, 531–2; see also H Fingarette 'Disabilities of Mind and Criminal Responsibility—A Unitary Doctrine' (1976) 76(2) *Columbia Law Review* 236, 238–9).

[6] P McCandless '"Curses of Civilization:" Insanity and Drunkenness in Victorian Britain' (1984) 79 *British Journal of Addiction* 49; see also R Porter *Flesh in the Age of Reason: The Modern Foundations of Body and Soul* (London: Norton, 2003) 399; D Rabin 'Drunkenness and Responsibility for Crime in the Eighteenth Century' (2005) 44 *Journal of British Studies* 457, 466; J Warner 'The Naturalization of Beer and Gin in Early Modern England' (1997) 24 *Contemporary Drug Problems* 373, 374.

[7] Porter *Flesh in the Age of Reason* 399; N Walker *Crime and Insanity in England (Vol 1: The Historical Perspective)* (Edinburgh: Edinburgh University Press, 1968) 177.

[8] Rabin 'Drunkenness and Responsibility for Crime' 476; see also McCandless '"Curses of Civilization"' 52; D Rabin *Identity, Crime and Legal Responsibility in Eighteenth Century England* (Basingstoke: Palgrave Macmillan, 2004) 18; M Valverde *Law's Dream of Common Knowledge* (Princeton: Princeton University Press, 2003) 150–1.

[9] Rabin 'Drunkenness and Responsibility for Crime' 459.

[10] Porter *Flesh in the Age of Reason* 399.

[11] Matthew Hale, *Historia placitorum coronae* (The history of the pleas of the crown) (1st American edn by W A Stokes and E Ingersoll, Vol 1 Philadelphia, 1847) [32], in The Making of Modern Law database <http://galenet.galegroup.com/servlet/MOML> (last accessed 26 September 2011). In relation to the practical disregard for the prohibition on intoxication as an excuse, see Rabin 'Drunkenness and Responsibility for Crime' 457–8.

outlines—may be regarded as invoking what Rabin refers to as an 'informal' plea.[12] Rabin develops a useful typology of intoxication cases in the eighteenth century, according to which drunkenness pleas fell into two camps: a 'simple' drunkenness plea, in which individuals argued in a general way for diminished responsibility from drink, and a plea linking intoxication and insanity.[13]

Of those individuals who raised a 'simple' drunkenness plea, Rabin argues that they were asserting 'that the crime was out of their usual, sober character, that it would not have happened but for the influence of alcohol, and that they had no malicious intent when they committed the crime'.[14] Based on my analysis of the *Old Bailey Proceedings* (*OBPs*), an example of this formulation of an informal intoxication plea is provided by the trial of George Stone for theft and burglary:

> Court: Did he appear drunk, mad or insane?
> Cooley (witness): He rather appeared in liquor.
> Prisoner's defence: I was very much in liquor and don't know what I did.... [I] had got a little more beer than ordinary... I have got a wife and five small children. I never did such a thing in all my life.
> Guilty of stealing. Transported for seven years.[15]

In this and similar cases of a 'simple' drunkenness plea, defendants were effectively blaming their offence on the intoxicating effects of liquor.[16]

Those individuals who linked claims to drunkenness with insanity were attempting to associate the crimes they committed while under the effects of alcohol with 'the uncontrollable behaviour expected of those deemed non compos mentis'.[17] A number of the references to intoxication in the *OBPs* fit the profile of this type of informal plea. An example is provided by the trial of William Edwards for theft and burglary:

> Court: A little drink would bring on the disorder?
> Gosner (apothecary at Bethlem Hospital): Very suddenly, I believe the first occasion of the disorder was from that.
> ...
> Court (to prisoner): Have you anything further to say in [sic] your own behalf?
> Prisoner: Only that I am seized at intervals with lunacy, and I cannot account for it; I have had relapses these twelve years.
> Not guilty.[18]

---

[12] 'Drunkenness and Responsibility for Crime' 458. While Rabin refers to an 'informal intoxication defence', the unrefined nature of structures of criminal liability seems to warrant the looser term plea instead.

[13] See Rabin *Identity, Crime and Legal Responsibility* 79 and Rabin 'Drunkenness and Responsibility for Crime' 469.

[14] 'Drunkenness and Responsibility for Crime' 471–2. According to Rabin, this type of informal plea based on intoxication was more likely to be raised by men than women because 'the image of a drunk woman... might incur only more disapproval': *Identity, Crime and Legal Responsibility* 79.

[15] *OBP*, George Stone, 12 September 1787 (t17870912–15).

[16] Rabin *Identity, Crime and Legal Responsibility* 80.

[17] Rabin 'Drunkenness and Responsibility for Crime' 473, 475. Rabin suggests that women defendants more commonly featured in this category of informal intoxication plea: see *Identity, Crime and Legal Responsibility* 83.

[18] *OBP*, William Edwards, 20 October 1784 (t17841020–10).

This extract exposes the close connection between insanity and intoxication that pertained in this era, with the latter being regarded as either a cause or a species of the former. The effect of intoxication was thought to be akin to that of insanity, as it was held to render the defendant 'disturbed in her mind', or 'out of his mind', or to ensure that he 'did not know what he did'.[19] With evidence from an apothecary, Williams Edwards' trial record also provides an example of early reliance on individuals with specialist knowledge of intoxication. I discuss the development of an expertise on intoxication in the next section of this chapter.

As these two types of intoxication plea suggest, drunkenness was operating as a basis for informal exculpation of individuals charged with offences. These two types of plea were closely connected, both conceptually and in practice, in a way that reflected the then largely unelaborated conditions of criminal liability. As the close connection between insanity and intoxication suggests, the criminal law employed a minimally differentiated conceptualization of the abnormal mental states that might exculpate an individual.[20] The informal process of exculpation was characterized by conceptual indeterminacy. This indeterminacy in the criminal law may be interpreted as an incident of what Nicola Lacey has referred to as 'a thin doctrine of capacity as a condition of criminal responsibility'.[21] Mindful of the state of development of a notion of criminal responsibility at this time, what Rabin interprets as recognition of a 'spectrum of culpability' might more accurately be attributed to the loose or 'thin' conception of responsibility then pertaining, and the nebulous boundary between (what would now be) factors in mitigation and affirmative defences that accompanied it.

In the context of unelaborated legal structures of liability and responsibility, and in advance of a sophisticated account of the way in which intoxication affected a defendant's mental state, a robust common knowledge of alcohol and its effects provided an animating framework for exculpation on the basis of intoxicated incapacity. Paralleling the informal insanity plea, common knowledge of intoxication and its effects was part of what Lacey calls 'local knowledge', which informed 'widely accepted judgments about criminality' in the task of determining liability in

---

[19] See *OBP*, Mary Jones, 18 May 1768 (t17680518-39); *OBP*, Thomas Haycock, 28 June 1780 (t17800628-34); and *OBP*, Thomas Baggot, 28 June 1780 (t17800628-113) respectively.

[20] Connecting her study of eighteenth-century criminal trials to the broader idea of a 'culture of sensibility' that rose to the fore in the 1700s, Rabin interprets the intoxication cases to reveal the existence of a notion of 'partial responsibility, a spectrum of culpability' in the criminal law: see 'Drunkenness and Responsibility for Crime' 477. According to Rabin, the possibility of diminished but not abrogated responsibility, whereby 'drunkenness might place one closer to the excusable end without implying innocence', evidences 'gradations of responsibility': 'Drunkenness and Responsibility for Crime' 476-7. However, it seems to me that the notion of criminal responsibility was not sufficiently elaborate at this time to support such a sophisticated conceptualization.

[21] N Lacey 'Responsibility and Modernity in Criminal Law' (2001) 9(3) *Journal of Political Philosophy* 249, 261. Lacey argues that, in this era, a defendant's capacities were merely components of his or her character, which was the object of evaluation during a trial (263). Rabin herself appears to acknowledge the interconnectedness of considerations of what she refers to as the 'language of excuse' and character in the eighteenth-century trial context: see *Identity, Crime and Legal Responsibility* 112-31.

the eighteenth-century criminal trial.[22] It was common knowledge about intoxication that gave meaning to what Rabin calls the 'brief suggestions' that were used to 'associate the crime and the accused with intoxicated incoherence', rendering these 'brief suggestions' intelligible within informal legal practices.[23] A plea based on a behaviour—the consumption of alcohol—which was familiar to key participants in the trial process enhanced its acceptability as an excuse. As Joel Eigen writes, in raising intoxication, defendants were attempting 'to enlist the sympathy of the jury by overtly appealing to their own leisure activities'.[24] In a way that is similar to proof of insanity at the same point in time, the significance of common knowledge of intoxication in this era meant that ordinary people could give evidence about and evaluate a defendant's drunkenness.[25] The generalized social meaning of drunkenness—which was built on but not limited to experiential knowledge of alcohol and its effects—formed the knowledge context against which an expertise on intoxication developed.

'The nature of her mania was madness from drink':[26] the Development of Expertise on Intoxication

Social concerns about widespread alcohol consumption, which had appeared by the end of the eighteenth century, were amplified and elaborated by the appearance of expert knowledge about alcohol in the nineteenth century. The appearance of expert knowledges about alcohol consumption and its effects was itself part of a larger intellectual history of changing knowledge practices across the century.[27] As I discuss in Chapter 6, on the level of elite knowledges, this development encompassed new objects of knowledge, and spawned new specializations and new intellectual-cum-social groups. Reflecting its place in a wider if loose alliance of knowledges about public health and public order which arose in the Victorian era, the burgeoning expert or specialist knowledge about intoxication encompassed bureaucratic or administrative, scientific, and medical, as well as an emergent psychiatric, knowledge. Each of these specialist knowledges shared a depiction of intoxication—by alcohol, and to a much lesser extent, by drugs such as opium—as a genuine object of expertise, about which it was possible to offer intelligible explanations about cause and effect.

---

[22] Lacey 'Responsibility and Modernity in Criminal Law' 265.
[23] Rabin 'Drunkenness and Responsibility for Crime' 468. As Joel Eigen writes, 'no experts were needed to explain the effects of liquor' to juries—it was well known that alcohol could 'inflame passions, cloud thinking and inhibit the will:' J P Eigen *Witnessing Insanity: Madness and Mad Doctors in the English Court* (New Haven: Yale University Press, 1995) 168.
[24] *Witnessing Insanity* 168; see also Rabin *Identity, Crime and Legal Responsibility* 79.
[25] See, for example, the trial of Thomas Taplin (*OBP*, Thomas Taplin, 28 June 1780 (t17800628-18)), in which a friend of Taplin's testified that 'when he gets in liquor [the defendant] is void of his senses'. In relation to insanity, see Chapter 6.
[26] *OBP*, Emma Brown, 6 May 1878 (t18780506-499).
[27] For discussion, see S Collini *Public Moralists: Political Thought and Intellectual Life in Britain, 1850–1930* (Oxford: Clarendon Press, 1991).

Medical and emergent psychiatric knowledge about intoxication—which focused on the effect of alcohol on individuals—was one particular subset of this diffused expert knowledge. In keeping with the changed emphasis of developing psychiatric knowledge—from intellectual defect to 'malfunctions in impulse control'—individual will had a prominent place here.[28] Among medical and psychiatric experts, it is clear that a variety of attitudes and beliefs about drunkenness abounded.[29] These can be usefully divided into two sets of attitudes.

One set of expert medical attitudes regarding drunkenness held that it was a matter of individual choice and was thus within an individual's control. This attitude was given additional impetus by the temperance movement. As Martin Wiener suggests, the temperance movement was 'probably the single most powerful and widespread social "cause" of the century', 'deeply coloring accepted notions of social respectability'.[30] The new 'respectability' insisted upon 'duty and the ability of men to maintain self-management, an insistence that fit ill with drunkenness'.[31] Wiener points to judicial statements condemning intoxication and argues that, although these sorts of statements had been made in court before, in the second half of the nineteenth century, they were enforced in a novel way.[32] This declining tolerance for intoxication and the interpersonal violence it was believed to cause is also evident in the increase in the prosecution and punishment of public drunkenness (itself an offence) and drunken killings in the second half of the century.[33] At the same time, an excuse based on intoxication was becoming less likely to prevent a murder conviction, although it continued to be taken into account to mitigate punishment in non-capital cases.[34]

Another set of expert medical attitudes about drunkenness depicted intoxicated individuals as suffering from what Wiener refers to as 'diminished responsibility for drink'.[35] This latter set of attitudes, which arose at the end of the nineteenth century, was accompanied by a 'less autonomous image of drunkards', meaning that individuals were not thought to be wholly culpable for their condition.[36] This set of attitudes fed the growing approval of medical treatment for drunkenness apparent in the last decades of the century (although, as historians

---

[28] See M Wiener *Reconstructing the Criminal: Culture, Law and Policy in England, 1830–1914* (Cambridge: CUP, 1990) 26.
[29] For further discussion, see M Valverde *Diseases of the Will: Alcohol and the Dilemmas of Freedom* (Cambridge: CUP, 1998) 49.
[30] M Wiener *Men of Blood: Violence, Manliness and Criminal Justice in Victorian England* (Cambridge: CUP, 2004) 255.
[31] *Men of Blood* 261. For a discussion of the gender dimensions of expert attitudes to alcohol, see M Valverde '"Slavery from Within:" The Invention of Alcoholism and the Question of Free Will' (1997) 22(3) *Social History* 251.
[32] Wiener *Men of Blood* 260.
[33] *Men of Blood* 256.
[34] K J M Smith *Lawyers, Legislators and Theorists: Developments in English Criminal Jurisprudence 1800–1957* (Oxford: Clarendon Press, 1998) 341.
[35] M Wiener *Reconstructing the Criminal* 295.
[36] *Reconstructing the Criminal* 294.

have noted, this treatment was moral or disciplinary rather than medical[37]). An illustration of this set of attitudes is provided by the inebriates' legislation that was enacted towards the end of the century. The Habitual Drunkards Act 1879 applied to a person who 'by reason of habitual intemperate drinking of intoxicating liquors' was 'at time dangerous to himself or herself or to others, or incapable of managing himself or herself and his or her affairs'.[38] Those classed as 'habitual drunkards' could choose to go to asylums, but, once there, could be detained against their will and forced to undergo a course of treatment.[39] The 1879 Act was followed by the Inebriates Act 1898 (which substituted the Latinate term 'inebriates' for the morally-laden reference to 'habitual drunkards').[40] Under the 1898 Act, judges could sentence 'habitual inebriates' to detention in inebriate reformatories for up to three years, in addition to any other punishment that might be imposed.[41] As scholars have suggested, this legislation applied to a subset of those who drank to excess, although it is indicative of a broader problematizing of alcohol consumption, and formed a useful locus for medical expertise.[42]

These two sets of expert attitudes toward drunkenness were neither mutually exclusive, nor unconnected to attitudes to insanity or mental incapacity more generally. As Mariana Valverde argues, both popularly and medically, inebriety was regarded as a 'hybrid object', 'part vice, part disease'.[43] In Valverde's words, there was a 'sort of refusal to medicalise' intoxication, based on the idea that doctors should not waste their time with 'social misfits'.[44] Valverde suggests that efforts to medicalize habitual drunkenness or alcoholism (through diagnostic entities such as 'moral insanity' and 'dipsomania') were not successful because the courts and ordinary people believed that 'heavy drinkers, if they really tried, could stop their destructive behaviour'.[45] The persistence of the idea of individual culpability for drunkenness within a discourse of diminished responsibility for drink is the key to the social meaning of intoxication that emerged by the end of the period. The durability of this idea of personal culpability for drunkenness is reflected in the

---

[37] See, for example, G Johnstone 'From Vice to Disease? The Concepts of Dipsomania and Inebriety, 1860–1908' (1996) 5 *Social and Legal Studies* 37. Johnstone argues that the main goal of reform, reformers, and reformatories was moralization, specifically focused on irresponsibility and inefficiency, rather than medicalization.

[38] 'An Act to Facilitate the control and cure of Habitual Drunkards' 60 & 61 Vict. c.60. See G Johnstone, 'From Vice to Disease?' for discussion.

[39] Valverde *Diseases of the Will* 77–8; see also Wiener *Reconstructing the Criminal* 295.

[40] *Reconstructing the Criminal* 297.

[41] M Ajzenstadt, and B Burtch 'Medicalization and Regulation of Alcohol and Alcoholism: The Professions and Disciplinary Measures' (1990) 13 *International Journal of Law and Psychiatry* 127, 138; D Garland *Punishment and Welfare: A History of Penal Strategies* (Aldershot: Gower, 1985) 20.

[42] See Valverde '"Slavery from Within"' and G Johnstone 'From Vice to Disease?'.

[43] Valverde *Diseases of the Will* 51. Valverde argues that the hybrid status of intoxication meant that it was easily assimilated into the late Victorian branch of evolutionary science of degeneration theory in which 'bodily features were moralized and moral vices were blamed for causing physical degeneration'. See also H Rimke and A Hunt 'From Sinners to Degenerates: The Medicalization of Morality in the Nineteenth Century' (2002) 15(1) *History of the Human Sciences* 59, 73–9.

[44] Valverde *Diseases of the Will* 49–50.

[45] *Diseases of the Will* 2.

contemporaneous development of the law on intoxicated offending, which I discuss below.

The rise of an expert knowledge about intoxication impacted on the criminal trials concerning intoxicated offenders. The *OBP* trial records reveal the involvement of medical witnesses in court processes, and also expose the still inchoate distinction between claims to incapacity based on intoxication and those based on insanity (which was undergoing a process of formalization at the same time). For example, in the trial of William Murray for murder, in 1869, John Spencer Ferris, a member of the Royal College of Surgeons, is recorded as stating that 'constant habitual drunkenness of that sort would provide a diseased state of the brain; an inflammatory condition'.[46] Individuals such as Ferris testified alongside ordinary people, who continued to give evidence about and evaluate a defendant's intoxication. For instance, in the 1871 trial of James Alexander Mills, who was charged with shooting at the trustee of his bankrupt estate, John Ckibb, a fellow publican, testified:

[W]hen sober he was a very good man indeed—I never saw him in a greater state of excitement than he was on the 9th—I don't think he was able to judge the consequences of his actions, and I made a remark to that effect when I left him.[47]

The authority of ordinary people to detect and evaluate drunkenness represented an element of continuity with the previous era. In part because of the idea that doctors were thought to be wasting their time with 'social misfits', and in part because of the ubiquity of alcohol consumption, intoxication did not become exclusively the subject of expert knowledge in the nineteenth century. Particularly when compared with the development of expert medical knowledge about insanity by the same time, intoxication and its effects on individuals was not elite subject matter. As I discuss in Chapter 3 in relation to knowledge of mental incapacity in general, as a result of the rise of an expert knowledge, the knowledge ordinary people had regarding mental incapacity must be seen in a different light. The rise of expert or specialized knowledges about intoxication by alcohol produced a lay knowledge of intoxication. I take up this point below.

The Formalization of the Law of Intoxicated Offending

As discussed above, the advent of mass intoxication had produced new subjects of legal processes—individuals who were 'in liquor' at the time of their offence—but it did not immediately throw up new legal concepts. In the nineteenth century, informal practices around intoxicated offending began a process of formalization via which a legal entity of intoxication would be created. Reflecting the uncertainty that prevailed at the start of this era about the way in which intoxication affected criminal liability, the first half of the nineteenth century was marked by

---

[46] *OBP*, William Murray, 12 July 1869 (t18690712-652).
[47] *OBP*, James Alexander Mills, 18 September 1871 (t18710918-695).

inconsistent judicial approaches to intoxicated offending.[48] Prefiguring the development of the dual meaning of intoxication for the criminal law that would emerge by the end of the century (as exculpatory abnormality and morally culpable conduct), some judges made 'cautious concessions to the new [social] tolerance' for alcohol,[49] while other judges denied the exculpatory effect of intoxication. The decision of *Grindley* is evidence of a generous approach: Justice Holroyd held that, although intoxication could not excuse, if the material question was whether an act was pre-meditated or done with a 'sudden heat and impulse' (as in the case of murder), intoxication could be taken into account.[50] This direction was disapproved in the 1835 decision of *Carroll*, in which the Court took a more stringent line. In *Carroll*, Justice Park held that drunkenness was not relevant to the question of intention. Reviewing earlier case law, Justice Park stated that 'there would be no safety for human life if [*Grindley*] was to be considered as law'.[51] The rule in *Carroll* was itself overruled in *Cruse* in 1838, where the Court held that intoxication was relevant to the 'question of intention: a person may be so drunk as to be unable to form any intention at all, and yet may be guilty of great violence'.[52]

The indeterminacy of the relationship between intoxication and criminal liability, and the inconsistency in the relevant case law, was addressed in the middle of the century. In a way that reflects the rise of a capacity conceptualization of criminal fault at this time, intoxication came to be conceptualized as affecting an individual's *capacity* to form intent.[53] This idea that intoxication potentially led to incapacity to form intent can be traced to the decision of *Monkhouse* in 1849. In *Monkhouse*, Justice Coleridge referred to the 'general rule' (now defunct) that juries are to presume a man [sic] to do what is the natural consequence of his act, and then stated that if an individual is proved to have been intoxicated, the question becomes 'was he rendered by intoxication entirely incapable of forming the intent charged?'. In *Monkhouse*, the Court instructed the jury that the accused's intoxication could not be considered unless it was 'such as to prevent [the individual] restraining himself from committing the act in question, or to take away from him the power of forming any specific intention'.[54] No definition of 'specific intention' was provided by the Court in *Monkhouse* or in subsequent cases. From this point

---

[48] McCord 'The English and American History' 376; R Smith *Trial by Medicine: Insanity and Responsibility in Victorian Trials* (Edinburgh: Edinburgh University Press, 1981) 85.
[49] Walker *Crime and Insanity in England (Vol 1)* 178.
[50] *R v Grindley* (1819) 1 C & M 8, extracted in *DPP v Beard* [1920] AC 479, 495.
[51] *Rex v Carroll* (1835) 7 C & P 145. See also M J Wiener 'Judges and Jurors: Courtroom Tensions in Murder Trials and the Law of Criminal Responsibility in Nineteenth Century England' (1999) 17 *Law and History Review* 467, 490–1.
[52] *Reg v Cruse* (1838) 8 C & P 541, cited in *DPP v Beard* [1920] AC 479, 497; see also *Reg v Meakin* (1836) 173 ER 132.
[53] On capacity, see Lacey 'Responsibility and Modernity in Criminal Law'. As Lacey argues, between the eighteenth and twentieth centuries, the English criminal process was marked 'by a broad movement from ideas of responsibility as founded in character to conceptions of responsibility as founded in capacity:' 'Responsibility and Modernity in Criminal Law' 250. See also N Lacey 'Psychologising Jekyll, Demonising Hyde: The Strange Case of Criminal Responsibility' (2010) 4 *Criminal Law and Philosophy* 109.
[54] *R v Monkhouse* (1849) 4 Cox CC 55, cited in *DPP v Beard* [1920] AC 479, 497–8.

onwards, although the term 'specific intent' was used, it was not used in all cases of intoxicated offending, nor used consistently.[55] There was no indication in the case law as to how offences involving 'specific intention' were to be identified other than by 'judicial designation'.[56] In the twentieth century, aided by the creation of appellate courts, 'specific intent' would be invested with a distinct, technical meaning, denoting the intent required for an offence, over and above the intent to do the particular physical act that formed the external component of the offence.[57]

The standard account of the appearance of the notion of 'specific intent' and the outlines of a recognizable legal entity of intoxication over these decades is one of judicial clemency: developments in the law are depicted as efforts to ameliorate the harshness of the prohibition on taking intoxication into account for the purposes of conviction.[58] But the premise of the judicial clemency account of the development of intoxication law—the 'severity' of the common law—does not withstand close inspection. While, as in the previous era, intoxication did not constitute formal grounds for exculpation, it formed the basis of informal pleas, and, as Wiener argues with regard to homicide, intoxication became *less* not more likely to be admitted as an excuse or a mitigating factor over the nineteenth century.[59] Rather than mitigating the 'severity of the common law' and by contrast with judicial activity in other areas (such as infanticide), judges seem to have had a role in tightening up the way evidence of intoxication could be used to avoid a conviction, or in mitigation of sentence.

The development of the law on intoxication in this period is most accurately understood as one aspect of broader processes of formalization by which criminal law principles and practices more generally solidified into the form they take in the current era. As I discuss in Chapter 3, the central trend captured by what I call formalization is the movement away from the flexible and overtly moral-evaluative aspect of the early modern criminal law towards more rigid processes and technical and precise rules that have come to comprise the law in the current era. By this account, it is not so much that the case law from *Grindley* in 1819 onwards represents judicial mitigation of the 'severity of the common law',[60] but rather that, prompted by the formalization of other parts of the criminal law, including

---

[55] S Gough 'Intoxication and Criminal Liability: The Law Commission's Proposed Reforms' (1996) 112 *Law Quarterly Review* 335, 343.
[56] Smith *Lawyers, Legislators and Theorists* 241.
[57] *DPP v Majewski* [1977] AC 443, 478–9 per Lord Simon; *R v Heard* [2007] 3 WLR 475, 485; McCord 'The English and American History' 383; J Horder 'Sobering Up? The Law Commission on Criminal Intoxication' (1995) 58(4) *Modern Law Review* 534; see also Law Commission for England and Wales *Intoxication and Criminal Liability* (Cm 7526) (Law Com No 314, 2009).
[58] This judicial clemency account has a wide currency among practitioners and academics. See, for example, *DPP v Majewski* [1977] AC 443, 471 per Lord Elwyn-Jones LC and 496 per Lord Edmund-Davies; G Dingwall, 'Intoxicated Mistakes and the Need for Self-Defence' (2007) 70(1) *Modern Law Review* 127, 129; McCord 'The English and American History' 378; Rabin 'Drunkenness and Responsibility' 458; Smith *Lawyers, Legislators and Theorists* 100–2.
[59] Indeed, according to Wiener, in assault trials at the end of the nineteenth century, drunkenness became primarily an aggravating rather than mitigating factor: see Wiener *Men of Blood* 258.
[60] *DPP v Beard* [1920] AC 479, extracted in *DPP v Majewski* [1977] AC 443, 452; see also *DPP v Majewski* [1977] AC 443, 488 per Lord Salmon.

the insanity doctrine, the parameters of the law relating to intoxicated offending were gradually defined and limited and an intoxication doctrine came to be understood as a discrete and circumscribed component of the criminal law corpus. This emerging law of intoxication centred on a notion of 'specific intent', to which I return below.

From this point in the development of the law related to intoxicated offending, it became possible to detect the outlines of a recognizable legal entity of intoxication. But despite the nascent development of a notion of 'specific intent' by the second half of the nineteenth century, the pace of the development of the law was slow and uneven. The *OBP*s trial records provide evidence of the range of approaches to the relevance of intoxication persisting in the last decades of the nineteenth century. Throughout this period, the *OBP*s indicate that evidence of intoxication continued to form a basis for claims that an individual had not formed the requisite intent ('I can assure you that though I was guilty of the sin of drunkenness, I had no intention of committing a burglary';[61] 'All I can say is that at the time I committed my act I had been drinking, and drunken persons don't know exactly what they do'[62]), and seems to have constituted an ingredient in some acquittals.[63] In addition, intoxication continued to provide grounds for recommendations to mercy ('Unanimously recommended to mercy by the Jury in consequence of his drunkenness, and the absence of the child's mother'[64]).

Further evidence of the slow pace of the formalization of the law on intoxicated offending is provided by the conceptual connection between intoxication and insanity, which, as K J M Smith points out, subsisted throughout the century.[65] Insanity and intoxication were regarded as intimately connected, although the exact nature of the connection between the two was disputed.[66] On the one hand, intoxication was conceptualized as a species of insanity, and there is evidence of this approach in the case law.[67] Such an approach rested on the apparent similarity of the conduct of insane and intoxicated defendants (an approach that would be challenged both by the increasingly moralistic view of alcohol consumption and the development of expert knowledges about both insanity and intoxication). In Wiener's words, drunkenness, 'when viewed in the form of *delirium tremens* and other physical disorders associated with perpetual drunkenness' was amenable to

---

[61] See *OBP*, Charles Wright, 30 November 1863 (t18631130-77).
[62] *OBP*, Emma Brown, 6 May 1878 (t18780506-499).
[63] See for example, *OBP*, James Hoddinott, 3 April 1854 (t18540403-563) (where an acquittal seemed to flow from a combination of the defendant's drunkenness, an external blow from a policeman's staff, and his good character), and *OBP*, Susannah McKenzie, 2 July 1855 (t18550702-723) (where liquor, the shock of the baby's death, and the possibility of accidental suffocation all seemed to play a part).
[64] *OBP*, William Smith, 24 November 1851 (t18511124-61).
[65] Smith *Lawyers, Legislators and Theorists* 239-40.
[66] McCandless '"Curses of Civilization"' 52, 54; Valverde *Diseases of the Will* 47-8.
[67] See, for instance, the decision of *Wheeler and Batsford v Alderson*, where the Court described intoxication as 'in truth temporary insanity; the brain is incapable of discharging its proper functions: there is temporary mania—but that species of derangement, when the exciting cause is removed, ceases' ((1831) 3 Hog Ecc 574, 602, extracted in A C E Lynch 'The Scope of Intoxication' [1982] *Criminal Law Review* 139, 141).

redescription as insanity.[68] On the other hand, intoxication and insanity were also conceptualized as distinct if affiliated entities and, again, there is evidence of this approach in the case law.[69] Even after a distinction between intoxication and insanity appeared, the two remained incompletely separated for legal purposes. It was not until the House of Lords decision in *Beard's Case* in the first decades of the twentieth century that the *M'Naghten* test was decisively rejected on the basis that it was inapplicable to an assessment of the effect of intoxication on criminal responsibility. In *Beard's Case*, Lord Birkenhead stated that there was a distinction between 'the defence of insanity in the true sense caused by excessive drinking' and 'the defence of drunkenness which produces a condition such that a drunken man's mind becomes incapable of forming a specific intention'.[70]

In addition to decisively rejecting the relevance of the *M'Naghten Rules* to cases of intoxication, *Beard's Case* also marked another step in the process of formalization of the law on intoxicated offending. This step entailed the explication of the relationship between intoxication and criminal fault via the elaboration of the meaning of 'specific intent'. In *Beard's Case*, the Court stated that, where a 'specific intent is an essential element in the offence, evidence of a state of drunkenness rendering the accused incapable of forming such an intent should be taken into consideration' in determining where he or she had in fact formed intent.[71] Although it is arguable that the reference to 'specific intent' in *Beard's Case* did not mean anything particular in the context,[72] the decision has been taken as proof of the existence of a doctrine of 'specific intent', rather than a more nebulous notion of 'specific intent', by this time. The *Beard* approach to intoxication, fault, and 'specific intent' was adopted in subsequent appellate judgments,[73] including by the House of Lords in *DPP v Majewski*.

The development of a doctrine of 'specific intent' enabled the courts to carve out a principled way of circumscribing the exculpatory effect of intoxication and to deal

---

[68] Wiener 'Judges and Jurors' 503; see also Wiener *Men of Blood* 272.
[69] A distinction between insanity ('alcoholic mania') and intoxication was drawn in the 1881 decision of *Davis* (*R v Davis* (1881) 14 Cox CC 563; see also Singh 'History of the Defence of Drunkenness' 541), where Justice Stephen stated that 'drunkenness is one thing, and the diseases to which drunkenness leads are different things' (extracted in 'History of the Defence of Drunkenness' 541). The jury was directed to return a verdict of 'not guilty by reason of insanity' if they thought the defendant had been suffering a distinct disease of the mind caused by drinking, and if by that reason, he did not know his act was wrong (see 'History of the Defence of Drunkenness' 541).
[70] *DPP v Beard* [1920] AC 479, 500. The Court concluded that insanity and intoxication are different defences, and that it is 'inconvenient to use the same language in charging juries in relation to different defences' (506).
[71] *DPP v Beard* [1920] AC 479, 499. In reaching this conclusion, the Court criticized the Court of Criminal Appeal in *R v Meade* [1909] 1 KB 895 for connecting exculpatory intoxication with the ability to foresee consequences: *Beard's Case* at 504–5; see also Singh, 'History of the Defence of Drunkenness' 543.
[72] See Law Commission for England and Wales *Legislating the Criminal Code: Intoxication and Criminal Liability* (Law Com No 229, 1995) para 3.8; see also J C Smith 'Intoxication and the Mental Element in Crime' in *Essays in Memory of Professor F.H. Lawson* (London: Butterworths, 1986) 122.
[73] In *Bratty v Attorney-General for Northern Ireland* [1963] AC 386, Lord Denning stated *obiter* that if a 'drunken man is so drunk that he does not know what he is doing, he has a defence to any charge...in which a specific intent is essential' (410). Similarly, in *Attorney-General for Northern Ireland v Gallagher* [1963] AC 349, Lord Denning stated that 'if a man is charged with an offence in which a specific intention is essential...then evidence of drunkenness which renders him incapable of forming that intention, is an answer' (381).

with intoxicated defendants in distinct ways, without impinging on the more general principles applicable to all defendants.[74] In this sense, the rise of 'specific intent' can be interpreted along the same lines as the since-altered rule that a defendant is presumed to have intended the probable consequences of his or her acts.[75] By the time of *Beard's Case*, the rule regarding the probable consequences of a defendant's act, which had been a 'general understanding', had hardened into a presumption of law.[76] As Lacey argues, the presumption provided a solution to 'the problem of knowledge co-ordination', allowing courts to refer to a defendant's 'interior mental world' without requiring close investigation of that world.[77] The doctrine of 'specific intent' is amenable to a parallel analysis: the idea of 'specific intent' refers to a subjective mental state but actually rests on a generalized construction of the altered capacities of intoxicated individuals. In referring to capacity to form intent, the doctrine of 'specific intent' collapses a question of fact (did the defendant form the requisite intent?) into the question of capacity (was the defendant capable of forming the requisite intent?).[78] This generalized construction—that intoxication affects an individual's ability to form 'sophisticated' intentions—is held on 'physiological grounds', and based on either 'the personal experience of judges or folk wisdom or a combination of the two'.[79] The significance of lay knowledge of intoxication (invoked in an idea of 'folk wisdom') is that it functions to forestall certain arguments about what is known and not known about intoxication. I discuss the significance of lay knowledge in the penultimate section of this chapter.

The Apogee of Formalization?: *DPP v Majewski*

The formalization of the law of intoxication took a large step forward with the House of Lords decision of *DPP v Majewski*, which also sets out the current law of intoxication. The significance of this decision is such that it is worth considering closely. Majewski was involved in a bar brawl and was charged with three counts of assault occasioning actual bodily harm and three counts of assaulting a police officer in the execution of his duty. Majewski claimed he 'completely blanked out' and was

---

[74] As Stephen Gough argues, the doctrine of 'specific intent' worked to distinguish certain kinds of offences—those that specifically required intent—from the general milieu, which merely required 'malice', effectively a negligence standard that intoxication would not negate: Gough 'Intoxication and Criminal Liability' 344.
[75] As Keith Smith argues, the 'underlying rationale' of 'specific intent' offences may be seen as 'derivative' of this rule: *Lawyers, Legislators and Theorists* 241.
[76] E Griew 'States of Mind, Presumptions and Inferences' in P Smith (ed) *Criminal Law; Essays in Honour of JC Smith* (London: Butterworths, 1987) 69.
[77] N Lacey 'In Search of the Responsible Subject: History, Philosophy and Social Sciences in Criminal Law Theory' (2001) 64(3) *Modern Law Review* 350, 370.
[78] A D Gold 'An Untrimmed "Beard": The Law of Intoxication as a Defence to a Criminal Charge' (1976–77) 19 *Criminal Law Quarterly* 34, 42.
[79] See McCord 'The English and American History' 384, 378.

'Since the days of Noah': the Law of Intoxicated Offending 187

unaware of what he was doing because he had consumed alcohol and drugs (a mix of amphetamines and barbiturates). The trial judge had directed the jury that they were to 'ignore the subject of drink and drugs as being in any way a defence' to the assaults.[80] Majewski was convicted on all counts and appealed. The Law Lords unanimously upheld his convictions. The *Majewski* decision provides that voluntary intoxication may be used to prove that an individual did not form the requisite *mens rea* for offences of 'specific intent'.[81] By contrast, in relation to a residual category of offences of 'basic intent', such as assault, an individual's voluntary intoxication cannot be taken into account when determining whether he or she formed the *mens rea* required by the offence.

In restricting the admissibility of evidence of voluntary intoxication for offences of 'basic intent', the *Majewski* Court had to confront the significance of Section 8 of the Criminal Justice Act 1967. This statutory provision had altered the common law presumption, to which I referred above, that a man [sic] may be taken to have intended the natural and probable consequences of his actions. Section 8 of the 1967 Act provides that the jury is not 'bound in law' to infer intention in this way, but is to determine what the defendant intended or foresaw 'by reference to all the evidence'.[82] This provision might have been interpreted to invalidate any attempt to restrict the kind of evidence that could be taken into account in cases of intoxicated offending. However, the *Majewski* Court held that the reference in Section 8 to 'all the evidence' was a reference to 'all the *relevant* evidence', which meant that 'if there is a substantive rule of law that in crimes of basic intent, the factor of intoxication is irrelevant... evidence with regard to it is quite irrelevant'.[83] By adopting this reasoning, and constructing the question about the admissibility of evidence of intoxication as one of law rather than of evidence, the Law Lords justified the restriction on the admissibility of evidence of intoxication in 'basic intent' offences.

Over and above the baseline rule that voluntary intoxication may be adduced as evidence in relation to an offence of 'specific intent' but not in relation to offences of 'basic intent', there have been two sources of ambiguity about what *Majewski* decided. The first source of ambiguity relates to the distinction between 'specific intent' and 'basic intent' offences. The Lords seem to have used the terms in three different ways.[84] It was the approach that depicted 'basic intent' offences as those

---

[80] Extracted in *DPP v Majewski* [1977] AC 443, 467 per Lord Elwyn-Jones.
[81] See *DPP v Majewski* [1977] AC 443.
[82] As a result of this statutory provision, the presumption about intention no longer exists as a matter of substantive law: see *R v Sheehan; R v Moore* [1975] 1 WLR 739, 743; for analysis, see Lacey 'In Search of the Responsible Subject' 370.
[83] *DPP v Majewski* [1977] AC 443, 475 per Lord Elywn-Jones; see also 484 per Lord Salmon and 497 per Lord Edmund Davies.
[84] Suggesting that 'specific intent' is similar to 'ulterior intent', Lord Elwyn-Jones cited with approval a passage from *DPP v Morgan* [1976] AC 182, which stated that crimes of 'basic intent' are those in which the *mens rea* does not go beyond the *actus reus* (*DPP v Majewski* [1977] AC 443, 471). Lord Simon seemed to adopt a similar if more expansive approach, defining 'specific intent' offences as those where the prosecution must 'prove that the purpose for the commission of the act extends to the intent expressed or implied in the definition of the crime' (*DPP v Majewski* [1977] AC 443, 479). Last, a number of the Lords appeared to suggest that 'basic intent' offences are those where

where recklessness will suffice for liability that became the settled approach to *Majewski* and the doctrine of intoxication,[85] although, relatively recently, the orthodoxy of this approach was called into question.[86] The second source of ambiguity stemming from the *Majewski* decision relates to the way in which evidence of voluntary intoxication is to be treated where an individual is charged with an offence of 'basic intent'. Again, on this point, the comments in *Majewski* could be interpreted in three different ways: first, that, where an intoxicated defendant was charged with a 'basic intent' offence, the prosecution would be required to prove only the *actus reus* of the offence;[87] or, second, evidence of voluntary intoxication in offences of 'basic intent' would be taken to provide the *mens rea* for the offence (on the basis that the defendant was reckless as to the risk of becoming intoxicated);[88] or, third, that evidence of voluntary intoxication is to be

recklessness will suffice for liability (*DPP v Majewski* [1977] AC 443, 474–5 per Lord Elwyn-Jones; 479 per Lord Simon; 498 per Lord Russell). See generally A R Ward, 'Making Some Sense of Self-Induced Intoxication' (1986) 45(2) *Criminal Law Journal* 247, 247–8.

[85] See, for example, *R v Caldwell* [1982] AC 341, 355 per Lord Diplock.

[86] In *R v Heard* [2007] 3 WLR 475, the Court of Appeal upheld the defendant's conviction for the sexual assault of a police officer. Heard had appealed on the basis that the offence was one of 'specific intent' and that therefore evidence of his voluntary intoxication should have been admissible. In dismissing the appeal, the Court of Appeal commented *obiter* that 'specific intent' is aligned to 'ulterior intent' and defined 'specific intent' offences as those which require 'proof of a state of mind addressing something beyond the prohibited act itself, namely its consequences' (485). According to this approach to *Majewski*, the distinction between 'basic intent' and 'specific intent' offences is a distinction between 'intention as applied to acts considered in relation to their purposes' ('specific intent') and 'intention as applied to acts apart from their purposes' ('basic intent') (485). Thus, because sexual assault required merely intentional touching, it was a 'basic intent' offence (481).

[87] See Law Commission for England and Wales *Intoxication and Criminal Liability* (Law Com No 127, 1993) para 3.17. In a comment that exposes the moralized dimension of the law on intoxication, in *DPP v Majewski* [1977] AC 443, Lord Elwyn-Jones stated that the defendant's conduct in voluntarily 'reducing himself by drugs or drink' provides 'the evidence of *mens rea*, of guilty mind certainly sufficient for crimes of basic intent' (474–5). On this interpretation, the defendant's intoxication effectively substitutes for the *mens rea* for a 'basic intent' offence: see Horder 'Sobering Up?' 536; G Williams *Textbook of Criminal Law* (London: Stevens, 1978) 428. Some commentators have concluded that this creates a situation of strict liability: see C Mitchell 'The Intoxicated Offender—Refuting the Legal and Medical Myths' (1988) 11 *International Journal of Law and Psychiatry* 77, 84; M T Thornton 'Making Sense of Majewski' (1980–81) 23 *Criminal Law Quarterly* 464, 484–5.

[88] Support for this second possible interpretation of the *Majewski* decision is provided by several of the Law Lords' opinions. For example, Lord Simon stated that 'a mind rendered self-inducedly insensible (short of *M'Naghten* insanity), through drink or drugs...is as wrongful a mind as one which consciously contemplates the prohibited act' (*DPP v Majewski* [1977] AC 443, 479; see also *R v Hardie* (1985) 80 Cr App R 157, 162 per Parker LJ). Lord Elwyn-Jones, Lord Edmund-Davies and Lord Russell were also prepared to regard voluntary intoxication as a form of recklessness. Lord Elwyn-Jones, for instance, stated that a person who 'of his own volition takes a substance which causes him to cast off the restraints of reason and conscience' adopts a 'reckless course of conduct and recklessness is enough to constitute the necessary *mens rea* in assault cases' (474–5). This overtly moralized approach means that voluntary intoxication is effectively one of the forms of *mens rea* for offences of 'basic intent': A Dashwood 'Logic and the Lords in Majewski' [1976] *Criminal Law Review* 532, 538. As critics of *Majewski* have noted, this approach to intoxication shifts the inquiry back in time to the point at which the defendant became intoxicated, thus contravening the correspondence principle which requires that *mens rea* and *actus reus* coincide in time in order to ground liability, and adopts a broad lay, as opposed to legal, definition of recklessness: see Dashwood 'Logic and the Lords in Majewski' 541; S Gardner 'The Importance of Majewski' (1994) 14(2) *Oxford Journal of Legal Studies* 279, 281; Law Commission for England and Wales *Intoxication and Criminal Liability* paras 4.34–4.35.

'Since the days of Noah': the Law of Intoxicated Offending   189

disregarded in deciding whether the defendant formed the *mens rea* required for the offence.[89] It is this third interpretation of the *Majewski* discussion of 'basic intent' that now seems to be orthodox. Of the possible interpretations of *Majewski*, this third interpretation does not involve an effective abrogation of the *mens rea* requirement of the offence. It does, however, significantly alter the context in which the defendant's state of mind is determined. This interpretation of *Majewski* means that, when considering the liability of a defendant charged with a 'basic intent' offence, the jury is asked the rather artificial question of whether he or she would have had the relevant *mens rea* if he or she had been sober.[90]

Before turning to the developments that have taken place since *Majewski* was decided, it is worth noting the criticisms to which the decision has been subject. The first of the two broad lines of criticism of *Majewski* runs along the lines that the rules governing voluntary intoxication contravene the basic principles of criminal liability.[91] As the Law Commission observes, if the normal rules of *mens rea* operated in cases of voluntary intoxication, a defendant who was unaware of the risk of harm resulting from his or her conduct would have to be acquitted.[92] But, the restriction on the admissibility of evidence of voluntary intoxication in relation to offences of 'basic intent' means that this is not necessarily the case—the *mens rea* required of an intoxicated defendant is constructed without reference to one of the factual elements of the offence (or perhaps derived from the act of getting intoxicated in the first place).[93] Because it excludes an ingredient of the fact scenario—self-induced intoxication—from the adjudication process, the *Majewski* rule excludes certain intoxicated offenders from the standard subjectivist conception of *mens rea*.[94] In this respect, the law represents a half-way house of criminal

---

[89] As Lord Elwyn-Jones stated, juries should be instructed that they 'can ignore the subject of drink or drugs as being in any way a defence' to charges of 'basic intent' (*DPP v Majewski* [1977] AC 443, 476). This interpretation of *Majewski* was upheld in the Court of Appeal decisions of *R v Woods* (1982) 74 Cr App Rep 312 and *R v Richardson and Irwin* (1999) 1 Cr App Rep 392.

[90] Horder 'Sobering Up?' 541–2.

[91] A number of commentators critique *Majewski* on this basis: see, for example, Law Commission for England and Wales *Intoxication and Criminal Liability* (Law Com No 127, 1993) para 3.2; R D Mackay *Mental Condition Defences in the Criminal Law* (Oxford: Clarendon Press, 1995) 148; G Virgo 'The Law Commission Consultation Paper on Intoxication and Criminal Liability: Part 1: Reconciling Principle and Policy' [1993] *Criminal Law Review* 415, 418; Williams *Textbook of Criminal Law* 424.

[92] Law Commission for England and Wales *Intoxication and Criminal Liability* para 1.6.

[93] This construction of the law of intoxicated offending contravenes the principle that the burden of proof of all elements of the offence is on the prosecution as per *Woolmington v DPP* [1935] All ER 1. As Robinson writes in the US context, the law on intoxication relies on 'rough-and-ready rules that only roughly approximate the results dictated by the culpability principle' (P Robinson 'Causing the Conditions of One's Own Defense: A Study of the Limits of Theory in Criminal Law Doctrine' (1985) 71(1) *Virginia Law Review* 1, 13). In relation to the act of getting intoxicated in the first place, while it may be labelled reckless, this amounts to a lay usage of that term because the recklessness relates simply to the fact of becoming intoxicated, not to the foreseeability of the risk of harm (Smith 'Intoxication and the Mental Element in Crime' 125; Virgo 'The Law Commission Consultation Paper on Intoxication and Criminal Liability' 418).

[94] This subjectivist conception holds that the cardinal mental state or fault element in the criminal law of the late modern era is subjective fault, where an individual is judged according to what they knew, perceived, or intended at the time of the offence. The compromise extends beyond subjective mental states because, in cases of negligence liability, intoxicated mistakes are regarded as unreasonable as a matter of law: see Dingwall 'Intoxicated Mistakes'. For a critical analysis of subjectivism, see

liability, sitting between objective and subjective liability.[95] The second of the two broad lines of criticism of *Majewski* is that there is no clear or principled rationale for distinguishing between offences of 'basic intent' and offences of 'specific intent'.[96] This criticism feeds into a broader argument that the law on intoxicated offending is only explicable in public policy terms.[97] Several commentators argue that, in the absence of legal logic or principle, offences have been categorized as either offences of 'specific intent' or 'basic intent' on policy grounds.[98]

In the years since the *Majewski* decision was handed down, the ossification of the law around the notions of 'specific intent' and 'basic intent' has set the scene for what might turn out to be a retreat from the formalization trajectory that led to *Majewski*. Although a number of offences have been labelled offences of 'specific intent',[99] and other offences have been identified as offences of 'basic intent',[100] in the last few years, this offence-by-offence approach has been called into question. In 2009, the Law Commission stated that the view that all offences can be classified as

---

A Norrie *Crime, Reason and History: A Critical Introduction to Criminal Law* (London: Butterworths, 2001).

[95] As Lord Edmund-Davies stated in *Majewski*, the intoxication law represents 'a compromise between the imposition of liability upon inebriates in complete disregard of their condition (on the alleged ground that it was brought on voluntarily), and the total exculpation required by the individual's actual state of mind at the time he committed the harm in issue': see *DPP v Majewski* [1977] AC 443, 495.

[96] Norrie has referred to the 'basic intent'/'specific intent' distinction as a 'distinction without a real difference': see A Norrie *Law, Ideology and Punishment: Retrieval and Critique of the Liberal Idea of Criminal Justice* (London: Kluwer Academic Publishers, 1990) 172. A number of commentators have critiqued *Majewski* on this basis: see, for example, Smith 'Intoxication and the Mental Element in Crime' 129; Criminal Law Revision Committee *Fourteenth Report: Offences Against the Person* (Cmnd 7844, 1980) para 258; Law Commission for England and Wales *Legislating the Criminal Code: Intoxication and Criminal Liability* (Law Com No 229, 1995) para 3.27.

[97] This policy end has resulted in a law of intoxication that is acknowledged to be an uneasy compromise between the standard meaning of the *mens rea* requirement on the one hand, and the goals of deterrence and social protection on the other: S Bugg 'Intoxication and Liability: A Criminal Law Cocktail' (1984–1987) 5 *Auckland University Law Review* 144, 145; Hall 'Intoxication and Criminal Responsibility' 1054; Smith *Lawyers, Legislators and Theorists* 338; Virgo 'The Law Commission Consultation Paper on Intoxication and Criminal Liability' 415. Achieving this 'compromise' involves exempting voluntarily intoxicated defendants from the standard subjectivist conception of *mens rea*, and, in cases of negligence liability, regarding intoxicated mistakes as unreasonable as a matter of law.

[98] See, eg, Mackay *Mental Condition Defences* 150; Smith 'Intoxication and the Mental Element in Crime' 120. According to this criticism, the division of offences into those of 'specific intent' and those of 'basic intent' is a device utilized to restrict the number of outright acquittals of intoxicated defendants, while at the same time recognizing that 'severe cases of intoxication may result in a lack of *mens rea*:' Mackay *Mental Condition Defences* 150.

[99] The courts have held that offences of 'specific intent' include murder (*DPP v Beard* [1920] AC 479), an attempt to commit any offence (*Durante* [1972] 3 All ER 962), theft (*Ruse v Read* [1949] 1 KB 377) and wounding with intent under Offences Against the Person Act 1861, s 18 (*Bailey* [1983] 1 WLR 760).

[100] Offences of 'basic intent' include assault (*R v Burns* (1973) 58 Cr App R 364), assault occasioning actual bodily harm (*Majewski* [1977] AC 443, 499 per Lord Russell), criminal damage where the *mens rea* is alleged to be recklessness (*R v Caldwell* [1982] AC 341; *R v O'Driscoll* (1977) 65 Cr App R 50), involuntary manslaughter (*DPP v Newbury* [1977] AC 500, 509), maliciously inflicting wounds or grievous bodily harm under Offences Against the Person Act 1861, s 20 (*Bailey* [1983] 1 WLR 760), the offence of rape, as it was constructed prior to the Sexual Offences Act 2003 (*Majewski* [1977] AC 443, 500 per Lord Russell; *R v Eatch* [1980] Crim LR 650) and sexual assault in relation to touching per Sexual Offences Act 2003, s 3 (*R v Heard* [2007] 3 WLR 475, 485–6 per Hughes LJ).

either 'basic intent' or 'specific intent' offences was 'unhelpful' and seems to have backed away from the rigidity of an offence-by-offence approach to intoxicated offending.[101] The Law Commission acknowledged that the terms 'specific intent' and 'basic intent' are 'ambiguous, misleading and confusing', but nonetheless stated that, when properly understood, they refer to genuinely different mental or fault elements for criminal offences, and maintained that evidence of intoxication should only be able to be adduced in relation to some offences and not others.[102]

Although the Law Commission's recent report on the law of intoxication seems to represent a move away from a rigid approach to the way intoxication affects liability, even under the Commission's proposed reforms, the law will still operate on a premise about the genuineness of a distinction between two different types of mental states, howsoever they are called. This idea that the mental states denoted by the labels 'basic intent' and 'specific intent' are meaningfully different from each other is a feature of lay knowledge of intoxication. As Valverde suggests, lay opinion holds that 'people who are very drunk cannot form "higher" thoughts or complex intentions, but that they are capable of, and indeed particularly susceptible to, more "impulsive" acts'.[103] This means that it is not only the notion of 'specific intent', but also a distinction between 'specific intent' and 'basic intent' that rests on lay knowledge of intoxication. I pick up this point again in the penultimate section of this chapter.

Beyond the Bounds of *Majewski*: Amoral Intoxication

Three types of intoxication lie beyond the bounds of the *Majewski* decision. In each type, the defendant shares an attenuation, or complete absence, of moral fault in relation to the intoxication. Carving out these kinds of cases from the reach of *Majewski* represents an attempt to ensure that the law on intoxicated offending does not over-reach its moral foundations in the culpability associated with the consumption of alcohol and dangerous drugs. As Robinson writes, where a defendant caused the conditions of his or her own 'defence', but does so blamelessly, there is little justification for taking away his or her 'defence': he or she 'is no more blameworthy...than is the actor who has made no causal contribution' at all.[104] Where the moral culpability underpinning the legal approach to (voluntary) intoxication is absent, the effects of that approach are unpalatable. Thus, even in their exceptional status, the legal treatment of these three types of intoxication

---

[101] Law Commission for England and Wales *Intoxication and Criminal Liability* (Law Com No 214, 2009) para 2.22 and Part 2 more generally. The Commission proposed abandoning the use of the terms 'specific intent' and 'general intent'. The possibility that the 'basic intent'/'specific intent' approach to the law of intoxicated offending would prove problematic was foreshadowed by Stephen White: see S White 'Offences of Basic and Specific Intent' [1989] *Criminal Law Review* 271.
[102] *Intoxication and Criminal Liability* (Law Com No 214, 2009) paras 1.28 and 3.33–3.34; see paras 3.46–3.52 for the specific recommendations.
[103] Valverde '"Slavery from Within"' 258–9 and Valverde *Diseases of the Will* 196; see also McCord 'The English and American History' 384.
[104] Robinson 'Causing the Conditions of One's Own Defense' 8.

reflects the policy concerns permeating the law on intoxicated offending more broadly.

(i) Involuntary Intoxication

By contrast with voluntary intoxication, evidence of involuntary intoxication may be adduced in order to raise reasonable doubt as to whether the defendant formed the requisite *mens rea* of either 'basic intent' or 'specific intent' offences. While there is no definition of the term 'involuntary intoxication', the courts have adopted a narrow and moralized approach to classifying intoxication as 'involuntary'.[105] Although there is some evidence that a distinction between voluntary and involuntary intoxication first appeared some time ago,[106] the precise way in which involuntary intoxication relates to *mens rea* has been explicated only recently. Even if intoxication is involuntary, it will not assist a defendant unless the intoxication negatived *mens rea*.[107] In the controversial decision of *Kingston*, the courts considered the defendant's appeal against a conviction of indecent assault of a 15-year-old boy. Kingston claimed that, because he had been involuntarily intoxicated when his drink was laced with a drug, he should have been regarded as acting without the *mens rea* required for the offence. By contrast with the Court of Appeal, which allowed Kingston's appeal against conviction,[108] the House of Lords upheld the conviction and affirmed the trial judge's direction that Kingston could be acquitted only if his involuntary intoxication meant that he did not or might not have formed the intention to assault the boy. If Kingston had formed the requisite *mens rea*, which the jury found he had, the fact that his behaviour was affected by a drug administered without his knowledge was no defence.[109] In reaching this

---

[105] Consuming a seemingly non-alcoholic drink that has been laced with alcohol will be considered involuntary intoxication (*R v Allen* [1988] Crim LR 698) but underestimating the effect of alcoholic substances will not (*R v Eatch* [1980] Crim LR 650).

[106] In his treatise, referred to above, Matthew Hale refers to intoxication by the 'contrivance' of others, or as a result of treatment by a physician, which, in contrast to voluntary drunkenness, is an excuse for crime: see Matthew Hale, *Historia placitorum coronae* (The history of the pleas of the crown) (1st American edn, by WA Stokes and E Ingersoll, Vol 1 Philadelphia, 1847) [32], in The Making of Modern Law database <http://galenet.galegroup.com/servlet/MOML> (last accessed 26 September 2011). Similarly, in *R v Pearson* (1835) 2 Lew 144, the Court stated that a defendant 'made drunk by strategem or the fraud of another' is not responsible for his or her actions (extracted in *R v Kingston* [1995] 2 AC 355, 366 per Lord Mustill). Hale's comments about involuntary intoxication never received direct judicial endorsement (Smith *Lawyers, Legislators and Theorists* 340), and it is possible that, in this period, a distinction between voluntary and involuntary intoxication may have had academic rather than practical significance.

[107] As Lane LJ stated in *R v Sheehan; R v Moore* [1975] 1 WLR 739, 744, a 'drunken intent is nevertheless an intent'; see also *R v Bree* [2008] QB 131.

[108] The Court of Appeal reasoned that if 'drink or drug, surreptitiously administered, causes a person to lose his self-control and for that reason to form an intent which he would not otherwise have formed, it is consistent with the principle that the law should exculpate him because the operative fault was not his': extracted in *R v Kingston* [1995] 2 AC 355, 362–3.

[109] Evidence to this effect would have been relevant at sentencing but did not affect Kingston's liability for conviction: *R v Kingston* [1995] 2 AC 355, 364, 377 per Lord Mustill; see also M Redmayne *Expert Evidence and Criminal Justice* (Oxford: OUP, 2001) 151. In reaching this conclusion, the House of Lords declined to place any legal significance on the lack of culpability for

conclusion, the House of Lords cautioned against relying on earlier dicta on involuntary intoxication.[110]

(ii) Non-Dangerous Drugs

Although the traditional approach in the law of intoxication is that it applies to intoxication by all substances,[111] the courts have carved out an exception to the traditional approach in the case of consumption of so-called non-dangerous drugs.[112] In a thin line of case law, the courts have concluded that intoxication by non-dangerous drugs will not be subject to the *Majewski* rules unless, in taking the drug, the defendant was reckless, being aware of the risk of aggressive or uncontrollable conduct but going ahead anyway. The main authority for the special case of non-dangerous drugs is *Hardie* (and the earlier decision it purported to follow, *Bailey*).[113] Hardie had taken some Valium tablets and started a fire inside a flat. He was charged and convicted of two different criminal damage offences, both of which were 'basic intent' offences. The Court of Appeal quashed Hardie's convictions, holding that, even if he had taken excessive quantities of this type of drug, this could not 'in the ordinary way' raise a conclusive presumption against the admission of evidence of intoxication for the purposes of disproving *mens rea*. The Court reasoned that Valium was 'wholly different in kind from drugs which are liable to cause unpredictability or aggressiveness', stating that, if the jury found that

---

the way in which the defendant became intoxicated, preferring to leave the significance of the absence of moral blameworthiness to be dealt with at sentencing: see G R Sullivan 'Making Excuses' in A P Simester and A T H Smith (eds) *Harm and Culpability* (Oxford: Clarendon Press, 1996) 131–5 for discussion. In Alan Norrie's analysis, this subsequent consideration of moral blameworthiness represents a re-contextualization of the 'juridical individual' after the decontextualization that occurs at the point of conviction: see Norrie *Crime, Reason and History* 225–31.

[110] The House of Lords cautioned that *Pearson* was decided 'at a time when the law concerning the mental element of crime, and the particular place of intoxication within it, was in an early stage of development' and concluded that 'it would be unwise to found any principle at all' upon it (*R v Kingston* [1995] 2 AC 355, 367–8 per Lord Mustill). In relation to Hale's comments on involuntary intoxication, the *Kingston* Court concluded that 'legal concepts of criminal responsibility' were 'so different' when Hale was writing that they could not place any 'substantial reliance' on the commentary for the current doctrine of intoxication (*R v Kingston* [1995] 2 AC 355, 368).

[111] In *Lipman*, the Court stated that, for the purposes of criminal responsibility, there is 'no reason to distinguish between the effect of drugs voluntarily taken and drunkenness voluntarily induced': *Lipman* [1970] 1 QB 152, 156. The rationale for this approach is that 'the question for the law is the same in all cases...was the awareness of the defendant relatively impaired or sufficiently impaired by a substance that he has voluntarily consumed: Law Commission for England and Wales *Intoxication and Criminal Liability* (Consultation Paper No 127, 1993) para 1.11; see also Gough, 'Intoxication and Criminal Liability' 339; Williams *Textbook of Criminal Law* 418.

[112] The category of non-dangerous drugs has been drawn by the courts themselves (Law Commission for England and Wales *Legislating the Criminal Code: Intoxication and Criminal Liability* (Law Com No 229, 1995) para 1.38), again reflecting the absence of consideration of expert knowledge in the law on exculpatory intoxication. The special status of intoxication via non-dangerous drugs has been interpreted as a 'straight-forward policy judgment that some kinds of drug-taking will not be tolerated while others will': see Norrie *Crime, Reason and History* 118.

[113] *R v Hardie* (1985) 80 Cr App R 157. The decision in *Hardie* purported to follow *R v Bailey* [1983] 1 WLR 760, although in that case, the diabetic defendant's automatistic behaviour was assumed to be the result of failure to eat rather than the injection of insulin.

the defendant had been unable to appreciate the risks of his actions, it should consider whether taking the Valium itself was reckless.[114]

The way this particular vein of case law relating to intoxication by non-dangerous drugs has opened up exposes courts' reliance on lay knowledge about intoxication. The decisions of *Bailey* and *Hardie* reveal a reliance on what is generally known, or thought to be known, about the causes and effects of intoxication. In *Hardie*, the Court noted that 'the same rule applies to both self-intoxication by alcohol and intoxication by hallucinatory drugs... because the effects of both are well known and there is therefore an element of recklessness in the self-administration of the drug'.[115] The Court concluded that, by contrast, 'there was no evidence that it was known to the appellant or even generally known' that taking Valium could make a person aggressive or unable to appreciate risks to others.[116] Similarly, as an explanation for exempting consumption of insulin from the reach of *Majewski*, the *Bailey* Court said that while 'it is common knowledge that those who take alcohol to excess or certain sorts of drugs may become aggressive or do dangerous or unpredictable things', there is no such knowledge about the effect of insulin.[117] As one commentator has argued, the category of non-dangerous drugs depends on what most people are supposed to believe about the drug, rather than any objective pharmacological properties of it.[118]

(iii) Alcoholism

Like intoxication via non-dangerous drugs and involuntary intoxication, the special status of intoxication resulting from alcoholism represents the moral limits of the *Majewski* approach. Where an individual's intoxication is the result of a disease, his or her moral culpability is attenuated such that the *Majewski* rules appear unjust. Unlike intoxication, alcoholism (or chronic alcohol dependency) has been accepted as a disease for the purposes of the criminal law. Where intoxication can be shown to result from alcoholism, it will be able to be adduced as the basis for an insanity plea or a diminished responsibility plea, rather than (merely) an intoxication plea.[119] Because insanity is generally available across the spectrum of criminal offences, the claim that a 'disease of the mind' is the result of alcoholism may be raised where a defendant is charged with either a 'specific intent' or 'basic intent' offence. Although alcoholism for the purposes of diminished responsibility (and insanity) has been interpreted more expansively in recent decisions (no longer requiring that the defendant must have consumed his or her first drink involuntari-

---

[114] *R v Hardie* (1985) 80 Cr App R 157, 163.
[115] *R v Hardie* (1985) 80 Cr App R 157, 162.
[116] *R v Hardie* (1985) 80 Cr App R 157, 163.
[117] *R v Bailey* [1983] 1 WLR 760, 765-6.
[118] C Mitchell 'Intoxication, Criminality and Responsibility' (1990) 13 *International Journal of Law and Psychiatry* 1, 2.
[119] As a disease, alcoholism may form a 'disease of the mind' as required for the defence of insanity (*DPP v Beard* [1920] AC 479, 501; see also *R v Davis* (1881) 14 Cox CC 563) or what was an 'abnormality of mind' as required by the 1957 version of diminished responsibility (*Attorney-General for Jersey v Holley* [2005] 2 AC 580; *R v Tandy* [1989] 1 WLR 350).

ly to distinguish alcoholism from ordinary intoxication[120]), the condition and thus its exculpatory potential, is still strictly delimited.[121]

Lay Knowledge of Intoxication in Criminal Law

The result of the legal developments canvassed above is that, in the current era, the law of intoxicated offending comprises a complex set of rules. Against the background of the medical and psychiatric expertise about the effect of intoxication on individuals that arose in the nineteenth century, the formalization of an informal exculpatory plea produced a legal entity of intoxication that is now most accurately conceptualized as a 'doctrine of imputation'. But the more moral-evaluative grounding of the law belies the technical contours of the law on intoxicated offending, and the fact that the development of an expertise about intoxication went only some way toward covering the field of knowledge practices in criminal law. Space remained in criminal law practices for what I have called lay knowledge of intoxication. As mentioned above, and as I discuss in Chapter 3, the development of an expert knowledge of intoxication meant that the knowledge of ordinary people has to be seen in a different light. It was only as a result of the cleaving out of a set of expert knowledges from an undifferentiated general, common, or everyday knowledge about intoxication that it became possible to talk of a lay or non-expert knowledge of intoxication—of alcohol and of other drugs (perhaps by analogy with alcohol). I suggest that this type of knowledge of intoxication continues to play a role in criminal law practices on intoxicated offending.

One way of thinking about lay knowledge of intoxication relates to its practical role, as a basis for lay evaluation of claims based on intoxication. Because the question of whether an individual formed the requisite *mens rea* for an offence committed while intoxicated is a question of fact, where it is raised, the jury has a potentially significant role in assessing intoxication. The rules comprising the law on intoxication exclude intoxication from the consideration of jurors (or magistrates, when they act as fact-finders) in the large number of cases in which the defendant is charged with a 'basic intent' offence, but, if a defendant is charged with a 'specific intent' offence, the issue of whether he or she formed the requisite intent

---

[120] For most of the life of the 1957 version of diminished responsibility, if an intoxicated defendant is charged with murder, he or she was able to rely on this doctrine to reduce their charge to manslaughter if they could prove that they sustained injury to the brain causing gross impairment of judgment, or that they were unable to resist the impulse to have the first drink (*Tandy* [1989] 1 WLR 350; *R v Inseal* (CA, 10 May 1991)). Recently, the Court of Appeal has moved away from this strict approach to what constitutes involuntary consumption of alcohol in the context of chronic addiction. Referring the 'current understanding of alcoholism and alcohol dependency syndrome', in those cases where observable brain damage has not occurred, the jury should determine a defendant's substantial impairment by reference to the effect of the alcohol consumed as a 'direct result' of the illness or disease: see *R v Wood (Clive)* [2009] 1 WLR 496; see also *R v Stewart* [2009] 2 Cr App R 500. It is reasonable to expect that the new formulation of diminished responsibility—around an 'abnormality of mental functioning'—would also encompass alcoholism. On diminished responsibility, see Chapter 9.
[121] For discussion, see J Tolmie 'Alcoholism and Criminal Liability' (2001) 64(5) *Modern Law Review* 688.

although intoxicated is decided by the jury.[122] Over and above the role of lay knowledge as it informs lay evaluation by jurors, lay knowledge of intoxication informs the decision-making of legal actors—including judges, magistrates, prosecution, and defence counsel. As I discuss in Chapter 3 (and also in Chapter 6 in relation to insanity), legal actors rely on lay knowledge in relation to mental incapacity—legal expertise is mixed with lay knowledge or non-expertise when it comes to matters such as intoxication. As a result, the role of lay knowledge in criminal process does not begin and end with lay adjudication.

By contrast with the role of lay knowledge, the practical role of expert knowledge of intoxication, in the form of expert evidence, is more circumscribed. It is notable that, in the current era, and relative to other mental incapacity doctrines, expert medical or scientific evidence has a low profile in the process of proving an intoxicated defendant's mental state. Expert evidence is sometimes adduced in support of the claim of intoxication, as it was in the case of *Majewski*.[123] But, not only is there no requirement of expert evidence, there are dicta to indicate that knowledge of the effects of intoxication is properly a matter of non-expert knowledge.[124] The low profile of expert evidence in cases in which intoxication is pleaded indicates that it is lay rather than expert knowledge that governs the fact-finding context of the intoxicated offending. As Valverde has written in relation to alcohol licensing laws, 'knowledges of alcohol and of alcohol's effects on human bodies are regarded as lay rather than expert knowledges'.[125] In part because medical and scientific experts have made few inroads into the law on intoxication, there has been little attempt to articulate the different effects of different substances, and, in practice, it seems that the law on intoxication applies to all intoxicants by way of analogy with alcohol, which is the intoxicant that has most often come to the attention of the courts. This is also the intoxicant with which lay people are most likely to be familiar.

Stretching above its practical role in any particular instance, my study of the law of intoxication leads me to suggest that lay knowledge has a further, more discursive

---

[122] Given the large number of 'basic intent' offences compared to 'specific intent' offences, and recalling the policy concerns informing this area of criminal law, it is possible to interpret the restriction on jury consideration of the effect of intoxication to certain cases as the product of judicial mistrust of jury decision-making in intoxication cases (see, eg, Gold 'An Untrimmed "Beard"' 85). There is some support for this interpretation of the law of intoxication in the case law. In *Majewski* [1977] AC 443, the Court expressed concern about sympathetic juries who may too readily acquit a defendant if evidence of voluntary intoxication was open to them: 475 per Lord Elywn-Jones; for a contrasting view, see the Australian decision of the *Queen v O'Connor* [1980] 146 CLR 64, 79 per Barwick CJ).

[123] *DPP v Majewski* [1977] AC 443; see also *R v O'Connor* (1994) 15 Cr App R 473. In both of these cases the defendants had consumed drugs and alcohol and, although there was no discussion on the point in the judgments, it is possible that expert evidence was admissible because the effect of combining alcohol with other drugs could not be assumed to be common knowledge.

[124] In the Scottish case of *Kennedy v HM Advocate* (1944) JC 171, the High Court stated that 'medical evidence is not necessary to establish the plea' of intoxication: rather, 'evidence of conduct given by laymen may be perfectly competent evidence to support the plea' (178 per Lord Justice-General Normand, cited in *Bratty v Attorney-General for Northern Ireland* [1963] AC 386, 413 per Lord Denning).

[125] Valverde *Law's Dream of Common Knowledge* 190. See also McCord 'The English and American History' 372.

part to play in criminal law practices. In my analysis, lay knowledge of intoxication has two specific roles and one further, more overarching role in criminal law. First, it bolsters the legal rules comprising the law on intoxicated offending in that it sustains the particularly complex and technical rules that make it up. As Valverde claims, and as mentioned above, the particular distinction between 'basic' and 'specific' intent seems to map onto lay beliefs about intoxication. In her words, the distinction between 'two modes of consciousness/volition'—'specific intent' and 'basic intent'—translates into the 'lofty language of legal doctrine' the common-sense, everyday views of the effects of alcohol on humans.[126] As mentioned above, lay opinion holds that 'people who are very drunk cannot form "higher" thoughts or complex intentions, but that they are capable of, and indeed particularly susceptible to, more "impulsive" acts'.[127] Even absent empirical data bearing this out, it is clear that the legal discourse on intoxicated offending is constructed as if it were accurate. For example, in the 1981 decision of *Lawrence*, Lord Hailsham commented *obiter* that 'since the days of Noah, the effects of intoxication have been known to induce the state of mind described in English as recklessness, and not to inhibit it, and for that matter to remove inhibitions in the field of intention and not to destroy intention'.[128] Lord Hailsham's comment suggests that, as a matter of common knowledge, intoxication may affect the mind to the extent of recklessness (whether understood in a legal or a popular way) but not disturb intention. A legal distinction between 'specific intent' and 'basic intent' offences is constructed as if it tracks a genuine division between different mental states—and naturalizes that division.

In addition, lay knowledge of intoxication and its effects has a second role in criminal law practices. Viewed as a whole, the part played by lay knowledge—in connecting the restrictions on the law of intoxication with moral culpability and with an idea about genuinely different mental states—may be interpreted as a bridge linking the intoxication law with the dominant subjective principles of *mens rea* or fault. As mentioned above, the law on voluntary intoxication as it applies to 'basic intent' offences represents a half-way house of criminal liability: it is neither a wholly subjective nor a wholly objective form of *mens rea*. But, as Valverde has written about criminal cases generally, '"common knowledge" acts to forestall arguments about what a person did or did not know about alcohol in general and about his or her bodily capacities in particular'.[129] Because knowledge about intoxication and its effects is non-expert knowledge and is constructed as 'common', the individual can be presumed to know what 'everyone' knows.[130] In this way, references to non-expert knowledge about intoxication function to connect the general or objective (what everyone knows or is assumed to know) and the

---

[126] Valverde *Diseases of the Will* 196.
[127] Valverde, '"Slavery from Within"' 258–9 and Valverde *Diseases of the Will* 196.
[128] *R v Lawrence* [1981] 2 WLR 524, 530. There is an ambiguity in this comment between the idea of recklessness as subjective foresight of risk and recklessness as culpably indifferent attitude to risk.
[129] Valverde *Diseases of the Will* 191.
[130] Valverde refers to this as a 'duty to know' drunkenness—a kind of 'imperative knowledge' and a practice of responsibilizing private individuals: see *Law's Dream of Common Knowledge* 169–72.

particular or subjective (what the individual him or herself knows). Thus, within a dominant subjective rationale for liability, references to lay knowledge about intoxication function to justify what can be considered to be the artificial form of liability—absent a specific ingredient of the fact scenario—for 'basic intent' offences individuals commit while intoxicated.

More generally again, there is a further role for lay knowledge of intoxication that I suggest is important in criminal law practices. This role for lay knowledge is derived from an assessment of the rhetorical force of expert scientific knowledge (which I discuss in Chapter 3). In relation to knowledge practices in the natural sciences, Steve Fuller has argued that worldly power is exercised by rhetorically drawing attention *away* from the fact that it also intervenes in that world and *to* the fact that the knowledge represents the world.[131] The deployment of lay knowledge of intoxication—to connect the restrictions on the law of intoxication with moral culpability and with an idea about genuinely different mental states—works in a similar way in criminal law practices: with its everyday or commonsense connotations, it rhetorically draws attention *to* the idea of a morally neutral or descriptive statement of fact, and *away* from the idea of construction and contingency. As a construction of the material world, lay knowledge about intoxication, as deployed in criminal law, does not map onto an empirical reality but rather constitutes a particular story or narrative about that reality. The deployment of lay knowledge of intoxication in criminal law practices works to enmesh the moral-evaluative with the descriptive, obscuring the former beneath the latter, and rendering what is a partial and contingent account apparently true and universal.[132]

The Janus-face of the Law of Intoxicated Offending

With a close account of the law on intoxicated offending outlined, it is now possible to say something more about the controversy that continues to dog the law on intoxication. That controversy derives not just from a tension between principle and policy-driven pragmatism. Rather, it finds its roots in the Janus-face of the law, which encodes two different conceptualizations of intoxication—intoxication as exculpatory abnormality, on the one hand, and intoxication as morally culpable conduct, on the other. I discuss each of these two conceptions in turn, before pointing to evidence that suggests that these two conceptions are held in a fine balance in criminal law.

In criminal law schemas, intoxication is understood as a species of mental incapacity and the doctrine encodes an idea of the abnormality of an intoxicated

---

[131] S Fuller 'Disciplinary Boundaries and the Rhetoric of the Social Sciences' in E Messer-Davidow et al (eds) *Knowledge: Historical and Critical Studies in Disciplinarity* (Charlottesville and London: University of Virginia Press, 1993) 126 (emphasis added).

[132] It has been argued that the legal notion of the 'reasonable person' achieves a similar mix of the normative and the descriptive: see M Moran *Rethinking the Reasonable Person: An Egalitarian Reconstruction of the Objective Standard* (Oxford: OUP, 2003).

individual.[133] The construction of abnormality and its pejorative connotations is evident for instance in *Majewski*, where Lord Elwyn-Jones referred to an individual who 'consciously and deliberately takes alcohol and drugs...in order to escape from reality...and thereby *disables* himself from taking the care he might otherwise take'.[134] In the case of intoxication (as opposed to other types of mental incapacity, such as insanity), this abnormality is temporary and not that uncommon—it is something a significant percentage of the population have experienced at least once. The ubiquity of intoxication poses a challenge for a construction of the intoxicated individual as abnormal and, as a result, this construction is a more tenuous one than that of the individual raising an insanity claim, for example. However, resting on the general absence of a disaggregation of alcohol and other intoxicants in the criminal law, the notion of abnormality subsists in the criminal law of England and Wales, even as intoxication pleas are less rare than those of insanity, for instance.[135]

Alongside exculpatory abnormality, the legal entity of intoxication encodes an idea of intoxication as morally culpable conduct. This conception of intoxication is evident in the way in which intoxication has been quarantined from the law on automatism (which relates to unwilled or unconscious conduct)—on the basis that individuals seeking to rely on intoxication to defeat a criminal charge are not wholly free from fault. In addition, as discussed above, this idea about intoxication as morally culpable conduct is evidenced in the way in which certain types of intoxication—involuntary intoxication, intoxication from non-dangerous drugs, and that resulting from the disease of alcoholism—have been carved out from the reach of *Majewski* in an attempt to ensure that the law on intoxicated offending does not over-reach its moral foundations in individual culpability. In *Majewski*, Lord Edmund-Davies contrasted cases of voluntary intoxication by drugs or alcohol with those excuses in which 'the actor is wholly free from fault in relation to the onset of a mental state'.[136] The idea of moral fault is also evident in the *Majewski* line of reasoning (itself now largely out of favour) that holds that getting intoxicated in the first place provides the requisite culpability for criminal liability.[137] The idea

---

[133] See further Chapter 2.
[134] *DPP v Majewski* [1977] AC 443, 471 (emphasis added).
[135] The use of a largely undifferentiated notion of an intoxicant—alcohol or any illicit drug—for criminal liability is itself part of a broader disconnection between the legal regimes regulating drug use (eg Misuse of Drugs Act 1971) and scientific knowledge of variable drug harms. It seems that it is frustration with this disconnect that has led to the creation of the Independent Scientific Committee on Drugs, comprising various medical professionals (<http://www.drugscience.org.uk>), and the publication of research conducted on its behalf. Some of this research rates alcohol as the most harmful of drugs, taking into account both harm to users and harm to others: see D J Nutt et al 'Drug Harms in the UK: A Multicriteria Decision Analysis' (2010) 376 (6 November) *The Lancet* 1558. These same frustrations seem to be behind a call to adapt drug policy so as to regulate so-called 'legal highs': see J Birdwell et al *Taking Drugs Seriously: A Demos and UK Drug Commission Report on Legal Highs* (2009) available at <http://www.ukdpc.org.uk/index.shtml> (last accessed 29 September 2011).
[136] *DPP v Majewski* [1977] AC 443, 487.
[137] Lord Elwyn-Jones stated that the defendant's conduct in voluntarily 'reducing himself by drugs or drink' provides 'the evidence of *mens rea*, of guilty mind certainly sufficient for crimes of basic intent.' (*DPP v Majewski* [1977] AC 443, 474–5). See also *R v Hardie* (1985) 80 Cr App R 157, 162 per Parker LJ.

of intoxication as morally culpable conduct exposes the evaluative dimension of the law, which underlies its apparently precise and technical terminology.

These two contradictory conceptualizations of intoxication—as exculpatory abnormality and morally culpable conduct—are suspended in a fine balance. Some evidence of this is provided by the perennially unimplemented proposal for an *offence* of dangerous or criminal intoxication. The idea of an offence of intoxication is difficult to swallow because such an offence would make overt the connection between intoxication and criminal liability, sabotaging the popular myth that intoxication is some kind of 'defence' to a criminal charge. The idea of an offence of intoxication has been on the law reform table for some decades. A set of reform proposals, which are broadly critical of *Majewski*, has centred on the creation of an offence of what has been called either 'dangerous intoxication' or 'criminal intoxication'. In its 1975 report, the Butler Committee proposed the creation of an offence of 'dangerous intoxication', which would have been available as an alternative charge to another serious offence.[138] Building on the unimplemented Butler proposal, in 1993, the Law Commission canvassed the introduction of an offence that it called 'criminal intoxication'. This offence would have applied where an intoxicated defendant caused the harm proscribed by a number of enumerated offences (most of which involved personal violence or property damage).[139] The proposals for an offence of 'dangerous intoxication' or 'criminal intoxication' have been criticized. One concern has been the catch-all nature of such an offence.[140] Another concern relates to social perceptions about the seriousness of the offence.[141] In addition, concerns have been raised about the difficulty of proving that the defendant's awareness was 'substantially impaired', as required under the formulation of the offence the Law Commission considered.[142] Behind these

---

[138] United Kingdom *Report of the Committee on Mentally Abnormal Offenders* (Cmnd 6244, 1975) (Butler Report). The Butler Report provided that it would be an offence for 'a person while voluntarily intoxicated to do an act (or make an omission) that would amount to a dangerous offence if it were done or made with the requisite state of mind for such offence' (para 18.54). A 'dangerous offence' for this purpose was an offence of violence (assault occasioning actual bodily harm or death), sexual assault, or criminal damage so as to endanger life (para 18.55). The offence would have been one of strict liability for the offences to which it applied (para 18.57).

[139] Law Commission for England and Wales *Intoxication and Criminal Liability* (Law Com No 127, 1993). According to this offence, a person would be 'intoxicated' when he or she had taken anything that caused his or her awareness or control to be 'substantially impaired'. It would be immaterial that the defendant lacked the *mens rea* for the offence or was in a state of automatism at the time he or she performed the *actus reus*.

[140] In the course of its discussion of offences against the person, the Criminal Law Revision Committee (CLRC) reported that the offence of 'dangerous intoxication' was an insufficiently sharp tool to label appropriately the type of defendants who might fall within the boundaries of the offence (CLRC *Fourteenth Report: Offences Against the Person* (Cmnd 7844, 1980) para 261).

[141] In rejecting their own 1993 proposal in 1995, the Law Commission expressed concerns about the possibility that the offence would be perceived by defendants as less serious than the primary offence with which the defendant was charged: see *Legislating the Criminal Code: Intoxication and Criminal Liability* (Law Com No 229, 1995) paras 5.10–5.11.

[142] This latter difficulty was said to open the door to expert evidence, and to be likely to add to the length and cost of trials (Law Commission for England and Wales *Legislating the Criminal Code: Intoxication and Criminal Liability* (Law Com No 229, 1995) para 5.11; see also F Boland 'Intoxication and Criminal Liability' (1996) 60 *Journal of Criminal Law* 100, 105). The Law Commission

particular concerns about an offence of 'dangerous' or 'criminal intoxication', there is a general if nebulous concern that such an offence is socially and politically unpalatable in that it impinges on what is otherwise, at least in relation to alcohol, a legally and socially sanctioned activity.

---

noted that some of those who responded to the Consultation Paper favoured an offence of criminal intoxication where it was limited to circumstances in which the intoxication caused the criminal behaviour (para 5.15). However, the Commission rejected this amendment on the basis that it would entail 'formidable problems of proof' (para 5.16). Thus, in its final report on intoxication, the Law Commission did not recommend the creation of a new offence of 'criminal intoxication' (para 5.18).

8
Gender, 'Madness', and Crime: the Doctrine of Infanticide

This chapter addresses the gender dimension of 'madness' and crime via a study of the infanticide doctrine. The subject of gender, 'madness' and crime has been of most interest to feminist scholars. Like feminist studies of law more generally, the subject of gender, 'madness', and crime has been approached with a critical eye on the distribution of power.[1] Feminist scholars have pointed out the ways in which women offenders are depicted as doubly-deviant, transgressing gender norms as well as legal norms.[2] As my analysis of infanticide shows, gender norms are crucial for understanding this part of the mental incapacity terrain.

As I discuss in Chapter 2, infanticide is a mental incapacity doctrine on my account of the mental incapacity terrain in criminal law. Infanticide is distinctive in that it is both a partial defence to a charge of murder or manslaughter, as well as a distinct homicide offence, and it applies exclusively to women who kill a biological child where the child is under the age of 12 months.[3] In its restriction to women, infanticide is thus a rare instance of the overt gendering of the legal subject—gender differences, which are more often implicit in legal doctrines and practices, are made explicit on the face of the law of infanticide.[4] In addition to providing a specific focus for consideration of the wider and more nebulous flow of currents of meaning around gender, 'madness', and crime, my study of infanticide exposes the gendered character of abnormality as it is constructed within criminal law.

The two main arguments advanced in this chapter concern the broad continuities in the meanings given to women's 'madness' at the point of intersection with

---

[1] In this respect, feminist legal theory and critical legal studies have shared concerns. As Nicola Lacey argues, there are strong continuities between strains of feminist legal theory and critical legal studies, in that both share a strategy of what she calls 'recontextualisation as critique': see N Lacey *Unspeakable Subjects: Feminist Essays in Legal and Social Theory* (Oxford: Hart, 1998) ch. 7.

[2] See K Kendall 'Beyond Reason: Social Constructions of Mentally Disordered Female Offenders' in W Chan et al (eds) *Women, Madness and the Law: A Feminist Reader* (London: GlassHouse Press, 2005) 41–57. Women's biology has featured prominently in these ideas of deviance. See for discussion, L Seal *Women, Murder and Femininity: Gender Representations of Women Who Kill* (Basingstoke: Palgrave Macmillan, 2010) 50–1.

[3] See Infanticide Act 1938 (1 & 2 Geo. VI c.38), s 1(1) and 1(2) as amended by Coroners and Justice Act 2009.

[4] For discussion, see C Smart 'The Woman of Legal Discourse' in K Daly and L Maher (eds) *Criminology at the Crossroads: Feminist Readings in Crime and Justice* (Oxford: OUP, 1998) 21–36; and Lacey *Unspeakable Subjects* ch. 7.

crime. The first of these arguments is that these broad continuities permit the doctrine of infanticide to slide between the categories of offence and defence, or, more precisely, between charge and plea, meaning that the doctrine itself is most accurately understood as both/either partially exculpatory and/or partially inculpatory. The second main argument is that a particular gendered social type—the infanticidal woman—has come to determine the legal issue of an infanticide defendant's criminal responsibility, and the acts of infanticide have come to be read as an instantiation of abnormality for criminal law purposes. In the current era, the doctrine of infanticide is sustained by a lay or non-expert knowledge about the interrelation of gender, 'madness', and crime, which, when overlaid with the social meanings accorded to childbirth and motherhood, over-determines the legal evaluation of infanticidal women and their acts in criminal law.

Proscribing Infanticide: 'Lewd Women' and 'Bastard' Children

Infanticide has a longer history as the practice of killing unwanted children—of various ages, and by men and women—than as legally proscribed conduct. Historians suggest that the practice of infanticide was a familiar part of pre-modern and early modern social life. These periods were ones in which the social landscape was marked by the sexual vulnerability of women employed as servants, heavy stigma attached to unwed mothers, a lack of options for fertility control, and high infant mortality.[5] In the second half of the sixteenth century, concern with women's sexual activity, the criminal activities of the poor, and the financial burden of illegitimate children on parish resources combined to move prosecutions for fornication, bastardy, and similar crimes from church courts to royal courts.[6] Parliament passed a series of personal control laws, which reflected concern about social disorder. One such law was the 'poor law' of 1576,[7] under which women with illegitimate children faced imprisonment on the basis that they were defrauding the parish of the funds that were used to support such children (and that should have been used to relieve the 'true poor'). Under this law, unmarried women faced social and legal pressure to reveal the name of the fathers of illegitimate children so that local authorities could try to ensure that the fathers supported them. Peter Hoffer and N E H Hull have speculated that the severity of the 'poor law'

---

[5] See generally S Shahar *Childhood in the Middle Ages* (New York: Routledge, 1992) 126–7. Even after infanticide became legally proscribed, prosecutions, and certainly convictions, represented only a small slice of all acts of infanticide that took place: R Dickinson and J Sharpe, 'Infanticide in Early Modern England: The Court of Great Sessions at Chester, 1650–1800' in M Jackson (ed) *Infanticide: Historical Perspectives on Child Murder and Concealment, 1550–2000* (Aldershot: Ashgate, 2002) 43.

[6] See P Hoffer and N E H Hull *Murdering Mothers: Infanticide in England and New England 1558–1803* (New York: New York University Press, 1984) 12. As these authors discuss, and in a way that also reflects extant anxieties about gender, accusations of witchcraft also became the object of royal law and royal prosecution at about this time (28–31).

[7] 18 Eliz. I c. 3.

'counselled the poor to conceal bastardy pregnancy and perhaps murder their bastard newborns'.[8]

Concern with women's sexual 'immorality', illegitimacy, and poverty coalesced in a statute dealing specifically with newborn child murder by single women, enacted in 1624.[9] The 1624 Act created a species of constructive crime, an offence paralleling murder and a legal presumption that a woman concealing the death of her illegitimate child had murdered it. The Act provided that, where 'lewd women' concealed the death of a 'bastard child', 'the said mother so offending shall suffer death as in the case of murther'.[10] With a presumption of murder on evidence of concealment of death, the 1624 Act introduced special evidential rules to apply to cases in which single women were alleged to have killed their children. The presumption was designed to avoid the problems that beset murder trials at common law, where it was necessary to prove that the child was born alive and then killed.[11] In murder trials where there were no witnesses to the birth, the prosecution had to rely on 'presumptive or circumstantial evidence' that a child had been born alive.[12] Character evidence and circumstantial evidence were sometimes sufficient to obtain a conviction, but, in general, murder convictions under the common law proved difficult to secure.[13] The 1624 Act provided that, if a woman could produce a witness to testify that the child had been born dead, she could avoid conviction and death. However, as several writers point out, it was often difficult for unmarried women to secure a witness to the birth because of the secrecy of the affair or seduction that led to it.[14]

As it reflects extant structures of liability and responsibility (then incompletely separated from each other), the offence created in the 1624 Act—a constructive crime, paralleling murder, which was based on a presumption that a woman concealing the death of her illegitimate newborn had murdered it—is helpfully

---

[8] Hoffer and Hull *Murdering Mothers* 15.
[9] 21 Jac. I. c.27. The Act was titled 'An Act to Prevent the Destroying and Murthering of Bastard Children' and is known as the 'Concealment of Birth of Bastards' Act 1624.
[10] Extracted in Hoffer and Hull *Murdering Mothers* 20. The reference to 'lewd women' connoted unmarried women. At this time, marriage was not regulated by the state. As a result, as C Smart writes, 'the condition of being married or not married was more fluid' than in the current era: 'The Woman of Legal Discourse' 29. Married women, as well as married and unmarried men, and any individuals accused of killing children other than newborns, were excluded from the reach of the 1624 Act, but could still face murder charges: see M Jackson *New-Born Child Murder: Women, Illegitimacy and the Courts in Eighteenth Century England* (Manchester: Manchester University Press, 1996) 43–5.
[11] J M Beattie *Crime and the Courts in England 1660–1800* (Oxford: OUP, 1986) 113.
[12] Such evidence included accounts of the defendant woman's behaviour and reputation, and a variety of physical signs, such as signs of violence on the child's body and estimates of whether the child had gone to full term. Other physical signs included the amount of air in a dead baby's lungs—if a baby's lungs floated, it was thought to have breathed and therefore to have died after birth—and the form of the dead baby's hands—if clenched in a fist, this was taken to indicate that the baby had been born dead: see, for example, *OBP*, Maria Jenkins, 18 September 1765 (t17650918-40) and *OBP*, Ann Mabe, 27 February 1718 (t17180227-25) respectively.
[13] M Jackson *New-Born Child Murder* 32.
[14] J M Beattie 'The Criminality of Women in Eighteenth Century England' in D K Weisberg (ed) *Women and the Law: A Social History Perspective* (Cambridge MA: Schenkman Publishing, 1982) 202–3.

understood via Fletcher's pattern of 'manifest criminality'.[15] This structure of criminal liability was, according to Fletcher, the dominant 'pattern of criminality' until the end of the eighteenth century.[16] One of the features of liability under 'manifest criminality' is that the commission of a crime is 'objectively discernible at the time that it occurs': as a crime, 'the act must manifest, on its face, the actor's criminal purpose'.[17] The concealment of the birth of a 'bastard child' fits here because the act of concealing is treated as an act that, to borrow Fletcher's words, 'meets an objective standard of liability'.[18] A single woman's act of 'murthering' an illegitimate child and concealing its death was constructed as intelligible and purposeful behaviour.[19] Further, under this law, a woman's actions were accorded a particular significance for the purposes of determining criminal liability. While the individual mental states that might accompany the act of infanticide—intent or perhaps motive to preserve reputation and status—are obliquely countenanced in the Act, liability is grounded in the lethal action itself. As Fletcher writes, when liability is structured according to the principles of 'manifest criminality', the 'criminal act is treated as a substantive condition of liability'.[20]

To refute the allegation of concealment and the attendant presumption of murder, those charged under the 1624 Act could raise a 'benefit of linen' or 'preparation' plea, in which a woman demonstrated that she had prepared for the arrival of her baby, or a 'want of help' plea, in which she claimed that she had unsuccessfully sought assistance in childbirth.[21] An illustration of the successful use of these informal pleas is provided by the record of Mary Campion's trial for killing her newborn:

> The Prisoner said, that she was not near her time; and no proof was made that the Child was Born alive; and she being found to make good Provision for the Child against the Birth, she was deemed to be out of the Statute and so she was Acquitted.[22]

Conversely, the absence of evidence that the defendant had sought help or had prepared for the baby could inculpate her:

---

[15] See my Chapter 3 for detailed discussion.
[16] G P Fletcher *Rethinking Criminal Law* (Oxford: OUP, 2000) 61.
[17] *Rethinking Criminal Law* 116, 232. So, when criminal liability is structured according to 'manifest criminality', 'thieves could be seen thieving; they could be caught in the act': *Rethinking Criminal Law* 80.
[18] *Rethinking Criminal Law* 89.
[19] As Dana Rabin argues, a single woman's act of killing her baby was seen as a 'reasoned, premeditated (though immoral and criminal) act': see *Identity, Crime and Legal Responsibility in Eighteenth Century England* (Basingstoke: Palgrave Macmillan, 2004) 97.
[20] Fletcher *Rethinking Criminal Law* 232. Fletcher illustrates this aspect of 'manifest criminality' with reference to larceny, where, under 'manifest criminality', the 'primary inquiry was the act of larceny' and intent is a 'subsidiary issue' (86). Regarding mental states, the 1624 Act is also notable for the elision between what would now be identified as separate phenomena with distinct legal significance, motive and intention: a motive for concealing a dead illegitimate baby (loss of reputation and status, for example) substituted for intention to kill it.
[21] See R W Malcolmson 'Infanticide in the Eighteenth Century' in J S Cockburn (ed) *Crime In England 1550–1800* (London: Methuen, 1977) 198 and Rabin *Identity, Crime and Legal Responsibility* 95–6 for discussion.
[22] *OBP*, Mary Campion, 11 December 1689 (t16891211-26).

The Prisoner could say little in her Defence, it did not appear that she made any Provision for the Birth of the Child, nor was she heard to cry out, or us'd any endeavour to discover it, as the Statute of King James I [the 1624 Act] in such Cases requires. The Fact being clear, upon the whole the Jury found her Guilty of the Indictment.[23]

In the absence of sophisticated conceptions of proof and formal rules of evidence, these informal pleas were designed to challenge the authenticity of the manifest meaning of the act of concealment. As the act of concealing the death of an illegitimate baby was, *prima facie*, indicative of having killed it, evidence of preparation or 'want of help' undercut this manifest meaning by casting doubt on it (why would a woman kill a baby when she had prepared for it or sought help to ensure it was born alive?).

Indicating the strength of concerns with immorality and the economic and social problems posed by single women and illegitimate children, prosecutions and convictions under the 1624 Act were initially high, but the Act came to be observed with less and less strictness and, eventually, it was 'largely disregarded'.[24] The radical change from the first decades after 1624 was the result of developments both within and beyond the criminal justice system. Within the criminal justice system, the first of two sets of developments concerned changes in the mode of criminal trial. As I discuss in detail in Chapter 6, up to 1700, criminal trial process was changing such that 'truth was becoming internal to the trial procedure',[25] and changes from 1700 were associated with the rise of the adversarial trial process. With greater emphasis on proof, concealment of an illegitimate birth came to be regarded as an insufficient basis for a capital charge.[26] The second, connected set of changes related to the status of the Bloody Code, which came to be criticized both for the severity of the law on the books and the unpredictability of punishment that, in practice, accompanied it. Against a backdrop marked by these legal developments, eighteenth-century judges seem to have worked to avoid the imposition of capital punishment in infanticide cases.[27]

---

[23] *OBP*, Ann Gardner, 15 January 1708 (t17080115-1).
[24] Malcolmson 'Infanticide in the Eighteenth Century' 197. In her study of Old Bailey trials from the 1700s, Rabin finds that there were no convictions under the Act after 1775: see *Identity, Crime and Legal Responsibility* 99. As Mark Jackson notes, the decline of the 1624 Act was accompanied by a trend to try women accused of killing their newborns (even single women) for murder under the common law, where such trials continued to be beset by problems of proof, and women tended to be discharged or acquitted of murder: *New-Born Child Murder* 151.
[25] See A Duff et al *The Trial on Trial (Vol 3): Towards a Normative Theory of the Criminal Trial* (Oxford: Hart Publishing, 2007) 40.
[26] See Beattie *Crime and the Courts in England* 124. As Beattie suggests, William Blackstone's Commentaries on the Laws of England (1775) suggests that the severity of the 1624 statute was mitigated in practice by shifting the burden of proof to the Crown: see *Crime and the Courts in England* 122.
[27] *Crime and the Courts in England* 203. In the absence of an alternative verdict to conviction under the 1624 Act, the majority of single women accused of killing their newborns were acquitted: see M Jackson 'The Trial of Harriet Vooght: Continuity and Change in the History of Infanticide' in M Jackson (ed) *Infanticide: Historical Perspectives on Child Murder and Concealment 1550–2000* (Aldershot: Ashgate, 2002) 6.

Beyond the bounds of the criminal courtroom, the eighteenth century saw changes in attitudes to women, illegitimacy, and poverty, each of which was an ingredient in infanticide trials. As Mark Jackson argues, as a result of these changes, a 'humanitarian' approach to infanticide rose to the fore, affecting the social meanings of infanticide.[28] According to this 'humanitarian' approach, unmarried women who were alleged to have concealed, abandoned, or murdered their illegitimate newborns did so because of their modesty and virtue, and not because they were cruel and unnatural. The 'humanitarian' approach emphasized the social pressures unmarried women faced, and also criticized the lack of responsibility shown by men—the 'seducers of women'—for their sexual behaviour: although 'neither the actions nor the criminality of men' featured in legal investigations, infanticidal women came to be regarded as 'passive, compassionate, pitiable and innocent'.[29] While on the face of the law, their conduct remained criminal, social meanings changed such that women who were charged with killing their newborns were to be pitied, and punishment avoided if possible.

The aggregate effect of the changes both within and beyond the criminal justice system in this era was to pave the way for the appearance in criminal courtrooms of informal pleas to newborn child killing based on mental incapacity. In this era, claims to exculpation on the basis that a defendant woman was not in her 'senses',[30] or did not know what she was 'about',[31] were made alongside other informal claims to exculpation such as the 'benefit of linen' plea.[32] Such claims already had a history of success as bases for an informal insanity plea in the common law murder trials of married women charged with killing their newborns.[33] These types of claims based on mental incapacity came to enjoy greater prominence over the course of the 1700s.[34] An illustration of their successful extension to single women is provided by the trial record of Isabella Buckham, who was acquitted of the murder of her 'male bastard child' in 1755. In her defence, she is recorded as saying:[35]

> I was not in my senses; I do not know what I said or did. Had I been in my senses I should have been very loth to have parted with it.

Over the course of the eighteenth century, judges and juries became increasingly aware of 'the physical and mental distress associated with labour' and the idea that this led women to act 'irrationally'.[36] This meant that claims to exculpation on the

---

[28] See Jackson *New-Born Child Murder* 113–23.
[29] *New-Born Child Murder* 118.
[30] *OBP*, Sarah Hunter, 28 June 1769 (t17690628-27).
[31] *OBP*, Diana Parker, 17 September 1794 (r17940917-46).
[32] The 'benefit of linen' claim was raised in the trial of Diana Parker, for example. *OBP*, Diana Parker, 17 September 1794 (t17940917-46).
[33] See Rabin *Identity, Crime and Legal Responsibility* 98.
[34] Rabin argues that the rise of informal exculpation based on mental incapacity around the time of childbirth is a discrete product of the broader intellectual culture of the eighteenth century. According to Rabin, 'in the context of a culture of sensibility', an explanation for killing a newborn 'that pointed to a temporary "phrenzy" brought on by a single women's illegitimate pregnancy was received as sincere, inevitable and exculpatory:' *Identity, Crime and Legal Responsibility* 108–9.
[35] *OBP*, Isabella Buckham, 4 December 1755 (t17551204-27).
[36] M Jackson 'Infanticide: Historical Perspectives' (1996) 146 *New Law Journal* 416, 417.

basis of mental stress at the time of giving birth and in the period following it came to have greater probity. Overall, the increasing prominence of claims to exculpation based on 'phrenzy' at the time of childbirth over the course of the eighteenth century heralded the profound shift in the legal meaning of infanticide (as it would later be called).[37]

The greater probity these claims to 'phrenzy' enjoyed in the eighteenth century was both a part of and fed into broader, social dynamics around gender. The rise of informal exculpation based on mental incapacity around the time of childbirth has been interpreted by Dana Rabin as a product of the intellectual culture of the eighteenth century, which had particular gender inflections.[38] However, neither the degree nor the pace of change in the legal meaning of killing a newborn over the seventeenth and eighteenth centuries should be overstated. An element of continuity between these centuries is revealed when taking into account the situation of married women who killed their newborn children. Even though the 'vast majority' of trials of women alleged to have killed their newborns took place under the 1624 Act,[39] properly conceptualized, the history of the law of infanticide includes the treatment of married women tried for the common law offence of murder of their newborns. When looking at these cases, something of the deep roots of an association between the mental distress of childbirth and child killing (and thus the genesis of the current construction of infanticide as abnormality) becomes evident. While unmarried women were charged with concealing their dead newborns under the 1624 Act, married women alleged to have killed their newborns continued to be charged with murder under the common law.[40] Some married women charged with child murder drew on an informal insanity plea in responding to charges. Such claims were likely to be successful because, as Rabin acknowledges, while the criminal explanation for an unmarried woman killing her newborn was readily cognizable (she was 'treacherous, threatening and active'), the possibility that a married woman could have committed the same act was 'so shocking and so unlikely' that it could only be the product of insanity.[41]

---

[37] Rabin concludes that the strength of this explanation for the act of killing a newborn was such that, by the end of the 1700s, 'the crime itself became evidence of madness that required little or no supporting testimony about marital status or mental alienation': D Rabin 'Bodies of Evidence, States of Mind: Infanticide, Emotion and Sensibility in Eighteenth-Century England' in M Jackson (ed) *Infanticide: Historical Perspectives on Child Murder and Concealment 1550–2000* (Aldershot: Ashgate, 2002) 73, 79. It seems to me, however, that this is somewhat precipitous: my analysis suggests that the emergence of these ideas and their rise to prominence took place gradually over the eighteenth and nineteenth century.

[38] See Rabin *Identity, Crime and Legal Responsibility*. In Rabin's words, 'in the context of a culture of sensibility', an explanation for killing a newborn 'that pointed to a temporary "phrenzy" brought on by a single women's illegitimate pregnancy was received as sincere, inevitable and exculpatory' (108–9). Thus, according to Rabin, the eighteenth-century image of women who killed their newborns as passive agents of the crime is in stark contrast with the seventeenth-century image of unmarried women as 'treacherous, threatening and active': *Identity, Crime and Legal Responsibility* 102.

[39] Beattie *Crime and the Courts in England* 114.

[40] *Crime and the Courts in England* 113.

[41] Rabin *Identity, Crime and Legal Responsibility* 98.

'Out of her usual senses':[42] Infanticide and Incapacity

By 1800, the practice of treating leniently women alleged to have killed their newborns contrasted starkly with the severe treatment prescribed under the 1624 Act. Dissatisfaction with what was at least formally a severe law led to calls for the repeal of the 1624 Act and there were several reform attempts in the last decades of the eighteenth century.[43] The successful bill was proposed by Lord Ellenborough and passed into law in 1803. This Act provided that women acquitted of the murder of their children, and thus spared the death penalty, could be charged in the alternative with an offence of concealment of birth of the dead baby, for which the maximum penalty was two years' imprisonment.[44] The alternative offence of concealment was designed to mitigate the difficulties of proof in baby death cases, as it provided an alternative charge where there was insufficient proof of a live birth or killing. The new Act made few concessions to changing social attitudes to women who killed their children, however, or to the case made by those advocating criminal law reforms. As several commentators note, it was designed not to reduce the harshness of the previous statute, but to ensure more convictions of women who killed their children by reigning in the latitude of the courts in dealing with suspects.[45] Like the 1624 Act, the 1803 Act (initially) applied exclusively to unmarried women.[46]

While the introduction of an alternative offence of concealment in the 1803 Act reflected the older structure of criminal liability referred to above (whereby the act of a mother concealing the birth of her dead baby constituted liability as per 'manifest criminality'[47]), the conditions, such as those relating to proof, which underpinned this liability structure were changing. Under the 1803 Act, there was no presumption of murder where a woman had concealed her dead baby, and so it was necessary for the prosecution to show that the child died after birth. A number of prosecutions failed because the possibility that the baby was born dead could not be conclusively ruled out.[48] Even if there was some evidence that the baby had been killed, a woman might still be convicted of concealment and avoid a murder

---

[42] *OBP*, Jane Harrington, 18 September 1854 (t18540918-1068).
[43] For discussion, see Jackson *New-Born Child Murder* 158–68.
[44] 43 Geo. III c.58. The Act was entitled 'An Act for the Further Prevention of Malicious Shooting and Attempting to Discharge Loaded Fire-arms'. . . and for repealing 'An Act to Prevent the Destroying and Murthering of Bastard Children".
[45] See, for example, Jackson *New-Born Child Murder* 177.
[46] In 1828, the concealment provision became an offence in itself and the reach of the statute was extended to married women. For discussion, see R Smith *Trial by Medicine: Insanity and Responsibility in Victorian Trials* (Edinburgh: Edinburgh University Press, 1981) 145. A concealment offence, which applies to men and women, still exists in England and Wales. Section 60 of the Offences Against the Person Act 1861 provides that 'any person' can be charged with concealment, and the offence will apply whether or not the child had been born alive or dead. The maximum penalty is two years in prison.
[47] See further A Loughnan 'The Strange Case of the Infanticide Doctrine' (2012) 32(4) *Oxford Journal of Legal Studies*.
[48] See, for example, *OBP*, Julia Barry, 8 December 1825 (t18251208-16).

conviction. Where a trial resulted in a conviction of concealment rather than murder, evidence of preparation, 'want of help', and good character seemed to work in the prisoner's favour. The 1832 trial record of Maria Poulton, alleged to have killed her illegitimate baby by strangulation, provides an illustration.[49] In her defence, the defendant stated that: 'In the state of mind I was in, I was unconscious of what I said or did'. One acquaintance testified that the prisoner had 'uniformly borne the character of an inoffensive mild woman', and another stated that Poulton had prepared for the birth. She was convicted of concealment rather than murder and sentenced to two years' imprisonment. As this case suggests, after the passage of the 1803 Act, leniency continued to feature in the courts' treatment of women charged with killing their newborns, and the 1803 Act had patchy success in facilitating prosecutions and convictions of women who killed their infants.

Something of the modern character of infanticide—structured around an explicit association of infanticidal conduct and mental incapacity—can be detected from the first decades of the nineteenth century. The appearance of a diagnostic entity of puerperal insanity (also known as puerperal psychosis or puerperal mania) boosted change in this direction. Reflecting the increasingly strong cultural association between childbirth, danger, and risk, puerperal insanity was thought to be one of a number of 'unfavourable medical occurrences' that could follow the intense strain of childbirth.[50] This diagnostic entity, which was affiliated with another novel construct, 'moral insanity', entered the medical arena in the 1820s and 1830s, and reflected the emergence of a body of 'alienists' identifying and treating mental conditions.[51] Puerperal insanity readily gained currency among 'alienists' and, by mid-century, it had established a firm place in the insanity discourse. It was regarded as a discrete disease, characterized by depression, hallucinations, and acute anxiety.[52] While the causes of puerperal insanity were disputed, it was widely accepted as a serious condition, which, in particular cases, resulted in self-harm and violence directed towards the infant and others. In Joel Eigen's words, 'puerperal insanity was not mere confusion: its natural *result* was an impulse to destroy one's new-born child'.[53] This feature of puerperal insanity implicated it in the question of criminal liability for child killing by mothers because the disorder was understood to *cause* such criminal conduct. The belief that there was a causal relationship between puerperal insanity and child killing was central to the way in which, over the second half of the nineteenth century, the law of infanticide would develop.

---

[49] *OBP*, Maria Poulton, 17 May 1832 (t18320517-65).
[50] H Marland 'At Home with Puerperal Mania: The Domestic Treatment of the Insanity of Childbirth in the Nineteenth Century' in P Bartlett and D Wright (eds) *Outside the Walls of the Asylum: The History of Care in the Community 1750–2000* (London: Athlone Press, 1999) 46.
[51] See 'At Home with Puerperal Mania' 45–6. See my Chapter 6 for discussion of the development of an expert knowledge of 'madness'.
[52] J P Eigen 'Criminal Lunacy in Early Modern England: Did Gender Make a Difference?' (1998) 21(4) *International Journal of Law and Psychiatry* 412.
[53] 'Criminal Lunacy in Early Modern England' 413.

The development of an expert psychiatric language connecting 'phrenzy' to the physical process of childbirth meant that a variety of professionals could all be called to give evidence in trials of women accused of killing their newborn children—to include obstetric practitioners, midwives, general practitioners, and alienists.[54] Indeed, what would now be identified as expert evidence seems to have been a prominent feature in infanticide trials since this time. The broad acceptability of expert evidence about infanticide was the product of several interrelated factors. It was due in part to the distinctive status of midwives, who possessed specialist knowledge about childbirth and related matters such as the death of newborn children,[55] but who were also members of the defendant's local community. The acceptability of expert evidence about newborn child murder was also the result of the difficulty of determining whether a child had been born alive, an issue on which surgeons and others were called to give evidence. In addition, the entry of expert evidence in trials where mothers were charged with killing their children was facilitated by the fact that the offence was a form of homicide. As Roger Smith notes, because medical experts had been required to give evidence in contexts such as coronial inquiries, there was an 'established institutional framework' into which medical evidence linking 'lunacy' and infanticide could be placed.[56] The factors that ensured the ready acceptance of expert evidence pertaining to child killing by women also grounded the increasing social acceptability of psychological and psychiatric knowledge about, and clinical diagnosis of, the phenomenon.[57]

The rise to prominence of psychiatric and psychological knowledge in courtroom assessment of a mother's act of killing her newborn child over the course of the nineteenth century reflected in part the strategic utility of such knowledge. A clinical diagnosis based on such knowledge provided a means of accommodating the variety of exculpatory narratives that featured in the criminal trials of such women. Facilitated by the open-textured character of psychiatric labels such as puerperal insanity, 'the plea of mental disorder extended to cases where the accused was clearly not insane but was very upset, behaving oddly, facing the distress of destitution or was feeble-minded'.[58] As a result, and in a way that pre-figures the current debate about the relevance of context to a defendant's responsibility (evidenced in the judgment in *Kai-Whitewind*, discussed in the final section of

---

[54] An example of reliance on experts in infanticide trials is provided by the trial of Harriet Farrell: see *OBP*, Harriet Farrell, 19 February 1829 (t18290219-62).

[55] See G Böhme 'Midwifery as Science: An Essay on the Relationship between Scientific and Everyday Knowledge' in N Stehr and V Meja (eds) *Society and Knowledge: Contemporary Perspectives in the Sociology of Knowledge and Science* (New Brunswick: Transaction Publishers, 2005) 379–85.

[56] R Smith *Trial by Medicine: Insanity and Responsibility in Victorian Trials* (Edinburgh: Edinburgh University Press, 1981) 148.

[57] As Joel Eigen writes, it seems that 'specialist witnesses believed their pronouncements would resonate intuitively with the court and the jury for whom puerperal mania was hardly an esoteric, clinical discovery whose features had to be explained': see J P Eigen *Unconscious Crime: Mental Absence and Criminal Responsibility in Victorian London* (Baltimore: Johns Hopkins University Press, 2003) 83.

[58] H Marland 'Getting Away with Murder?: Puerperal Insanity, Infanticide and the Defence Plea', in M Jackson (ed) *Infanticide: Historical Perspectives on Child Murder and Concealment 1550–2000* (Aldershot: Ashgate, 2002) 168, 186.

this chapter), the plea of mental disorder encompassed consideration of a defendant woman's lethal acts, her conduct or behaviour more generally as well as her broader circumstances. In Smith's words, jury decisions in cases involving women charged with child killing reveal 'a willingness to associate distressful circumstances with distress of reason'.[59] Such a 'willingness' both depended upon and reproduced a porous boundary between women's mental state and their circumstances, resulting in a long-lasting legal construction of women offenders such as those alleged to have committed infanticide as over-determined or hyper-contextualized.[60]

The blurred line between distressing circumstances and distress of reason, or between 'sad' and 'mad' women, reflected ordinary or non-specialist understandings of 'madness', rather than a desire on the part of medical professionals to prescribe the significance of the acts of women killing their newborns.[61] The rise of an expert knowledge of mental incapacity and childbirth—possessed and espoused by 'medical men'—has been interpreted as the 'medicalization' of infanticide. The reference to the 'medicalization' is a reference to the notion that any special status at law is dependent on pathologization: thus, infanticide defendants are depicted as most properly the subjects of medical rather than legal attention, and treatment rather than punishment.[62] However, this approach, with its specific focus on the advent of expert medical (and specifically psychiatric and psychological) knowledge, fails to grasp thoroughly what my analysis suggests is the long and strong association between gender, childbirth, and 'madness' relating to child killing by mothers, and its currency beyond the bounds of a professionalizing elite. In addition, the argument about 'medicalization' does not pay sufficient attention to what has been referred to as the way in which medicine 'became much more important as a source of intellectual resources for understanding the world' in the Victorian era.[63] While in this period there were increasing points of interconnection between medicine and deviance, this was a complex development—reflecting in part a re-articulation of humanitarian concerns within 'scientific' language. The particular associations between gender, 'madness', and crime were taken up and amplified by, rather than invented within, expert medical

---

[59] Smith 'Trial by Medicine' 149.

[60] As hyper-contextualized or over-determined by social forces, women offenders are less autonomous than the archetypal subject of the law: thus, it is not so much that infanticidal defendants are depicted in legal doctrines and practices as 'mad' as opposed to 'bad', but rather that they are 'sad': see T Ward 'The Sad Subject of Infanticide: Law, Medicine and Child Murder 1860–1938' (1999) 8(2) *Social and Legal Studies* 163.

[61] Ward 'The Sad Subject of Infanticide' 166.

[62] Several feminists and critical scholars have argued that infanticide is marked by 'medicalization': see, for example, H Allen *Justice Unbalanced: Gender, Psychiatry and Judicial Decisions* (Milton Keynes: Open University Press, 1987) 56–7; D Nicolson 'What the Law Giveth, it Also Taketh Away: Female-Specific Defences to Criminal Liability' in D Nicolson and L Bibbings (eds) *Feminist Perspectives on Criminal Law* (London: Cavendish Press, 2000) 171; and F Raitt and M S Zeedyk *The Implicit Relation of Psychology and Law: Women and Syndrome Evidence* (Philadelphia: Routledge, 2000) 9.

[63] C Lawrence *Medicine in the Making of Modern Britain, 1700–1920* (London: Routledge, 1994) 71. The development of an elite or specialist knowledge about mental incapacity and childbirth was part of a broader development of medical specialisms in the nineteenth century. For discussion of the development of the medical profession, see *Medicine in the Making of Modern Britain* 55–83.

discourse.[64] Viewed in this way, the changing meanings of infanticide would seem to reflect something more complex than an idea that medical knowledge overstepped a pre-existing and solid boundary beyond which it might not go.[65]

The interaction between an emergent expertise about gender, 'madness', and crime and ordinary people's attitudes and beliefs was dynamic. At this time, ordinary people's understanding of 'madness' was 'growing into' medical conceptions. As Roy Porter argues in relation to 'madness' in general, and as I discuss in Chapter 6, the development of expert medical knowledge 'emerged on the basis of "natural beliefs" about madness already well entrenched within common culture'.[66] Such beliefs had a strong moral dimension. According to Martin Wiener, moral issues were 'starkly clear', and, with their basis in this shared morality, penal and medical discourse had 'many points of contact', up to the mid-Victorian era.[67] This meant that expert discourses shared moral precepts with generalized social discourses, around responsibility, for instance. The effect of the close connection between non-expert and expert knowledge about insanity following childbirth was that moral-evaluative decisions about women's (attenuated) responsibility for killing their young children were underscored by both lay and scientific knowledge. Although the relevant body of scientific knowledge would later fragment, at least until the end of the nineteenth century, it formed a solid under layer for the lenient practices that would be formalized in the infanticide doctrine.

In a way that parallels the developments in knowledges brought to bear on other mental incapacity doctrines, as the development of an expertise about mental incapacity and childbirth emerged out of common knowledge, the process created a lay or non-expert knowledge of the same. As I discuss in Chapter 3, this type of knowledge is most accurately understood as lay because it is defined by its non-expert quality. As it concerns socially ratified attitudes and beliefs about the interaction of gender, 'madness', and crime, this lay knowledge has a significant impact of legal evaluation and adjudication of women who killed their young children. The strength of these gender meanings—initially common to both expert and non-expert knowledges—has come to determine the legal issue of a defendant's criminal responsibility, and to mean that the acts of infanticide have come to be read as an instantiation of abnormality for criminal law purposes.

---

[64] As Lucia Zedner argues, 'psychiatric diagnoses were built on traditional, exculpatory legal discourse to provide a formidable case for acquitting the infanticidal mother': see L Zedner *Women Crime and Custody in Victorian England* (Oxford: Clarendon Press, 1991) 89.

[65] See N Rose 'Beyond Medicalisation' (2007) 369 *The Lancet* 700–2 for a critique of the idea of 'medicalization'.

[66] See R Porter *Mind-Forg'd Manacles: A History of Madness in England from the Restoration to the Regency* (London: Athlone Press, 1987) 33.

[67] M J Wiener *Reconstructing the Criminal: Culture, Law and Policy in England, 1830–1914* (Cambridge: CUP, 1990) 21, 123.

Liability, Responsibility, and the 'Infanticidal' Type

A common set of gender constructions formed the central plank of both emergent expert psychiatric and psychological knowledge and lay or non-expert knowledge about women killing their newborn children. The Victorian era was marked by what Smith calls a 'network of correspondences between woman, nature, passivity, emotion and irresponsibility'.[68] On the one hand, the effect of these correspondences was that 'all women were seen to be closely bound to their biology, and the psyche was thought to be intimately connected with the reproductive cycle, the health or pathology of which directly determined their mental health'.[69] This meant that 'with women, madness lay in essential constitutional weakness'—women were in effect predisposed to insanity.[70] Beliefs that women's mental conditions were closely related to or determined by biology were common to expert medical and lay discourses.[71] The diagnostic entity of puerperal insanity fitted neatly here because, as discussed above, the mental disorder was thought to flow from the physical strains of childbirth. On the other hand, this network of gendered meanings involved the construction of women as passive subjects, 'heavily determined by social forces, the antithesis of the autonomous, rational masculine self'.[72] As a result of these gender constructions, during the Victorian era, a compassionate view of a woman's act of killing her newborn solidified—based on sympathy for her weak physical and moral state, for the physical pain a woman suffered giving birth without assistance, and on a conception of the 'fallen woman' who was not a fully independent agent.[73]

By the end of the nineteenth century, these gendered constructions coalesced to create a particular social type, the infanticidal woman. The combination of the strength of the expert psychological and psychiatric discourse, and the fact that an impulse to kill the child was thought to be a particular feature of puerperal insanity, meant that, according to this social type, a woman's conduct was *caused* behaviour, for which she had at most limited moral responsibility. This idea formed the basis for the practice—which preceded the reformation of the law—of treating infanticide defendants as having attenuated legal responsibility. By this point, the early Victorian emphasis on denunciation and deterrence of criminal offenders had given way to a view whereby they were thought to be 'less wicked, but also less

---

[68] R Smith *Trial by Medicine: Insanity and Responsibility in Victorian Trials* (Edinburgh: Edinburgh University Press, 1981) 143.

[69] L Zedner 'Women, Crime and Penal Responses: A Historical Account' (1991) 14 *Crime and Justice* 336.

[70] Eigen 'Criminal Lunacy in Early Modern England' 414–16. Exculpatory narratives, loosely based in ideas of women's constitutional weakness, also feature in cases in which women were charged with other offences: see, for example, *OBP*, Emily Newbar, 5 February 1894 (t18940205-246).

[71] 'Criminal Lunacy in Early Modern England' 412.

[72] T Ward 'Legislating for Human Nature: Legal Responses to Infanticide, 1860–1938', in M Jackson (ed) *Infanticide: Historical Perspectives on Child Murder and Concealment, 1550–2000* (Aldershot: Ashgate, 2002) 251.

[73] 'Legislating for Human Nature' 251.

rational and less autonomous than formerly'.[74] The infanticidal woman was just such an offender. While on the face of the law, the action of child killing by mothers remained straightforwardly criminal, leniency and mercy gave 'practical expression', to borrow Smith's phrase, to a different set of meanings.[75] Although the law was not amended until 1922,[76] the particular social type on which it would be formulated—the infanticidal woman, with circumscribed personal responsibility for her acts—was established by the end of the 1800s.

As well as creating a particular social type, the dense network of meanings around gender had the effect of over-determining the legal significance of the infanticidal woman's act of killing her child. The network of meanings, shared by experts and non-experts, combined in a particular way to ensure that the act of a mother killing her child came to be understood as an instantiation of abnormality for both moral and criminal law adjudication purposes. By this idea that the act of infanticide became an instantiation of abnormality, I mean to suggest something other than what might be called evidence or proof of abnormality: as the instantiation of exculpatory abnormality, the infanticidal act itself comprises rather than merely evidences the abnormality that characterizes the defendant woman, linking her lethal act (as caused) to her legal responsibility (as attenuated). As the instantiation of abnormality, a 'mad' defendant's conduct has a thick significance in legal evaluation and adjudication practices, permitting 'madness' to be 'read off' her conduct in legal processes. As I discuss in Chapter 3, the thick significance of a 'mad' defendant's conduct arises from the intimate connection between the conceptual and the evidentiary on the mental incapacity terrain—what counts as 'madness' for criminal law purposes is what is manifest as 'madness' within criminal doctrines and practices.[77] On my analysis, even as the meanings given to the acts themselves changed (such that infanticide came to be illustrative of 'manifest

---

[74] Wiener *Reconstructing the Criminal* 307.

[75] Smith *Trial by Medicine* 154. The increasingly popular idea that a woman's actions in killing her child were not properly her acts, and that she deserved sympathy rather than condemnation, seems to lie behind the empirical data that indicates that, after a mid-Victorian panic about infanticide in the 1860s, prosecutions for concealment fell and sentences grew shorter: see Wiener *Reconstructing the Criminal* 269. There is also evidence to suggest that infanticide defendants were particularly likely to be found unfit to plead in this period: see Eigen *Unconscious Crime* 83.

[76] Proposals to amend the 1803 Act were first introduced in the parliamentary session of 1872, and then again in 1880, 1908, and 1909. Each Bill proposed attempted to introduce a specific homicide offence for all women who killed their newly born babies. Each of the unsuccessful Bills faced problems derived from larger issues such as concern with the dilution of the law of murder and judicial-versus-Home Office discretion over capital punishment and none was successful: see N Walker *Crime and Insanity in England (Vol 1: The Historical Perspective)* (Edinburgh: Edinburgh University Press, 1968) 129–31. As Walker discussed, the evidence before the Capital Punishment Commission (1866) indicated that lay and professional opinion opposed a law that did not distinguish between murders by mothers of infants and other types of murders. The Commission acknowledged that it was 'established practice' for the Home Office to advise that the death penalty be commuted in infanticide cases.

[77] This is part of what I suggest is the persistence into the current era of older ideas about the way in which 'madness' becomes known and is proved for criminal law purposes. See Chapter 3 for discussion.

madness' rather than 'manifest criminality'), the acts of infanticidal woman defendants retained this thick significance in law.[78]

Until this point in time, it was still accurate to regard a claim of mental incapacity as a claim for exculpation of a defendant woman charged with killing her child. But the effect of the social type, the infanticidal woman, was such that, when the law comprising the current doctrine of infanticide developed in the first decades of the twentieth century, infanticide would crystallize as both an offence and a defence. That is, mental incapacity would operate to (partially) exculpate a defendant woman (who might otherwise be liable for murder of the infant), but also (partially) inculpate her (in that she would be liable for conviction of a manslaughter-equivalent offence, if charged with infanticide). Broad continuities in the meanings given to gender, 'madness', and crime sustain this dual nature of infanticide in the criminal law of the current era, something that evidences the multiple roles mental incapacity doctrines have in criminal law.[79]

Of Imbalance and Disturbance: the Current Law of Infanticide

The social and legal dynamics assessed above found their full expression in the formulation of the current law on infanticide. It appeared in two stages in the first decades of the twentieth century. In the first stage, the Infanticide Act 1922 created a new offence, called infanticide, which was subject to the same penalty structure as manslaughter, and which constituted a defence to a charge of murder. The novel nomenclature—infanticide—applied to a novel legal formulation.[80] The Act stipulated that, to be liable for infanticide, a woman must have caused the death of a 'newly born' child, when her 'balance of mind' was 'disturbed' by the effect of childbirth. The reasons for this particular formulation of the infanticide provision are not clear.[81] In the second stage of the formulation of the current law, there was an expansion of the scope of 'newly born'. After the courts took a strict view of the

---

[78] See further Loughnan 'The Strange Case of the Infanticide Doctrine' (2012) 32(4) *Oxford Journal of Legal Studies*.

[79] See Chapter 2 for a discussion of these roles—inculpation, imputation, and a procedural role, as well as exculpation.

[80] As Nigel Walker suggests, the 'new and technical' label, infanticide, by contrast with murder, lacked emotional association: see Walker *Crime and Insanity in England (Vol 1)* 134. The Bill that became the Act had initially provided that, if the defendant woman had not recovered from 'the effect of giving birth to the child' when she killed it, she could be convicted of manslaughter rather than murder. However, in the course of debate in the House of Lords, Lord Birkenhead criticized the Bill on the basis that the alternative verdict of manslaughter was already available, and on the basis that the phrase 'the effect of giving birth to the child' was too wide: see Ward 'Legislating for Human Nature' 264.

[81] Walker suggests that this phraseology, which was the result of an amendment proposed by Lord Birkenhead, may have been drafted so the provision would be 'self-justifying' in that it made the basis of giving special treatment to this particular species of homicide (the mother's state of mind) clear on the face of the statute: *Crime and Insanity in England (Vol 1)* 131. By way of an alternative interpretation, Ward suggests that the reference to a defendant's disturbed mind was intended to cover women whose knowledge of right and wrong was affected: 'Legislating for Human Nature' 264. On this interpretation, the infanticide provision represents a parallel to the law of insanity that artfully

reach of that part of the new provision,[82] and critics pointed out 'the gap between the medical view of maternal mental disorder and its legal reconstruction',[83] a parliamentary proposal to broaden the scope of infanticide was drafted in 1936.[84] The Bill that became the Infanticide Act 1938, however, was a later one, proposed by Lord Dawson of Penn. By contrast with the 1922 Act's reference to 'newly born', the 1938 Act set a 12-month age limit for the child and introduced an additional clause providing that a defendant mother's mind could be disturbed by 'the effects of lactation' (breastfeeding) as well as by 'the effect of giving birth'. The current law of infanticide is contained in Section 1(1) of the Infanticide Act 1938, which makes infanticide an independent homicide offence, and Section 1(2) of the Act, which makes infanticide available as an alternative verdict when a defendant is charged with murder or, since 2009, with manslaughter.[85]

The current law of infanticide may be broken into three components. First, the infanticide doctrine is available only to a woman who kills her own child. This component encodes what was, by the time of the 1922 and 1938 Acts, the long-standing special status accorded to women who kill their infants. This special status meant that the creation and maintenance of a specific category of homicide for women in the first decades of the twentieth century was regarded as a legitimate and uncontroversial legal development. The second component of the infanticide doctrine is the requirement that the 'balance' of the defendant woman's mind must have been 'disturbed' at the time of the act or omission leading to the death of her child. As I discuss below, significantly, a mere temporal connection between mental disturbance and *actus reus* suffices for infanticide.[86] The third component of the current law is the requirement that the disturbance of the defendant's mind be caused 'by reason of her not having fully recovered from the effect of giving birth' or from 'the effect of lactation'. These physiological processes form the aetiological basis for the diminished mental capacity that is central to the doctrine.

---

succeeded in encoding lenient treatment for defendants but avoided the indefinite detention that followed a successful insanity plea: see more generally Ward 'The Sad Subject of Infanticide' 174.

[82] In the case of *R v O'Donoghue* ((1927) 20 Cr App Rep 132), the Court of Criminal Appeal confirmed a trial judge opinion that a 35- day old baby was not 'newly born'. O'Donoghue was applied in *Hale* (*R v Hale*, The Times, 22 July 1936), a case in which a married, middle class woman with a history of depression killed her three-week old baby.

[83] See Ward 'The Sad Subject of Infanticide' 174.

[84] The Infanticide Bill 1936 covered the killing of children up to the age of eight and expanded the definition of a defendant mother's state of mind to include 'distress and despair arising from solicitude for her child or extreme poverty or other causes': extracted in Ward 'The Sad Subject of Infanticide' 172–3. According to Walker, the breadth of this provision meant it would have had little chance of passing through Parliament but, in any event, it lapsed before it could be considered: *Crime and Insanity in England (Vol 1)* 132.

[85] The provision was amended by the Coroners and Justice Act 2009, which extended the reach of infanticide by providing that it function as an alternative charge to a charge of either murder or manslaughter, and act as a partial defence to either of these offences.

[86] Unlike the defence of insanity, for example, the Infanticide Act 1938 does not require that the defendant show that her knowledge of the nature and quality of her act was affected by a 'defect of reason' resulting from a 'disease of the mind': see *M'Naghten Rules* as discussed by the House of Lords in *Bratty v Attorney-General for Northern Ireland* [1963] AC 386 and my Chapter 5.

In my analysis, the three components of the infanticide doctrine raise three points of scholarly interest. The first of these relates to the *mens rea* required for the offence (or impliedly admitted if infanticide is raised by the defence). The *mens rea* or fault element is not clear on the face of the infanticide provision. Although the statutory provision states that a woman charged with or pleading infanticide would, 'notwithstanding that the circumstances were such that but for the provisions of this Act', have been liable for murder, it had not been clear until recently if an infanticidal woman had to have the *mens rea* for murder. Recently, both the issue of the *mens rea* of infanticide and the precise relationship between infanticide and murder has been resolved. In *Gore*, the Court of Criminal Appeal determined that the inclusion of the term 'wilful' in the infanticide provision was wide enough to cover both intent and recklessness, and found that Parliament had intended to create an offence that covered situations wider than those covered by murder.[87] The Court stated, *obiter*, that there was no requirement that all the ingredients of the offence of murder be proved before a defendant could be convicted of infanticide.[88] To me, it is striking that, before it was resolved, uncertainty about the *mens rea* of infanticide did not stand in the way of either convictions or pleas of infanticide, hinting that, in relation to infanticide, the centre of gravity for criminal law adjudicative purposes lies elsewhere (as I discuss below).

The second point of interest regarding the current law relates to the relationship between the requirement that the defendant woman's mind be 'disturbed' and the *actus reus* of killing, the external element of infanticide. The relationship between the specified mental incapacity and the *actus reus* looks different from other such relationships elsewhere in criminal law. As a number of commentators note, the connection required is merely temporal—the infanticide law does not specify that a defendant woman's mental disturbance must cause her to kill her child.[89] Requiring a mere temporal coincidence between the defendant's incapacity and her lethal act obscures the de facto relation between mental disturbance and the killing under the law of infanticide: based on my analysis of the social type, the infanticidal woman, I suggest that infanticide operates via an implicit assumption that the defendant woman's *actus reus* of killing is caused or determined behaviour. It is this that is behind the 'simplified' relationship between mental incapacity and the *actus reus* of the offence in the Infanticide Acts 1922 and 1938, which created what Nigel Walker refers to as a 'virtual presumption' that the woman actor was not fully responsible by reason of mental illness.[90] This 'virtual presumption' forecloses the question of the defendant's responsibility for her offence. In foreclosing the

---

[87] See *R v Gore (Lisa Therese) (Deceased)* [2007] EWCA Crim 2789.
[88] See *R v Gore (Lisa Therese) (Deceased)* [2007] EWCA Crim 2789, [33]–[34]. This has now been confirmed by the amendments to the Infanticide Act 1938 contained in the Coroners and Justice Act 2009, which extend the reach of infanticide as a defence to a charge of either murder or manslaughter.
[89] Allen *Justice Unbalanced* 27.
[90] Walker *Crime and Insanity in England (Vol 1)* 135. In Walker's words, 'if a mother kills her last-born child in its first year of life, the law more or less invites us to treat her as having done so in an abnormal state of mind'. Walker refers to this as the 'unique feature of infanticide' (136); see also R D Mackay *Mental Condition Defences in the Criminal Law* (Oxford: OUP, 1995) 211.

question of the defendant's criminal responsibility, the infanticidal woman is in effect decreed to have attenuated responsibility for her actions. This idea of partial responsibility is encoded both in infanticide as a plea and as a charge, that is, it is present when infanticide operates to partially inculpate or partially exculpate.[91] On this reading, the infanticidal woman's partial responsibility flows from the generalized social construction of an infanticidal type, which substitutes for an individualized inquiry into a defendant's mental capacities at the time of the offence.[92]

The third point of interest regarding the current law of infanticide relates to the precise significance of its external element, the act of killing. Here, it seems that the act of killing is the key to the 'virtual presumption' of partial responsibility encoded in the provision. Thus, the external element of infanticide is more significant than the Latin term *actus reus* itself implies—it operates as more than a mere threshold for liability. As I discuss in Chapter 3, in my thinking, the 'mad' defendant's act is a part of the broader picture of his or her conduct, and the significance of that conduct lies in the enmeshment of the conceptual and evidentiary aspects of 'madness'.[93] In relation to infanticide, the centre of gravity of the doctrine is its external element, the killing, and the law of infanticide rests on the manifest meaning of this conduct, the act of a mother killing her child. By eliding a distinction between the descriptive aspects of infanticide (a woman kills her infant at the same time as having a mind disturbed by childbirth or lactation) and its evaluative aspects (this action under these conditions warrants partial liability), a finding of partial responsibility for killing (whether in conviction for a charge or in the acceptance of a plea) flows straightforwardly from the construction of the act of infanticide as an instantiation of abnormality.

In addition, there is a further consequence of this construction of abnormality for the purposes of the law of infanticide. Because the mental disturbance underpinning infanticide is dependent on giving birth or lactating, it is necessarily a time-bound condition. This presents a potential problem for the task of assessing criminal responsibility, because, like 'temporary insanity', the exculpating condition may no longer be present by the time of the criminal trial. Concern about 'temporary insanity' has shadowed the law of insanity since its formalization in the *M'Naghten Rules*.[94] However, the physiological basis of the infanticide doctrine seems to have provided a neat justification for legal acceptance of the temporary nature of mental disturbance following childbirth or lactation.[95] Because the

---

[91] See further Chapter 2.
[92] See further Loughnan 'The Strange Case of the Infanticide Doctrine'.
[93] By this reference to the connection between the conceptual and evidentiary, I suggest that meaning resides in conformity between the thing itself and the idea of the thing. See further Chapter 3.
[94] See K J M Smith *Lawyers, Legislators and Theorists: Developments in English Criminal Jurisprudence 1800–1957* (Oxford: OUP, 1998) 223–32 for discussion.
[95] The physiological basis of infanticide has been subject to sustained and heavy criticism. Many legal commentators have expressed doubt about the validity of a clinical foundation for the infanticide doctrine and most contemporary scientific studies reject the notion that there is a distinct mental disorder following childbirth or connected to lactation: by way of example of legal commentary, see, *Report of the Committee on Mentally Abnormal Offenders* (Cmnd 6244, 1975) ('Butler Report')

physical processes leading to the mental disturbance are themselves temporary, so too is the defendant woman's abnormality. Stretching above this, the physiological basis of infanticide in the effects of childbirth or lactation is significant for another reason: in providing that women's mental disturbance has a physical base in common reproductive practices (giving birth and breastfeeding), the doctrine of infanticide naturalizes women's abnormality. As feminist theorists argue, the physiological basis of this abnormality means that abnormality is simultaneously exceptional and unexceptional.[96] The result is that, as Hilary Allen suggests, assertions of women's 'feminine normality' can either 'shore up or undercut' the ascription of criminal responsibility: thus, it is equally possible for women to come to rest on either side of the non-responsibility/responsibility divide,[97] or, via the specific legal form of infanticide, on both sides. And, indeed, as a successful infanticide charge or plea results in a conviction and sentence as if the defendant had been convicted of manslaughter, it seems that such women come to rest in a half-way house of partial responsibility.[98]

It is in light of this assessment of abnormality that the role of expert psychiatric and psychological evidence in infanticide trials should be understood. As is the case in trials involving claims of diminished responsibility, expert evidence about a defendant's disturbed mental state is a practical necessity for the doctrine of infanticide.[99] Beyond its practical role, my reflections on the potentially normal abnormality, or unexceptional exceptionality, of women who kill their children suggests that expert evidence is one of the ways in which infanticidal women are constructed as abnormal for the purposes of the criminal law: by interpreting women's actions in the psychiatric language of disorder and disturbance, they are constructed as exceptional and pathological legal subjects. Writing about

---

para 19.23; in relation to scientific commentary, see, for example, V Dobson and B Sales 'The Science of Infanticide and Mental Illness' (2000) 6 *Psychology, Public Policy and Law* 1098. In addition, it is now widely accepted that physiological factors related to childbirth and lactation are 'much less important' than the psychological stresses of child-care: See A Wilczynski 'Mad or Bad? Child-Killers, Gender and the Courts' (1997) 37(3) *British Journal of Criminology* 432. In particular, the reference to the 'effects of lactation' in the Infanticide Act 1938 has been heavily criticized. It has been argued that this clause in the infanticide doctrine had no scientific basis even at the time of the passage of the 1938 Act and was included merely to make the 12-month age limit of the child victim 'plausible': see Walker *Crime and Insanity in England (Vol 1)* 132.

[96] According to Allen, an 'exclusive legal exemption' for the new mother who kills her child conjures up two contradictory conceptions of maternal attachment. On the one hand, exempting a new mother from responsibility for killing her child makes the mother's attack 'unthinkable' unless it is the result of some pathology. On the other hand, connecting the woman's violent act with her physiology suggests a 'natural maternal violence' which cannot be subject to the usual legal restraints: *Justice Unbalanced* 28.

[97] *Justice Unbalanced* 50.

[98] I suggest that the kind of difference invoked at this half-way house point is most accurately understood as one of kind. See Chapter 9 for a discussion in relation to diminished responsibility.

[99] Mackay argues that expert reports are 'vital' as to how a plea progresses. Although there is no requirement that a defendant suffer from a recognized mental disorder in order to be charged with or plead infanticide, most of the expert reports reviewed by Mackay included clinical diagnoses (such as postnatal depression): see R D Mackay, 'Infanticide and Related Diminished Responsibility Manslaughters: An Empirical Study', Law Commission for England and Wales *Murder, Manslaughter, and Infanticide* (Law Com No 304, 2006) Appendix D: paras 23–5.

infanticide, insanity, and diminished responsibility, Alan Norrie argues that 'psychiatry was the means of introducing a satisfactorily circumscribed compassion into the legal rules': this ensures that the criminal law achieves a contextualization of the defendant that falls short of subsuming the law's voluntarist inquiry about criminal behaviour beneath a determinist medical account of behaviour.[100] Norrie's argument is compelling and it is clear that the separation of infanticide from murder and its presentation in 'medical terms' has enabled the law to 'maintain a general punitive stance to a social problem, laced with an unthreatening show of compassion in the individual(ised) case'.[101]

'[T]his sad case':[102] What Legal Actors Know about Infanticide

In the recent decision of *Kai-Whitewind*, the Court of Appeal rejected the appeal brought by a woman convicted of the murder of her three-month-old baby, Bidziil.[103] Kai-Whitewind had not admitted the killing—her counsel had adduced evidence to the effect that the baby died of natural causes—and the possibility of an alternative homicide charge and/or conviction—infanticide—was not raised by either the prosecution or defence, at trial or on appeal. However, prompted by the unusual facts of the case, the Court of Appeal considered it appropriate to offer some comments, *obiter*, on whether infanticide should have been raised in the appellant's case. Lord Justice Judge, delivering the judgment of the Court, observed:

The appellant was a woman of good character with two children. She had apparently given them natural maternal love and affection before she gave birth to Bidziil. He was conceived in the course of an alleged rape.... Immediately after the birth she underwent some unspecified level of depression... Within a very short period, for understandable reasons,... [Bidziil] was cared for by her mother, and not by her. All this inevitably weakened the natural bonding process... It was in those circumstances that the baby was killed, less than three months after the appellant had given birth to him.[104]

These aspects of the facts of the case led Lord Justice Judge to question 'whether, as a matter of substantive law, infanticide should extend to circumstances subsequent to the birth, but connected with it, such as the stresses imposed on a mother by the absence of natural bonding with her baby'.[105]

---

[100] A Norrie *Crime, Reason and History: A Critical Introduction to Criminal Law* (London: Butterworths, 2001) 191. Norrie argues that medical knowledge permits some consideration of the defendant's social context without exposing the connection between social context and criminal behaviour that the criminal law attempts to obscure: *Crime, Reason and History* 190.
[101] *Crime, Reason and History* 191.
[102] *R v Kai-Whitewind* (Chaha'oh Niyol) [2005] 2 Cr App R 457, 484.
[103] *R v Kai-Whitewind* (Chaha'oh Niyol) [2005] 2 Cr App R 457.
[104] *R v Kai-Whitewind* (Chaha'oh Niyol) [2005] 2 Cr App R 457, 482-3.
[105] *R v Kai-Whitewind* (Chaha'oh Niyol) [2005] 2 Cr App R 457, 484.

The Court of Appeal expressed further concern about the law of infanticide as it relates to the case of a mother 'who has in fact killed her infant [but] is unable to admit it', observing that:

This may be because she is too unwell to do so, or too emotionally disturbed by what she has in fact done, or too deeply troubled by the consequences of an admission of guilt on her ability to care for any surviving children. When this happens, it is sometimes difficult to produce psychiatric evidence relating to the balance of the mother's mind. Yet, of itself, it does not automatically follow from denial that the balance of her mind was not disturbed; in some cases, it may indeed help to confirm that it was.[106]

In his judgment, Lord Justice Judge concluded that 'the law relating to infanticide is unsatisfactory and outdated. The appeal in this sad case demonstrates the need for a thorough re-examination.'[107]

Lord Justice Judge's comments suggest that circumstantial factors affect a woman's responsibility for the act of killing, and, further, that the meaning of the acts of a 'mother who has in fact killed her infant [but] is unable to admit it' is evidently that she is mentally disturbed. These comments rely on and encode a particular set of apparently self-evident 'truths' about the interaction of gender, childbirth, and mental illness that clearly engaged the sympathies of the Court in *Kai-Whitewind*. These 'truths' represent what I have been calling lay knowledge about child killing by mothers. Even though it is espoused by legal actors, it is a non-expert form of knowledge. As I discuss above (and also in Chapter 3 and Chapter 6 in relation to insanity), legal actors rely on lay knowledge in relation to mental incapacity—legal expertise is mixed with lay knowledge or non-expertise.[108] This type of knowledge is enlisted in support of the current law of infanticide elsewhere in legal debates.[109] Indeed, the longevity of infanticide law is in significant part due to continuity in the particular social meanings given to infanticidal women and infanticidal acts, which I discussed above and which underpin the responsibility-attribution practices. The social meanings given to infanticidal

---

[106] *R v Kai-Whitewind* (Chaha'oh Niyol) [2005] 2 Cr App R 457, 484.

[107] *R v Kai-Whitewind* [2005] 2 Cr App R 457, 484.

[108] See Chapter 3 in general, and see Chapter 6 in relation to insanity and Chapter 7 in relation to intoxication.

[109] This reliance on such lay knowledge is evident in law reform proposals. For instance, unlike the Butler Report, which had concluded that there were no advantages gained by a separate infanticide provision, the Criminal Law Revision Committee (CLRC) recommended retaining and extending the doctrine of infanticide: see *Fourteenth Report: Offences Against the Person* (Cmnd 7844, 1980) para 102. The Committee acknowledged that the 'medical principles' underlying the Infanticide Act 1938 are 'not proven' but considered that the 'types of situations' that the courts are currently taking into account in cases of infanticide, such as family stress and poverty, 'should continue to fall within the ambit of the offence' (para 105). According to the CLRC, each of these considerations 'rests on a mental disturbance resulting in a real sense from childbirth' (para 105). In its report, the CLRC stated that 'in cases now dealt with as infanticide it is a matter of human experience that the mental disturbance is connected with the fact of birth ... even where it is primarily related to environmental or other stresses consequent upon the birth' and, to ensure such matters could genuinely be considered, proposed that the infanticide provision should be broadened to provide that the balance of a woman's mind was disturbed 'by reason of the effect of giving birth or circumstances consequent upon that birth' (para 105).

women and infanticidal acts have proved remarkably durable: they are now sustained without consensus among expert medical professionals regarding the idea of mental disturbance following childbirth or lactation.[110]

In its 2005 multi-stage review of the law of homicide, the Law Commission gave serious consideration to Lord Justice Judge's comments, both about the scope of infanticide and the situation of a defendant 'who has in fact killed her infant [but] is unable to admit it'. In its consultation paper, the Law Commission considered an abolitionist position, and three options (minimal, moderate, and radical) for retaining but reforming infanticide law. The Commission made a provisional proposal in favour of minimal reform, retaining infanticide in its current form but removing the statutory reference to lactation, and raising the age limit of the child victim to two years.[111] In rejecting the moderate and radical reform proposals, the Commission rejected a requirement that the act or omission leading to the infant's death be causally connected to the defendant's 'disturbance of mind', reasoning that, without a causal requirement, environmental factors which may influence a defendant's state of mind may be taken into account.[112] In general, the Law Commission's proposal to retain the doctrine reflects the broad and continuing acceptability of infanticide as a distinct category of homicide, and the special status accorded to women who kill their infants that the law encodes.

In addressing the issue raised by Lord Justice Judge of a defendant not being able to admit to the acts comprising the offence, the Law Commission noted that, as also applies to diminished responsibility, a procedure exists whereby such a defendant can make a case that his or her illness itself prevented disclosure to doctors and counsel. The Commission suggested that, if the evidence is unopposed, it will be in the interests of justice for such evidence to be received by an appeal court.[113] Despite concluding that the existing procedure was satisfactory, the Law Commission went on to make a proposal that a different procedural rule should apply in infanticide trials.[114] By way of justification for a special procedural rule for infanticide trials, *contra* diminished responsibility trials, the Law Commission

---

[110] For a well-known account of one set of expert views in favour of the law, see D Maier-Katikin and R Ogle 'A Rationale for Infanticide Laws' [1993] *Criminal Law Review* 903–14. Despite the absence of scientific consensus, the legal doctrine of infanticide remains closely wedded to its physiological basis. Some evidence of this is provided by the response the Law Commission received to its question, included in its Consultation Paper, about whether the doctrine of infanticide should be available to all carers of infants: *A New Homicide Act for England and Wales?* (Law Com No 177, 2005) paras 9.87–9.92. In its final report, the Commission noted that there was little support for making infanticide available to 'other carers' and concluded that the doctrine should continue to be restricted to biological mothers (paras 8.29, 8.31).

[111] *A New Homicide Act for England and Wales? An Overview* (Law Com No 177, 2005) paras 9.75–9.78.

[112] The Commission stated that the cause of the mental disturbance should have only an 'evidential relevance', that is, going to whether or not the mind was disturbed or disordered. The Commission concluded that this approach ensures that evidence supporting infanticide can evolve as medical practice evolves: see *A New Homicide Act for England and Wales? An Overview* para 9.63.

[113] Law Commission, *Murder, Manslaughter and Infanticide* (Law Com No 304, 2006) para 8.45, referring to Criminal Appeal Act 1968, s 23(2).

[114] The Commission proposed that, in cases where a defendant mother is convicted of the murder of her child of one year or less, the judge should have the power to order a 'medical examination of the

Consultation Paper referred to the 'chasm' between the mandatory penalty for murder and an 'appropriate' sentence in infanticide cases.[115] The special procedural rule was not implemented when changes were made to infanticide by the Coroners and Justice Act 2009, and, in my view, the Commission's proposal would have represented an unfortunate development. While ostensibly motivated by the disparity between a life sentence for murder and what would be likely to be a non-custodial sentence for infanticide, the now-rejected proposal was founded on a particular set of attitudes and beliefs about gender, 'madness', and crime, which are more usually naturalized in law.

The sympathy for infanticidal women, which is palpable in Lord Justice Judge's judgment and in the Law Commission report, has an analogue in sentencing practices relating to infanticide. Statistics relating to infanticide convictions reveal the virtual abandonment of custodial punishment for one species of homicide offence.[116] Studies conducted in England and Wales show that infanticide convictions attract lenient penalties.[117] For instance, in *Sainsbury*, the Court of Appeal quashed the trial judge's 12-month custodial sentence and substituted it with a three-year probation order. The Court of Appeal stated that, far from the welfare of society demanding a custodial sentence, this course would 'risk' the welfare of society.[118] Similarly, although in relation to a defendant charged with manslaughter for killing her infant, in *Lewis*, the Court of Appeal again quashed a 12-month custodial sentence and substituted it with a three-year probation order. The Court emphasized that Lewis needed treatment, making this a condition of the order.[119] The leniency following a conviction for infanticide (spilling over to manslaughter where the facts are comparable) strongly suggests that defendants are viewed with a high level of sympathy and compassion, and that the infanticide defendant is regarded as less dangerous than other killers.

There is an interesting coda to the lenient sentencing practices attendant to the law of infanticide. It is commonly acknowledged that infanticide is rare, as either a charge or a plea,[120] but, in those sentencing decisions available, it is possible to

---

defendant' within 28 days after the end of the trial: *Murder, Manslaughter and Infanticide* para 8.46. This proposal has since been rejected by the government.

[115] Law Commission *A New Homicide Act for England and Wales? An Overview* para 9.105.

[116] As the Law Commission noted, sentencing practices in infanticide cases are in sharp contrast with sentencing provisions contained in recent legislation: *A New Homicide Act for England and Wales? An Overview* para 9.73.

[117] Of the infanticide convictions reviewed by Mackay in the study commissioned for the Law Commission, the vast majority of defendants were given non-custodial sentences: *Murder, Manslaughter and Infanticide*, Appendix D, [20]. Of the 59 cases decided in 1979–1988, to which the Court referred in *Sainsbury*, there were no custodial sentences handed down: see *R v Sainsbury* (1989) 11 Cr App R (S) 533, 534.

[118] *R v Sainsbury* (1989) 11 Cr App R (S), 535.

[119] *R v Lewis* (1989) 11 Cr App R (S) 577, 579.

[120] In his empirical study, conducted for the Law Commission, R D Mackay found that there were 49 convictions for infanticide between 1990 and 2003: see *Murder, Manslaughter and Infanticide*, Appendix D para 7. Reflecting the large number of cases in which a plea of infanticide is accepted in the course of pre-trial negotiations, only two of these verdicts resulted from jury trials (Appendix D paras 17–18).

detect a faint idea that 'madness' (and its product, the act of infanticide) is its own punishment. This seems to be the import of Lord Russell's comments in *Lewis*, where he stated that the defendant's behaviour was 'wicked, and a young life has been lost. That must never be forgotten. We imagine it will not be forgotten by her.'[121] Depicting the defendant's 'madness' (and its product, the act of infanticide) as its own punishment again exposes legal emphasis on the defendant's act—as an instantiation of abnormality. The significance of the infanticidal woman's act of killing is such that it can act as a punishment, replacing formal penal sanction. Assessed together with the absence of custodial penalties for what is a homicide offence, it seems that, in infanticide, the actual or forecast realization of what a defendant woman has done is punishment enough.

---

[121] *R v Lewis* (1989) 11 Cr App R (S) 577, 579.

9
Differences of Degree and Differences of Kind: Diminished Responsibility

Where successful, an accused pleading diminished responsibility receives a manslaughter rather than a murder conviction.[1] As a result, diminished responsibility is typically regarded as partially exculpatory, distinguishing individuals on the basis that both their criminal liability and their criminal responsibility is reduced or impaired, but not abrogated. As I suggest in Chapter 2, useful insights are to be gained by viewing diminished responsibility (and infanticide) as Janus-faced, both partially exculpatory and partially inculpatory, or sliding between my two subcategories of exculpatory and non-exculpatory mental incapacity doctrines. As I discuss in that chapter, this involves thinking about diminished responsibility in relation not only to (the offence of) murder but also to (the exculpatory doctrine of) insanity, which, if successful, results in a special verdict ('not guilty by reason of insanity'). In this chapter, I take up this point about the Janus-faced nature of diminished responsibility with the aim of exposing what kind of difference is encoded in the diminished responsibility doctrine, or, to put it another way, analysing what kind of difference diminished responsibility makes to the individual who raises it. My analysis of the development of a doctrine of diminished responsibility from its origins in nineteenth-century Scotland shows that the sort of difference encoded in the diminished responsibility doctrine is most accurately thought of as one of kind, as opposed to one of degree.

In brief, first appearing at a time when the boundary between factors relating to liability and mitigating factors remained porous, diminished responsibility developed as a free-standing mental incapacity doctrine, and formalized into a discrete partial defence to murder in the Scottish law. Even as a jurisprudence developed around diminished responsibility following its import to England and Wales—with the concept developing in a dialectical relation with both *M'Naghten* insanity and lay knowledge about incapacity—the precise way in which an 'abnormality of mind' (now, an 'abnormality of mental functioning') affected an individual for criminal law purposes remained ambiguous. In the decades since diminished responsibility was first introduced to England and Wales, the ambiguity surrounding the doctrine (does it relate to the actor or the act?) has come to be more

---

[1] Homicide Act 1957, s 2(1), as amended by Coroners and Justice Act 2009, s 52. A manslaughter conviction attracts sentencing discretion.

problematic, generating a close practical and strategic reliance on expert psychiatric and psychological evidence (and thus on expert knowledge), and, most recently, the momentum for a change in the law to include an express requirement that a quasi-causal relationship exist between the abnormal mental state and the prohibited act of killing. The result of these developments over time is that the difference diminished responsibility makes is no longer under-determined, but over-determined.

'Without being insane in the legal sense': the Development of Diminished Responsibility in Scotland

Three aspects of Scots criminal law at the end of the nineteenth century were significant in the formation of what would come to be called diminished responsibility. The first of these was the Scots law on insanity, which encompassed a notion of partial insanity, providing that a 'penalty should be reduced in proportion to the degree of impairment of responsibility—the worse the accused's mental condition the less the sentence'.[2] A defendant's partial insanity could be taken into account via particular sentencing practices, and it was these practices which formed the second aspect of the Scots criminal law that facilitated the development of a doctrine of diminished responsibility. By contrast with England, where the Criminal Lunatics Act 1800 had been enacted to regulate the sentencing of insane defendants and those found 'insane on arraignment', contemporary Scots sentencing practices concerning those with abnormal mental states were more informal and flexible. From the early nineteenth century, Scots courts took 'mental weakness' into account as a factor that might mitigate sentence or lead to a recommendation of mercy.[3] According to Gerald Gordon, by the mid-nineteenth century, it was 'common' for juries to make 'recommendations to mercy on the ground of mental weakness'.[4] The informality of criminal law practices at this stage meant that there was nothing unique about 'mental weakness' and thus, in Gordon's words, 'no

---

[2] See G H Gordon *The Criminal Law of Scotland* (Edinburgh: W Green, 2000) 455. Although the difference between English and Scots law on the issue of partial insanity had been glossed over following the Articles of Union in 1707, it amounted to a genuine and significant difference in the two legal traditions: N Walker *Crime and Insanity in England (Vol 1: The Historical Perspective)* (Edinburgh: Edinburgh University Press, 1968) 140–1. In at least formally requiring something like total insanity to acquit a defendant, Scots law paralleled English law: Walker *Crime and Insanity in England (Vol 1)* 140. See Chapter 5 for a discussion of how 'total insanity' as an informal law of insanity might be interpreted in the English context.

[3] L Farmer *Criminal Law, Tradition and Legal Order: Crime and the Genius of Scots Law 1747 to the Present* (Cambridge: CUP, 1997) 153–4. Significantly, in this era, there was no firm distinction between factors relating to conviction (defences) and those relating to sentence (mitigation). In capital cases, such as murder, conviction meant death unless a prisoner was granted mercy through the royal prerogative: Gordon *The Criminal Law of Scotland* 453, 458. This led juries to try to encourage the royal prerogative through the practice of issuing 'verdicts of guilty with a recommendation as to mercy or mitigation of sentence' to reflect any extenuating circumstances of the defendant: Scottish Law Commission *Insanity and Diminished Responsibility* (Discussion Paper 122, 2003) para 3.1 and Scottish Law Commission *Insanity and Diminished Responsibility* (Report 195, 2004) para 3.1. The defendant's abnormal mental state was one such extenuating circumstance.

[4] Gordon *The Criminal Law of Scotland* 453.

"doctrine" was necessary' to account for mitigation on the basis of diminished responsibility.[5]

These two aspects of Scots criminal law in the middle of the nineteenth century were accommodated within what constituted the third basis for the development of diminished responsibility, the category of culpable homicide in the Scots law of homicide.[6] In the first half of the nineteenth century in Scotland, culpable homicide was used as a category of offence by what Lindsay Farmer labels 'an increasingly organized and interventionist prosecutorial system', to charge defendants in a range of situations that had not previously been prosecuted, such as accidental death caused by machinery or vehicles.[7] As the category of culpable homicide grew in importance over the course of the century, it came to be defined in positive terms, 'on the basis of the degree of blame of each of the accused as this could be determined from the circumstances of the case'.[8] As Farmer argues, the need to distinguish between the defendant's act and his or her state of mind led to the formulation of a test by which the defendant's state of mind could be judged.[9] Judges had to articulate both the distinctiveness and the relevance of mental states generally, and 'mental weakness' in particular, to the ascription of criminal responsibility. In Gordon's words, the 'anomalous position of the fixed penalty for murder meant that the effect of diminished responsibility on sentence had to be "justified", to be "rationalized"'.[10] What would come to be called diminished responsibility had to be given some conceptual basis in the law of murder, which would explain why a conviction for culpable homicide was more appropriate in a particular instance than a conviction for murder. Significantly (although for reasons which seem unclear), it was in the law of homicide, 'rather than in any more fashionable scientific theory of alienation', that a justification for the idea that mental states could affect culpability was sought.[11]

It was against this backdrop that the two decisions that mark the origins of diminished responsibility (a term in use since at least 1844[12]) appeared. These two decisions illustrate the interaction of the Scots law of insanity, sentencing practices, and the structure of the law of homicide in facilitating the development of diminished responsibility in Scotland. The first of these decisions is *Alexander*

---

[5] Gordon *The Criminal Law of Scotland* 453.
[6] Culpable homicide was distinct from manslaughter in English law, which, since the sixteenth century, had denoted killings in the absence of premeditation, such as those committed 'in the heat of passion.' See J M Beattie *Crime and the Courts in England 1660–1800* (Oxford: OUP, 1986) 79–80 and J M Kaye, 'The Early History of Murder and Manslaughter' (1967) 83 *Law Quarterly Review* 365, 369–70.
[7] Farmer *Criminal Law, Tradition and Legal Order* 153. Unlike murder, which automatically attracted the death penalty, a conviction for culpable homicide gave the judge discretion in sentencing: Scottish Law Commission *Insanity and Diminished Responsibility* (Discussion Paper 122, 2003) para 3.1.
[8] *Criminal Law, Tradition and Legal Order* 154.
[9] *Criminal Law, Tradition and Legal Order* 154.
[10] Gordon *The Criminal Law of Scotland* 453.
[11] Farmer *Criminal Law, Tradition and Legal Order* 154.
[12] See Walker *Crime and Insanity in England (Vol 1)* 142.

Dingwall, concerning an accused charged with the murder of his wife.[13] Lord Deas, who played a central role in the emergence of diminished responsibility, presided over the trial. In his summing up, Lord Deas set out the grounds for a verdict of culpable homicide, as opposed to murder, stating that these grounds included the 'unpremeditated and sudden nature of the attack', 'the prisoner's habitual kindness to his wife', the fact that 'there was only one stab wound', and that 'the prisoner appeared not only to have been peculiar in his mental constitution but to have had his mind weakened by successive attacks of disease', which might have been caused by 'a stroke of the sun in India'.[14] Lord Deas concluded by stating that 'the state of the mind of a prisoner... might... be an extenuating circumstance, although not such as to warrant an acquittal on the ground of insanity'.[15]

In the same year as *Dingwall*, Lord Deas presided over the case of *McLean*, concerning an accused charged with theft by housebreaking.[16] McLean was convicted, but it was with a recommendation to leniency on the basis that he had a 'weak intellect'.[17] In his speech, Lord Deas stated that it was appropriate for a judge to take into account mental weakness in passing sentence, whether or not the jury had recommended leniency. Lord Deas stated:

[W]ithout being insane in the legal sense, so as not to be amenable to punishment, a prisoner may yet labour under that degree of weakness of intellect or mental infirmity which may make it both right and legal to take that state of mind into account, not only in awarding the punishment, but in some cases, even in considering within what category of offences the crime shall be held to fall.[18]

As these brief extracts suggest, the condition of the two defendants in *Dingwall* and *McLean* did not amount to legal insanity. Lord Deas' differentiation between 'weakness of intellect or mental infirmity' and insanity might suggest that the latter was clear. However, by way of contrast with England, there was no 'precise test of criminal insanity' in Scotland at this time: the *M'Naghten Rules* were 'merely interesting news'.[19] As it was, Dingwall and McLean's impaired mental states were among a number of factors to be considered, such as the accused's character and the nature of the killing, each of which might reduce his or her charge from murder to culpable homicide.[20] Reflecting the absence of a robust distinction between defences (which impacted on conviction) and mitigating factors (which

---

[13] *Dingwall* (1867) 5 Irv 466.
[14] *Dingwall* (1867) 5 Irv 466, 479.
[15] *Dingwall* (1867) 5 Irv 466, 480. The jury returned a verdict of culpable homicide, and Dingwall was sentenced to 10 years' penal servitude.
[16] *McLean* (1876) 3 Couper 334. McLean was regarded as an imbecile and had once been a certified lunatic. Theft by housebreaking was a capital charge but one for which the death penalty was no longer considered appropriate: see Gordon *The Criminal Law of Scotland* 461.
[17] *The Criminal Law of Scotland* 461.
[18] *McLean* (1876) 3 Couper 334, 336, extracted in Gordon *The Criminal Law of Scotland* 461.
[19] As a result, Lord Deas' direction in *Dingwall* was 'less remarkable' than it would have been in England. See Walker *Crime and Insanity in England (Vol 1)* 144.
[20] Gordon *The Criminal Law of Scotland* 453.

impacted on sentence), an accused's impaired mental state was grouped together with what are now regarded as general mitigating factors (such as good character).

For my purposes in analysing the sort of difference diminished responsibility makes, what is notable about Lord Deas' directions in *Dingwall* and *McLean* is their imprecision. Lord Deas did not regard mental abnormality as affecting criminal responsibility in a unique way.[21] Thus, it was in a rather indeterminate way that an impaired 'mental constitution' was held to warrant conviction of culpable homicide as opposed to murder. According to Lord Deas, these abnormal states had a profound if unspecified effect on the defendants' liability for their offences. Even as Lord Deas' views about diminished responsibility 'gained ready acceptance' among his contemporaries in the decades after the decisions of *Dingwall* and *McLean*,[22] the Scots concept of diminished responsibility remained open-textured and flexible. Various mental states were articulated as the base of the defence: phrases such as 'mental weakness', 'mental aberration', 'unsoundness of mind', and 'partial insanity' peppered the case law.[23] These labels for mental abnormality short of insanity, each of which was partly descriptive and partly prescriptive, were premised on the idea that there was something distinct about diminished responsibility and that such a mental state had a qualitative significance for criminal liability. What was clear was that the abnormal 'state of mind' had to pertain at the time of the killing (recently, this temporal connection has been replaced with a quasi-causal requirement, as I discuss below). But the precise way in which 'the state of mind of a prisoner...might...be an extenuating circumstance, although not such as to warrant an acquittal on the ground of insanity'[24] remained indeterminate. This indeterminacy about the precise nature of the difference diminished responsibility makes would linger after diminished responsibility was introduced in England and Wales in the form of statutory doctrine.

Setting the development of diminished responsibility at this juncture in the middle of the nineteenth century in a larger frame, it is possible to detect, in diminished responsibility, traces of broader changes in the idea of criminal responsibility in English and Scots law that were taking place around this time. As Nicola Lacey argues in relation to the English law, between the eighteenth and twentieth centuries, a loose or thin formulation of criminal fault, whereby responsibility was assumed, gave way to a thicker and more robust concept of fault or *mens rea* which was itself the object of investigation at trial.[25] The references to the defendant's 'weakness of intellect or mental infirmity' that were included in the directions given in *Dingwall* and *McLean* reflect a capacity conceptualization of criminal fault. In addition, it is notable that these abnormal mental states were regarded as something that, in Farmer's words, 'could be proved as a question of

---

[21] *The Criminal Law of Scotland* 460–1.
[22] *The Criminal Law of Scotland* 461.
[23] See *The Criminal Law of Scotland* 461–3 for discussion of these cases.
[24] *Dingwall*, per Lord Deas, extracted in Gordon *The Criminal Law of Scotland* 460.
[25] N Lacey 'Responsibility and Modernity in Criminal Law' (2001) 9(3) *Journal of Political Philosophy* 249, 261. For a discussion of change in the concept of 'dole' in the Scots law at this time, see Farmer *Criminal Law, Tradition and Legal Order* 147–60.

fact'.[26] The development of diminished responsibility in Scots law was premised on the 'factualisation' of *mens rea*, and may be regarded as an instance of what Lacey has referred to as the rise of a 'primarily capacity-based and heavily psychologised notion of *mens rea*' that marked 'the core of the late modern general part of the criminal law'.[27] This development produced a conception of criminal responsibility that could be 'explicated in technical, legal terms, and hence legitimated as a form of specialist knowledge underpinning an impersonal mode of judgment'.[28]

Precisely what constituted diminished responsibility was subjected to further explication in the first half of the twentieth century, prior to its import to England and Wales. Scots courts attempted to define and limit the scope of diminished responsibility. In the decision of *Savage* in 1923, Lord Alness gave this definition of diminished responsibility:

> It is very difficult to put in a phrase, but it has been put this way: that there must be aberration or weakness of mind; that there must be some form of mental unsoundness; that there must be a state of mind which is bordering on, though not amounting to, insanity; that there must be a mind so affected that responsibility is diminished from full responsibility to partial responsibility—in other words, the prisoner in question must be only partially accountable for his actions. And I think one can see running through the cases that there is implied... that there must be some form of mental disease.[29]

This address to the jury became the authoritative test of diminished responsibility in Scotland. The factors enumerated by Lord Alness were regarded as cumulative in nature, and the test for diminished responsibility became difficult to satisfy.[30] This strict approach to diminished responsibility has been revised in recent decades, with the High Court in *Galbraith* concluding that, in order to be successful, a diminished responsibility plea did not require that all the *Savage* conditions be met or that the defendant's condition amount to one bordering on insanity.[31]

---

[26] *Criminal Law, Tradition and Legal Order* 157.
[27] Lacey 'Responsibility and Modernity in Criminal Law' 266.
[28] 'Responsibility and Modernity in Criminal Law' 267–8. For a discussion of the historical development of criminal responsibility practices, see N Lacey 'Psychologising Jekyll, Demonising Hyde: The Strange Case of Criminal Responsibility' (2010) 4 *Criminal Law and Philosophy* 109.
[29] *HM Advocate v Savage* 1923 SLT 659, 661. The restriction of the Scots defence of diminished responsibility in the first half of the twentieth century has been interpreted as a defensive move on the part of the judiciary. According to Gordon, the scope of the defence was restricted because judges feared that the defence would 'lead to many murderers escaping their just deserts' and because some judges believed the doctrine of diminished responsibility was 'illogical and anomalous': see Gordon *The Criminal Law of Scotland* 463.
[30] Scottish Law Commission *Insanity and Diminished Responsibility* (Report No 195, 2004) para 3.2. In *Carraher* (*Carraher v HM Advocate* 1946 JC 108), in which the *Savage* statement of the law was approved (117), the Court stated that the defence of diminished responsibility was 'anomalous' in the Scots law and concluded that it should not be given wider scope than it has already been accorded (119).
[31] *Galbraith v HM Advocate* (No 2) 2002 JC 1, 8; see also Scottish Law Commission *Insanity and Diminished Responsibility* (Report 195, 2004) paras 3.3–3.7. The Scottish Law Commission proposed a statutory version of diminished responsibility that was incorporated into the Criminal Justice and Licensing Act 2010. For discussion, see R M Mackay 'The Coroners and Justice Act 2009—Partial Defences to Murder (2) The New Diminished Responsibility Plea' [2010] *Criminal Law Review* 290, 302.

As the *Savage* decision suggests, by this point in time, diminished responsibility was conceptualized 'as doing something to the "quality of the act" as if it were an exculpatory plea and not a plea in mitigation of sentence'.[32] But I suggest that this constitution as an exculpatory plea rather than a plea in mitigation was contingent. It was dependent on the restriction of diminished responsibility to murder, and a tight but still unspecified connection between the abnormal mental state and prohibited act. As a result, although still somewhat amorphous, the kind of difference diminished responsibility made stretched across any neat distinction between the act and the actor. The idea that diminished responsibility affected the 'quality' of a defendant's act, from which it was difficult to disentangle the actor him or herself, would give mental disorder (and, eventually, expert medical evidence) an enhanced position in the doctrine. Once a statutory version of the doctrine was introduced into England and Wales, mental disorders, and expert evidence of them, would together come to play a significant role in decision-making around diminished responsibility.

'In the light of modern knowledge': the Introduction of Diminished Responsibility in England and Wales

The first serious consideration of diminished responsibility by English authorities dates from the middle years of the twentieth century, when the Royal Commission on Capital Punishment (1949–1953) considered whether to import the Scots law into England and Wales. The Scots law of diminished responsibility would have been known to English legal commentators from around the time of its inception in the second half of the nineteenth century. As I discuss in Chapter 5, a broad ranging debate about the *M'Naghten Rules* took place in England over the last decades of the nineteenth century, and, although this debate encompassed issues such as volitional impairment, punishment versus treatment, and the culpability of insane defendants, some sort of doctrine of diminished responsibility affecting the category of offence and/or sentence was not discussed.[33] By the time of the Royal Commission mid-century, criticism of the *M'Naghten Rules* had amplified and several professional medical organizations had come to advocate the introduction of diminished responsibility as a remedy for its deficiencies.[34] Having received submissions both in favour of and against the adoption of

---

[32] Gordon *The Criminal Law of Scotland* 465.
[33] See my Chapter 5; see also K J M Smith *Lawyers, Legislators and Theorists: Developments in English Criminal Jurisprudence 1800–1957* (Oxford: Clarendon Press, 1998) 223–32; M Wiener *Reconstructing the Criminal: Culture, Law and Policy in England, 1830–1914* (Cambridge: CUP, 1990) 269–76. Similarly, the Scots defence did not receive serious attention in the first decades of the twentieth century when, for example, it might have been examined by the Atkin Committee on Insanity and Crime, which reported in 1923. The lack of consideration given to diminished responsibility may have reflected the English commentators' preoccupation with the *M'Naghten Rules* in these decades.
[34] For discussion, see Walker *Crime and Insanity in England (Vol 1)* 147–8.

diminished responsibility, the Royal Commission recommended against introducing diminished responsibility into the English and Welsh law, although it observed that diminished responsibility operated satisfactorily in Scotland.[35]

Despite the conclusion of the Royal Commission, diminished responsibility was introduced into the law of England and Wales within the space of a few years. In the wake of the publication of the Royal Commission report, a group of barristers and Members of Parliament formed the Heald Committee to push for change in the criminal law. The Heald Committee produced a report, *Murder: some suggestions for the reform of the law relating to murder in England* (1956), which recommended a set of changes to the criminal law, including changes relating to the law of insanity.[36] Rather than attempt to improve the *M'Naghten Rules*, the report recommended diminished responsibility be adopted, to be available to reduce a charge of murder to manslaughter. It was the Heald Committee report that pushed the Cabinet to examine its attitude to diminished responsibility and the Heald proposal that was taken up by Parliament in the 1956–57 parliamentary session. The Homicide Bill introduced in that session contained a partial defence of diminished responsibility, available only to murder, and also restricted the scope of the death penalty to certain kinds of murder. The parliamentary debates on the Bill indicate that it was capital punishment rather than diminished responsibility that was the major preoccupation at the time—the provision on diminished responsibility seems to have been uncontroversial and became law with the passage of the Homicide Act 1957.

The 1957 Act provided that a defendant charged with murder would be liable for manslaughter instead if he or she suffered from an 'abnormality of mind' that 'substantially' impaired his or her 'mental responsibility' for the killing.[37] Section 2 of the Act stated that the burden of proof of diminished responsibility lay with the defence and that, where successful, a defendant who pleaded diminished responsibility would be convicted of manslaughter rather than murder (a conviction attracting sentencing discretion).[38] The section stipulated that the requisite 'abnormality of mind' had to arise from 'arrested or retarded development

---

[35] United Kingdom *Royal Commission on Capital Punishment Report* (Cmd 8932, 1953) para 413, 403. The Commission justified this awkward conclusion by arguing that, if diminished responsibility was introduced in England, it would have to become part of the general law rather than just operate as a defence to murder. The Commission's terms of reference were restricted to the law of murder, and it did not consider that 'so radical an amendment to the law of England would be justified for this limited purpose' (para 413). Rather than adopt diminished responsibility, the Royal Commission recommended (unsuccessfully) that the insanity defence be extended.

[36] See Walker *Crime and Insanity in England (Vol 1)* 149.

[37] Homicide Act 1957, s 2.

[38] Courts have a range of sentencing options including imprisonment, up to and including life, a hospital order, a probation or supervision order, a suspended sentence, a restriction order and an absolute discharge: see Law Commission for England and Wales *Partial Defences to Murder* (Law Com 290, 2004) Appendix B, para 22. Of diminished responsibility pleas granted over 1997–2001, about 49 per cent resulted in restriction orders and 46 per cent resulted in prison terms, supervision orders and suspended sentences (para 22).

of mind' or 'any inherent causes' or be 'induced by disease or injury'. The availability of diminished responsibility was (and remains) narrowly circumscribed around murder.[39]

The introduction of diminished responsibility into English and Welsh criminal law was a reaction to the restricted nature of the *M'Naghten Rules* governing insanity. As a number of commentators note, the introduction of diminished responsibility was intended to counter the effects of the narrow, cognitive *M'Naghten* test for insanity.[40] In a comment that presaged the subsequent development of a jurisprudence of diminished responsibility—in a dialectical relation with both *M'Naghten* insanity and lay understandings of incapacity—Major Lloyd-George stated in his Second Reading Speech in the House of Commons, that the 'new defence' will be open to:

those who, although not insane in this [*M'Naghten*] legal sense, are regarded in the light of modern knowledge as insane in the medical sense, and those who, not insane in either sense, are seriously abnormal, whether through mental deficiency, inherent causes, disease or injury.[41]

The import of diminished responsibility from north of the border seems to have provided a convenient means of injecting flexibility into the law on insanity and of effectively amending insanity (as it related to murder) with limited risk. As Keith Smith argues, the proposal to introduce the Scots doctrine was appealing in that 'rather than being a complete conceptual leap in the dark, it had been tested in action (albeit as part of the Scots legal system) for nearly a century without noticeable subversion of orthodox notions of criminal responsibility'.[42]

---

[39] Even within the bounds of the offence of murder, diminished responsibility is not available as a (partial) defence to a charge of attempted murder: *R v Campbell* [1997] Crim LR 495. Under the Law Commission's proposals relating to the law of homicide, diminished responsibility would be available only to reduce first degree murder to second degree murder. See *A New Homicide Act for England and Wales?* (Law Com 177, 2005).

[40] See, for example, K W M Fulford 'Value, Action, Mental Illness and the Law' in S Shute, J Gardner and J Horder (eds) *Action and Value in the Criminal Law* (Oxford: Clarendon Press, 1993) 279–310, 299–300; J E Hall Williams 'The Homicide Act 1957' (1957) 20(4) *Modern Law Review* 381, 383; G Hughes 'The English Homicide Act of 1957: The Capital Punishment Issues, and Various Reforms in the Law of Murder and Manslaughter' (1959) 49(6) *Journal of Criminal Law, Criminology and Police Science* 521, 525–6; S Prevezer 'The English Homicide Act: A New Attempt to Revise the Law of Murder' (1957) 57(5) *Columbia Law Review* 624, 638; R F Sparks '"Diminished Responsibility" in Theory and Practice' (1964) 27(1) *Modern Law Review* 9, 31; B Wootton 'Diminished Responsibility: A Layman's View' (1960) 76 *Law Quarterly Review* 224, 227.

[41] *Hansard* (HC) (1956–57) (Series 5) vol 560, col 1154 (15 November 1956). Although insanity was not amended, it was envisaged that an insanity plea would be less common once diminished responsibility was introduced: *Hansard* (HC) (Series 5) (1956–57) vol 560, col 1252–3 (15 November 1956).

[42] Smith *Lawyers, Legislators and Theorists* 329; see also Walker *Crime and Insanity in England (Vol 1)* 149.

The Current Doctrine of Diminished Responsibility

As a result of the Coroners and Justice Act 2009, the law of diminished responsibility has been amended. The revised law provides that diminished responsibility is available where a killing is explained by an 'abnormality of mental functioning', arising from a 'recognised medical condition', which has 'substantially impaired' the defendant's 'ability' to understand the nature of his or her conduct, form a rational judgment, or exercise self-control, and the 'abnormality provides an explanation for the defendant's act in doing or being a party to the killing'.[43] This change in the law was the outcome of the Law Commission's review of the law of homicide. The Law Commission proposed modernizing the definition of diminished responsibility 'so that it is clearer and better able to accommodate developments in expert diagnostic practice'.[44] The Commission proposed that diminished responsibility be retained in the same form—as a partial defence—reducing first degree murder to second degree murder according to their proposed (but as yet unimplemented) restructure of homicide.[45] Given that the mandatory life sentence would apply to first degree murder, a successful diminished responsibility plea would continue to provide a means of introducing discretion in sentencing, as had been the case under Section 2(1) of the Homicide Act 1957, as originally drafted.

In order to offer an analysis of diminished responsibility up to the current era, and to lay the ground for a discussion of the way in which diminished responsibility is decided in the next section, I offer a close discussion of the current law here. There are four components of the new diminished responsibility doctrine, and I structure my discussion around them.

(i) 'Abnormality of mental functioning'

A defendant seeking to raise diminished responsibility must suffer from an 'abnormality of mental functioning', the phrase that replaced 'abnormality of mind', which was used in the 1957 Act. The phrase 'abnormality of mental functioning' had been proposed by the Law Commission, on the basis that psychiatrists prefer 'mental functioning' to 'mind'.[46] The Law Commission's reasoning suggests that this new phraseology represents an update of the law, but not one that is intended to radically change diminished responsibility. Given this, but mindful of the other

---

[43] Coroners and Justice Act 2009, s 52, amending Homicide Act 1957, s 2.
[44] Law Commission for England and Wales *Murder, Manslaughter, and Infanticide* (Law Com No 304, 2006) para 5.107. By this time, criticisms of diminished responsibility were longstanding. Both the Butler Committee and the Criminal Law Revision Committee (CLRC) considered the provision relating to diminished responsibility to be unsatisfactory on the basis of its ambiguous construction: see United Kingdom *Report of the Committee on Mentally Abnormal Offenders* (Cmnd 6244, 1975) (Butler Report) para 19.5; and Criminal Law Revision Committee *Fourteenth Report: Offences Against the Person* (Cmnd 7844, 1980) paras 91–2 respectively.
[45] *Murder, Manslaughter, and Infanticide* (Law Com No 304, 2006) para 5.83. At the time of writing, these changes to the law of homicide have not been implemented.
[46] *Murder, Manslaughter, and Infanticide* (Law Com No 304, 2006) para 5.114.

changes to diminished responsibility made by the 2009 Act (which I discuss below), it seems likely that, like 'abnormality of mind', 'abnormality of mental functioning' will be defined broadly.[47] Whether a particular defendant has the requisite abnormal mental state is a question of fact for the jury, although the question of whether a particular clinical condition can give rise to such a state is a question of law.[48] A diverse set of clinical conditions had been held to ground an 'abnormality of mind' for the purposes of diminished responsibility.[49]

The scope of the phrase 'abnormality of mind' had developed in part in a dialectical relation with insanity, and specifically with the 'disease of the mind' limb of the *M'Naghten Rules*. Early judicial discussion of the phrase 'abnormality of mind' drew express comparisons with insanity, according to which the phrase was defined in contradistinction with 'disease of the mind'. In *Byrne*, the first diminished responsibility case to go before the Court of Criminal Appeal, 'abnormality of mind' was interpreted to encompass psychopathy, thus ensuring that volitional incapacity could found a claim of diminished responsibility. In *Byrne*, which involved a defendant who had killed a woman and mutilated her body, all the medical evidence suggested that Byrne was a sexual psychopath who had impulses that were very difficult or impossible to control. The trial judge directed the jury to the effect that, if Byrne had an impulse or urge that was so strong that he found it difficult or impossible to resist, but that he was otherwise normal, diminished responsibility was not available to him.[50] In allowing Byrne's appeal, and substituting a conviction of manslaughter for murder, the Court of Criminal Appeal stated that the phrase 'abnormality of mind' appeared to be:

> wide enough to cover the mind's activities in all its aspects, not only perception of physical acts and matters and the ability to form a rational judgment as to whether an act is right or wrong, but also the ability to exercise will-power to control physical acts in accordance with that rational judgment.[51]

According to the Court of Criminal Appeal, an 'abnormality of mind' that results in an 'inability to exercise will power to control physical acts...is...sufficient to entitle the accused to the benefit' of diminished responsibility.[52] In the *Byrne*

---

[47] See Mackay 'The Coroners and Justice Act 2009—partial defences to murder (2)'.
[48] *R v Spriggs* [1958] 1 QB 270, 274; *R v Byrne* [1960] 2 QB 396, 403 per Lord Parker CJ.
[49] These conditions include Asperger's Syndrome (*R v Reynolds (Gary)* [2004] EWCA Crim 1834), battered women's syndrome (*R v Hobson* [1998] 1 Cr App R 31), depression (*R v Ahluwalia* (1993) 96 Cr App R 133), pre-menstrual tension (*R v Graddock* [1981] Current L Ybk 476), psychopathy (*R v Byrne* [1960] 2 QB 396), reactive depression (*R v Seers* (1984) 79 Cr App R 261; *R v Dietschmann* [2003] 1 AC 1209), and schizophrenia (*R v Weekes* [1999] 2 Cr App R 520).
[50] Referred to in *R v Byrne* [1960] 2 QB 396, 401 per Lord Parker CJ.
[51] *R v Byrne* [1960] 2 QB 396, 403 per Lord Parker CJ.
[52] *R v Byrne* [1960] 2 QB 396, 404 per Lord Parker CJ. The effect of the *Byrne* decision was that the defence of diminished responsibility in English law was wider than its Scots equivalent at the time: Scottish Law Commission *Insanity and Diminished Responsibility* (Report No 195, 2004) para 3.25. In its recent review of the defence of diminished responsibility, the Scottish Commission took the view that the exclusion of psychopathic personality disorder was too sweeping and recommended that, in a reformulated, statutory defence, diminished responsibility 'should not be excluded solely by virtue of the fact that at the relevant time the accused had any form of personality disorder': see Scottish Law Commission *Insanity and Diminished Responsibility* (Report No 195, 2004) para 3.34.

decision, the Court side-stepped the well-rehearsed argument that volitional incapacity was problematic because of the difficulty of distinguishing between impulses that were unable to be resisted and those that were merely unresisted. According to the *Byrne* Court, whether mere difficulty, as opposed to inability, to control one's acts, will ground a plea of diminished responsibility will depend on whether the difficulty is 'so great' as to amount to a 'substantial impairment of the accused's mental responsibility for his act'.[53] The Court concluded that the question of precisely when the difficulty of controlling oneself is sufficiently great is 'scientifically insoluble' and must be determined by the jury 'in a broad, common-sense way'.[54]

This reasoning exposes the other side of the dialectical relation in which a jurisprudence of 'abnormality of mind' developed. 'Abnormality of mind' also developed in relation to lay or non-expert attitudes and beliefs about mental incapacity. Although it may have been prompted at least initially by the uncertain status of the *M'Naghten Rules* in Scotland,[55] referencing 'abnormality of mind' to lay rather than legal meanings of insanity constitutes an attempt to both update and legitimate the law on exculpatory abnormality. In *Byrne*, the Court referred with approval to the Scots case law on diminished responsibility, which provided that 'substantially impaired' 'mental responsibility' involves a 'mental state which in popular language (not that of the *M'Naghten Rules*) a jury would regard as amounting to partial insanity or being on the border-line of insanity'.[56] Given the *Byrne* Court's notable confidence in lay evaluation of a 'scientifically insoluble' issue (of unresisted versus unable-to-be-resisted impulses), it is clear that lay or non-expert as well as expert medical knowledge about abnormality is relevant to the inquiry about what constitutes 'abnormality of mind' for the purposes of diminished responsibility. Indeed, this is the import of Major Lloyd-George's comment, extracted in full above, that the new defence of diminished responsibility was to be open to those who were insane in the 'legal sense', the medical sense, and 'those who, not insane in either sense, are seriously abnormal'.[57]

---

[53] *R v Byrne* [1960] 2 QB 396, 404 per Lord Parker CJ.
[54] *R v Byrne* [1960] 2 QB 396, 404 per Lord Parker CJ.
[55] See Scottish Law Commission *Insanity and Diminished Responsibility* (Report No 195, 2004) para 2.6 for discussion.
[56] *R v Byrne* [1960] 2 QB 396, 404 per Lord Parker CJ. In the year after *Byrne*, in the Court of Criminal Appeal decision of *Rose*, the trial judge's direction to the effect that 'abnormality of mind' was to be understood 'in terms of the borderline between legal insanity and legal sanity' was labelled a 'serious and vital misdirection': *Rose v R* [1961] AC 496, 508 per Lord Tucker. However, the Court stated that if 'insanity is to be taken into consideration, as undoubtedly will usually be the case, the word must be used in its broad, popular sense' (508). According to the Court in *Rose*, whether a direction is made using the words 'borderline' and 'insanity' will depend on the particular case: it will not be 'helpful' in all cases (508). Again, in the decision of *Seers* (*R v Seers* (1984) 79 Cr App R 261), the Court of Appeal concluded that a judicial direction that 'abnormality of mind' required a 'condition on the borderline of insanity' was a material misdirection (265). The Court concluded that reference to insanity was merely 'one way of assisting the jury to determine the degree of impairment of mental responsibility in the appropriate case' which would not apply in all circumstances (264).
[57] *Hansard* (HC) (Series 5) (1956–57) vol 560, col 1154 (15 November 1956).

The development of an expansive jurisprudence of 'abnormality of mind', encompassing volitional incapacity and independent of *M'Naghten* insanity, is, to a significant extent, a product of the restricted scope of diminished responsibility as a partially exculpatory doctrine available only to murder (as opposed to a full exculpatory doctrine, like self-defence, available across the board of criminal offences). Because a successful plea of diminished responsibility does not result in a complete acquittal, the consequences of accommodating volitional incapacity here are more circumscribed than if it was a part of the law of insanity (which was haunted by the spectre of volitional incapacity from the nineteenth century until the inter-war era[58]). In addition, and for my purposes, most interestingly, the tight circumscription of the scope of diminished responsibility around the act of killing also permits lingering ambiguity about the precise effect an 'abnormality of mental functioning' has (does it affect the act or the actor or either/both?). I return to this point below.

(ii) 'A recognised medical condition'

'A recognised medical condition' provides the aetiology of the relevant 'abnormality of mental functioning'. In the 1957 version of diminished responsibility, the question was whether the 'abnormality of mind' was the result of one of a tripartite set of causes, 'a matter to be determined on expert evidence'.[59] The 1957 version of diminished responsibility had required that the defendant's 'abnormality of mind' arise from either 'a condition of arrested or retarded development of mind', 'any inherent causes' or 'disease or injury'.[60] In its reform proposal, (which introduced

---

[58] See Chapter 5.
[59] *R v Byrne* [1960] 2 QB 396, 403 per Lord Parker CJ. Yet, none of the three causes has a defined or agreed psychiatric meaning: S Dell *Murder into Manslaughter: The Diminished Responsibility Defence in Practice* (Oxford: OUP, 1984) 39; Law Commission for England and Wales *Murder, Manslaughter, and Infanticide* (Law Com No 304, 2006) para 5.111; R D Mackay 'Diminished Responsibility and Mentally Disordered Killers' in A Ashworth and B J Mitchell (eds) *Rethinking English Homicide Law* (Oxford: OUP, 2000) 62. The causes gradually acquired legal meaning through a thin line of appellate level case law. In 1994, the Court of Appeal heard the case of *Sanderson* (*R v Sanderson* (1994) 98 Cr App R 325), in which the cause of Sanderson's 'abnormality of mind' was disputed: Sanderson's defence counsel adduced psychiatric evidence that he suffered from paranoid psychosis while the prosecution adduced evidence that Sanderson's paranoia was the result of drug abuse. In allowing Sanderson's appeal on the basis that the trial judge had misled the Court over the aetiology of 'abnormality of mind', the Court of Appeal stated *obiter* that 'induced by disease or injury' referred to 'organic or physical injury or disease of the body, including the brain' and that 'any inherent cause' covered functional mental illness (336 per Lord Roch). In *O'Connell* (*R v O'Connell* [1996] EWCA Crim 1552), the defendant had been taking a sleeping drug on prescription. The Court of Appeal stated that the drug's 'rapid absorption and elimination from the body' precluded it from grounding an 'injury' for the purposes of Section 2, Homicide Act 1957 (extracted in R D Mackay, 'The Abnormality of Mind Factor in Diminished Responsibility' [1999] *Criminal Law Review* 117, 123–4). This reasoning indicated that an 'injury' for the purposes of diminished responsibility had to be more than transitory.
[60] As the parliamentary debates at the time diminished responsibility was introduced indicate, they were intended to circumscribe the scope of the otherwise broad phrase, 'abnormality of mind'. According to the Lord Chancellor, the purpose of the bracketed causes was to 'limit the generality of the words "abnormality of mind" and to bring the law into line with the Scots doctrine:' *Hansard* (HL) (Series 5) vol 202, col 358 (7 March 1957). The bracketed causes were modelled on the definition of 'mental defectiveness' in the Mental Deficiency Act 1927, s 1(2). However, as Griew has pointed out, in the Mental Deficiency Act 1927, the causes were not words of limitation but were intended to

the phrase 'a recognised medical condition'), the Law Commission stated that an advantage of the new phrase was that it ensured that the law was no longer constrained by a 'fixed and out-of-date set of causes'.[61] It seems likely that the new terminology will mean that diminished responsibility will continue to be wide enough to accommodate both mental disorders and physical disorders that have an impact on mental functioning.[62] However, R M Mackay has posited that, with its reference to 'a recognised mental condition', the reformulated doctrine of diminished responsibility contained in the Coroners and Justice Act 2009 may narrow the scope of the law, to exclude, for instance, so-called 'mercy killing' cases. Mackay posits that the new phraseology may work to prevent the 'benevolent conspiracy' between the court and experts that was possible under the obscure wording of the old diminished responsibility doctrine.[63]

In its previous incarnation (under the tripartite aetiology that applied until 2009), diminished responsibility was interpreted so as to exclude those who might be regarded as culpable for their diminished condition. Exposing the significance of moral culpability in the law relating to intoxication, those individuals whose 'abnormality of mind' and impaired mental responsibility arose from intoxication fell without the boundaries of diminished responsibility.[64] The courts also prevented intoxication from supplementing the presence of other factors that, in combination, might have brought the defendant within the bounds of diminished responsibility.[65] But, unlike intoxication, the disease of alcoholism (or alcohol dependency syndrome) had been held to be an 'inherent cause' for the purposes of diminished responsibility. Until recently, the question of what constitutes alcoholism has been interpreted narrowly. In a way that reflected a 'black and white' approach to impaired control, this approach to alcoholism meant that unless the defendant was wholly incapable of resisting the impulse to drink, he or she could not plead diminished responsibility on the basis of his or her disease.[66] However, in the recent decision of *Stewart*, the court recognized that, even in the

---

suggest 'however arising or caused'. This mismatch between their original purpose and that to which they were put in the 1957 Act leads Griew to label the causes 'a remarkably inept reconstruction' of the 1927 Act: E Griew 'The Future of Diminished Responsibility' [1988] *Criminal Law Review* 75, 77.

[61] Law Commission for England and Wales *Murder, Manslaughter, and Infanticide* (Law Com No 304, 2006) para 5.114.

[62] See Mackay 'The Coroners and Justice Act 2009—Partial Defences to Murder (2)'. As the Law Commission stated, what matters is the effect of the condition on the individual.

[63] 'The Coroners and Justice Act 2009—Partial Defences to Murder (2)' 294–5. Mackay also posits that, given the changes to the defence of provocation (now 'loss of control') that were enacted at the same time in the Coroners and Justice Act 2009, it will be more difficult to raise both 'loss of control' and diminished responsibility (295).

[64] See *R v Sanderson* (1994) 98 Cr App R 325. I discuss the significance of moral culpability in relation to intoxication in Chapter 7.

[65] In *Dietschmann*, the House of Lords held that diminished responsibility is available to an intoxicated defendant only if his or her abnormality played a part in substantially impairing his or her mental responsibility for the killing 'despite the drink': *R v Dietschmann* [2003] 1 AC 1209, 1227 per Lord Hutton.

[66] In *Tandy*, the Court of Appeal approved the trial judge's direction that the defendant could not avail herself of the defence of diminished responsibility if she had voluntarily had her first drink of the day: *R v Tandy* [1989] 1 WLR 350, 357.

absence of evidence of brain damage, 'at some levels of severity, what might appear to be voluntary drinking might be inseparable from the defendant's underlying [alcohol dependency] syndrome', and thus be part of such a syndrome, and able to form the basis of a diminished responsibility plea.[67]

Viewed with the kind of difference invoked by diminished responsibility in mind, the restrictions on the scope of this part of the doctrine take on a particular gloss. The use of the aetiology of mental 'abnormality' to exclude consideration of intoxication and merely transient abnormal conditions (and to circumscribe consideration of alcoholism) for the purposes of diminished responsibility represents an attempt to delimit the exculpatory scope of diminished responsibility. In addition, over and above this, it has the effect of ensuring that the doctrine is based on qualitative as opposed to merely quantitative impairment. I take up this point in the next subsection, concerning the specific kind of impairment which must result from 'a recognised medical condition'.

(iii) 'Substantially impaired' D's 'ability' to Understand the Nature of the Conduct, Form a Rational Judgment or Exercise Self-Control

The third component of diminished responsibility relates to the specific kind of effect a defendant's 'abnormality of mental functioning' should have on him or her. Here, the relevant part of the provision centres on an idea of the defendant's 'ability' (the term that replaces reference to an individual's 'mental responsibility', which had been the terminology of the 1957 version of diminished responsibility[68]). The use of the term 'ability' in the newly-formulated provision may have resulted from its use by Lord Parker CJ in *Byrne*, who stated that the reference to 'mental responsibility' in the 1957 version of the doctrine required the jury to consider 'the extent to which the accused's mind is answerable for his physical acts', including 'the extent of his physical ability to exercise will power to control his physical acts'.[69] In relation to 'ability', the statutory provision contains two subparts—one that relates to the extent of the requisite effect on a defendant ('substantially impaired') and the other that relates to the human capacities that

---

[67] See *R v Stewart* [2009] 2 Cr App R 500, 509. See also *R v Wood* [2009] 1 WLR 496.

[68] The term 'mental responsibility' had no antecedents in either English or Scots law and had been the subject of significant criticism. Although the term 'mental responsibility' appeared to be a precise and technical component of the defence and, thus, at least partially within the purview of expert witnesses (S C Hayes 'Diminished Responsibility: The Expert Witness' Viewpoint' in S Yeo (ed) *Partial Excuses to Murder* (Sydney: Federation Press, 1991) 145, 155), as the Butler Committee pointed out, 'mental responsibility...is either a concept of law or a concept of morality; it is not a clinical fact relating to the defendant' (Butler Report para 19.5; see also Mackay 'Diminished Responsibility and Mentally Disordered Killers' 62; B J Mitchell, 'Putting Diminished Responsibility Law into Practice: A Forensic Psychiatric Perspective' (1997) 8(3) *Journal of Forensic Psychiatry* 620, 621; G Williams *Textbook of Criminal Law* (London: Stevens, 1978) 624.

[69] *R v Byrne* [1960] 2 QB 396, 403 per Lord Parker CJ. Mackay posits that this dicta prompted the legislative drafts to prefer the term 'ability' to the term 'capacity' which had been the wording of the Law Commission's draft. See Mackay 'The Coroners and Justice Act 2009—Partial Defences to Murder (2)' 295.

must be affected ('to understand the nature of D's conduct; to form a rational judgment; or to exercise control'). In relation to the extent of the effect on the defendant, it seems likely that 'substantially impaired' will be accorded the same meaning as it was given per the 1957 formulation, given the use of the same phrase in the new Act. 'Substantially impaired' has been held to mean that the requisite impairment need not be total, but must be more than 'trivial or minimal'.[70] In relation to the types of capacities that must be affected—encompassing cognitive and volitional capacities—which are spelled out here for the first time, it is notable that each of the elements appears to be inspired by *Byrne*.[71]

The third component of diminished responsibility, 'substantial impairment', is the centre of gravity of the doctrine. It is through this component of diminished responsibility that the doctrine has been able to accommodate a range of levels of culpability because, if the plea is granted, the impairment is thought to satisfy a certain threshold.[72] In normative criminal law scholarship, the requirement that the defendant's 'abnormality of mental functioning' be 'substantially impaired' is regarded as the moral-evaluative aspect of diminished responsibility.[73] So, approached from this perspective, in effect, the doctrine requires that the defendant's 'abnormality' is of such consequence in the context of the offence that his or her 'legal liability for it ought to be reduced'.[74] As this suggests, and as several commentators note, in practice, the scope of diminished responsibility expands and contracts depending on the morality of the case,[75] or on the basis of the sympathy the defendant elicits, perhaps accounting for the success

---

[70] *R v Lloyd* [1967] 1 QB 175, 178–9 per Edmund Davies J.
[71] This has been pointed out by R M Mackay who notes that in spelling out what abilities need to be impaired, 'abnormality of mental functioning' is now narrower than 'abnormality of mind': see Mackay 'The Coroners and Justice Act 2009—Partial Defences to Murder (2)' 297. The first element—'to understand the nature of D's conduct'—is similar to the first limb of *M'Naghten* insanity (296).
[72] As the Court stated in *Wood*, 'the culpability of the defendant in diminished responsibility manslaughter may sometimes be reduced almost to extinction, while in others, it may remain very high': *R v Wood* [2010] 1 Cr App R (S) 6, 15.
[73] As Alan Norrie argues in relation to s 2(1), 'while "abnormality of mind" draws upon a psychiatric view of the causes of mental illness, it is hitched to a moral-legal judgment' through the requirement of a substantial impairment. See A Norrie *Crime, Reason and History: A Critical Introduction to Criminal Law* (London: Butterworths, 2001) 183.
[74] Griew 'The Future of Diminished Responsibility' 82. Indeed, wording along these lines had been proposed by the Butler Committee and the CLRC. Both Committees had advocated abolition of the mandatory penalty for murder and concluded that, if this reform was enacted, the diminished responsibility defence would be unnecessary. If the mandatory penalty was retained, the Butler Committee proposed reformulating the defence by replacing the reference to 'abnormality of mind' with a reference to 'mental disorder', as defined in the civil law, and by explicitly directing the jury to determine whether that disorder was such as to be 'an extenuating circumstance which ought to reduce the offence to manslaughter' (Butler Report para 19.17). The CLRC considered this formulation to be insufficiently tight and advocated a version that required that the specified 'mental disorder' be 'a substantial enough reason to reduce the offence to manslaughter' (para 93).
[75] See, for example, K J M Smith and W Wilson, 'Impaired Voluntariness and Criminal Responsibility: Reworking Hart's Theory of Excuses—the English Judicial Response' (1993) 13 *Oxford Journal of Legal Studies* 69, 89; Williams *Textbook of Criminal Law* 629.

(at least under the old version of the doctrine) of so-called 'mercy killers' who raise diminished responsibility.[76]

The 'substantially impaired' component of diminished responsibility is typically, if implicitly, understood to mean that what the doctrine connotes, in the abstract and in practice, is a certain *degree* of impairment. As the Court stated in *Walden*, the term 'substantially impaired' 'connotes a question of degree and questions of degree are questions of fact in each case'.[77] The prominence of the language of degree in diminished responsibility has generated a predominant scholarly understanding that it connotes a quantitative rather than qualitative difference. But I suggest this scholarly understanding has obscured another, deeper sense of difference connoted by diminished responsibility—difference in kind. On its face, this idea of the difference connoted by diminished responsibility seems counter-intuitive because the law is replete with the language of degree—evident in the name of the doctrine itself as well as in elements such as 'substantially impaired'. But, when examined as a whole, and taking into account the ways in which diminished responsibility is proved (with close reliance on expert evidence and clinical diagnoses), diminished defendants can be seen to be constructed as different in kind, rather than degree. I discuss this point in the final section of this chapter.

(iv) 'Abnormality of mental functioning' Provides 'an explanation for D's act in doing/being a party to the killing'

The reformulated diminished responsibility provision introduced by the Coroners and Justice Act 2009 stipulates that there must be a quasi-causal relationship between the defendant's 'abnormality of mental functioning' and his or her acts in relation to the killing. In providing that the 'abnormality of mental functioning' offers 'an explanation' (as opposed to 'the' or 'the sole' explanation) for the killing, the new diminished responsibility provision contemplates that only those individuals whose 'abnormality of mental functioning' caused, or was 'a significant contributory factor in causing', the relevant conduct will be able to succeed in their claim for a partial defence.[78] This new component of the doctrine of diminished responsibility followed the Law Commission's recommendations that a defendant's abnormality of mind (or developmental immaturity, according to their formulation) must form 'an explanation' for his or her conduct.[79] A quasi-causal connection between the defendant's 'abnormality of mental functioning' and

---

[76] See, for example, Mitchell 'Putting Diminished Responsibility Law into Practice' 631–2; W Wilson *Criminal Law: Doctrine and Theory* (London: Longman, 2003) 247.
[77] *R v Walden* [1959] 1 WLR 1008, 1012.
[78] Coroners and Justice Act 2009, s 52(1B), amending Homicide Act 1957, s 2.
[79] Law Commission for England and Wales *Murder, Manslaughter, and Infanticide* (Law Com No 304, 2006) para 5.124; see also Law Commission for England and Wales *Partial Defences to Murder* (Law Com No 290, 2004) para 5.95. According to the Commission, this would ensure an 'appropriate connection' between the abnormality and the killing, but leaves open the possibility that other factors (such as provocation) may also have been operative at the time the killing occurred (*Murder, Manslaughter, and Infanticide* para 5.124).

his or her homicidal acts means that the defendant's mental abnormality must precipitate the killing he or she commits.[80] With this new quasi-causal requirement, diminished responsibility has moved closer to infanticide, which, as I suggest in Chapter 8, works on the implicit assumption that the defendant woman's actions in killing her child are caused actions.

The 1957 version of diminished responsibility did not specify a particular connection between a defendant's 'abnormality of mind' and his or her 'acts or omissions in doing or being party to the killing'. But, those in favour of the recent reform in this direction argued that this was something like a de facto requirement of diminished responsibility.[81] However, the requirement of a quasi-causal connection between the defendant's 'abnormality' and his or her homicidal acts is just one of several possible formulations of the relationship between the abnormal mental state and criminal conduct under diminished responsibility. On the one hand, the connection between 'abnormality of mind' and a defendant's homicidal conduct may be merely temporal, that is, the doctrine may require that the defendant suffer from an 'abnormality of mind' *at the time* he or she kills. There is also another possible formulation of the connection between 'abnormality of mind' and the defendant's homicidal acts—his or her abnormality may mean that he or she did not form the requisite *mens rea* for murder. Diminished responsibility provisions constructed in this way—as putative rather than affirmative defences—are in place in other jurisdictions.[82]

It is possible to mount a critique of the introduction of a quasi-causal requirement to diminished responsibility on several bases. On an abstract level, an approach that assumes or requires that mental abnormality cause the killing conflates two separate ideas—excuse and causation. As Michael Moore argues in relation to insanity, properly understood, exculpatory doctrines based on mental

---

[80] R M Mackay queries whether this requirement will make diminished responsibility harder to satisfy than insanity, which has no such limitation: see Mackay 'The Coroners and Justice Act 2009—Partial Defences to Murder (2)' 300.

[81] The Judicial Studies Board specimen direction on diminished responsibility made reference to the caused nature of the defendant's conduct. See for discussion, *R v Ramchurn* [2010] 2 Cr App R 3. See also Law Commission for England and Wales *Murder, Manslaughter, and Infanticide* (Law Com No 304, 2006) para 5.122; J Horder *Excusing Crime* (Oxford: OUP, 2004) 155. In *R v Egan* [1992] 4 All ER 470, the Court of Appeal denied diminished responsibility to an intoxicated defendant on the basis that it was the consumption of alcohol, rather than internal abnormality, which caused him to kill (479). The decision in *Egan* was disapproved by the House of Lords in *Dietschmann* (*R v Dietschmann* [2003] 1 AC 1209, 1225). In *Dietschmann*, the House of Lords rejected the idea that a defendant's 'abnormality of mind' must be the sole cause of the killing, interpreting the defence of diminished responsibility to require that it must be one although not the sole cause for the defendant's conduct (1217).

[82] See P Arenella 'The Diminished Capacity and Diminished Responsibility Defenses: Two Children of a Doomed Marriage' (1977) 77(6) *Columbia Law Review* 827, 828–9 and S J Morse 'Diminished Capacity' in S Shute, J Gardner and J Horder (eds) *Action and Value in Criminal Law* (Oxford: Clarendon Press, 1993) 239, 240–1 for discussion. However, this type of connection between 'abnormality of mind' and the defendant's homicidal conduct was specifically disallowed on the face of both the 2009 and the 1957 versions of diminished responsibility in England and Wales: because diminished responsibility is constructed such that a diminished defendant would otherwise be liable for murder, the doctrine comes into effect, at least in principle, only once the *mens rea* and *actus reus* of murder have been proved or admitted.

incapacity excuse defendants because of their incapacity, not because that incapacity causes criminal acts. According to Moore, conflating causation and excuse obscures the legal (and moral) basis of excusing in either incapacity or lack of opportunity.[83] On an empirical level, it is arguable that diminished responsibility had not been restricted to those defendants whose abnormalities caused them to kill. According to G R Sullivan, empirically, most pleas of diminished responsibility involve a claim that the 'abnormality of mind' precipitated the killing, but, in some cases, such as those in which the defendant is intellectually impaired, the issue of what caused the defendant to kill is severable from an inquiry into whether he or she was responsible for that killing.[84] Given this, and although more than one cause can be considered under the new formulation, the approach to causation taken in the reformulated diminished responsibility provision is likely to narrow the scope of diminished responsibility.

Viewed in the light of my assessment of the historical development of diminished responsibility, the inclusion of a causation requirement appears as an over-determination of what had been an under-determined aspect of the doctrine. As discussed above, there are good reasons to conclude that the foundational Scots version of diminished responsibility actually relied only on a temporal connection between mental abnormality and the act of killing. This temporal connection meant that the defendant's 'abnormality of mind' must have been operative or in some way pertained at the time of the killing, but did not mean that it precipitated the killing (the stricter requirement). This type of connection left open the question of precisely *how* a defendant's 'abnormality of mind'/ 'abnormality of mental impairment' impairs his or her criminal responsibility. It was this looser type of connection that seems to have been envisaged at the time of the development of the Scots plea of diminished responsibility. Up until 2009, the effect of the looser connection between abnormality and criminal responsibility was to raise expert medical evidence to a position of prominence as it provided a means by which the descriptive issue of the defendant's mental state ('abnormality of mind' resulting from one of the specified causes) and the evaluative issue (whether that state amounted to a 'substantial' impairment of 'mental responsibility') could be joined. The new version of the plea seems set to continue to depend on expert evidence. I pick up this point again in the next section of this chapter.

Where causation does seem to be an appropriate consideration for diminished responsibility is in relation to those cases in which appellants argue that their mental states were such that they were unable to instruct their lawyers to raise diminished responsibility at trial. These cases concern the 'rare' instances in which it is argued that 'fresh evidence shows that the appellant's responsibility at the time of killing was indeed sufficiently diminished...and that there is a persuasive reason why the defence was not advanced at trial'.[85] In relation to the latter, the question is

---

[83] M S Moore 'Causation and the Excuses' (1985) 73 *California Law Review* 1091, 1148.
[84] G R Sullivan 'Intoxicants and Diminished Responsibility' [1994] *Criminal Law Review* 152, 160.
[85] *R v Erskine; R v Williams* [2010] 1 WLR 183, 201, regarding Criminal Appeal Act 1968, s 23.

if the 'mental illness itself' was a 'material cause' of the decision not to run diminished responsibility.[86] In the joint decision of *R v Erskine; R v Williams*, the Court of Appeal held that there was 'unequivocal contemporaneous evidence' which suggested that the decision in Erskine's trial not to advance diminished responsibility was not a strategic decision but was 'irredeemably flawed'.[87] By contrast, in *R v Latus*, the Court held that the decision not to run diminished responsibility was caused not by the illness but by a tactical choice not to allow the defence to be investigated.[88] In the latter case, the appeal was denied.

Professional Actors and Expert Knowledge: Deciding Diminished Responsibility

Legal experts—judges, prosecution, and defence counsel—and medical experts now dominate decision-making in relation to diminished responsibility. In terms of legal experts, on their face, the rules about the way in which diminished responsibility may be raised in court suggest the primacy of defence counsel. Reflecting the 'long established policy of the law that the defendant is presumed to be in full possession of his faculties until the contrary is shown', it is up to the defendant to raise diminished responsibility.[89] Because a plea of diminished responsibility entails admitting that the defendant did the *actus reus* with the *mens rea* (thus exposing him or her to conviction for murder), diminished responsibility has been called an 'optional defence'.[90] The 'optional defence' status of

---

[86] *R v Diamond* [2008] EWCA Crim 923, [23]. See also *R v Neaven* [2007] 2 All ER 891.

[87] *R v Erskine; R v Williams* [2010] 1 WLR 183, 207. The Court admitted the fresh evidence, and substituted a conviction of manslaughter on the grounds of diminished responsibility.

[88] *R v Latus* [2006] EWCA Crim 3187. See also *R v Shickle* [2005] EWCA Crim 1881, in which the Court concluded that there was 'no reasonable explanation for failing to adduce the evidence of diminished responsibility at the trial' ([64]) and declined to grant the appeal. Concern with these kinds of cases was perhaps behind the Criminal Cases Review Commission (CCRC) submission to the Law Commission, in which they called for the abolition of diminished responsibility (*Murder, Manslaughter, and Infanticide* (Law Com No 304, 2006) para 5.91).

[89] Criminal Law Revision Committee *Fourteenth Report: Offences Against the Person* (Cmnd 7844, 1980) para 95. The procedural rule that only the defence may raise diminished responsibility parallels the rule relating to raising automatism, and both rules may be interpreted as products of presumptions made in the criminal law. In relation to automatism, the presumption is the 'presumption of mental capacity' ensuring that an act can be presumed to be voluntary unless there is evidence to rebut this presumption.

[90] *R v Campbell* (1987) 84 Cr App R 255; see also Mackay 'Diminished Responsibility and Mentally Disordered Killers' 77. Unlike the notable case of infanticide, which is a discrete category of homicide, it is not possible to be charged with 'manslaughter by reason of diminished responsibility'. Both the Butler Report and the CLRC Report on *Offences Against the Person* proposed that, subject to the defendant's consent and where there was clear evidence indicating that a defence can be made out, the prosecution should be able to indict the defendant for manslaughter (Butler Report para 19.19; CLRC *Fourteenth Report* para 95–6). In formulating this proposal, both the Butler Committee and the CLRC focused on the practical advantages of pleading diminished responsibility, including that the indictment accurately reflected the trial outcome; that a trial for murder would not further damage the accused's mental state; and that decision-making would not be left to the jury when the Crown's own evidence pointed to diminished responsibility (Butler Report para 19.19; CLRC *Fourteenth Report* para 95). Although these proposals have not been implemented, the effect of the change in the way in

diminished responsibility means that the prosecution may not raise diminished responsibility, unless the defence puts the defendant's state of mind in issue by raising insanity, in which case the prosecution may raise diminished responsibility as an alternative.[91] The judge may not raise diminished responsibility: the most the judge may do ('at least in cases where the defendant is represented by counsel') is to point out the evidence of diminished responsibility to the defence, leaving it to them to decide whether to make the plea.[92] Possibly reflecting the Scots law, the burden of proof for diminished responsibility is on the defendant, and the standard of proof is the legal standard.[93]

Although the rules about raising diminished responsibility suggest that defence counsel occupy the most prominent position regarding diminished responsibility, taking into account legal practices, the picture is more equivocal. As a result of changes in the way in which the claims to diminished responsibility are decided, there has been a shift in the balance of decision-making in diminished responsibility cases toward the prosecution, who determines whether to contest a plea of dimin-

which diminished responsibility is decided—to allow the prosecution to accept a plea of diminished responsibility in cases where the medical evidence is unequivocal—is such that the concerns of the Butler Committee and the CLRC have been addressed without reform to the way in which offences are charged. The status quo was noted with approval by the Law Commission: *Murder, Manslaughter, and Infanticide* (Law Com No 304, 2006) paras 5.102–5.106.

[91] Criminal Procedure (Insanity) Act 1964, s 6.

[92] *R v Campbell* (1987) 84 Cr App R 255, 260 per Lord Kennedy CJ; see also *R v Kooken* (1982) 74 Cr App R 30, 34. The Court in *Campbell* reasoned that because s 2(1) of the Homicide Act 1957 provides that 'it shall be for the defence to prove' diminished responsibility, and because 'the judge's knowledge of the evidence available in relation to the issue of diminished responsibility will inevitably be limited', it should be left to defence counsel to choose to run the defence (at 259–60). This wording is unchanged by the 2009 Act and thus diminished responsibility continues to be an 'optional defence'.

[93] Regarding the burden of proof, see Homicide Act 1957, s 2; this section of the 1957 Act was unchanged by the 2009 amendments. In relation to the standard of proof, see *R v Dunbar* [1958] 1 QB 1 at 11–12, in which the Scots law was taken into consideration. If the prosecution adduces evidence of diminished responsibility (because the defence has raised insanity), the standard of proof is beyond all reasonable doubt: see *R v Grant* [1960] Crim LR 424. In relation to the standard of proof, diminished responsibility differed from the now-defunct provocation defence: in raising provocation, the defence bore only an evidential burden of proof: *Attorney-General for Jersey v Holley* [2005] 2 AC 580, 612. It has been argued that different standards and burdens of proof for provocation/now 'loss of control' and diminished responsibility caused jurors confusion as the defences were able to be run simultaneously (see, for example, A P Simester et al *Simester and Sullivan's Criminal Law: Theory and Doctrine* (Oxford: Hart, 2010) 401–2, 715–16). Although several law reform bodies have concluded that the burden of proof for diminished responsibility should be an evidentiary one as was the case with provocation (Butler Report para 19.18; CLRC *Fourteenth Report* para 94), the Law Commission expressly recommended against changes to the burden of proof in its report on partial defences (*Partial Defences to Murder* (Law Com No 290, 2004), para 5.91) and briefly affirmed the status quo in its report on reform to the law of homicide (*Murder, Manslaughter, and Infanticide* para 5.105). Given the parallel with the law of insanity, justifications for the burden and standard of proof for diminished responsibility echo those offered for the reverse burden in relation to insanity. Thus, one explanation proffered is that the knowledge required to make out the defence of diminished responsibility is uniquely within the province of the accused (see, for example, P W Ferguson, 'Reverse Burdens of Proof' (2004) 22 *Scots Law Times* 133, 138; Law Commission for England and Wales *Partial Defences to Murder* para 5.90). This justification is based on the assumed difficulty of assessing abnormal mental states for the purposes of the defence, and its popularity helps to account for the prominence of expert evidence in diminished responsibility cases. See my Chapter 6 for discussion of the issue of assessing abnormal mental states in the context of insanity.

ished responsibility, and the judge who accepts or rejects any prosecution–defence arrangement.[94] This shift has occurred with the rise in the importance of pre-trial decision-making. In a move that seems to reflect institutional pressure on prosecution services to process cases speedily, the requirement that a plea of diminished responsibility go to the jury was abrogated by the Court of Appeal in *Cox*, decided in 1968. In this case, the Court of Appeal concluded that, in cases where 'the medical evidence available, in the possession of the prosecution as well as the defence', indicated 'perfectly plainly' that it would have been proper to accept a plea of diminished responsibility, it is open to the prosecution to accept that plea and avoid a murder trial.[95]

These changes to the way in which diminished responsibility is decided heralded a significant change in the practical operation of the law. In a way that prefigures the recent changes to the way in which unfitness to plead is decided, which I discuss in Chapter 4, the rule permitting the prosecution to accept a plea of diminished responsibility in (what are at least formally) unequivocal cases means that the issue of the defendant's mental abnormality is in the hands of legal actors and medical professionals. Thus, even though it is not possible to charge diminished responsibility manslaughter, the law is such that the situation is now as close to that as possible without such a change. In those cases in which the medical evidence is 'perfectly plainly' to the effect that the defendant killed under conditions of diminished responsibility, the doctrine in effect becomes a preliminary issue, determining whether or not a trial will go ahead. In the decades since the decision in *Cox*, decision-making in relation to diminished responsibility has altered such that the majority of diminished responsibility pleas are now accepted by the prosecution.[96]

As so many diminished responsibility pleas are accepted prior to trial, the shift in the balance of power between various legal experts has also entailed a shift away from lay evaluation of diminished responsibility claims. In evaluating and adjudicating diminished responsibility claims, lay actors initially had a greater role than

---

[94] See Mackay 'Diminished Responsibility and Mentally Disordered Killers' 62. Perhaps the most well-known instance of a judge rejecting an agreement to accept a plea to manslaughter on the basis of diminished responsibility occurred in the case of the 'Yorkshire Ripper'. See *R v Sutcliffe* The Times, 30 April 1981.

[95] *R v Cox* [1968] 1 WLR 308, 311. The *Cox* Court was motivated by the practical considerations of the time and monetary cost of a trial, as well as the 'anxiety and uncertainty' defendants face while murder trials take place. The Court in *Cox* offered no further explanation for treating diminished responsibility differently from insanity, which must go to the jury: see *Bratty v Attorney-General for Northern Ireland* [1963] AC 386.

[96] Law Commission for England and Wales *Murder, Manslaughter, and Infanticide* (Law Com No 304, 2006) para 5.96; Law Commission for England and Wales *Partial Defences to Murder* (Law Com No 290, 2004) Appendix B, para 20; Mackay 'Diminished Responsibility and Mentally Disordered Killers' 61. Under these conditions, it is possible that some diminished responsibility claims which are accepted by the prosecution would have been rejected by a jury (Mackay 'Diminished Responsibility and Mentally Disordered Killers' 63), effectively enlarging the scope of the plea. In his recent study for the Law Commission, Mackay found that, of the cases in which diminished responsibility was raised, the prosecution accepted a plea in 77 per cent of the cases (*Partial Defences to Murder* (Law Com No 290, 2004) Appendix B para 20). Of the cases in which the plea was contested by the prosecution (23 per cent), only 22 per cent were successful (Appendix B para 21).

they now do. When the plea was first introduced into the criminal law in England and Wales, and prior to *Cox*, all findings of diminished responsibility had to be made by a jury,[97] although, unless there was 'other evidence which can displace or throw doubt on that evidence', it was not open to the jury to reject unanimous medical evidence of 'abnormality of mind'.[98] But, in those instances where experts differed as to whether the defendant was suffering from 'diminished responsibility', the decision to grant or deny the plea lay with the jury. In *Byrne*, Lord Parker CJ stated that, with regard to the issue of the defendant's 'abnormality of mind', 'medical evidence is no doubt of importance, but the jury are entitled to take into consideration all the evidence including the acts or statements of the accused and his demeanour'.[99] Lord Parker CJ went on to state that:

> They [the jury] are 'not bound to accept the medical evidence if there is other material before them which, in their good judgment, conflicts with it and outweighs it, [bearing in mind that] the question involves a decision not merely as to whether there was some impairment... but whether such impairment can properly be called 'substantial', a matter upon which juries may quite legitimately differ from doctors.[100]

The balance between lay people and medical experts evoked in *Byrne* fell away within a short period of time following the introduction of diminished responsibility into England and Wales. With a majority of diminished responsibility pleas accepted by the prosecution, juries are only involved in the minority of cases—those in which the plea is contested.[101]

A declining role for lay actors does not sound a knell for lay knowledge. Because legal actors—including judges, prosecution, and defence counsel—rely on lay knowledge of mental incapacity, the role of lay knowledge in criminal process does not begin and end with lay adjudication, meaning that its significance is not coterminous with decision-making by a jury, for instance. As I discuss in Chapter 3, in relation to the decision-making around mental incapacity more generally, legal actors can be seen to be lay when it comes to the issue of mental incapacity, although they are in different subject positions when compared with lay people. This is not to deny legal actors their status as experts—but it is to suggest that these individuals are lay vis-à-vis mental incapacity. In relation to diminished responsibility, legal actors combine their lay knowledge of incapacity with their expert knowledge of legal processes. Thus, a decision about whether to

---

[97] *R v Matheson* [1958] 1 WLR 474. In interpreting the Homicide Act 1957 to require that a jury evaluate the claim to the defence, the Court in *Matheson* simply stated that the issue 'must be left to the jury, just as the issue must be if the defence is insanity' (*R v Matheson* [1958] 1 WLR 474, 480 per Lord Goddard).
[98] *R v Matheson* [1958] 1 WLR 474, 480.
[99] *R v Byrne* [1960] 2 QB 396, 403–4; see also *R v Jennion* [1962] 1 WLR 317, 322; *R v Tandy* [1989] 1 WLR 350, 356; *R v Khan* (Dawood) [2010] 1 Cr App R 74, 86.
[100] *R v Byrne* [1960] 2 QB 396, 403, 404.
[101] Reflecting the contested nature of pleas coming before juries, Mackay's recent research indicated that only 22 per cent of the cases in which the defence was contested by the prosecution were successful: Law Commission for England and Wales *Partial Defences to Murder* (Law Com No 290, 2004) Appendix B para 21; see also Mackay 'Diminished Responsibility and Mentally Disordered Killers' 62.

Differences of Degree and Differences of Kind: Diminished Responsibility 249

accept a plea of diminished responsibility will involve both a lay knowledge of the relevant condition forming the basis of the plea, and an expert knowledge of the way in which, in the context of all the circumstances of the case, such a plea would be received in court.

Nonetheless, in relation to diminished responsibility, it seems that expert psychological and psychiatric knowledge, and evidence based on it, has a deep significance in this part of the mental incapacity terrain. In this respect, diminished responsibility is similar to insanity, and may be contrasted with intoxication, for instance. This significance is in part a practical one. As the Law Commission recently concluded, expert evidence is 'crucial' to the viability of a claim to diminished responsibility.[102] Even in the absence of a statutory requirement that expert evidence be adduced in support of a plea of diminished responsibility (*contra* insanity and unfitness to plead), empirical studies bear out the claim that expert medical evidence is 'crucial' in diminished responsibility cases.[103] Indeed, it is appropriate to think of expert evidence as a de facto requirement of the plea, placing expert knowledge at its heart. Given this, it is significant that the recent reform to diminished responsibility was accompanied by a renewed emphasis on a clear division of labour between experts and the jury, preserving the 'ultimate issue'—that the defendant's state was indeed such that he or she was 'substantially impaired'—as solely one for the jury.[104]

---

[102] Law Commission for England and Wales *Murder, Manslaughter, and Infanticide* (Law Com No 304, 2006) para 5.111; see also Law Commission for England and Wales *Partial Defences to Murder* (Law Com No 290, 2004) Appendix B para 28. In relation to the former version of diminished responsibility, the Court of Appeal in *R v Dix* (1982) 74 Cr App R 306 stated that expert evidence about the defendant's 'abnormality of mind', its causes, and the question of whether the defendant's 'mental responsibility' was 'substantially impaired' was 'essential' to a diminished responsibility defence (*R v Dix* (1982) 74 Cr App R 306, 311 per Lord Shaw). According to the *Dix* Court, although Section 2(1) does not require that medical evidence is adduced in support of a defence of diminished responsibility, 'it makes it a practical necessity if the defence is to begin to run at all' (*R v Dix* (1982) 74 Cr App R 306, 311 per Lord Shaw).

[103] In the study commissioned by the Law Commission, Mackay found a total of 366 expert reports in the court files of 157 diminished responsibility cases (Law Commission for England and Wales *Partial Defences to Murder* (Law Com No 290, 2004) Appendix B para 24). Mackay found that these reports were commissioned in approximately equal numbers by the prosecution and defence (Appendix B para 25). The study found that the primary diagnoses given to defendants seeking to rely on diminished responsibility were depression, schizophrenia, personality disorder, and psychosis, in descending order of popularity (Appendix B para 26). Taking into account the kind of diagnoses identified in these reports, the Law Commission concluded that the defence succeeds where there is 'a clear psychosis' or, 'in other cases (such as depression), its success is related to whether there is an established prior medical condition and its severity' (*Partial Defences to Murder* para 5.84).

[104] In its report, the Law Commission recorded as one of the virtues of its proposal that it makes the relationship between the role of the expert and the role of the jury 'clearer' (*Partial Defences to Murder* para 5.117). Mackay's study found that expert witnesses were commenting on the issue of 'substantial impairment of mental responsibility' in 69 per cent of cases (Law Commission for England and Wales *Partial Defences to Murder* (Law Com No 290, 2004) Appendix B para 32; see also Law Commission for England and Wales *Murder, Manslaughter, and Infanticide* (Law Com No 304, 2006) para 5.118; see also Griew 'The Future of Diminished Responsibility' 82; Mitchell 'Putting Diminished Responsibility Law into Practice' 622. Some writers have suggested that psychiatrists and other experts are willing participants in this intrusion into the jury role (see, for example, Griew 'The Future of Diminished Responsibility' 84). However, the Royal College of Psychiatrists' submission to the Law Commission expressed support for the legal view that the expert should not comment on the 'ultimate

Beyond its practical role in particular cases, expert psychiatric and psychological evidence has a more diffused significance that transcends any specific decision. Various accounts of the role expert evidence plays in relation to diminished responsibility have been offered. In relation to the operation of diminished responsibility, some commentators have suggested that expert evidence operates to expand the scope of the doctrine.[105] Another account of the significance of expert medical knowledge for the diminished responsibility doctrine assesses the value of the evidence from a more ideological perspective, suggesting that expert evidence provides a way of manipulating the strictures of legal standards for exculpation.[106] Evidence in support of these arguments is provided by the inclusion of homicides which are 'essentially non-pathological reactions to stressful life events' within the bounds of diminished responsibility.[107] A third account of the significance of expert medical evidence for diminished responsibility is mounted in terms of the legitimation of legal processes. Here, the significance of expert evidence supports what Tony Ward calls the 'dual authority of science and lay consensus', which he argues underpins mental incapacity doctrines such as diminished responsibility historically.[108] As this last account suggests, lay as well as expert knowledge is relevant to legitimation: because the (most) controversial claims to diminished responsibility—those in which a plea is not accepted by the prosecution or, more rarely, in which the judge insists on the defendant going to trial on a charge of murder—are those that are adjudicated by a jury, lay knowledge as employed in lay evaluation also performs a legitimating role in relation to diminished responsibility.

issue': *Murder, Manslaughter, and Infanticide* (Law Com No 304, 2006) paras 5.117–5.120 for discussion.

[105] Griew suggests that reliance on expert psychiatric and psychological evidence is a device for stretching the scope of s 2(1) in practice: 'The Future of Diminished Responsibility' 84. Mackay suggests that judges admit expert psychiatric and psychological evidence on the question of whether the defendant's 'mental responsibility' was 'substantially impaired' in order to assist the jury in the difficult task of assessing the genuine capacities and choices of the defendant: R D Mackay *Mental Condition Defences in the Criminal Law* (Oxford: Clarendon Press, 1995) 192.

[106] Norrie argues that 'psychiatric testimony operates to stretch irresponsibility beyond the narrow bounds of the legal test' and thus operates as a 'safety valve' for the law—it provides the means of introducing a satisfactorily circumscribed compassion into the legal rules' of insanity and diminished responsibility: *Crime, Reason and History* 190–1.

[107] A P Simester et al *Simester and Sullivan's Criminal Law* 719; see also W Wilson *Criminal Law: Doctrine and Theory* (London: Longman, 2003) 250. Simester et al argue that, once given diagnostic labels (such as 'reactive depression'), conditions arising from external circumstances can be brought within diminished responsibility. One species of such homicides is 'mercy killings', where those who kill are believed to have been motivated by laudable considerations such as ending the suffering of a loved one who is ill. In one empirical study, Mackay identified 22 homicides described as 'mercy killings' between 1982–1991 in England and Wales: of these, only one murder verdict was returned: 'Diminished Responsibility and Mentally Disordered Killers' 79. In another study, Mackay found that each of the three defendants in homicides described as 'mercy killings' was successful in arguing diminished responsibility: Law Commission for England and Wales *Partial Defences to Murder* (Law Com No 290, 2004) para 5.40. The Law Commission sounded a note of caution in relation to these sorts of cases, stating that 'where there are "deserving cases" or non-medical grounds such as "mercy killings", they need to be addressed honestly and openly rather than disguised as cases or issues of diminished responsibility: *Partial Defences to Murder* (Law Com No 290, 2004) para 5.94.

[108] See T Ward 'Observers, Advisors, or Authorities? Experts, Juries and Criminal Responsibility in Historical Perspective' (2001) 12 *Journal of Forensic Psychiatry* 105.

Differences of Degree and Differences of Kind: Diminished Responsibility 251

By way of contribution to this scholarly discussion about expert medical evidence, I suggest that its significance lies in part in its contribution to the particular construction of the subject of diminished responsibility. This becomes apparent when we take a step back to think about knowledge rather than evidence. Here, it is useful to recall my discussion of the kind of difference shared by mental incapacity doctrines. As I discuss in Chapter 2, the process of construction of subjects of the law takes place in and through legal processes. There, I suggest that a particular idea of difference marked defendants relying on mental incapacity doctrines out from other defendants. With regard to diminished responsibility, I suggest that, in making the defendant the subject of specialist language of pathology via the evidence adduced, expert knowledge assists in constructing the diminished defendant as abnormal. The difference invoked is a difference of kind rather than degree. Again, as I discuss in Chapter 2, this qualitative difference is both a requirement of the doctrine and a construction of the individuals ('diminished', 'disabled', 'impaired') who seek to rely on it. When the scholarly frame is extended to take into account the evidentiary and procedural aspects of mental incapacity, it becomes evident that 'madness' for criminal law purposes has particular formal qualities, which together mark out the features of the mental incapacity terrain.[109]

On my analysis of diminished responsibility, beneath the language of degree, another kind of difference is operating. As the Law Commission has put it in relation to the requirement of a 'medically recognisable basis' for diminished responsibility:

> The distinction between what is normal and abnormal is one of degree and can be difficult to draw. The requirement of a medically recognisable basis provides both a doctrinal justification (that a person suffering a medically recognisable abnormality of mind lacks full responsibility for his or her acts) and a practical limitation on the ambit of the defence. Without it, there would be a serious risk of an 'evaluative free for all'.[110]

This requirement of a 'medically recognisable basis' delineates the boundaries of diminished responsibility, providing a way of drawing a line at the point of abnormality. But the process of drawing a line is not just about drawing a line at some point—it entails a reconstruction that ensures that the altogether more slippery idea of a quantitative difference (how substantial is substantial?) is made to resemble a firmer qualitative difference, which, on my analysis, is the core of the construction of abnormality for criminal law purposes.

Women seem to be particularly amenable to the construction as abnormal or different in kind via diminished responsibility. Although the recent Law Commission report, *Partial Defences to Murder*, concluded that diminished responsibility does not operate 'in a way which involves gender discrimination',[111] there does

---

[109] These formal qualities are, on the one hand, that 'madness' is constructed as it is dispositional, and, on the other hand, that it can be 'read off' conduct by different participants in the criminal justice process. See further my 'manifest madness' analysis in Chapter 3.

[110] Law Commission for England and Wales *Partial Defences to Murder* (Law Com No 290, 2004) para 5.74.

[111] *Partial Defences to Murder* (Law Com No 290, 2004) para 5.33.

appear to be a multifaceted gender bias in the operation of diminished responsibility. Women are over-represented among defendants granted the plea.[112] In addition, the prosecution is more likely to accept a plea of diminished responsibility for women defendants than for men.[113] Women are also more likely than men to be granted the plea at trial.[114] Once granted a diminished responsibility plea, women are more likely to be sentenced to probation or supervision orders as opposed to prison sentences.[115] The gender bias in the operation of diminished responsibility suggests an underlying consensus about gender, violence, and mental abnormality in both legal processes and lay attitudes and beliefs.[116]

Concurrent with the changes in the type of actors involved in and the type of knowledges in use in diminished responsibility, its success rate has declined. In the years immediately following the Homicide Act 1957, diminished responsibility was a frequently successful plea.[117] As the Law Commission concluded, the figures indicate that there has been 'a consistent fall in the successful use of diminished responsibility in recent years'.[118] Various reasons for the decline have been offered, including that there has been less use for diminished responsibility since the suspension of the death penalty in 1965 (for those types of murder to which it had continued to apply), or that its territory shrunk with the expansive approach to the partial defence of provocation, which prevailed from the 1980s until the early 2000s (I discuss the relationship between diminished responsibility and provocation in the final section of this chapter).[119] It is also possible that jurors

---

[112] Aileen McColgan finds that women indicted for murder over 1996–97 were about twice as likely as men to be convicted of manslaughter under s 2(1): 'General Defences' in D Nicolson and L Bibbings (eds) *Feminist Perspectives on Criminal Law* (London: Cavendish Press, 2000) 137, 140; see also Law Commission for England and Wales *Partial Defences to Murder* (Law Com No 290, 2004) Appendix B para 8.

[113] *Partial Defences to Murder* para 5.36 and Appendix B para 21.

[114] *Partial Defences to Murder* paras 5.34, 5.39 and Appendix B para 21.

[115] *Partial Defences to Murder* Appendix B para 23.

[116] I take this up in my discussion of the law on infanticide: see Chapter 8.

[117] In her study of the operation of the defence in the first two years of its life, Barbara Wootton finds that a diminished responsibility plea was accepted in more than two thirds of cases where the defence was argued (Wootton 'Diminished Responsibility: A Layman's View' 225). However, by 1986–88, the success rate of the defence had dropped to 42 per cent (Mackay *Mental Condition Defences* 181). The numbers of successful pleas has declined further in the years since then. Mackay found that there were 78 cases in which the diminished responsibility defence was successful in 1992 but only 49 in 1996 (Mackay 'The Abnormality of Mind Factor in Diminished Responsibility' 117). In a recent study commissioned by the Law Commission for England and Wales, Mackay found that between 1997 and 2001, there were a total of 171 successful pleas of diminished responsibility (*Partial Defences to Murder* (Law Com No 290, 2004) Appendix B para 6).

[118] *Partial Defences to Murder* Appendix B para 5. The introduction of the defence of diminished responsibility has been accompanied by a decline in the use of insanity (and unfitness to plead) in murder trials (Mackay 'Diminished Responsibility and Mentally Disordered Killers' 59 and Mackay *Mental Condition Defences* 181; Walker *Crime and Insanity in England (Vol 1)* 158), which suggests that diminished responsibility has been raised by defendants who previously would have relied on the insanity defence (Mackay 'Diminished Responsibility and Mentally Disordered Killers' 56; Sparks '"Diminished Responsibility" in Theory and Practice' 32).

[119] As reflected in the House of Lords decision of *R v Smith (Morgan)* [2001] 1 Cr App R 3, under this approach, the objective part of the provocation test was interpreted such that particular characteristics of the defendant (including, in that case, depression) could be attributed to the reasonable man for the purposes of determining the degree of self-control that could be expected of him. This approach

(and perhaps judges and lawyers) have come to be more cynical about the use of labels of mental illness to (partially) exculpate those who are charged with criminal acts.[120] Over and above all this, another broader extra-legal current may be affecting diminished responsibility practices. Given the prominence of expert evidence in the doctrine, it is not unreasonable to suggest that broader social changes associated with late modernity, and its paradigmatic decline in the faith in experts, may play into the reception of claims to diminished responsibility, backed up by the de facto requirement of expert evidence.[121] It is notable that it is in this context that a quasi-causal link between the 'abnormality of mental functioning' and the killing—tightening up the relationship between the two—has been introduced.

The Difference Diminished Responsibility Makes

In criminal law scholarship, the predominant way of conceptualizing the difference diminished responsibility makes is in terms of degree. On the basis that certain conditions that affect a defendant's mental capacity are relevant to liability (not just to sentence), but merely *reduce* rather than abrogate his or her criminal responsibility, extant conceptual analyses of diminished responsibility have coalesced around the idea of diminished responsibility as a partial excuse. On this approach, diminished responsibility is located within a schema of defences by normative type, a schema I discuss in Chapter 2. There are two streams of analysis of diminished responsibility as a partial excuse, and I discuss each in turn.

In the first stream of normative analysis, scholars critique diminished responsibility for its incoherence. For instance, in relation to the 1957 version of the doctrine, Edward Griew argues that diminished responsibility has 'clumsily compacted' two ideas—impaired capacity and diminished liability—'by virtue of a "third idea"', reduced culpability.[122] According to this analysis, diminished responsibility is structured such that a reduction in sentence depends on a defendant's reduced capacity, which is itself considered to reduce blameworthiness for the killing he or she committed. This structure is criticized because it assumes that

---

to provocation was disapproved in *Attorney-General for Jersey v Holley* [2005] 2 AC 580 in 2005. The Privy Council held that the only characteristics of the defendant that were relevant to the objective test are his or her age and sex (*Attorney-General for Jersey v Holley* [2005] 2 AC 580, 591 per Lord Nicholls). The pre-*Holley* approach to provocation that encompassed abnormal mental states may have meant that some matters in which diminished responsibility would have been raised were instead decided via provocation.

[120] There was some evidence of these concerns in the empirical survey of popular attitudes to partial defences to murder, conducted by Barry Mitchell, and commissioned for the Law Commission's 2004 report. Mitchell concluded that survey participants accepted expert evidence when it was 'clear and unequivocal' but also expressed 'some cynicism or skepticism about the reliability of psychiatric evidence' in relation to diminished responsibility (Law Commission for England and Wales *Partial Defences to Murder* (Law Com No 290, 2004) Appendix C para 77).

[121] See Chapter 6 for a discussion in the context of insanity.

[122] Griew 'The Future of Diminished Responsibility' 81–2.

liability for punishment is something that can be *impaired*.[123] But, as Richard Sparks points out in a widely-cited analysis, 'to say that we are less willing to blame ... a man if he does something wrong surely does not mean "we are willing to blame him less, if he does something wrong"'.[124] Even if liability could be said to be impaired, it is not clear precisely how a defendant's diminished capacity reduces his or her culpability. A number of theorists conclude that the process of reducing liability on the basis of capacity in effect tracks moral-evaluative lines, meaning that the plea succeeds for those defendants whose liability for killing *ought* to be reduced.[125] Some of the theorists who critique diminished responsibility on the basis of its incoherence conclude that the doctrine should either provide full exculpation,[126] or that it should be abolished.[127] Other theorists conclude that, despite the theoretical incoherence of diminished responsibility, in practice, it operates in a pragmatic way.[128]

By contrast, in the second of the two streams conceptualizing diminished responsibility as a partial excuse, scholars defend the doctrine as a coherent instantiation of criminal law principles. Thus, in Herbert Fingarette's words, a successful diminished responsibility plea marks out a defendant who 'did have sufficient rationality to grasp the criminal purport of his conduct up to a significant point, though not its full heinousness'.[129] Here, diminished responsibility is analogous to insanity, merely weakening rather than destroying the propriety of assigning responsibility to a defendant for his or her acts. The difference between diminished responsibility and insanity becomes one of degree.[130] In Martin Wasik's analysis, as partial excuses, diminished responsibility and provocation (now replaced by 'loss of control') may be thought to be midway on a 'scale of excuse', with excuses with the maximum 'moral pressure for exculpation' (such as automatism) at one end, and those which 'may be morally significant [but] are outweighed by practical and policy considerations' (such as good motive) at the other.[131] On this basis, commentators in this stream hold that diminished responsibility and provoca-

---

[123] Sparks '"Diminished Responsibility" in Theory and Practice' 18.
[124] '"Diminished Responsibility" in Theory and Practice' 16.
[125] See, for example, Griew 'The Future of Diminished Responsibility' 82; Horder *Excusing Crime* 155; Smith and Wilson, 'Impaired Voluntariness and Criminal Responsibility' 89. In speculating about how the defence might work in practice, Griew posits that, in deciding whether to grant a defence of diminished responsibility, the jury may 'set the defendant's abnormality and its effects upon him against the character of the offence': 'The Future of Diminished Responsibility' 83.
[126] See, eg, Sparks '"Diminished Responsibility" in Theory and Practice' 17.
[127] See, eg, Arenella 'The Diminished Capacity and Diminished Responsibility Defenses' 863–5.
[128] See, eg, Griew 'The Future of Diminished Responsibility' 87; N Lacey 'Partial Defences to Homicide: Questions of Power and Principle in Imperfect and Less Imperfect Worlds' in A Ashworth and B J Mitchell (eds) *Rethinking English Homicide Law* (Oxford: OUP, 2000) 111; Mackay 'Diminished Responsibility and Mentally Disordered Killers' 60 and Mackay *Mental Condition Defences* 185.
[129] H Fingarette 'Diminished Mental Capacity as a Criminal Defence' (1974) 37(3) *Modern Law Review* 264, 275.
[130] J Dressler 'Reaffirming the Moral Legitimacy of the Doctrine of Diminished Capacity: A Brief Reply to Professor Morse' (1984) 75(3) *Journal of Criminal Law and Criminology* 953, 960; R G Meakin 'Diminished Responsibility: Some Arguments for a General Defence' (1988) 52 *Journal of Criminal Law* 406, 407.
[131] M Wasik 'Partial Excuses in Criminal Law' (1982) 45(5) *Modern Law Review* 516, 524–5.

tion are 'not simply strange aberrations of an otherwise clear and self-evident distinction between excusing conditions and mitigating excuses'[132] or, more forcefully, that diminished responsibility 'falls entirely unexceptionally within the pattern of mental capacity defences'.[133]

These conceptions of diminished responsibility as, happily or unhappily, midway on a 'scale of excuse' have an analogue in the descriptive legal scholarship. Here, diminished responsibility is also depicted as positioned at something of a midway point, but it is viewed as midway between a point at which there is no judicial discretion in sentencing (ie under the mandatory penalty of life for murder) and a point where judicial discretion pertains, but a jury has no jurisdiction over the issue (ie if diminished responsibility is a factor in mitigation only). That is, in this body of legal scholarship, diminished responsibility is a product of the mandatory penalty for murder,[134] and the current, only minimally disaggregated law of homicide.[135] Viewed in the shadow of the mandatory penalty for murder, and within the broad structure of the law of homicide, on this account, diminished responsibility is regarded as a matter of practical necessity (even if otherwise undesirable). As the sentencing tail is wagging the diminished responsibility dog on this account, it implies that any difference connoted by diminished responsibility is more apparent than real. After all, if it could be dealt with on sentence, then perhaps there is nothing in particular to distinguish diminished defendants from any other defendants.

My analysis of the historical development of diminished responsibility leads me to conclude that diminished responsibility relies on an idea of difference that is most accurately thought of as one of kind rather than one of degree and I suggest that approaching it this way generates a closer understanding of the doctrine than existing accounts provide. Facilitated in part by the restriction of diminished responsibility to a particular kind of act—killing—diminished responsibility does not fit easily into the neat dichotomy between the act and actor that pervades scholarly thinking about defences. In a way that is clearer still with the addition of a requirement that a quasi-causal relation exist between the 'abnormality of mental functioning' and the act of killing under the new version of diminished responsibility, the doctrine does

---

[132] 'Partial Excuses in Criminal Law' 524.
[133] Fingarette 'Diminished Mental Capacity as a Criminal Defence' 274.
[134] The mandatory penalty is often invoked to explain the ongoing existence of diminished responsibility. See, for example, H Allen *Justice Unbalanced: Gender, Psychiatry and Judicial Decisions* (Milton Keynes: Open University Press, 1987) 117; Gordon *The Criminal Law of Scotland* 452. By corollary, several commentators have suggested that the diminished responsibility defence would be unnecessary if the mandatory penalty for murder was abolished (see, for example, Walker *Crime and Insanity in England (Vol 1)* 162; Law Commission for England and Wales *Partial Defences to Murder* (Law Com No 290, 2004) para 5.11).
[135] According to some writers, like the former partial defence of provocation, diminished responsibility owes its existence not so much to the mandatory penalty but to the structure of the law of homicide. According to this argument, because murder and manslaughter prohibit the same kind of conduct (killing), partial excuses are necessary to distinguish among defendants who fall within 'broad bands of culpability': Wasik 'Partial Excuses in Criminal Law' 530. As Wasik argues, partial defences accommodate pressure for the recognition of moral and legal subdivision in the law of homicide ('Partial Excuses in Criminal Law' 530).

something to the 'quality of the act' (as discussed above), but in a way that thoroughly implicates the actor. Understanding diminished responsibility to connote a qualitative rather than a quantitative difference takes seriously the notion of abnormality, which has been a consistent feature of the doctrine over time, and helps to account for the significance of expert medical evidence in decision-making around diminished responsibility. It is this idea of difference—difference in kind rather than difference in degree—that can be seen to underpin the way in which diminished responsibility slides between a doctrine of (partial) exculpation and one of (partial) inculpation: in effect, it is a doctrine that renders the defendant *differently* liable.

Some evidence in support of this analysis of diminished responsibility is provided by the recent judicial discussions of the appropriate boundary between it and the now-defunct provocation defence (which was abolished by the Coroners and Justice Act 2009 and replaced with the 'loss of control' defence).[136] These discussions revolved around the kind of characteristics that could be accorded to the reasonable person and be taken into account for the objective component of provocation.[137] As is well known, the provocation defence provided that, where an individual would otherwise be liable for murder, he [sic] could be held liable for manslaughter instead, if he had lost self-control as a consequence of provocation, and the provocation was 'enough to make a reasonable man do as he did'.[138] Provocation was generally considered to comprise a subjective test—whether the defendant himself actually lost self-control because of something that counted as provocation—and an objective test—whether a reasonable person, faced with the provocation, would have lost self-control, and, if so, whether he would have acted as the defendant did. In relation to the objective test, the rather thorny issue for the courts was what characteristics could be accorded to the reasonable person so that the jury would take them into account in making a decision about the defendant's actions.[139]

---

[136] Coroners and Justice Act 2009, ss 54–6, amending Homicide Act 1957, s 3. The new Act replaced provocation with a partial defence to murder which requires that the defendant killed as a result of a 'loss of self-control' (which had a 'qualifying trigger') and a person of the defendant's same sex and age, 'with a normal degree of tolerance and self restraint', and in the circumstances of the defendant might have reacted in the same way. See A Norrie 'The Coroners and Justice Act 2009—Partial Defences to Murder (1) Loss of Control' [2010] *Criminal Law Review* 275 for discussion.

[137] The courts' answer to this question has varied according to whether the characteristic is alleged to have affected the gravity of the provocation or to have rendered the defendant less able to control him or herself (ie more provokable). In relation to the former, all kinds of characteristics including discreditable ones, may be taken into account if they become the subject of the taunt to which the defendant reacts. In relation to the latter, the approach has been more restrictive, with the reasonable person standard used to exclude 'unusual' people from the protection of the defence. In an early decision on this part of the reasonable person test, *DPP v Camplin* [1978] AC 705, the House of Lords held that, for the purposes of determining whether a reasonable person would have done as the defendant did, the reasonable person is to be accorded only the defendant's age and sex. See now Coroners and Justice Act 2009, s 54(1)(c), abolishing provocation as set down in Homicide Act 1957, s 3.

[138] See Homicide Act 1957, s 3.

[139] See further A P Simester et al *Simester and Sullivan's Criminal Law* 381.

Differences of Degree and Differences of Kind: Diminished Responsibility 257

At one end of the spectrum of possible approaches to this issue lies the House of Lords decision in *Smith (Morgan)*.[140] Here, the approach the Court adopted to the question of the characteristics of the reasonable person was expansive and openly moral-evaluative. In this case, the defendant was charged with killing a friend who he believed had stolen his carpenter's tools. At trial, Smith pleaded a lack of *mens rea*, provocation, and diminished responsibility. Smith was convicted of murder, and appealed, arguing against the trial judge's direction to the jury that it could not take his severe depressive illness into account when deciding whether an ordinary person would have lost his self-control. The House of Lords upheld the Court of Appeal decision, in which manslaughter was substituted for murder, and, in doing so, adopted an expansive approach to the scope of the objective component of provocation. The House of Lords held that the objective component of the defence means that 'the jury can legitimately "give weight to factors personal to the prisoner in considering a plea of provocation"'.[141] This meant that, if it grants provocation, the jury must conclude that 'the circumstances were such as to make the loss of self-control sufficiently *excusable* to reduce the gravity of the offence from murder to manslaughter'.[142] In his judgment, Lord Hoffman stated that the jury 'may think that there was some characteristic of the accused, whether temporary or permanent, which affected the degree of control which society could reasonably have expected of *him* and which it would be unjust not to take into account. If the jury take this view, they are at liberty to give effect to it.'[143] In Lord Hoffman's words, it would be 'wrong to assume that there is a neat dichotomy between the "ordinary person" contemplated by the law of provocation and the "abnormal person" contemplated by the law of diminished responsibility'.[144]

At the other end of the spectrum of possible approaches to the scope of provocation, and by contrast with the broad and overtly morally evaluative approach adopted in *Smith (Morgan)*, lies the 2005 Privy Council decision of *Attorney-General v Holley*[145] The Privy Council took a narrow approach to the question of which of the defendant's characteristics could be taken into account for the objective part of the provocation defence. The Privy Council concluded that the question for the jury was '[w]hether the provocative act or words and the defendant's response met the "ordinary person" standard prescribed by the statute is ... not the altogether looser question of whether, having regard to all the circumstances, the jury consider the loss of self-control was sufficiently excusable'.[146] The Privy Council stated that:

[t]he powers of self-control possessed by *ordinary* people vary according to their age and, more doubtfully, their sex. These features are to be contrasted with abnormalities, that is,

---

[140] *R v Smith (Morgan)* [2001] 1 Cr App R 31.
[141] *R v Smith (Morgan)* [2001] 1 Cr App R 31, 38 per Lord Slynn (extracting words of the Royal Commission on Capital Punishment Report 1953).
[142] *R v Smith (Morgan)* [2001] 1 Cr App R 31, 58.
[143] *R v Smith (Morgan)* [2001] 1 Cr App R 31, 58.
[144] *R v Smith (Morgan)* [2001] 1 Cr App R 31, 52.
[145] *Attorney-General v Holley* [2005] 2 AC 580.
[146] *Attorney-General v Holley* [2005] 2 AC 580, 593.

features not found in a person having ordinary powers of self-control. The former are relevant when identifying and applying the objective standard of self-control, the latter are not.[147]

As these comments make clear, the *Holley* decision tightened up the distinction between provocation and diminished responsibility, and in doing so, reinscribed a bright line between 'normality' and 'abnormality' in criminal law.

These judicial machinations about the characteristics that may be appropriately attributed to the reasonable person for the purposes of provocation reveal that, as Andrew Ashworth suggests, the provocation defence was for defendants who are in a broad sense mentally normal.[148] By contrast, the partially exculpatory doctrine of diminished responsibility applies to abnormal defendants. These machinations hint at the profound significance of the normal/abnormal distinction for the criminal law and the disruption that flows from any blurring of the boundaries between these two states.

---

[147] *Attorney-General v Holley* [2005] 2 AC 580, 591. In *R v James; R v Karimi* [2006] 1 Cr App R 440, the Court of Appeal held that *Holley*, rather than *Smith (Morgan)*, represented the English law.

[148] A Ashworth 'The Doctrine of Provocation' [1976] *Criminal Law Journal* 292, 312. Ashworth acknowledges, however, that it may not be the case that the law actually operates with such a clear distinction between diminished responsibility and provocation (314).

Bibliography

Ajzenstadt, M and Burtch, B 'Medicalization and Regulation of Alcohol and Alcoholism: The Professions and Disciplinary Measures' (1990) 13 *International Journal of Law and Psychiatry* 127.

Alldridge, P 'Forensic Science and Expert Evidence' (1994) 21(1) *Journal of Law and Society* 136.

Allen, H *Justice Unbalanced: Gender, Psychiatry and Judicial Decisions* (Milton Keynes: Open University Press, 1987).

Archard, D 'Philosophical Perspectives on Childhood' in J Fionda (ed) *Legal Concepts of Childhood* (Oxford: Hart Publishing, 2001).

Arenella, P 'The Diminished Capacity and Diminished Responsibility Defenses: Two Children of a Doomed Marriage' (1977) 77(6) *Columbia Law Review* 827.

Ashworth, A 'The Doctrine of Provocation' [1976] *Criminal Law Journal* 292.

—— *Principles of Criminal Law* (Oxford: Oxford University Press, 2009).

—— 'Child Defendants and the Doctrines of Criminal Law' in A Ashworth, E Clive, J Chalmers, F Leverick and L Farmer (eds) *Essays in Criminal Law in Honour of Sir Gerald Gordon* (Vol 8, Edinburgh Studies in Law, Edinburgh: Edinburgh University Press 2010).

Baker, E 'Human Rights, M'Naghten and the 1991 Act' [1994] *Criminal Law Review* 84.

Ball, C 'Young Offenders and the Youth Court' [1992] *Criminal Law Review* 277.

—— 'Youth Justice? Half a Century of Responses to Youth Offending' [2004] *Criminal Law Review* 28.

Bandalli, S 'Abolition of the Presumption of Doli Incapax and the Criminalisation of Children' (1998) 37(2) *The Howard Journal* 114.

Baron, M 'Excuses, Excuses' (2007) 1 *Law and Philosophy* 21.

Bartlett, R 'Legal Madness in the Nineteenth Century' (2001) 14(1) *Social History of Medicine* 107.

Beattie, J M 'The Criminality of Women in Eighteenth Century England' in D K Weisberg (ed) *Women and the Law: A Social History Perspective* (Cambridge MA: Schenkman Publishing, 1982).

—— *Crime and the Courts in England 1660–1800* (Oxford: Oxford University Press, 1986).

Bennion, F 'Mens Rea and Defendants Below the Age of Discretion' [2009] *Criminal Law Review* 757.

Bentley, M 'The Evolution and Dissemination of Historical Knowledge' in M Daunton (ed) *The Organisation of Knowledge in Victorian Britain* (Oxford: Oxford University Press, 2005).

Birdwell, J et al *Taking Drugs Seriously: A Demos and UK Drug Commission Report on Legal Highs* (2009) available at <http://www.ukdpc.org.uk/index.shtml> (last accessed 29 September 2011).

Böhme, G 'Midwifery as Science: An Essay on the Relationship between Scientific and Everyday Knowledge' in N Stehr and V Meja (eds) *Society and Knowledge: Contemporary Perspectives in the Sociology of Knowledge and Science* (New Brunswick: Transaction Publishers, 2005).

Boland, F 'Intoxication and Criminal Liability' (1996) 60 *Journal of Criminal Law* 100.
Bottoms, A and Dignan, J 'Youth Justice in Great Britain' (2004) 31 *Crime and Justice* 21.
Bugg, S 'Intoxication and Liability: A Criminal Law Cocktail' (1984–1987) 5 *Auckland University Law Review* 144.
Burke, P *A Social History of Knowledge: From Gutenberg to Diderot* (Cambridge: Polity Press, 2000).
Burney, I *Bodies of Evidence: Medicine and the Politics of the English Inquest, 1830–1926* (Baltimore: Johns Hopkins University Press, 2000).
Bynum, W F 'Rationales for Therapy in British Psychiatry 1780–1835' in A Scull (ed) *Madhouses, Mad-Doctors and Madmen: The Social History of Psychiatry in the Victorian Era* (London: Athlone Press, 1981).
—— *Science and the Practice of Medicine in the Nineteenth Century* (Cambridge: Cambridge University Press, 1994).
Cairns, D J A *Advocacy and the Making of the Adversarial Criminal Trial, 1800–1865* (Oxford: Clarendon Press, 1998).
Campbell, I *Mental Disorder and Criminal Law in Australia and New Zealand* (Sydney: Butterworths, 1988).
Cartwright, R 'Sleepwalking Violence: A Sleep Disorder, a Legal Dilemma and a Psychological Challenge' (2004) 161 *American Journal of Psychiatry* 1149.
Chalmers, J and Leverick, F *Criminal Defences and Pleas in Bar of Trial* (Edinburgh: W Green, 2006).
Chiswick, D 'Psychiatric Testimony in Britain: Remembering your Lines and Keeping to the Script' (1992) 15(2) *International Journal of Law and Psychiatry* 171.
Clark, M J '"Morbid Introspection," Unsoundness of Mind, and British Psychological Medicine c.1830–1900' in W F Bynum, R Porter, and M Shepherd (eds) *The Anatomy of Madness: Essays in the History of Psychiatry* (London: Routledge, 1988).
Collini, S *Public Moralists: Political Thought and Intellectual Life in Britain, 1850–1930* (Oxford: Clarendon Press, 1991).
Collins, H and Evans, R *Rethinking Expertise* (Chicago: University of Chicago Press, 2007).
Colman, A and Mackay, R D 'Excluding Expert Evidence: A Tale of Ordinary Folk and Common Experience' [1991] *Criminal Law Review* 800.
Colvin, E 'Exculpatory Defences in Criminal Law' (1990) 10 *Oxford Journal of Legal Studies* 381.
Constable, M *The Law of the Other: The Mixed Jury and Changing Conceptions of Citizenship, Law and Knowledge* (Chicago: University of Chicago Press, 1991).
Crofts, T 'Catching Up with Europe: Taking the Age of Criminal Responsibility Seriously in England' (2000) 17(4) *European Journal of Crime, Criminal Law and Criminal Justice* 267.
—— *The Criminal Responsibility of Children and Young Persons: A Comparison of English and German Law* (Aldershot: Ashgate, 2002).
Cross, R 'Reflections on Bratty's Case' [1962] *Law Quarterly Review* 236.
Cunningham, H *The Children of the Poor* (London: Blackwell, 1991).
Dalston, L 'Marvelous Facts and Miraculous Evidence in Early Modern Europe' (1991) 18 *Critical Inquiry* 93.
Dashwood, A 'Logic and the Lords in Majewski' [1976] *Criminal Law Review* 532.
Daunton, M 'Introduction' in M Daunton (ed), *The Organisation of Knowledge in Victorian Britain* (Oxford: Oxford University Press, 2005).
Davies, O *Witchcraft, Magic and Culture, 1736–1951* (Manchester: Manchester University Press, 1999).

Dear, P 'From Truth to Disinterestedness' (1992) 22(4) *Social Studies of Science* 619.

—— 'The Meanings of Experience' in K Park and L Dalston (eds) *The Cambridge History of Science Vol 3 Early Modern Science* (Cambridge: Cambridge University Press, 2006).

Dell, S 'Wanted: An Insanity Defence that Can be Used' [1983] *Criminal Law Review* 431.

—— *Murder into Manslaughter: The Diminished Responsibility Defence in Practice* (Oxford: Oxford University Press, 1984).

Dennis, I *The Law of Evidence* 4th edn (London: Sweet and Maxwell, 2010).

Diamond, B L 'The Origins of the "Right and Wrong" Test of Criminal Responsibility and its Subsequent Development in the United Sates: An Historical Survey' (1966) 53 *California Law Review* 1227.

—— 'On the Spelling of Daniel M'Naghten's Name' in D J West and A Walk (eds) *Daniel McNaughton: His Trial and the Aftermath* (Ashford: Gaskell Books, 1977).

Dickinson, R and Sharpe, J 'Infanticide in Early Modern England: The Court of Great Sessions at Chester, 1650–1800' in M Jackson (ed) *Infanticide: Historical Perspectives on Child Murder and Concealment, 1550–2000* (Aldershot: Ashgate, 2002).

Dingwall, G 'Intoxicated Mistakes and the Need for Self-Defence' (2007) 70(1) *Modern Law Review* 127.

Dobson, V and Sales, B 'The Science of Infanticide and Mental Illness' (2000) 6 *Psychology, Public Policy and Law* 1098.

Douglas, G 'The Child's Right to Make Mistakes: Criminal Responsibility and the Immature Minor' in G Douglas and L Sebba (eds) *Children's Rights and Traditional Values* (Aldershot: Ashgate, 1998).

Dressler, J 'Reaffirming the Moral Legitimacy of the Doctrine of Diminished Capacity: A Brief Reply to Professor Morse' (1984) 75(3) *Journal of Criminal Law and Criminology* 953.

—— 'Provocation: Partial Justification or Partial Excuse?' (1988) 51(4) *Modern Law Review* 467.

Dubber, M D 'Historical Analysis of Law' (1998) 16(1) *Law and History Review* 159.

—— and Farmer, L 'Introduction: Regarding Criminal Law Historically' in M D Dubber and L Farmer (eds) *Modern Histories of Crime and Punishment* (Stanford: Stanford University Press, 2007).

—— and Valverde, M 'Introduction: Perspectives on the Power and Science of Police' in M D Dubber and M Valverde, *The New Police Science: The Police Power in Domestic and International Governance* (Stanford: Stanford University Press, 2006).

Duff, R A *Trials and Punishments* (Cambridge: Cambridge University Press, 1986).

—— *Answering for Crime: Responsibility and Liability in the Criminal Law* (Oxford: Hart Publishing, 2007)

—— et al *The Trial on Trial (Vol 3): Towards a Normative Theory of the Criminal Trial* (Oxford: Hart Publishing, 2007).

Ebrahim, I, Fenwick, P, Marks, R and Peacock, K W 'Violence, Sleepwalking and the Criminal Law: Part 1: The Medical Aspects' [2005] *Criminal Law Review* 601.

Edmond, G 'The Law-Set: The Legal-Scientific Production of Medical Propriety' (2001) 26(2) *Science, Technology and Human Values* 191.

—— and Mercer, D 'Experts and Expertise in Legal and Regulatory Settings' in G Edmond (ed) *Expertise in Regulation and Law* (Aldershot: Ashgate, 2004).

Edwards, J 'Automatism and Criminal Responsibility' (1958) 21 *Modern Law Review* 375.

Eigen, J P '"I answer as a physician": Opinion as Fact in Pre-McNaughtan Insanity Trials' in M Clark and C Crawford (eds) *Legal Medicine in History* (Cambridge: Cambridge University Press, 1994).

Eigen, J P *Witnessing Insanity: Madness and Mad Doctors in the English Court* (New Haven: Yale University Press, 1995).

—— 'Criminal Lunacy in Early Modern England: Did Gender Make a Difference?' (1998) 21(4) *International Journal of Law and Psychiatry* 412.

—— 'Lesion of the Will: Medical Resolve and Criminal Responsibility in Victorian Insanity Trials' (1999) 33(2) *Law and Society Review* 425.

—— *Unconscious Crime: Mental Absence and Criminal Responsibility in Victorian London* (Baltimore: Johns Hopkins University Press, 2003).

—— 'Sense and Sensibility: Fateful Splitting in the Victorian Insanity Trial' in R A Melikan (ed) *Domestic and International Trials 1700–2000: The Trial In History Volume II* (Manchester; Manchester University Press, 2003).

—— 'Delusion's Odyssey: Charting the Course of Victorian Forensic Psychiatry' (2004) 27 (5) *International Journal of Law and Psychiatry* 395.

—— '"An Inducement to Morbid Minds": Politics and Madness in the Victorian Courtroom' in M D Dubber and L Farmer (eds) *Modern Histories of Crime and Punishment* (Berkeley: Stanford University Press, 2007).

—— and Andoll, G 'From Mad-Doctor to Forensic Witness: The Evolution of Early English Court Psychiatry' (1986) 8 *International Journal of Law and Psychiatry* 159.

Elliott, I D 'Automatism and Trial by Jury' (1967–1968) 6 *Melbourne University Law Review* 53.

Emmins, C 'Unfitness to Plead: Thoughts Prompted by Glenn Pearson's Case' [1986] *Criminal Law Review* 604.

Emsley, C *Crime and Society in England 1750–1900* (London: Pearson Longman, 2005).

Fairall, P 'Automatism' (1981) 5 *Criminal Law Journal* 335.

—— 'Voluntariness, Automatism and Insanity: Reflections on Falconer' (1993) 17 *Criminal Law Journal* 81.

Farmer, L 'The Obsession with Definition: The Nature of Crime and Critical Legal Theory' (1996) 5 *Social and Legal Studies* 57.

—— *Criminal Law, Tradition and Legal Order: Crime and the Genius of Scots Law 1747 to the Present* (Cambridge: Cambridge University Press, 1997).

—— 'Reconstructing the English Codification Debate: The Criminal Law Commissioners, 1833-45' (2000) 18(2) *Law and History Review* 397.

—— 'Arthur and Oscar (and Sherlock): The Reconstructive Trial and the "Hermeneutics of Suspicion"' (2007) 5(1) *International Commentary on Evidence* 1.

—— 'Time and Space in Criminal Law' (2010) 13 *New Criminal Law Review* 333.

—— *The Metamorphosis of Theft: Property and Criminalisation* (forthcoming).

Fennell, P 'The Criminal Procedure (Insanity and Unfitness to Plead) Act 1991' (1992) 55 *Modern Law Review* 547.

Fenwick, P 'Somnambulism and the Law: A Review' (1987) 5(3) *Behaviourial Sciences and the Law* 343.

—— 'Epilepsy, Automatism and the English Law' (1997) 16 *Medicine and the Law* 349.

Ferguson, P W 'Reverse Burdens of Proof' (2004) 22 *Scots Law Times* 133.

Fingarette, H 'Diminished Mental Capacity as a Criminal Defence' (1974) 37(3) *Modern Law Review* 264.

—— 'Disabilities of Mind and Criminal Responsibility—A Unitary Doctrine' (1976) 76(2) *Columbia Law Review* 236.

Fionda, J 'Youth and Justice' in J Fionda (ed) *Legal Concepts of Childhood* (Oxford: Hart Publishing, 2001).

Fletcher, G P 'Two Kinds of Legal Rules: A Comparative Study of Burden-of-Persuasion Practices in Criminal Cases' (1968) 77 *Yale Law Journal* 880.
—— 'The Right and the Reasonable' (1985) 98 *Harvard Law Journal* 949.
—— 'The Nature of Justification' in J Horder and J Gardner (eds) *Action and Value in Criminal Law* (Oxford: Clarendon Press, 1993).
—— *Rethinking Criminal Law* (Oxford: Oxford University Press, 2000).
Forbes, T *Surgeons at the Bailey: English Forensic Medicine to 1878* (New Haven: Yale University Press, 1985).
Foucault, M *Discipline and Punish: The Birth of the Prison* (New York: Pantheon Books, 1977).
—— *History of Madness* (London: Routledge, 2006).
Freckelton, I 'Rationality and Flexibility in Assessment of Fitness to Stand Trial' (1996) 19 (1) *International Journal of Law and Psychiatry* 39.
Freeman, M 'The James Bulger Tragedy: Childish Innocence and the Construction of Guilt' in A McGillivray (ed) *Governing Childhood* (Dartmouth: Aldershot, 1997).
Frost, G S *Victorian Childhoods* (Westport, CT: Praeger Publishers, 2009).
Fulford, K W M 'Value, Action, Mental Illness and the Law' in S Shute, J Gardner and J Horder (eds) *Action and Value in the Criminal Law* (Oxford: Clarendon Press, 1993).
Fuller, S 'Disciplinary Boundaries and the Rhetoric of the Social Sciences' in E Messer-Davidow et al (eds) *Knowledge: Historical and Critical Studies in Disciplinarity* (Charlottesville and London: University of Virginia Press, 1993).
Gardner, J 'The Gist of Excuses' (1998) 1(2) *Buffalo Criminal Law Review* 575.
—— *Offences and Defences: Selected Essays in the Philosophy of Criminal Law* (Oxford: Oxford University Press, 2007).
Gardner, S 'The Importance of Majewski' (1994) 14(2) *Oxford Journal of Legal Studies* 279.
Garland, D *Punishment and Welfare: A History of Penal Strategies* (Aldershot: Gower, 1985).
—— *The Culture of Control: Crime and Social Order in Contemporary Society* (Oxford: Oxford University Press, 2001).
Gelsthorpe, L 'Recent Changes in Youth Justice Policy in England and Wales' in E Weijers and A Duff (eds) *Punishing Juveniles: Principle and Critique* (Oxford: Hart Publishing, 2002).
Giddens, A *The Consequences of Modernity* (Cambridge: Polity Press, 1990).
—— *Modernity and Self-Identity: Self and Society in the Late Modern Age* (Berkeley: Stanford University Press, 1991).
—— 'Living in a Post-traditional Society' in U Beck et al (eds) *Reflexive Modernization: Politics, Tradition and Aesthetics in the Modern Social Order* (Stanford: Stanford University Press, 1994).
Gold, A D 'An Untrimmed "Beard": The Law of Intoxication as a Defence to a Criminal Charge' (1976–77) 19 *Criminal Law Quarterly* 34.
Goode, M 'On Subjectivity and Objectivity in Denial of Responsibility: Reflections on Reading Radford' (1987) 11 *Criminal Law Journal* 131.
Gordon, G H *The Criminal Law of Scotland* (Edinburgh: W Green, 2000).
Gotlieb, A E 'Intention, and Knowing the Nature and Quality of an Act' (1956) 19(3) *Modern Law Review* 270.
Gough, S 'Intoxication and Criminal Liability: The Law Commission's Proposed Reforms' (1996) 112 *Law Quarterly Review* 335.
Green, T A 'A Retrospective on the Criminal Trial Jury, 1200–1800' in J Cockburn and T A Green (eds) *Twelve Good Men and True: The Criminal Trial Jury 1200–1800* (Princeton: Princeton University Press, 1988).

Griew, E 'Let's Implement Butler on Mental Disorder and Crime!' [1984] *Current Legal Problems* 47.

—— 'States of Mind, Presumptions and Inferences' in P Smith (ed) *Criminal Law; Essays in Honour of JC Smith* (London: Butterworths, 1987).

—— 'The Future of Diminished Responsibility' [1988] *Criminal Law Review* 75.

Grubin, D 'Unfit to Plead in England and Wales, 1976–1988 A Survey' (1991) 158 *British Journal of Psychiatry* 540.

—— 'Regaining Unfitness to Plead: Patients found Unfit to Plead who Return for Trial' (1992) 2(2) *Journal of Forensic Psychiatry* 140.

—— 'What Constitutes Fitness to Plead?' [1993] *Criminal Law Review* 748.

Hacking, I *The Taming of Chance* (Cambridge: Cambridge University Press, 1990).

Hale, M *Historia placitorum coronae (The history of the pleas of the crown)* (1st American edn by W A Stokes and E Ingersoll, Vol 1 Philadelphia, 1847), in *The Making of Modern Law* <http://galenet.galegroup.com.ezproxy1.library.usyd.edu.au/servlet/MOML?af=RN&ae=F3704917452&srchtp=a&ste=14> (last accessed 26 September 2011).

Hall, J 'Intoxication and Criminal Responsibility' (1944) 57(7) *Harvard Law Journal* 1045.

Hall, R 'Presuming' (1961) 11(42) *The Philosophical Quarterly* 10.

Hall Williams, J E 'The Homicide Act 1957' (1957) 20(4) *Modern Law Review* 381.

Hart, H L A *Punishment and Responsibility: Essays in the Philosophy of Law* (Oxford; Oxford University Press, 2008).

Hay, D 'Property, Authority and the Criminal Law' in D Hay, P Linebaugh, J G Rule, E P Thompson and C Winslow (eds) *Albion's Fatal Tress: Crime and Society in Eighteenth Century England* (London: Allen Lane, 1975).

Haydon, D and Scraton, P '"Condemn a Little More, Understand a Little Less": The Political Context and Rights Implications of the Domestic and European Rules in the Venables-Thompson Case' (2000) 27(3) *Journal of Law and Society* 416.

Hayes, S C 'Diminished Responsibility: The Expert Witness' Viewpoint' in S Yeo (ed) *Partial Excuses to Murder* (Sydney: Federation Press, 1991).

Herrup, C *The Common Peace* (Cambridge: Cambridge University Press, 1987).

Ho, H L 'The Legitimacy of Medieval Proof' (2003–04) 19(2) *Journal of law and Religion* 259.

—— *A Philosophy of Evidence Law* (Oxford: Oxford University Press, 2008).

Hodgson, J 'Conceptions of the Trial in Inquisitorial and Adversarial Procedure' in A Duff et al *The Trial on Trial (Vol 2): Judgment and Calling to Account* (Oxford: Hart Publishing, 2006) 223.

Hoffer, P and Hull, N E H *Murdering Mothers: Infanticide in England and New England 1558–1803* (New York: New York University Press, 1984).

Horder, J 'Sobering Up? The Law Commission on Criminal Intoxication' (1995) 58(4) *Modern Law Review* 534.

—— *Excusing Crime* (Oxford: Oxford University Press, 2004).

Hörnle, T 'Social Expectations in the Criminal Law: The "Reasonable Person" in a Comparative Perspective' (2008) 11 *New Criminal Law Review* 1.

Howard, C and D'Orban, P T 'Violence in Sleep: Medico-Legal Issues and Two Case Reports' (1987) 17 *Psychological Medicine* 915.

Hughes, G 'The English Homicide Act of 1957: The Capital Punishment Issues, and Various Reforms in the Law of Murder and Manslaughter' (1959) 49(6) *Journal of Criminal Law, Criminology and Police Science* 521.

Jackson, M *New-Born Child Murder: Women, Illegitimacy and the Courts in Eighteenth Century England* (Manchester: Manchester University Press, 1996).

—— 'Infanticide: Historical Perspectives' (1996) 146 *New Law Journal* 416.

—— 'The Trial of Harriet Vooght: Continuity and Change in the History of Infanticide' in M Jackson (ed) *Infanticide: Historical Perspectives on Child Murder and Concealment 1550–2000* (Aldershot: Ashgate, 2002).

Jareborg, N *Scraps of Penal Theory* (Uppsala: Iustus Forlag, 2002).

Johnstone, G 'From Vice to Disease? The Concepts of Dipsomania and Inebriety, 1860–1908' (1996) 5 *Social and Legal Studies* 37.

Jones, C. A *Expert Witnesses: Science, Medicine and the Practice of Law* (Oxford: Clarendon Press, 1994).

Jones, T H 'Insanity, Automatism and the Burden of Proof on the Accused' (1995) 111 *Law Quarterly Review* 475.

Jordan, T E *Victorian Childhood: Themes and Variations* (New York, State University of New York Press, 1987).

Kadish, S 'Excusing Crime' [1987] *California Law Review* 257.

Kaye, J M 'The Early History of Murder and Manslaughter' (1967) 83 *Law Quarterly Review* 365.

Kean, A W G 'The History of the Criminal Liability of Children' (1937) 53 *Law Quarterly Review* 364.

Kearns, G and Mackay, R D 'The Trial of the Facts and Unfitness to Plead' [1997] *Criminal Law Review* 644.

Keating, H 'The Responsibility of Children in the Criminal Law' [2007] *Child and Family Law Quarterly* 183.

—— 'Reckless Children?' [2007] *Criminal Law Review* 546.

Kelman, M 'Interpretive Construction in the Substantive Criminal Law' (1980–1981) 33 *Stanford Law Review* 591.

Kendall, K 'Beyond Reason: Social Constructions of Mentally Disordered Female Offenders' in W Chan et al (eds) *Women, Madness and the Law: A Feminist Reader* (London: GlassHouse Press, 2005).

Kerlman, D. 'Was the Jury Ever Self-Informing?' in M. Mulholland and B. Pullan (eds) *Judicial Trials in England and Europe 1200–1700* (Manchester: Manchester University Press, 2003).

King, P 'Decision-Makers and Decision-Making in the English Criminal Law 1750–1800' (1984) 27(1) *Historical Journal* 25.

—— *Crime, Justice and Discretion in England 1740–1820* (Oxford: Oxford University Press, 2000).

Lacey, N 'A Clear Concept of Intention? Elusive or Illusory?' (1993) 56(5) *Modern Law Review* 621.

—— 'Abstraction in Context' (1994) 14(2) *Oxford Journal of Legal Studies* 255.

—— *Unspeakable Subjects: Feminist Essays in Legal and Social Theory* (Oxford: Hart Publishing, 1998).

—— 'Philosophy, History and Criminal Law Theory' (1998) 1 *Buffalo Criminal Law Review* 295.

—— 'Partial Defences to Homicide: Questions of Power and Principle in Imperfect and Less Imperfect Worlds' in A Ashworth and B J Mitchell (eds) *Rethinking English Homicide Law* (Oxford: Oxford University Press, 2000).

—— 'Philosophical Foundations of the Common Law: Social not Metaphysical' in J Horder (ed) *Oxford Essays in Jurisprudence* (Oxford: Oxford University Press, 2001).

—— 'Responsibility and Modernity in Criminal Law' (2001) 9(3) *Journal of Political Philosophy* 249.

Lacey, N 'In Search of the Responsible Subject: History, Philosophy and Social Sciences in Criminal Law Theory' (2001) 64(3) *Modern Law Review* 350.
—— 'Character, Capacity, Outcome: Towards a Framework for Assessing the Shifting Pattern of Criminal Responsibility in Modern English Law' in M D Dubber and L Farmer (eds) *Modern Histories of Crime and Punishment* (Stanford: Stanford University Press, 2007).
—— 'Space, Time and Function: Intersecting Principles of Responsibility Across the Terrain of Criminal Justice' (2007) 1 *Criminal Law and Philosophy* 233.
—— *Women, Crime and Character: From Moll Flanders to Tess of the D'Urbervilles* (Oxford: Oxford University Press, 2008).
—— 'Historicising Criminalisation: Conceptual and Empirical Issues' (2009) 72(6) *Modern Law Review* 936.
—— 'Psychologising Jekyll, Demonising Hyde: The Strange Case of Criminal Responsibility' (2010) 4 *Criminal Law and Philosophy* 109.
Landsman, S 'Of Witches, Madmen and Products Liability: An Historical Survey of the Use of Expert Testimony' (1995) 13 *Behavioral Sciences and the Law* 131.
—— 'One Hundred Tears of Rectitude: Medical Witnesses at the Old Bailey, 1717–1817' (1998) 16(3) *Law and History Review* 445.
Langbein, J H *Torture and the Law of Proof: Europe and England in the Ancien Regime* (Chicago: University of Chicago Press, 1977).
—— *The Origins of the Adversary Criminal Trial* (Oxford: Oxford University Press, 2003).
Larkin, E P and Collins, P J 'Fitness to Plead and Psychiatric Reports' (1989) 29(1) *Medicine, Science and the Law* 26.
Lawrence, C 'Incommunicable Knowledge: Science, Technology and the Clinical Art in Britain 1850–1914' (1986) 20(4) *Journal of Contemporary History* 503.
—— *Medicine in the Making of Modern Britain* (London: Routledge, 1994).
Lederman, E 'Non-Insane and Insane Automatism: Reducing the Significance of a Problematic Distinction' (1985) 34 *International and Comparative Law Quarterly* 819.
Levi, R and Valverde, M 'Knowledge on Tap: Police Science and Common Knowledge in the Legal Regulation of Drunkenness' (2001) 26(4) *Law and Social Inquiry* 819.
Levy, N and Bayne, T 'Doing without Deliberation: Automatism, Automaticity and Moral Accountability' (2004) 16(3) *International Review of Psychiatry* 209.
Loughnan, A 'Manifest Madness: Towards A New Understanding of the Insanity Defence' (2007) 70(3) *Modern Law Review* 397.
—— '"In a Kind of Mad Way": A Historical Perspective on Evidence and Proof of Mental Incapacity' (2011) 35(3) *Melbourne University Law Review* 1047.
—— 'Mental Incapacity Doctrines in Criminal Law' (2012) 15(1) *New Criminal Law Review* 1.
—— 'The Expertise of Non-Experts: Expert and Lay Knowledges of Intoxication in Criminal Law' in J Herring et al (eds) *Intoxication: Problematic Pleasures* (London: Routledge, 2012).
—— 'The Strange Case of the Infanticide Doctrine' (2012) 32(4) *Oxford Journal of Legal Studies*.
Lynch, A C E 'The Scope of Intoxication' [1982] *Criminal Law Review* 139.
Lynch, M 'Circumscribing Expertise: Membership Categories in Courtroom Testimony' in S Jasanoff (ed) *States of Knowledge: The Co-production of Science and Social Order* (London: Routledge, 2004).
Lyons, B 'Dying to be Responsible: Adolescence, Autonomy and Responsibility' (2010) 30(2) *Legal Studies* 257.

Mackay, R D 'The Automatism Defence—What Price Rejection?' (1983) 34(1) *Northern Ireland Legal Quarterly* 81.

—— 'Craziness and Codification—Revising the Automatism and Insanity Defences' in I Dennis (ed) *Criminal Law and Justice* (London: Sweet and Maxwell, 1987).

—— 'Fact and Fiction About the Insanity Defence' [1990] *Criminal Law Review* 247.

—— 'The Decline of Disability in Relation to the Trial' [1991] *Criminal Law Review* 87.

—— *Mental Condition Defences in the Criminal Law* (Oxford: Clarendon Press, 1995).

—— 'The Abnormality of Mind Factor in Diminished Responsibility' [1999] *Criminal Law Review* 117.

—— 'Diminished Responsibility and Mentally Disordered Killers' in A Ashworth and B J Mitchell (eds) *Rethinking English Homicide Law* (Oxford: Oxford University Press, 2000).

—— 'Mentally Abnormal Offenders: Disposal and Criminal Responsibility Issues' in M McConville and G Wilson (eds) *The Handbook of the Criminal Justice Process* (Oxford: Oxford University Press, 2002).

—— 'On Being Insane in Jersey: Part 3—The Case of Attorney General v O'Driscoll' [2004] *Criminal Law Review* 291.

—— 'Infanticide and Related Diminished Responsibility Manslaughters: An Empirical Study' Appendix D, Law Commission for England and Wales *Murder, Manslaughter, and Infanticide* (Law Com No 304, 2006).

—— 'Unfitness to Plead–Data on Formal Findings from 2002 to 2008' Appendix C, Law Commission for England and Wales *Unfitness to Plead: A Consultation Paper* (Law Com No 197, 2010).

—— 'The Coroners and Justice Act 2009—Partial Defences to Murder (2) The New Diminished Responsibility Plea' [2010] *Criminal Law Review* 290.

—— and Colman, A 'Equivocal Rulings on Expert Psychological and Psychiatric Evidence: Turning a Muddle into a Nonsense' [1996] *Criminal Law Review* 88.

—— and Kearns, G 'More Fact(s) About the Insanity Defence' [1999] *Criminal Law Review* 714.

—— and Kearns, G 'An Upturn in Unfitness to Plead? Disability in Relation to the Trial Under the 1991 Act' [2000] *Criminal Law Review* 532.

—— and Mitchell, B J 'Sleepwalking, Automatism and Insanity' [2006] *Criminal Law Review* 901.

——, Mitchell, B J and Howe, L 'Yet More Facts about the Insanity Defence' [2006] *Criminal Law Review* 399.

——, Mitchell, B J and Howe, L 'A Continued Upturn in Unfitness to Plead—More Disability in Relation to the Trial Under the 1991 Act' [2007] *Criminal Law Review* 530.

Macklem, T and Gardner, J 'Provocation and Pluralism' (2001) 64(6) *Modern Law Review* 815.

Maeder, T *Crime and Madness: The Origins and Evolution of the Insanity Defense* (New York: Harper and Row, 1985).

Maher, G 'Age and Criminal Responsibility' [2004–05] 2 *Ohio State Journal of Criminal Law* 493.

——, Pearson, J and Frier, B 'Diabetes Mellitus and Criminal Responsibility' (1984) 24(2) *Medicine, Science and Law* 95.

Maier-Katikin, D and Ogle, R 'A Rationale for Infanticide Laws' [1993] *Criminal Law Review* 903.

Malcolmson, R W 'Infanticide in the Eighteenth Century' in J S Cockburn (ed) *Crime In England 1550–1800* (London: Methuen, 1977).

Marland, H 'At Home with Puerperal Mania: The Domestic Treatment of the Insanity of Childbirth in the Nineteenth Century' in P Bartlett and D Wright (eds) *Outside the Walls of the Asylum: The History of Care in the Community 1750–2000* (London: Athlone Press, 1999).

—— 'Getting Away with Murder?: Puerperal Insanity, Infanticide and the Defence Plea' in M Jackson (ed) *Infanticide: Historical Perspectives on Child Murder and Concealment 1550–2000* (Aldershot: Ashgate, 2002).

McCandless, P '"Curses of Civilization:" Insanity and Drunkenness in Victorian Britain' (1984) 79 *British Journal of Addiction* 49.

McColgan, A 'General Defences' in D Nicolson and L Bibbings (eds) *Feminist Perspectives on Criminal Law* (London: Cavendish Press, 2000).

McCord, D 'The English and American History of Voluntary Intoxication to Negate Mens Rea' (1990) 11 *Journal of Legal History* 372.

McSherry, B 'Epilepsy, Automatism and Culpable Driving' (2002) 21 *Medicine and the Law* 133.

Meakin, R G 'Diminished Responsibility: Some Arguments for a General Defence' (1988) 52 *Journal of Criminal Law* 406.

Mitchell, B J 'Putting Diminished Responsibility Law into Practice: A Forensic Psychiatric Perspective' (1997) 8(3) *Journal of Forensic Psychiatry* 620.

—— 'Brief Empirical Survey of Public Opinion Relating to Partial Defences to Murder' Appendix C, Law Commission for England and Wales *Partial Defences to Murder*, (Law Com No 290, 2004).

—— et al 'Pleading for Provoked Killers: In Defence of Morgan Smith' (2008) 124 *Law Quarterly Review* 675.

Mitchell, C 'The Intoxicated Offender—Refuting the Legal and Medical Myths' (1988) 11 *International Journal of Law and Psychiatry* 77.

—— 'Intoxication, Criminality and Responsibility' (1990) 13 *International Journal of Law and Psychiatry* 1.

Mitchell, E W *Self-Made Madness: Rethinking Illness and Criminal Responsibility* (Aldershot: Ashgate, 2003).

Monahan, J 'Abolish the Insanity Defense? Not Yet' (1973) 26 *Rutgers Law Review* 719.

Moore, M S 'Causation and the Excuses' (1985) 73 *California Law Review* 1091.

Moran, M *Rethinking the Reasonable Person: An Egalitarian Reconstruction of the Objective Standard* (Oxford: Oxford University Press, 2003).

Moran, R *Knowing Right from Wrong: The Insanity Defense of Daniel McNaughtan* (New York: The Free Press, 1981).

—— 'The Origin of Insanity as a Special Verdict: The Trial for Treason of James Hadfield' (1985) 19(3) *Law and Society Review* 487.

—— 'The Punitive Uses of the Insanity Defence: The Trial for Treason of Edward Oxford (1840)' (1986) 9 *International Journal of Law and Psychiatry* 189.

Morris, N 'Somnambulistic Homicide: Ghosts, Spiders and North Koreans' (1951) 5 *Res Judicatae* 29.

Morse, S J 'Excusing the Crazy: The Insanity Defence Reconsidered' (1985) 58 *Southern California Law Review* 777.

—— 'Diminished Capacity' in S Shute, J Gardner and J Horder (eds) *Action and Value in Criminal Law* (Oxford: Clarendon Press, 1993).

Nicolson, D 'What the Law Giveth, it Also Taketh Away: Female-Specific Defences to Criminal Liability' in D Nicolson and L Bibbings (eds) *Feminist Perspectives on Criminal Law* (London: Cavendish Press, 2000).

Norrie, A *Law, Ideology and Punishment: Retrieval and Critique of the Liberal Idea of Criminal Justice* (London: Kluwer Academic Publishers, 1990).

—— *Crime, Reason and History: A Critical Introduction to Criminal Law* (London: Butterworths, 2001).

—— 'The Coroners and Justice Act 2009—Partial Defences to Murder (1) Loss of Control' [2010] *Criminal Law Review* 275.

Nutt, D J et al 'Drug Harms in the UK: A Multicriteria Decision Analysis' (2010) 376 (6 November) *The Lancet* 1558.

O'Malley, P *Risk, Uncertainty and Government* (London: Glasshouse Press, 2004).

Oldham, J C 'The Origins of the Special Jury' (1983) 50 *University of Chicago Law Review* 137.

—— 'On Pleading the Belly: A History of The Jury of Matrons' (1985) 6 *Criminal Justice History* 1.

Peay, J *Mental Health and Crime* (London: Routledge, 2010).

Platt, A and Diamond, B L 'The Origins of the "Right and Wrong" Test of Criminal Responsibility and its Subsequent Development in the United Sates: An Historical Survey' (1966) 53 *California Law Review* 1227.

Poole, A R 'Standing Mute and Fitness to Plead' [1968] *Criminal Law Review* 6.

Poovey, M *Making A Social Body: British Cultural Formation 1830–1864* (Chicago: University of Chicago Press, 1995).

Porter, R *Mind-Forg'd Manacles: A History of Madness in England from the Restoration to the Regency* (London: Athlone Press, 1987).

—— *Flesh in the Age of Reason: The Modern Foundations of Body and Soul* (London: Norton, 2003).

Prevezer, S 'The English Homicide Act: A New Attempt to Revise the Law of Murder' (1957) 57(5) *Columbia Law Review* 624.

—— 'Automatism and Involuntary Conduct' [1958] *Criminal Law Review* 440.

Rabin, D 'Bodies of Evidence, States of Mind: Infanticide, Emotion and Sensibility in Eighteenth-Century England' in M Jackson (ed) *Infanticide: Historical Perspectives on Child Murder and Concealment 1550–2000* (Aldershot: Ashgate, 2002).

—— *Identity, Crime and Legal Responsibility in Eighteenth Century England* (New York: Palgrave Macmillan, 2004).

—— 'Drunkenness and Responsibility for Crime in the Eighteenth Century' (2005) 44 *Journal of British Studies* 457, 466.

Rafter, N 'The Unrepentant Horse-Slasher: Moral Insanity and the Origins of Criminological Thought' (2004) 42(4) *Criminology* 979.

Raitt, F and Zeedyk, M S *The Implicit Relation of Psychology and Law: Women and Syndrome Evidence* (London: Routledge, 2000).

Redmayne, M *Expert Evidence and Criminal Justice* (Oxford: Oxford University Press, 2001).

Rimke, H and Hunt, A 'From Sinners to Degenerates: The Medicalization of Morality in the Nineteenth Century' (2002) 15(1) *History of the Human Sciences* 59.

Robinson, P 'Criminal Law Defences: A Systematic Analysis' (1982) 82(2) *Columbia Law Review* 199.

—— 'Causing the Conditions of One's Own Defense: A Study of the Limits of Theory in Criminal Law Doctrine' (1985) 71(1) *Virginia Law Review* 1.

—— *Structure and Function in Criminal Law* (Oxford: Clarendon Press, 1997).

Rogers, T P et al 'Fitness to Plead and Competence to Stand Trial: a Systematic Review of the Constructs and their Application' (2008) 19(4) *Journal of Forensic Psychiatry and Psychology* 576.

Rose, N 'Medicine, History and the Present' in C Jones and R Porter (eds) *Reassessing Foucault: Power, Medicine and the Body* (London: Routledge, 1994).

—— *Inventing Our Selves: Psychology, Power, and Personhood* (Cambridge: Cambridge University Press, 1996).

—— *Governing the Soul: The Shaping of the Private Self* 2nd edn (London: Free Association Press, 1999).

—— *Powers of Freedom: Reframing Political Thought* (Cambridge: Cambridge University Press, 1999).

—— 'Beyond Medicalisation' (2007) 369 *The Lancet* 700.

Scheffer, T 'Knowing How to Sleepwalk: Placing Expert Evidence in the Midst of an English Jury Trial' (2010) 35(5) *Science, Technology and Human Values* 620.

Schopp, R F *Automatism, Insanity and the Psychology of Criminal Responsibility* (Cambridge: Cambridge University Press, 1991).

Scull, A *Museums of Madness: The Social Organization of Insanity in Nineteenth-Century England* (London: Allen Lane, 1979).

—— 'The Social History of Psychiatry in the Victorian Era' in A Scull (ed) *Madhouses, Mad-Doctors and Madmen: The Social History of Psychiatry in the Victorian Era* (London: Athlone, 1981).

—— 'The Insanity of Place' (2004) 15(4) *History of Psychiatry* 417.

Seal, L *Women, Murder and Femininity: Gender Representations of Women Who Kill* (Basingstoke: Palgrave MacMillan, 2010).

Seddon, T *Punishment and Madness: Governing Prisoners with Mental Health Problems* (London: Routledge, 2007).

Shahar, S *Childhood in the Middle Ages* (New York: Routledge, 1992).

Shapin, S *A Social History of Truth: Civility and Science in Seventeenth-century England* (Chicago: University of Chicago Press, 1994).

—— *Never Pure: Historical Studies of Science as if it was Produced by People with Bodies, Situated in Time Space, Culture and Society, and Struggling for Credibility and Authority* (Baltimore: Johns Hopkins University Press, 2010).

Shapiro, B 'The Concept of "Fact": Legal Origins and Cultural Diffusion' (1994) 26(2) *Albion: A Quarterly Journal Concerned with British Studies* 230.

—— *A Culture of Fact, England, 1550–1720* (Ithaca: Cornell University Press, 2000).

Sharma, V D 'The Criminal Responsibility of Children in England' (1974) 3 *Anglo-American Law Review* 157.

Simester, A P 'Intoxication is Never a Defence' [2009] *Criminal Law Review* 3.

—— et al *Simester and Sullivan's Criminal Law: Theory and Doctrine* 4th edn (Oxford: Hart Publishing, 2010).

Singh, R U 'History of the Defence of Drunkenness in English Criminal Law' (1933) 49 *Law Quarterly Review* 528.

Smart, C 'The Woman of Legal Discourse' in K Daly and L Maher (eds) *Criminology at the Crossroads: Feminist Readings in Crime and Justice* (Oxford: Oxford University Press, 1998).

Smith, J C 'Intoxication and the Mental Element in Crime' in *Essays in Memory of Professor F.H. Lawson* (London: Butterworths, 1986).

—— 'Insanity—Available as a Defence in Summary Trials' [1997] *Criminal Law Review* 129.

Smith, K J M *Lawyers, Legislators and Theorists: Developments in English Criminal Jurisprudence 1800–1957* (Oxford: Clarendon Press, 1998).
—— and Wilson, W 'Impaired Voluntariness and Criminal Responsibility: Reworking Hart's Theory of Excuses—the English Judicial Response' (1993) 13 *Oxford Journal of Legal Studies* 69.
Smith, R *Trial by Medicine: Insanity and Responsibility in Victorian Trials* (Edinburgh: Edinburgh University Press, 1981).
Sparks, R F '"Diminished Responsibility" in Theory and Practice' (1964) 27(1) *Modern Law Review* 9.
Stumer, A *The Presumption of Innocence* (Oxford: Hart Publishing, 2010).
Sullivan, G R 'Intoxicants and Diminished Responsibility' [1994] *Criminal Law Review* 152.
—— 'Making Excuses' in A P Simester and A T H Smith (eds) *Harm and Culpability* (Oxford: Clarendon Press, 1996)
Sutherland, P J and Gearty, C A 'Insanity and the European Court of Human Rights' [1991] *Criminal Law Review* 418.
Suzuki, A *Madness at Home: The Psychiatrist, the Patient, and the Family in England 1820–1860* (Berkeley: University of California Press, 2006).
Tadros, V *Criminal Responsibility* (Oxford: Oxford University Press, 2005).
—— 'Crimes and Security' (2008) 71(6) *The Modern Law Review*, 940.
—— 'The Scope and Grounds of Responsibility' (2008) 11 *New Criminal Law Review* 91.
Tausz, D and Omerod, D C 'Fitness to Plead: Whether Defendant Found Unfit to Plead Permitted to Put Before Jury Defences of Lack of Intent and Provocation' [2002] *Criminal Law Review* 403.
Thornton, M T 'Making Sense of Majewski' (1980–81) 23 *Criminal Law Quarterly* 464.
Tolmie, J 'Alcoholism and Criminal Liability' (2001) 64(5) *Modern Law Review*, 688.
Valverde, M '"Slavery from Within:" The Invention of Alcoholism and the Question of Free Will' (1997) 22(3) *Social History* 251.
—— *Diseases of the Will: Alcohol and the Dilemmas of Freedom* (Cambridge: Cambridge University Press, 1998).
—— *Law's Dream of Common Knowledge* (Princeton: Princeton University Press, 2003).
—— 'Authorizing the Production of Urban Moral Order: Appellate Courts and Their Knowledge Claims' (2005) 39(2) *Law and Society Review* 419.
van Krieken, R 'Law's Autonomy in Action: Anthropology and History in Court' (2006) 15 *Social and Legal Studies* 574.
Virgo, G 'The Law Commission Consultation Paper on Intoxication and Criminal Liability: Part 1: Reconciling Principle and Policy' [1993] *Criminal Law Review* 415.
Walker, N *Crime and Insanity in England (Vol 1: The Historical Perspective)* (Edinburgh: Edinburgh University Press, 1968).
—— and McCabe, S *Crime and Insanity in England Volume 2: New Solutions and New Problems* (Edinburgh: Edinburgh University Press, 1973).
Ward, A R 'Making Some Sense of Self-Induced Intoxication' (1986) 45(2) *Criminal Law Journal* 247.
Ward, T 'Magistrates, Insanity and the Common Law' [1997] *Criminal Law Review* 796.
—— 'Law, Common Sense and the Authority of Science: Expert Witnesses and Criminal Insanity in England, CA 1840–1940' (1997) 6(3) *Social and Legal Studies* 343.
—— 'The Sad Subject of Infanticide: Law, Medicine and Child Murder 1860–1938' (1999) 8(2) *Social and Legal Studies* 163.

Ward, T 'Observers, Advisors, or Authorities? Experts, Juries and Criminal Responsibility in Historical Perspective' (2001) 12 *Journal of Forensic Psychiatry* 105.

—— 'A Terrible Responsibility: Murder and the Insanity Defence in England 1908–1939' (2002) 25 *International Journal of Law and Psychiatry* 361.

—— 'Legislating for Human Nature: Legal Responses to Infanticide, 1860–1938' in M Jackson (ed) *Infanticide: Historical Perspectives on Child Murder and Concealment, 1550–2000* (Aldershot: Ashgate, 2002).

—— 'English Law's Epistemology of Expert Testimony' (2006) 33(4) *Journal of Law and Society* 572.

Warner, J 'The Naturalization of Beer and Gin in Early Modern England' (1997) 24 *Contemporary Drug Problems* 373.

Wasik, M 'Partial Excuses in Criminal Law' (1982) 45(5) *Modern Law Review* 516.

Weisz, G 'The Emergence of Medical Specialization in the Nineteenth Century' (2003) 77 *Bulletin of Historical Medicine* 536.

Wells, C 'Whither Insanity?' [1983] *Criminal Law Review* 787.

West, D J and Walk, A (eds) *Daniel McNaughton: His Trial and the Aftermath* (Ashford: Gaskell Books, 1977).

White, S 'Offences of Basic and Specific Intent' [1989] *Criminal Law Review* 271.

—— 'The Criminal Procedure (Insanity and Unfitness to Plead) Act' [1992] *Criminal Law Review* 4.

—— *What Queen Victoria Saw: Roderick Maclean and the Trial of Lunatics Act, 1883* (Chichester: Barry Rose Law, 2000).

Wiener, M J *Reconstructing the Criminal: Culture, Law and Policy in England, 1830–1914* (Cambridge: Cambridge University Press, 1990).

—— 'Judges and Jurors: Courtroom Tensions in Murder Trials and the Law of Criminal Responsibility in Nineteenth Century England' (1999) 17 *Law and History Review* 467.

—— *Men of Blood: Violence, Manliness and Criminal Justice in Victorian England* (Cambridge: Cambridge University Press, 2004).

—— 'Criminal Law at the Fault Line of Imperial Authority: Interracial Homicide Trials in British India' in M D Dubber and L Farmer (eds) *Modern Histories of Crime and Punishment* (Stanford: Stanford University Press, 2007).

Wilczynski, A 'Mad or Bad? Child-Killers, Gender and the Courts' (1997) 37(3) *British Journal of Criminology* 432.

Williams, G 'The Criminal Responsibility of Children' [1954] *Criminal Law Review* 493.

—— *Textbook of Criminal Law* (London: Stevens, 1978).

—— 'The Theory of Excuses' [1982] *Criminal Law Review* 732.

Wilson, W *Criminal Law: Doctrine and Theory* 2nd edn (London: Longman, 2003).

——, Ebrahim, I, Fenwick, P and Marks, R 'Violence, Sleepwalking and the Criminal Law: Part 2: The Legal Aspects' [2005] *Criminal Law Review* 614.

Winnick, B J 'Reforming Incompetency to Stand Trial and Plead Guilty: A Restated Proposal and a Response to Professor Bonnie' (1995) 85(3) *Journal of Criminal Law and Criminology* 571.

Withington, P *Society in Early Modern England: The Vernacular Origins of Some Powerful Ideas* (Cambridge: Polity Press, 2010).

Woodbridge, F 'Some Unusual Aspects of Mental Irresponsibility in the Criminal Law' (1939) 29(6) *Journal of Criminal Law and Criminology* 822.

Wootton, B 'Diminished Responsibility: A Layman's View' (1960) 76 *Law Quarterly Review* 224

Yeo, S 'Clarifying Automatism' (2002) 25 *International Journal of Law and Psychiatry* 445.

Zedner, L 'Women, Crime and Penal Responses: A Historical Account' (1991) 14 *Crime and Justice* 336.
—— *Women Crime and Custody in Victorian England* (Oxford: Clarendon Press, 1991)
—— 'Pre-crime and Post-criminology?' (2007) 11(2) *Theoretical Criminology* 261.

REPORTS

Criminal Law Revision Committee, *Criminal Procedure (Insanity)* (Cmnd 2149, 1963)
Criminal Law Revision Committee *Fourteenth Report: Offences Against the Person* (Cmnd 7844, 1980)
Heald Committee *Murder: some suggestions for the reform of the law relating to murder in England* (1956)
Home Office *Report of the Departmental Committee on the Treatment of Young Offenders* (Cmd 2831, 1927)
Home Office *No More Excuses—A New Approach to Tackling Youth Crime in England and Wales* (Cmd 3809, 1997).
Home Office *Tackling Youth Crime, Reforming Youth Justice: A Consultation Paper* Tackling Youth Crime, Reforming Youth Justice: A Consultation Paper (London, Home Office, 1997).
Law Commission for England and Wales *Codification of the Criminal Law: A Report to the Law Commission* (Law Com No 143, 1985).
Law Commission for England and Wales *Legislating the Criminal Code: Intoxication and Criminal Liability* (Law Com No 229, 1995).
Law Commission for England and Wales *Partial Defences to Murder* (Law Com 290, 2004)
Law Commission for England and Wales *A New Homicide Act for England and Wales? An Overview* (Law Com No. 177, 2005).
Law Commission for England and Wales *Murder, Manslaughter, and Infanticide* (Law Com No 304, 2006).
Law Commission for England and Wales *Intoxication and Criminal Liability* (Cm 7526) (Law Com No 314, 2009).
Law Commission for England and Wales *Unfitness to Plead: A Consultation Paper* (Law Com No 197, 2010).
Scottish Law Commission *Insanity and Diminished Responsibility* (Discussion Paper 122, 2003)
Scottish Law Commission *Insanity and Diminished Responsibility* (Report 195, 2004)
Review of the Criminal Courts of England and Wales (Auld Report) (London, Home Office, 2001).
United Kingdom *Report of the Committee on Insanity and Crime* (Cmd 2005, 1924)
United Kingdom *Royal Commission on Capital Punishment 1949–1953* Report (Cmd 8932, 1953).
United Kingdom *Report of the Committee on Mentally Abnormal Offenders* (Cmnd 6244, 1975)

Index

abnormality
  automatism and 27
  criminal responsibility and 244
  dangerousness and 26–7, 29, 35
  difference and 23–4, 34–5, 39
  diminished responsibility and 27–8, 233–4, 251
  gendered idea of 57
  infancy as 30
  infanticide as 208
  insanity as 26–7
  intoxication and 199
  label of 25
  moralized idea of 116
  'normality' versus 6, 157
  notion of 6, 11, 16, 20–1, 56
  unfitness to plead and 29
affective conditions, *see* psychiatric conditions
Alderson, Baron 77
Allen, Hillary 32, 220
Alness, Lord 231
Alverstone, Lord 81n.74
Archard, David 94n.142
Ashworth, Andrew 127, 258
Atkin Committee on Insanity and Crime 85, 123, 232n.33
Auld Report 98–9
automatism, doctrine of
  abnormality and 27
  burden of proof 163
  dangerousness and 133
  definition 126–7, 129n.133
  development of discrete doctrine 122–5
  disposal power, possibility of 119n.84, 167
  empirical profile of 168
  evidence and procedure governing 159–70
  exculpatory, doctrine as 27, 103–35, 158, 161
  external cause 128–31
  general verdict 165–7
  informal claims 108–9
  insane/non-insane 103, 124
  insanity and 103, 109–13
  intoxication, caused by 131
  label of 124
  moral-evaluative aspect 132–3
  non-insane 119n.86
  presumption of mental capacity 160–1
  'prior fault' 131–3
  prototypical cases 108
  raising 162–3
  reform of 167
  requirements of 125–33
  self-control 54
  self-induced 124, 131
  total destruction of voluntary control 126–8
  tripartite construction 56, 104
  unconsciousness 115, 127
  voluntariness 122
  see also disability; insanity; medical conditions

Ball, C. 88n.112
Beattie, J. M. 106n.15, 206n.26
Bennion, Francis 91n.129
Bentley, Michael 44
Birkenhead, Lord 122n.103, 175n.5, 185, 216n.80
Butler Committee 83–4, 87n.107, 95n.145, 117n.71, 125, 130, 133n.157, 156n.104, 158n.113, 167n.153, 200, 219n.95, 235n.44, 241n.74, 245–6
Byrne, Justice 83n.79

capital punishment 5, 79, 85, 125, 232–3
  see also Royal Commission on Capital Punishment
children
  adultification of youth justice 91–2
  age of criminal responsibility 3, 30n.47, 67–70, 78, 88–9, 91–2
  anti-social behaviour orders 92
  'bastard' child/children 203–8
  birth and postnatal issues:
    breastfeeding/lactation 29, 57, 62, 217, 219–20, 223
    childbirth 15, 29, 62, 203, 217, 219–20, 223
    matrons, juries of 138
    medical practitioners of 211
    motherhood 203
    'phrenzy' 208, 211
    puerperal insanity/psychosis 210, 214
    registration of birth 70
    reproductive health 214
    specialist knowledge about 211–12
    stress related to 208, 214
  child defendants 63, 69–70, 78
  childhood:
    constructions of 91
    crimes 56–7, 94
    developmental psychology and 94n.142
    expert knowledge of 91
    incapacity and 80–1
    offending 57, 91, 93–4
    sentimentalization of 80
    social attitudes and beliefs about 94
    social meaning of 80, 91–2
    Victorian 80n.70

children (cont.)
  court system for juveniles 79
  crimes committed by 56–7, 94
  dangerousness of young offenders 91
  European Court of Human Rights and 101
  'good and evil', knowledge of 74, 90
  illegitimate 203–8
  imprisonment of 78
  juvenile delinquency 78, 80
  offending by 93–4
  politicization of child offending 91
  poverty and children's crimes 78–9
  puberty, physical process of 70n.14
  punishment of 78–9
  punitive approaches to 91
  reformatories 80
  sentencing for 89
  special status granted to 57, 78, 94
    mercy 69
  rehabilitation of young offenders 88
  'right and wrong', knowledge of 78
  young children:
    as abnormal 30
    as defendants 69
    social position of 69
  welfare approach to young offenders 88, 91, 93
  see also gender; infanticide; infancy
Coleridge, Justice 182
Colvin, Eric 23
Criminal Cases Review Commission (CCRC) 245n.88
Criminal Law Revision Committee (CLRC) 200n.140, 222n.109, 235n.44, 241n.74, 245–6
criminal responsibility 33, 50–1, 108, 125
  abstract structure of 7
  age of, *see* children
  attribution of 3, 18, 51
  capacity-based 45
  changes in the principles of 37n.79, 41n.4
  character-based 51
  denials of 8, 18–19
  fault, concept of 60, 144
  individual 6, 7, 42n.8, 45
  intoxication and 177, 185
  'mental responsibility' 233, 237, 239–40, 244, 249n.102, 250n.105
  non-responsibility 4–5, 7–8, 33, 51, 56, 62, 115, 150, 220
  ordinary principle of 34
  outcome-based 45
  partial 7, 51, 56–7, 62, 177n.20, 219–20, 224, 231
  personal responsibility, legal significance of 35, 80, 116, 215
  structures of 204
  time and 50–1
  see also liability
Cross, Rupert 110n.39

Dawson of Penn, Lord 217
Dear, Peter 139
Deas, Lord 229–30
defence
  categorizations of 18
  by function 20–2
  by normative type 18–19
  vs denials of responsibility 19
  excuse defences 21
  label of 17–20
  self-defence 18, 20, 96n.150, 162, 164, 238
Denning, Lord 118–19, 128, 156–7, 160, 162, 185n.73, 196n.124
Dennis, Ian 165n.144
Devlin, Lord Justice 27, 83n.79, 117–19, 131, 157, 162, 163
diminished responsibility
  abnormality and 27–8, 233–4, 251
  'abnormality of mind' 236–7, 243–4
  actus reus of 245
  aetiology, tripartite 239–40
  boundaries of 251
  burden of proof 233, 246
  Byrne decision, effect of 236–7
  causation 244
  character, considerations of 230
  conceptual basis of 228
  criminal fault and 230–1
  critique of 253–4
  culpable homicide 228–9
  current doctrine of 235–45
    abnormality of mental functioning 235–8, 242–5, 255
    explanation of D's act 242–5
    nature of the conduct, understanding the 240–2
    rational judgment 240–2
    recognised medical condition, a 238–40, 251
    substantially impaired ability 240–2
  decision-making in relation to 245–53, 256
  difference and 56n.63, 253–8
  evidence and procedure governing 238–40, 249–51
  as exculpatory doctrine 31, 256
  as excuse 31
    partial excuse 253–5
  expert knowledge 245–53
  gender bias and 251–2
  as inculpatory doctrine 31, 256
  infanticide and 220–1
  insanity law, compared 228, 231, 249, 254
  intoxication and 175, 179, 194, 239–40, 249
  introduction of, in England and Wales 232–5, 248
  Janus-faced 32, 226
  lay evaluation of 247–50
  Lord Deas, view of 229–30

Index

'loss of control' and 254, 256
M'Naghten insanity and 226, 232–4, 236–8
mens rea and 245, 257
'mental responsibility' 233, 237, 239–40, 244, 249n.102, 250n.105
'mercy killers' 242, 250n.107
murder and 234, 238, 245, 250, 255
'normal immaturity' 30n.50
'optional defence' status 245–6
practical operation of 247, 250
professional actors 245–53
provocation and 28n.39, 252, 254–8
'quality of the act' and 232, 256
raising 245–6
scope of 231, 240, 244, 250
Scottish:
   concept of 230
   development of 227–32
   origins of 226, 228–9
self-control and 256–8
sentencing practices 228–30
statutory provision 54
substantial impairment 241–2, 244, 249
successful use of 252
volitional incapacity 117, 237–8
Diplock, Lord 26, 30, 111, 127n.123, 188n.85
disability
   basis for insanity, rise of 122–5
   excuses 8, 21–5, 31n.54, 37
   incapacity and 14, 103–35
   learning 101
   medicalized notions of 43, 125, 134
   see also **automatism**; **insanity**; **medical conditions**; **psychiatric conditions**; **incapacity**
disposal 84–5, 110–11, 167–70
doli incapax, *see* **infancy**
Dubber, Markus Dirk 10
Duff, Antony 6n.4, 8n.10, 18–19, 46n.20, 71, 76n.43, 83, 97n.157, 138, 149

Edmund-Davies, Lord 131n.148, 183n.58, 187–8, 190n.95, 199
Eigen, Joel 113, 115n.64, 137, 145, 178, 210, 211n.57
Ellenborough, Lord 209
Elliot, I. D. 161n.124
Elwyn-Jones, Lord 31, 183n.58, 187–9, 196n.122, 199
Erle, Justice 78
European Convention on Human Rights 96, 100n.170
European Court of Human Rights 85n.99, 93n.140, 101
exculpation 3
   definition 7
   exculpatory mental incapacity doctrines 26–9, 62
   mental incapacity as a basis of 7–9
   mode/technique of 22–3

excuse(s)
   defence 21
   diminished responsibility 31–2, 253
   'disability excuse' 8, 21–5, 31n.54, 37
   excusing conditions 24
   mistake 21–2
   partial 255n.135
   reasonableness requirement 36n.73
   'status excuse' 30n.51, 75n.37

Farmer, Lindsay 10, 36, 50, 52n.44, 149n.73, 228, 230–1
fault, concept of 60, 144
Fingarette, Herbert 254
Fitzjames Stephens, James 12
Fletcher, George 19n.9, 51–3, 58–9, 108n.27, 140n.22, 165–6, 205
formalization
   account 40–4
   see also **infancy**; **insanity**; **intoxication**; **mental incapacity in criminal law**; **unfitness to plead**
Foucault, Michel 40n.1, 58
Fuller, Steve 198

Gardner, John 18n.7, 35
Garland, David 124n.110
gender
   abnormality and 57, 202–3, 215
   crime and 202–25
   diminished responsibility and 251–2
   feminist theory 29, 202, 212n.62, 220
   'infanticidal type'/woman 15, 28, 35, 57, 203, 214–16, 218–19, 225
   'lewd' women 203–8
   'madness' and 202–25
   meanings associated with 215–16
   reproductive practices 29, 214
   Victorian gender constructions 214
   see also **children**; **infanticide**
Giddens, Antony 47, 58n.67, 159
Goddard CJ, Lord 121
Gordon, Gerald 227–8, 231n.29
Gough, Stephen 186n.74
Griew, Edward 238n.60, 250n.105, 253–4
Grubin, Don 86

Hacking, Ian 152n.85
Hailsham, Lord 173n.1, 197
Hale, Matthew 12, 70, 73–4, 106, 175, 192–3
Heald Committee 233
Hewart, Lord 123n.107
Ho, H. L. 160n.118
Hoffman, Lord 257
Holroyd, Justice 182
Home Office, the (United Kingdom)
   discretion of 84n.92, 87n.109, 154
Horder, Jeremy 19n.10
Hörnle, Tatjana 35
Hutton, Lord 96n.150, 239n.65

278 Index

imputation
  intoxication as doctrine of 14n.25, 30–1, 195
  see also **intoxication**
incapacity, *see* **disability**; **mental incapacity**
inculpation 31
  diminished responsibility and 31–2
  infanticide and 32
  see also **diminished responsibility**; **infanticide**
infancy
  as abnormality 30
  conceptual interdependency:
    with insanity 72–5
    with unfitness to plead 68
  dangerousness and disposal 78–81
  doli incapax:
    abolition of 92–4
    criticism of 92n.135, 93
    defence of 90
    presumption of 69, 90–1
  dynamic of exclusion, rise of 92–4,
  dynamic of inclusion 68, 75, 78–81, 88–92, 102
  due process and 29
  fairness and special treatment 88–92
  formalization of 43, 68, 75–102
  mercy, role of in criminal process 69–72
  mixed approaches to 92
  political and social overtones 68
  special procedures for 91
  substantive criminal law:
    connection to 72–5
  symbolic significance 102
  see also **children**
infanticide
  as abnormality 57, 208, 213, 219–20, 225
  actus reus significance of 218–19
  admission of act of 222
  aetiological basis of 217
  'benefit of linen' plea 205, 207
  birth and postnatal issues:
    breastfeeding/lactation 29, 57, 62, 217, 219–20, 223
    childbirth 15, 29, 62, 203, 217, 219–20, 223
    matrons, juries of 138
    medical practitioners of 211
    motherhood 203
    'phrenzy' 208, 211
    puerperal insanity/psychosis 210, 214
    registration of birth 70
    reproductive health 214
    specialist knowledge about 211–12
    stress related to 208, 214
  capital punishment in cases of 206, 209
  concealment offence of 209–10
  criminal responsibility and 214–16
  current law of 216–21
  diminished responsibility and 220–1, 223
  disturbance of mind 217–19, 223
  evaluative aspects of 57, 62
  exculpatory doctrine, as 28–9, 32

  gendered construction of 224
  homicide, as distinct category of 223
  humanitarian approach 207
  incapacity and 209–13
  inculpation via 29–33
  'infanticidal type'/woman 15, 28, 35, 57, 203, 214–16, 218–19, 225
  insanity and 208, 211
  intoxication, comparison with 183
  lay knowledge of 222
  legal actors' knowledge of 221–5
  legal meaning of, shift in 208
  'lewd' women and 203–8
  'manifest criminality' as 209
  married women and 204, 208–9, 223–4
  medicalization of 212
  mens rea of 218–19
  moralization and 213–14
  murder, separation from 221
  newborn child murder 204–5, 208, 209
  partial responsibility 219–20, 224
  poor law, effect of the 203–4
  'preparation' plea 205
  procedural rules of 223–4
  proscribing act of 203–8
  psychiatry and 221
  physiology, product of 35
  puerperal insanity/psychosis 210–11
  reform of 223–4
  sentencing practices, sympathetic 224–5
  social meanings of 207, 220, 222–3
  socio-economic problems and 206–7
  'temporary insanity' 219–20
  'want of help' plea 205
  'wilful', use of term 218
  see also **children**; **gender**
insanity
  acquittal on the basis of 104–5
  arraignment, on 72, 75–8, 227
    see also **unfitness to plead**
  asylum movement, the 153–4
  automatism and 109–13, 162–3
  burden of proof 90n.122, 163–5
  consequentialist dimension of 135
  criminal responsibility and 125
  dangerousness and 104, 111–12, 133–5
  'defect of reason' 26n.31, 36n.73, 114, 117–21, 217n.86
  diminished responsibility and 228, 231, 249, 254
  disability, as a basis for 103, 116, 122–5
  'disease of the mind' 119, 130
  disposal 167–70
  empirical profile of 168
  evidence and procedure governing 159–70
  as exculpatory doctrine 26–27
  expert medical evidence 85–6, 146–7
  feigned 164
  flexible application of law 169

formalization of 43, 110, 116
indefinite detention 26n.34, 110–11, 167
infanticide and 208
informal plea of 103, 104–9
intellectual disability and 105
internal cause 117–20, 129–30
intoxication and 177, 184–5
irresistible impulse 123
label, inappropriateness of 123, 134
lay knowledge of 150–5
medical:
  evidence of 147, 150
  knowledge of 43, 85–6, 149
M'Naghten Rules 26n.31, 113–21
'moral' 113, 123
morality and 43, 112, 125
'partial' 78n.53, 106, 227
physical disorders and 118
pleas 72, 105, 111, 116
practical operation of the law 115, 168, 169n.165
presumption of sanity 160–1, 163
puerperal insanity 210
raising 162–3, 170
reform of 133–5
as a social problem, rise of 112, 116
risk and 104, 111, 134–5
scope of the doctrine 114, 148
special verdict 165–7
symbolic role of the law 116
temporary 219–20
ultimate issue 146, 157n.109, 249
uncontrollable impulse 123
'wild beast' insanity test 106–7
see also **automatism; disability**
intoxication, law of
abnormality and 31, 199
alcohol:
  alcohol dependency syndrome/
    alcoholism 31, 158, 173, 194–5, 240
  common knowledge about 48n.25
  drunkenness 24, 175–6, 178–80, 184–5
  licensing laws 48n.25, 196
  patterns of consumption 175, 178–81
  social tolerance for 182
amoral intoxication 191–5
  alcoholism 194–5
  involuntary 192–3
  non-dangerous drugs 193–4, 199
'basic intent' 190–1, 195, 197–8
capacity, to form intent 54, 182–3, 186
criminal intoxication:
  offence of 200–1
criminal responsibility and 177, 185
dangerous intoxication:
  offence of 200–1
DPP v Majewski 186–91
drugs:
  consumption of 31, 173, 187, 191
  hallucinatory 194

non-dangerous 193–4
pharmaceutical properties of 193–4
'diminished responsibility' from 175, 179, 194, 239–40, 249
effect(s) of 60, 177, 178, 196–7
as exculpatory abnormality 174, 182, 185–6, 200
expert knowledge, development of 178–81
formalization of 60, 173–4, 181–91
inebriates' legislation 180
infanticide, comparison with 183
informal intoxication plea, emergence of 174–8
insanity and 177, 184–5
involuntary 30–1, 192–3
Janus-face of law of 174, 198–201
lay knowledge of 54n.56, 60, 173, 181, 186, 195–8
local knowledge of 177–8
meanings related to 173–4
medical and psychiatric knowledge of 179–80
as morally culpable conduct 174, 199–200
OBPs trial records and 184
offence-by-offence approach 190–1
pleas:
  decline of 116
  informal 174–8
raising 175, 178
reform of 200
self-induced 173, 189
social profile of, changing 175
'specific intent' 54, 182–7, 190–1, 195, 197
temperance movement, the 179
voluntary 8, 14n.25, 30–1, 173, 187–9, 191–2
see also **abnormality; imputation**

Jackson, Mark 206–7
Jones, Carole 148
Juries
  evaluation by 154, 181, 196
  role of 4, 83–4, 98, 138–40, 158–9
  'special juries' 138
  see also **knowledge, lay**

Keating, Heather 91n.130
Kennedy, Lord 246n.92
Kilmuir, Viscount 127, 129n.132, 160n.121, 163n.134
knowledge, of 'madness'
changing knowledge context 113
common 47–8, 107, 136–43
coordination and legitimation 37n.79, 41n.4, 45–6
different types of 46–7
epistemology 57
expert medical 43, 44–9, 55, 59, 62, 63, 107, 113, 136–7, 143–50, 155–9, 245–53
folk 47
general 59
knowledge/knowers distinction 47n.23

Index

knowledge, of 'madness' (*cont.*)
  lay 47–8, 59–60, 86–7, 107, 136, 150–5, 195–8, 247–9
  of legal actors 221–5
  non-expert 44–9, 143–50, 155–9
  ontological 49, 151–2
  prudential 150–5
  psychiatric 45–6, 55, 136
  psychological 45–6, 136
  scientific 48n.27, 62, 155n.101
  see also '**manifest madness**'

Lacey, Nicola 7n.9, 10, 35, 45, 51, 144, 177, 182n.53, 186, 202n.1, 230–1
Landsman, Stephen 148n.67
Langbein, John 70–1, 174n.3
Larkin, E. P. and Collins, P. J. 86n.102
Law Commission for England and Wales 97–8, 100, 185n.72, 188–91, 200–1, 223–4, 235, 239, 242, 249, 251
  programme of reform 170
Lawton, Lord Justice 133
lay knowledge, *see* **knowledge**
liability
  objective and subjective 190
  ordinary principle of 34
  partial 57, 62, 219, 253–4
  participatory 96
  'patterns of liability' 51–3
  structures of 177, 204–5
  see also **criminal responsibility**
Lloyd-George, Major 48, 234, 237

Mackay, R. D. 8n.12, 100–1, 120, 124n.109, 163n.135, 165n.147, 167–9, 220n.99, 239, 241n.71, 243n.80
  and Kearns, G. 86n.102, 159n.114
  et al, study by 168–9, 224, 247–52
'manifest madness', 'madness'
  'absolute' character of 74
  common knowledge of 140
  conduct, significance of 49–57
  crime, intersection with 5, 51–5, 58, 141
  dispositional construction of 5, 13, 49–50
  epistemology of 57–64, 143
  expert knowledges of 58, 63n.83, 143–50
  formal qualities of 40, 49, 57, 251
  gender and 61n.76, 202–25
  infanticide and 202–25
  madness and crime, intersection of 39–64, 49–64
  'manifest criminality' compared with 51–4, 59
  medicalized character of 146
  naturalization of 'madness' 137–43
  ontology of 'madness' 49–57
  proof of 'madness' 142–3, 154, 159–60
  readability of 5, 13, 49–50, 58–61, 63
  reconstruction of 159–60
  religio-astrologic conceptions 137
  religious view of 137–8
  scientific-organic perspectives 137
  social and cultural attitudes to 138
  social meanings of 107
  testimony by 'ordinary' people 140
  terrain, topography of 39–40, 49, 57
  see also **knowledge, of 'madness'**; **insanity**; **mental incapacity in criminal law**
McColgan, Aileen 252n.112
M'Naghten, Daniel 74n.36, 113
  spelling of name 103n.1
M'Naghten Rules 26n.31, 113–21
  creation of 113–14
  'defect of reason' 117
  diminished responsibility and 226, 232–4, 236–8
  'disease of the mind' 117–20, 236
  insanity before *M'Naghten* 104–9
  irresistible impulse 114
  knowledge of wrongness 90n.122, 120–1
  'nature and quality' of the act 120–1
  presumption of sanity 160–1
  reform of 124–5
  reverse burden of proof 164–5
  scope of, expanding the 169n.165
  three limbs of 116–21
  wrong, meaning of 114
  see also **insanity**
medical conditions
  alcohol dependency syndrome/alcoholism 31, 158
  amnesia 99n.166, 115
  arteriosclerosis 118n.73
  brain/head injury 50, 131, 240
  'deaf and dumb' 69n.8, 71n.21, 77, 81, 99n.166
  diabetes 119–20, 129, 131, 157n.105, 167n.151
  epilepsy 5n.2, 118, 127–8, 134, 161
  hyperglycaemia 5n.2, 118, 129
  hypoglycaemia 128–30
  sleepwalking 118, 129–30, 157n.108
  unfitness and 99–100
  see also **disability**; **psychiatric conditions**
mental health, *see* **psychiatric conditions**
mental incapacity in criminal law
  change and continuity over time 40–4
  criminal non-responsibility and 33
  defences 17–20
  difference, label of 34–8
  disaggregation, early modern era 69
  as disciplinary hybrid 5
  doctrines of 3, 17–20
    category of 26
    formalization 13
    exculpatory 26–9
    non-exculpatory 29–33
  exculpation, as basis for 9
  formalization account 40–4
  lay knowledge of 86–7
  moralized notion of 116, 124, 133, 136, 149
  multidimensional approach 6, 39
  reasons for examining 3–6

reconstructing terrain of 17–25
roles of 16–17
   multiplicity of 16–17, 216
   reconceptualization of 16
social dimension of 60
social and political interest in 4
symbolic significance of 4
terrain, scope of 3, 8, 16–64
time and space 50–1
umbrella term of 6
violence and 119
see also **automatism; criminal law; insanity; manifest madness; mental health conditions**
Mitchell, Barry 253n.120
modernity 41n.2, 58, 143, 253
Moore, Michael 243–4
morality
   amorality 5
   'good and evil' 74
   insanity and 43, 112
   medicalization of 180n.43
   moral standards 121
moralization
   criminal law as instrument of 4, 116
   Victorian discourse of 112
Morris of Borthy-Gest, Lord 26, 163n.134
Morris, Norval 127
Mustill, Lord 192n.109

Nicholls, Lord 253n.119
Normand, Lord Justice-General 196n.124
Norrie, Alan 7, 42, 50, 128n.127, 190n.96, 193n.109, 221, 241n.73, 250n.106

Old Bailey Criminal Court 11, 194
Old Bailey Proceedings (OBPs)
   brief references in 140–1
   expert testimony 145–8, 152
   insanity and 107, 109
   intoxication and 176, 181, 184
   records 11–12
Onslow, Lord 106n.14
Ormrod, Lord Justice 161n.123
Otton, Lord Justice 99n.165

Parker CJ, Lord 240, 248
Parkin, Henry 57
Patten, John 95n.146
Poole, A. R. 76n.46
Poovey, Mary 143n.42
Porter, Roy 107, 137–8, 140–1, 213
provocation
   diminished responsibility and 28n.39, 252, 253–8
   history of 28n.39
psychiatric conditions
   anxiety 130
   delirium 115
   delusion 100n.167, 115
   depression 6, 130, 217n.82, 249n.103, 252n.119

'lesion of the will' 144
'lunacy' 144
mania 115
mental 'absence' 115
mental disorder 24, 50
'monomania' 144
mood disorder 100n.167
'moral insanity' 144
personality:
   change 50
   disorder 135, 249n.103
post-traumatic stress disorder 133
psychosis 249n.103
puerperal insanity/psychosis 210
reason, effect on 119
schizophrenia 236n.49, 249n.103
stress 130, 208
'unconsciousness' 115
unfitness to plead and 86
see also **disability; medical conditions; psychiatry**
psychiatry
   'alienists' 4, 144–5, 148, 210–11
   discipline of 4, 56n.61, 112
   infanticide and 221
   lexicon of 134
   'mad' doctors 145
   moralized discourse of deviance 55–6
   profession, rise of 112, 143–50
   psy-knowledge 5, 19
   psychology and 5, 55–6
   social profile of 124
see also **knowledge; psychiatric conditions**
psychology
   moralized discourse of deviance 55–6
   psychiatry and 5, 55–6
   social profile of 124
see also **knowledge**

Rabin, Dana 34, 105n.9, 108, 175–7, 205n.19, 206–8
Reading CJ, Lord 120
reasonableness 23
   excuse(s) and 36n.73
   reasonable person, the 35–7, 198n.132
responsibility, *see* **criminal responsibility**
Robinson, Paul 20–5, 30, 35, 37, 127, 132, 166, 191
Rose, Nikolas 135, 144, 153
Royal Commission on Capital Punishment 5, 85, 111n.41, 125, 215n.76, 232–3
see also **capital punishment**
Russell, Lord 188, 225

Salmon, Justice 99n.165, 183n.60
Sankey, Lord 122n.104
Scotland, *see* **diminished responsibility**
Scotland, Baroness 99n.163
Scottish Law Commission 100n.170, 231, 236n.52
Shapin, Steven 143n.38, 151–2
Shapiro, Barbara 139

Simester, A. P. et al 250n.107
Simon, Lord 187–8
Smith, Keith 105, 114–15, 125, 164, 184, 186n.75, 234
Smith, Roger 72n.28, 145n.52, 211–12, 215
socio-historical approach 9–11
Sparks, Richard 254
State Trial reports 11
Stephen, Justice 185n.69
subjectivity 3, 6, 51
  critical analysis of subjectivism 189n.94
  non-subjectivity 56
  'subjective criminality' 52, 53n.54
Sullivan, G. R. 244
Suzuki, Akihito 150n.77

Tadros, Victor 50
Taylor of Gosforth, Lord 126n.115
Tenth Programme of Law Reform 134
Tindal, Chief Justice 113
Tracy, Justice 106–7, 141
trial, criminal
  'accused speaks'/'lawyer free' 71–2
  by altercation 71–2, 139–40
  adversarial 105, 146–7
  effective processing by 137, 160, 162–3
  exculpatory 71–2
  by inquiry 138
  'lawyerization' 41–2
  medieval era, process 70–1
  by ordeal 138
    peine forte et dure 71n.21, 138
  'reconstructive' 149–50, 164–5
  summary:
    expansion of jurisdiction 79
    procedure in 87–8
  'trial of the facts', *see* unfitness to plead

unfitness to plead
  burden of proof 82
  communication, issues of 77
  comprehension, issues of 77
  conceptual interdependency:
    with infancy 68
    with insanity 72–5
  Consultation Paper (Law Commission) 97–102
  criteria for a finding of 99–102
  current era, in the 94–102
  dangerousness and disposal 75–81
  deciding unfitness/'trial of the issue':
    evidence in support of 83–6
    judge alone 98–9
    by jury 83–4, 98
  disposal, of unfit:
    detention 75–6
    range of options 83–5
  due process and 29
  dynamic of exclusion, rise of 92–102
  dynamic of inclusion 13, 43, 68, 75, 81–2, 88, 91–2, 94–5, 97, 101–2
  expert medical evidence 85–6
  fairness and special treatment 81–8
  formalization 43, 68, 75–102
  inability to participate in a trial 70
  inability to plead 70
  insanity on arraignment 68, 75–8
  lay knowledge of 86–7
  'mute by malice' 71, 99
  'mute by the visitation of God' 71, 73n.30, 77
  omnibus notion of 76
  plea, significance in medieval process 69–72
  raising unfitness, rule about 61–2
  'readability' of unfitness 62
  reform of 100–1
  special measures, use at trial 101–2
  substantive criminal law, connection to 72–5
  symbolic significance 102
  'trial of the facts' 83–4, 95–8

Valverde, Mariana 48, 180, 191, 196–7
victimhood 5, 62

Walker, Nigel 71n.20, 73n.32, 76n.44, 104, 107n.17, 154n.97, 166n.149, 215–18
  and McCabe, S. 87n.109
Ward, Tony 37n.80, 123, 151, 155, 216n.81, 250
Wasik, Martin 254–5
Weiner, M. J. 79–80, 110n.40, 112, 116, 145n.53, 154n.97, 179, 183–4, 213
Wells, Celia 121n.99
Williams, Glanville 121n.98, 127
Winnick, B. J. 101n.173
Woolf, Lord 164
Wootton, Barbara 252n.117

Zedner, Lucia 213n.64